ALSO AVAILABLE FROM

MANGA

ACTION

ANGELIC LAYER*
CLAMP SCHOOL DETECTIVES* (April 2003)
DIGIMON (March 2003)
DUKLYON: CLAMP SCHOOL DEFENDERS* (September 2003)
GATEKEEPERS* (March 2003)
GTO*
HARLEM BEAT
INITIAL D*
ISLAND
JING: KING OF BANDITS* (June 2003)
JULINE
LUPIN III*
MONSTERS, INC.
PRIEST
RAVE*
REAL BOUT HIGH SCHOOL*
REBOUND* (April 2003)
SAMURAI DEEPER KYO* (June 2003)
SCRYED* (March 2003)
SHAOLIN SISTERS* (February 2003)
THE SKULL MAN*

FANTASY

CHRONICLES OF THE CURSED SWORD (July 2003)
DEMON DIARY (May 2003)
DRAGON HUNTER (June 2003)
DRAGON KNIGHTS*
KING OF HELL (June 2003)
PLANET LADDER*
RAGNAROK
REBIRTH (March 2003)
SHIRAHIME: TALES OF THE SNOW PRINCESS* (December 2003)
SORCERER HUNTERS
WISH*

CINE-MANGA™

AKIRA*
CARDCAPTORS
KIM POSSIBLE (March 2003)
LIZZIE McGUIRE (March 2003)
POWER RANGERS (May 2003)
SPY KIDS 2 (March 2003)

ANIME GUIDES

GUNDAM TECHNICAL MANUALS
COWBOY BEBOP
SAILOR MOON SCOUT GUIDES

ROMANCE

HAPPY MANIA* (April 2003)
I.N.V.U. (February 2003)
LOVE HINA*
KARE KANO*
KODOCHA*
MAN OF MANY FACES* (May 2003)
MARMALADE BOY*
MARS*
PARADISE KISS*
PEACH GIRL
UNDER A GLASS MOON (June 2003)

SCIENCE FICTION

CHOBITS*
CLOVER
COWBOY BEBOP*
COWBOY BEBOP: SHOOTING STAR* (June 2003)
G-GUNDAM*
GUNDAM WING
GUNDAM WING: ENDLESS WALTZ*
GUNDAM: THE LAST OUTPOST*
PARASYTE
REALITY CHECK (March 2003)

MAGICAL GIRLS

CARDCAPTOR SAKURA
CARDCAPTOR SAKURA: MASTER OF THE CLOW*
CORRECTOR YUI
MAGIC KNIGHT RAYEARTH* (August 2003)
MIRACLE GIRLS
SAILOR MOON
SAINT TAIL
TOKYO MEW MEW* (April 2003)

NOVELS

SAILOR MOON
SUSHI SQUAD (April 2003)

ART BOOKS

CARDCAPTOR SAKURA*
MAGIC KNIGHT RAYEARTH*

TOKYOPOP KIDS

STRAY SHEEP (September 2003)

SHAOLIN 鈴 SISTERS

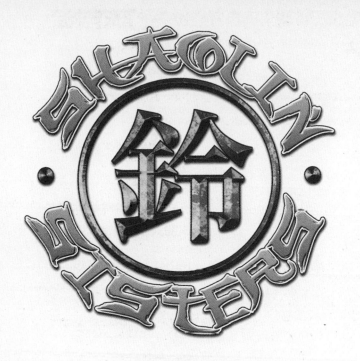

Volume 1

Story & Art
by
Narumi Kakinouchi

TOKYOPOP®
Los Angeles • Tokyo

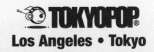

English Adaption - Alexander O. Smith
Editor - Rich Amtower
Retouch & Lettering - Paul Tanck
Graphic Design - Mark Paniccia
Cover Layout & logo Design - Patrick Hook

Senior Editor - Mark Paniccia
Managing Editor - Jill Freshney
Production Manager - Jennifer Miler
Art Director - Matthew Alford
VP of Production & Manufacturing - Ron Klamert
President & C.O.O. - John Parker
Publisher - Stuart Levy

Email: editor@TOKYOPOP.com
Come visit us online at www.TOKYOPOP.com

A ⊙ TOKYOPOP® Manga
TOKYOPOP® is an imprint of Mixx Entertainment, Inc.
5900 Wilshire Blvd. Suite 2000, Los Angeles, CA 90036

ISBN: 1-59182-024-3

First TOKYOPOP® printing: Feb 2003

10 9 8 7 6 5 4 3 2 1

Printed in the USA

"Touch my big sis... and you'll eat fist!"
-Julin

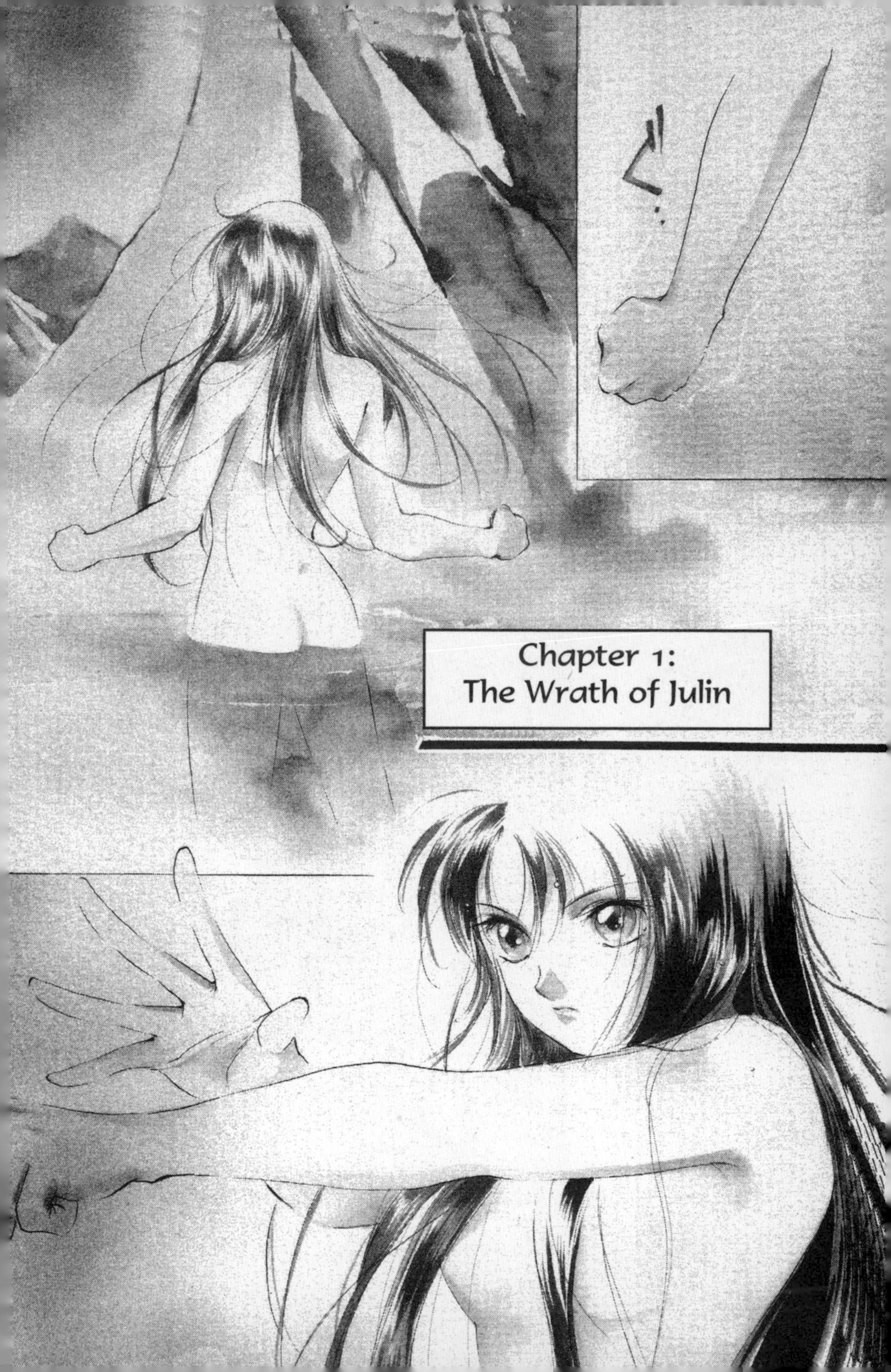
Chapter 1:
The Wrath of Julin

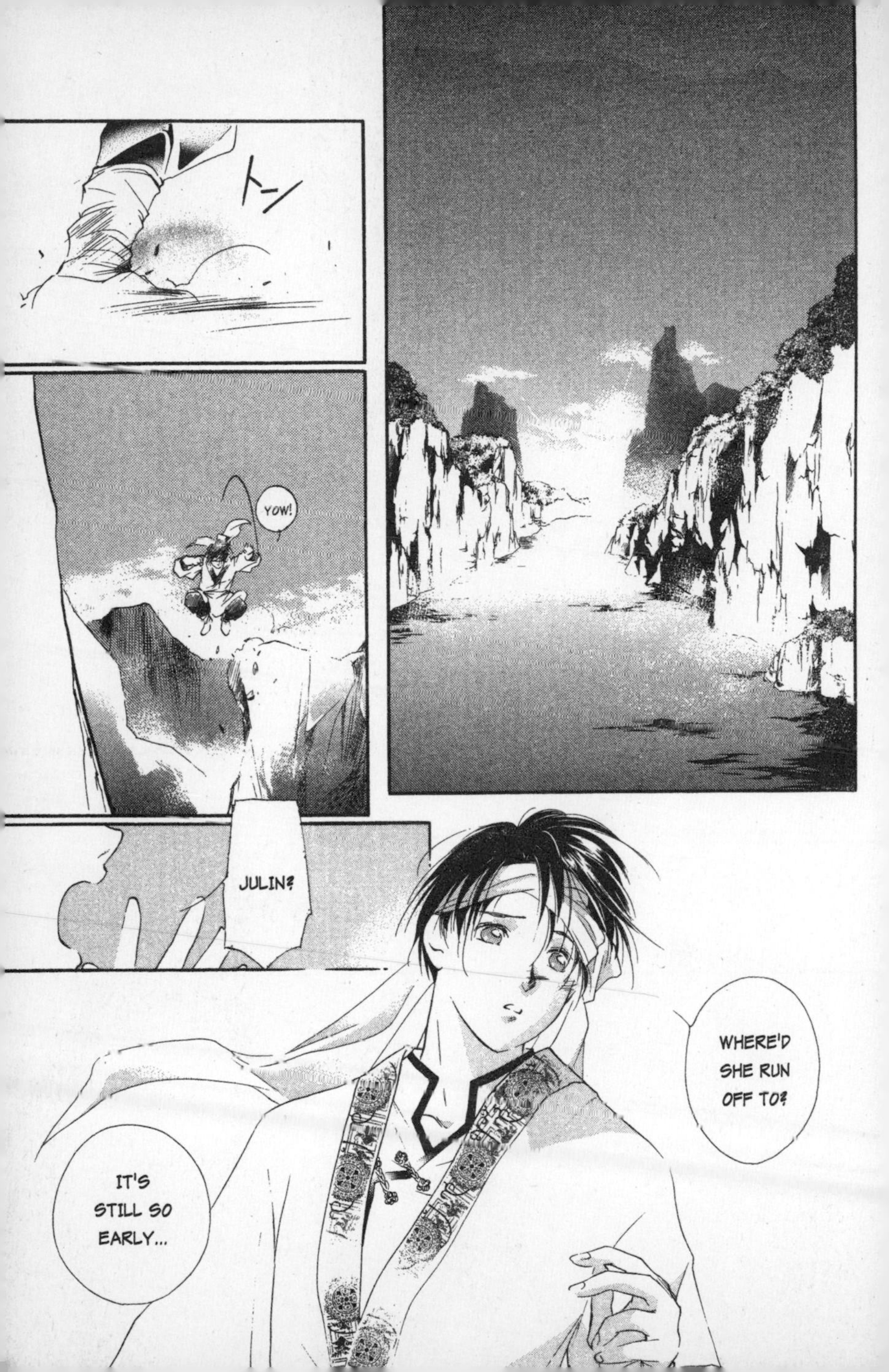
トン
YOW!
JULIN?
WHERE'D SHE RUN OFF TO?
IT'S STILL SO EARLY...

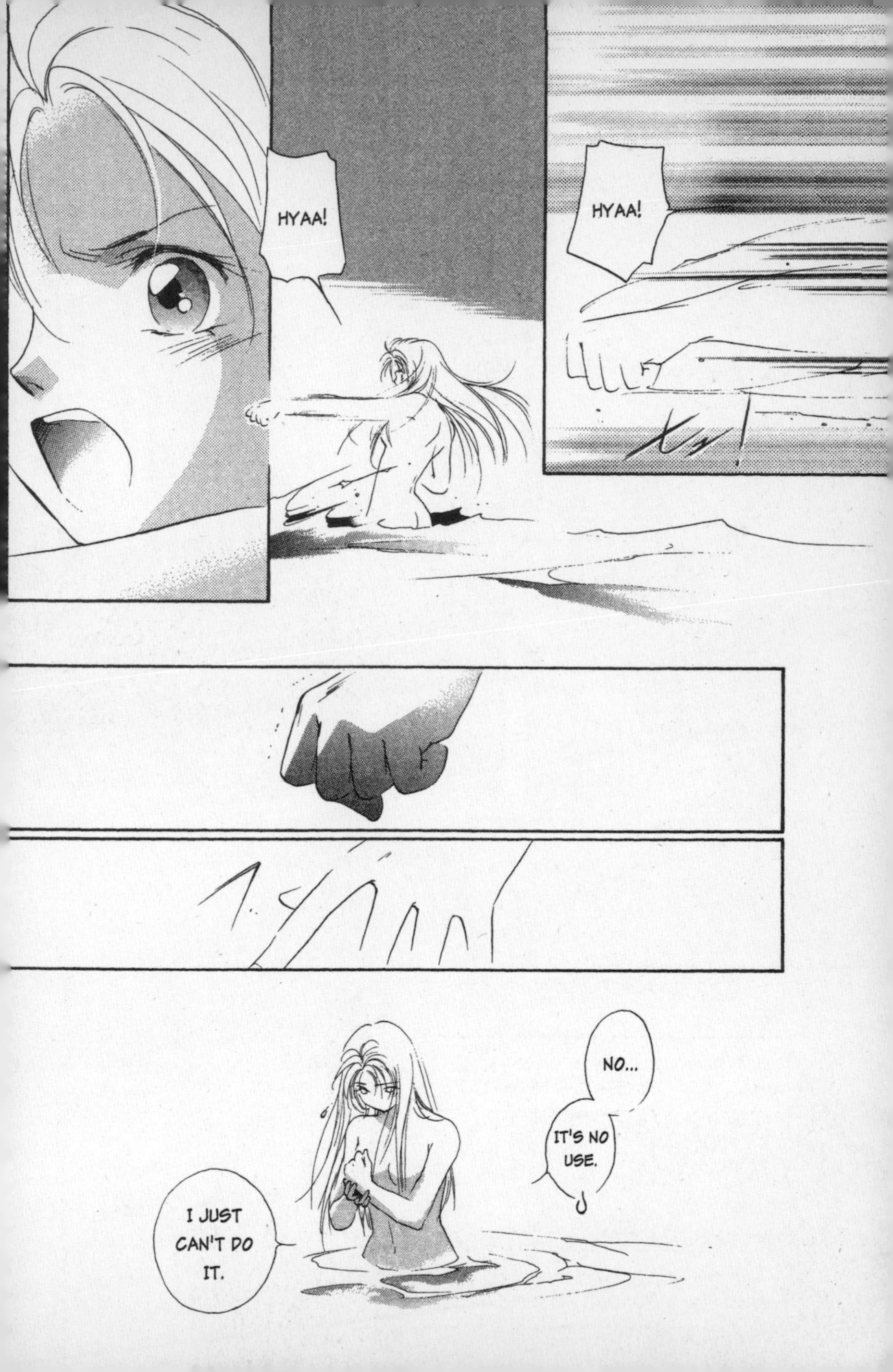

HYAA!
HYAA!
NO...
IT'S NO USE.
I JUST CAN'T DO IT.

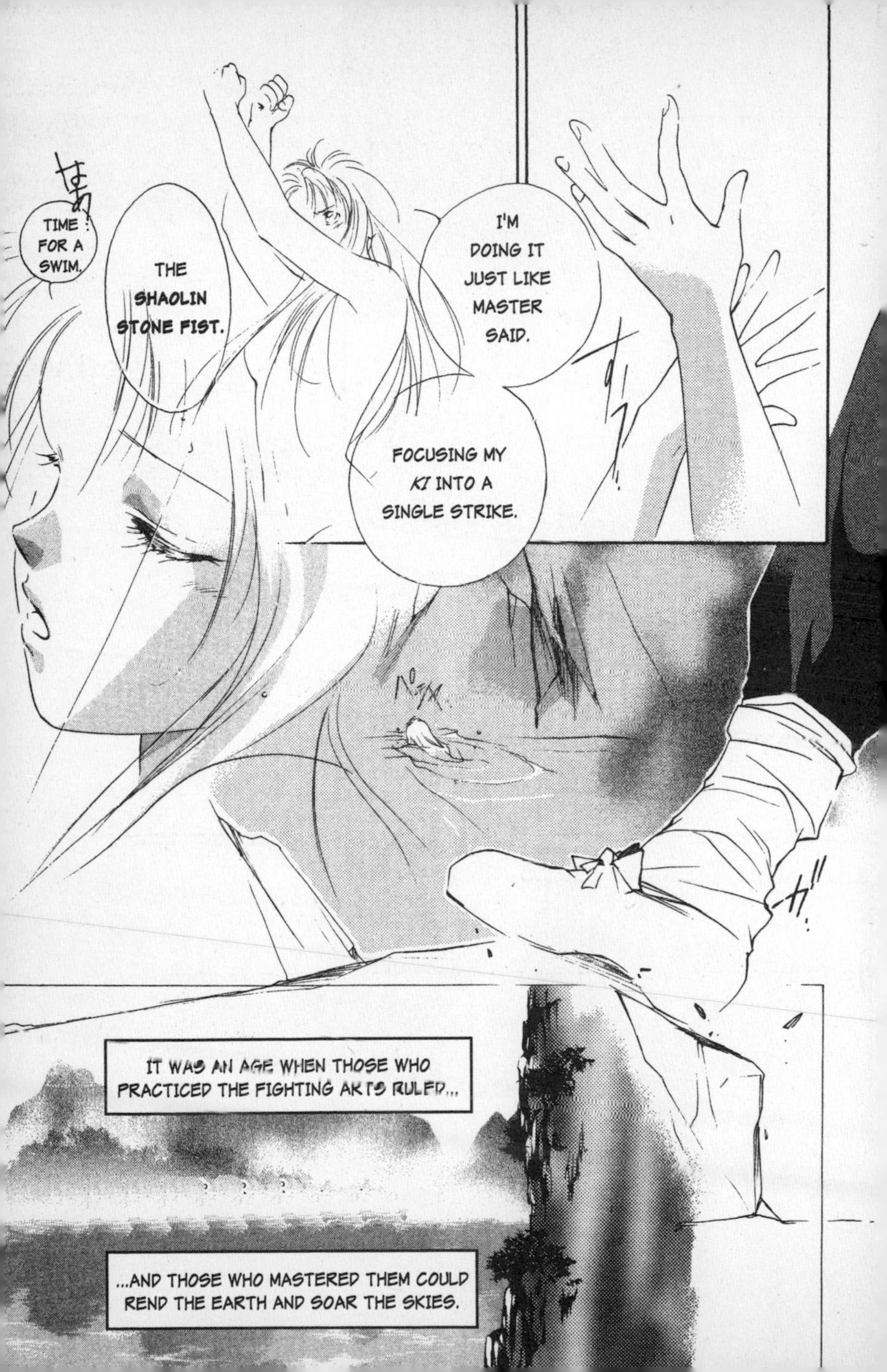
I'M DOING IT JUST LIKE MASTER SAID.
FOCUSING MY KI INTO A SINGLE STRIKE.
THE SHAOLIN STONE FIST.
TIME FOR A SWIM.
IT WAS AN AGE WHEN THOSE WHO PRACTICED THE FIGHTING ARTS RULED...
...AND THOSE WHO MASTERED THEM COULD REND THE EARTH AND SOAR THE SKIES.

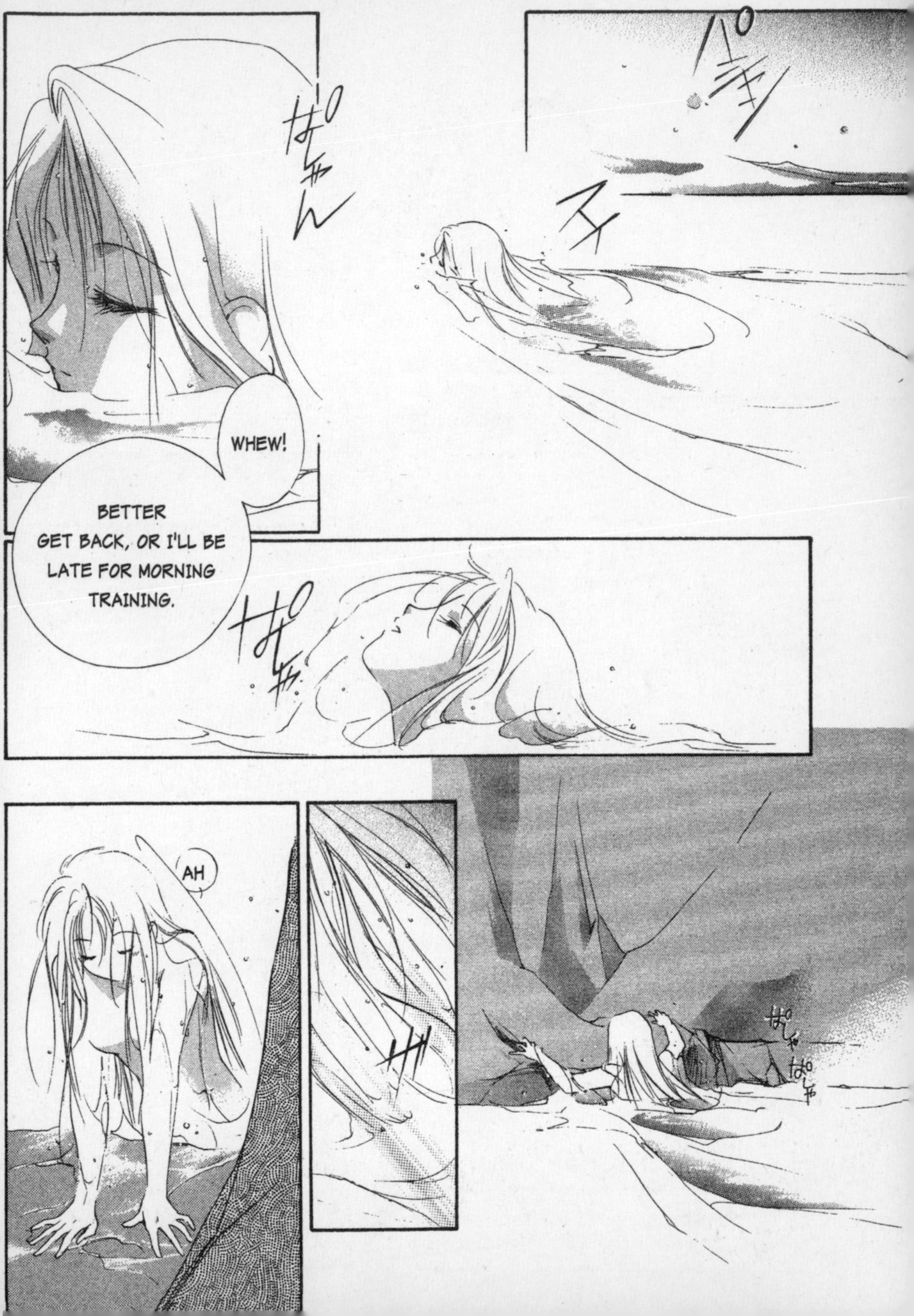
ぱしゃん
WHEW!
BETTER GET BACK, OR I'LL BE LATE FOR MORNING TRAINING.
AH

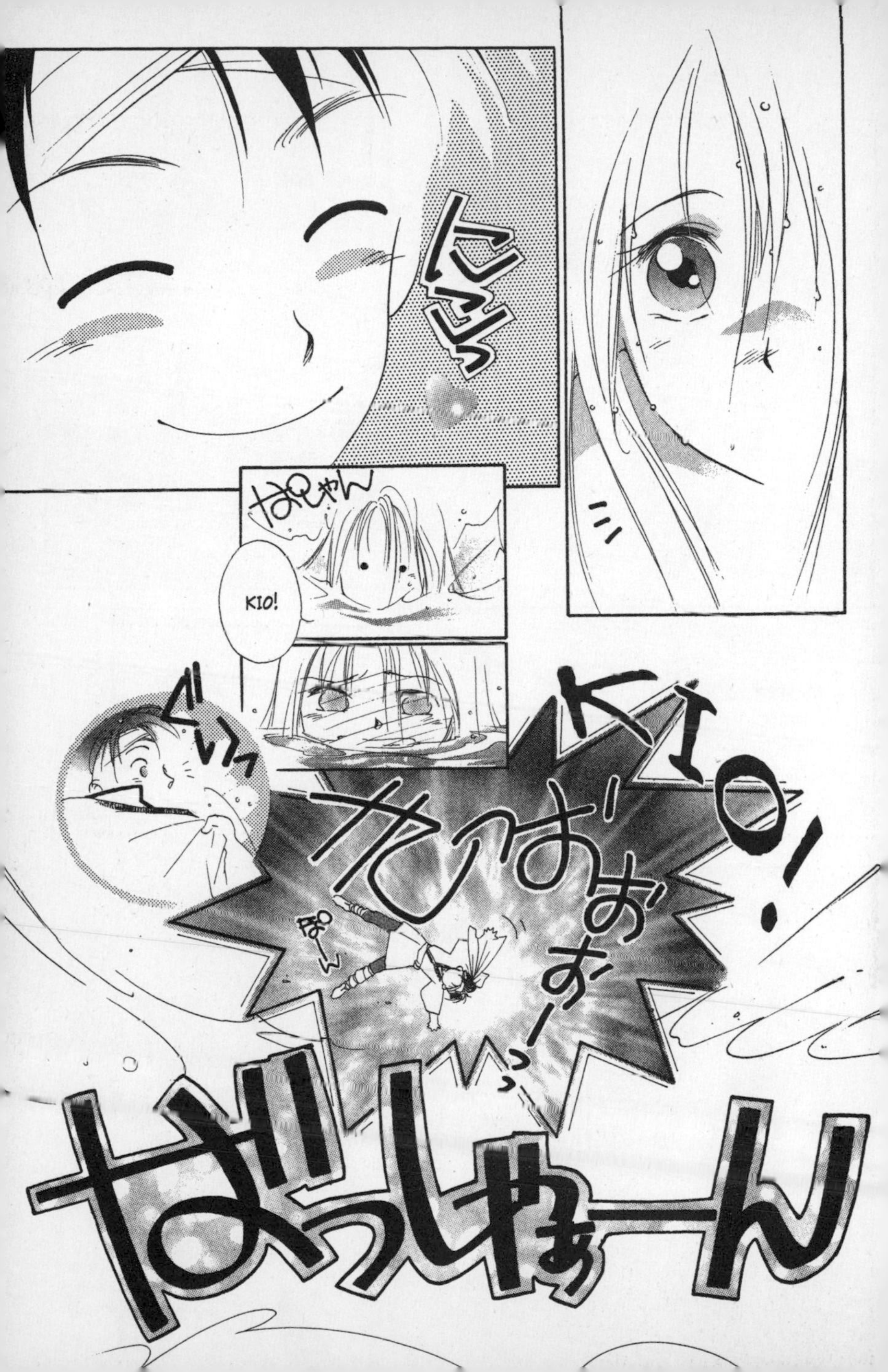
にこっ
ぱしゃん
KIO!
KIO!
ざっしゃーん

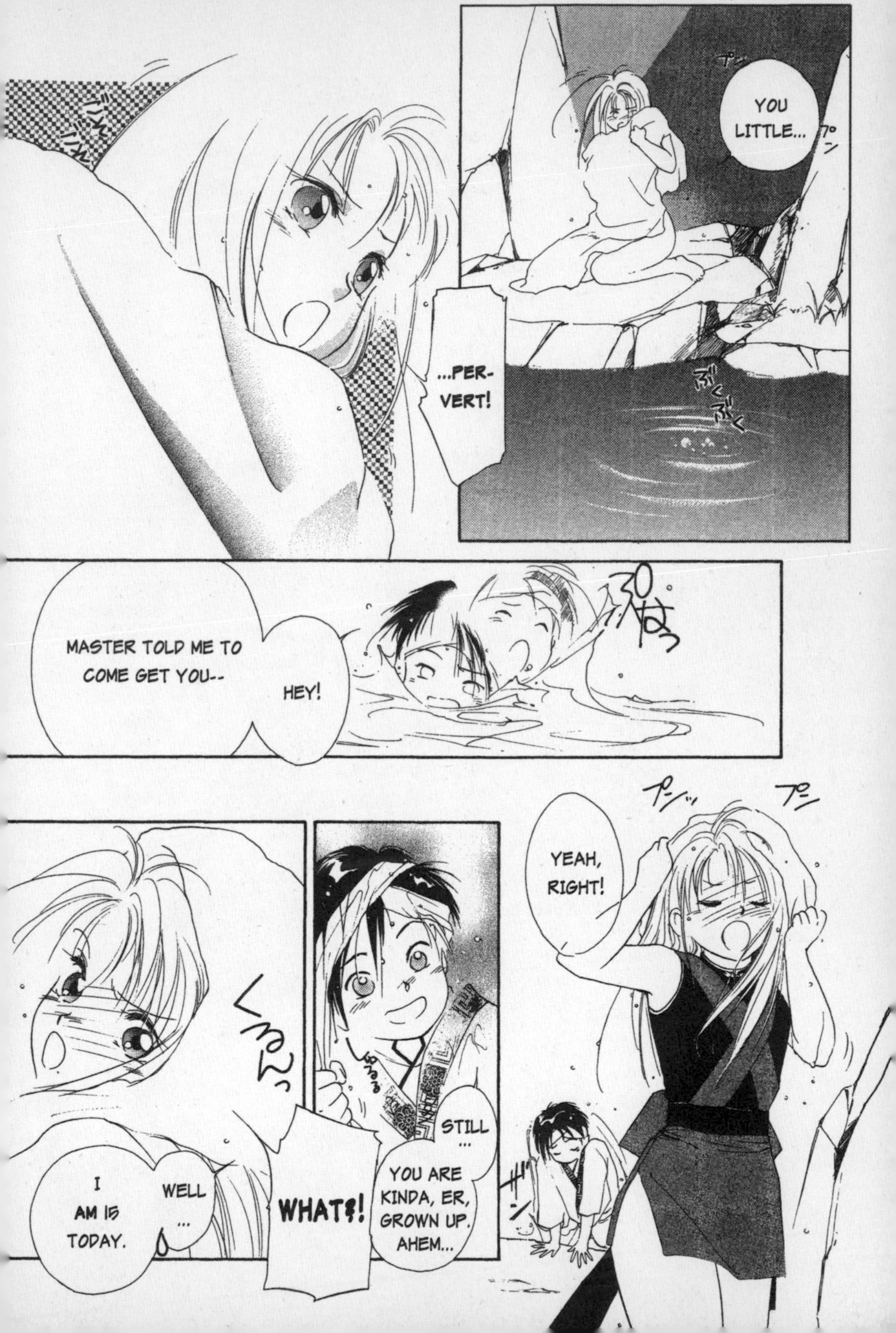

YOU LITTLE...
...PER-VERT!
MASTER TOLD ME TO COME GET YOU--
HEY!
YEAH, RIGHT!
STILL ...
YOU ARE KINDA, ER, GROWN UP. AHEM...
WHAT?!
WELL ...
I AM 15 TODAY.

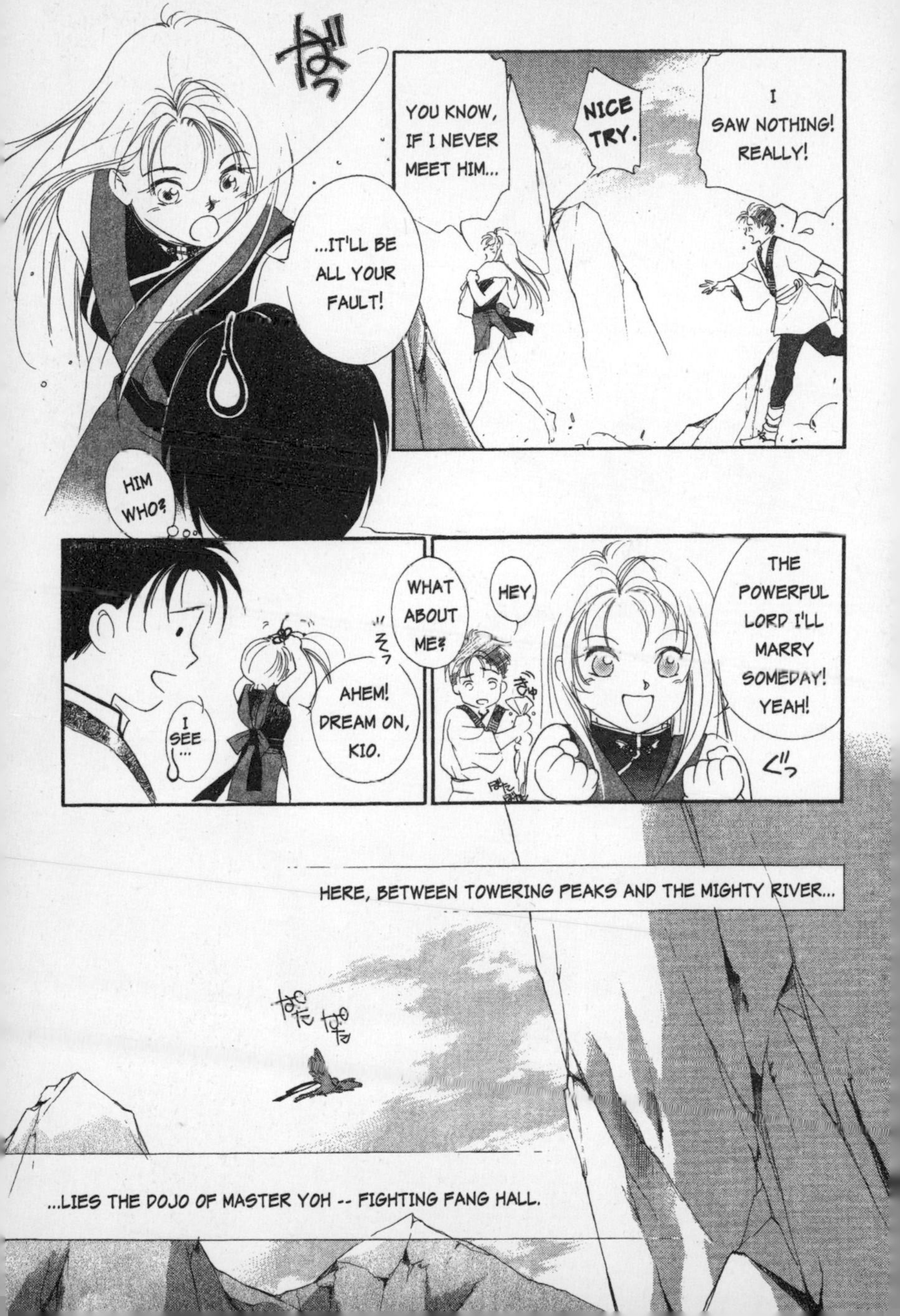
I SAW NOTHING! REALLY!
NICE TRY.
YOU KNOW, IF I NEVER MEET HIM...
...IT'LL BE ALL YOUR FAULT!
HIM WHO?
THE POWERFUL LORD I'LL MARRY SOMEDAY! YEAH!
HEY.
WHAT ABOUT ME?
AHEM! DREAM ON, KIO.
I SEE ...
HERE, BETWEEN TOWERING PEAKS AND THE MIGHTY RIVER...
...LIES THE DOJO OF MASTER YOH -- FIGHTING FANG HALL.

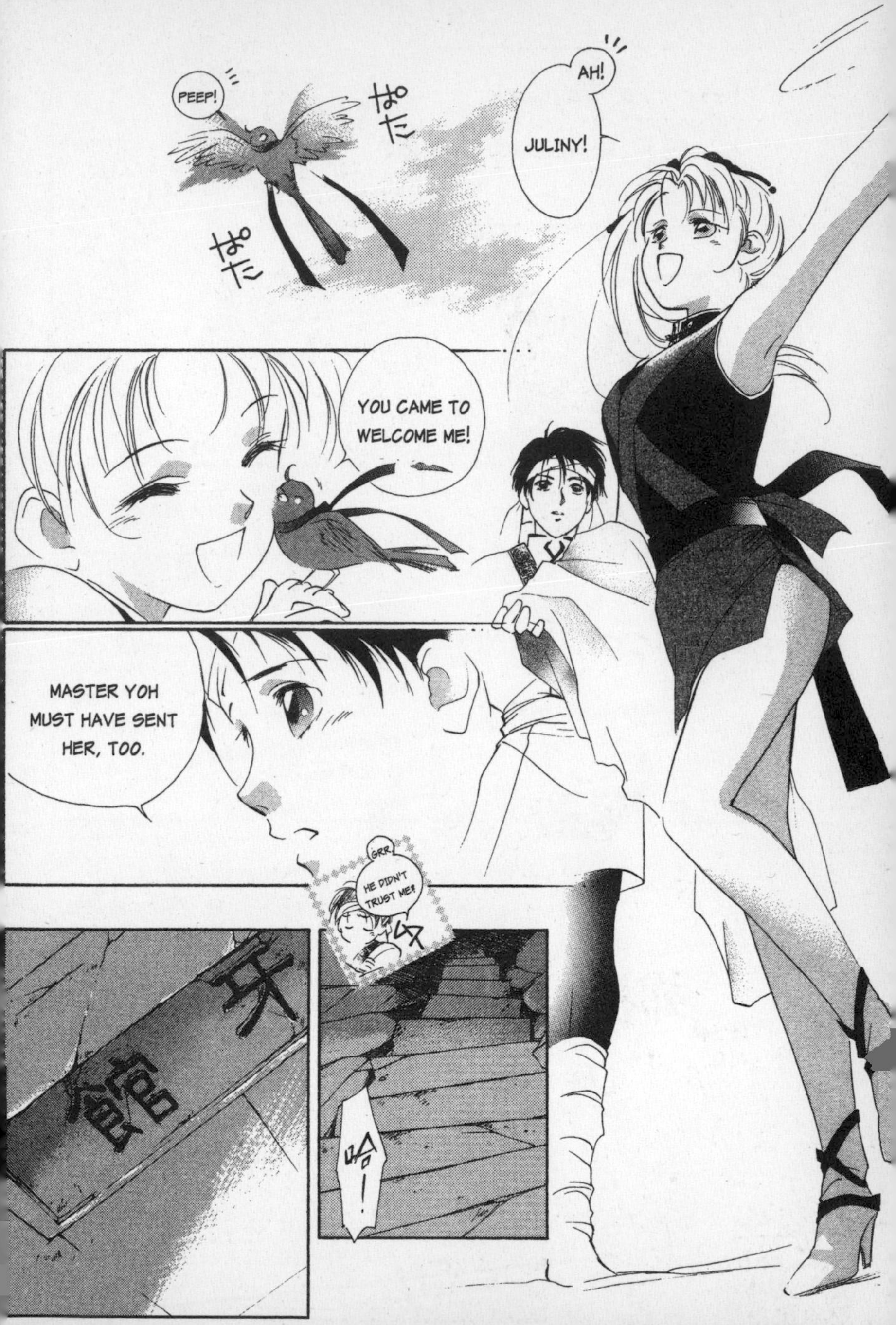
AH!
JULINY!
ぱた
ぱた
PEEP!
YOU CAME TO WELCOME ME!
MASTER YOH MUST HAVE SENT HER, TOO.
GRR.
HE DIDN'T TRUST ME!
ムス

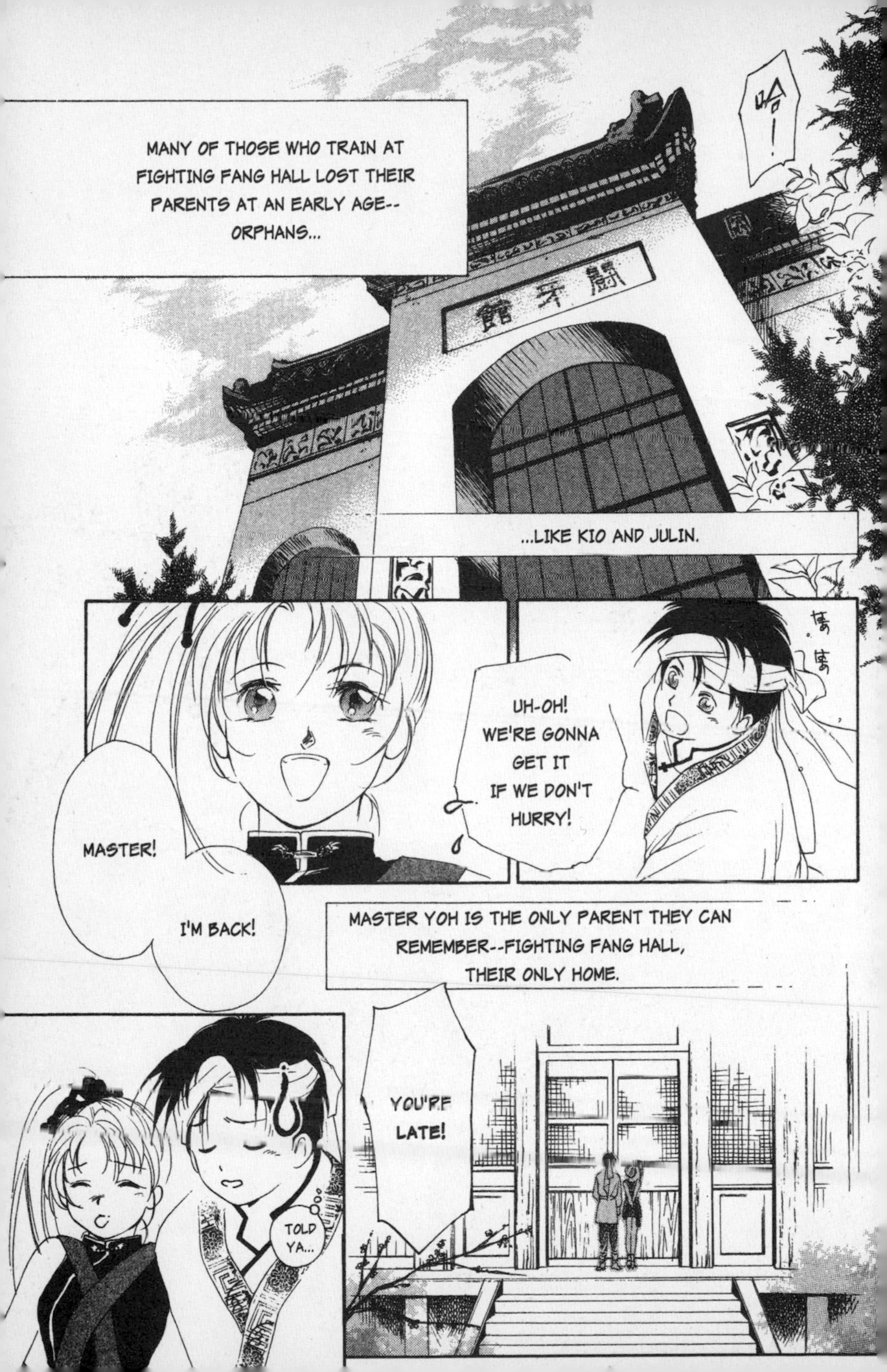
哈!
MANY OF THOSE WHO TRAIN AT FIGHTING FANG HALL LOST THEIR PARENTS AT AN EARLY AGE--ORPHANS...
...LIKE KIO AND JULIN.
UH-OH! WE'RE GONNA GET IT IF WE DON'T HURRY!
MASTER!
I'M BACK!
MASTER YOH IS THE ONLY PARENT THEY CAN REMEMBER--FIGHTING FANG HALL, THEIR ONLY HOME.
YOU'RE LATE!
TOLD YA...

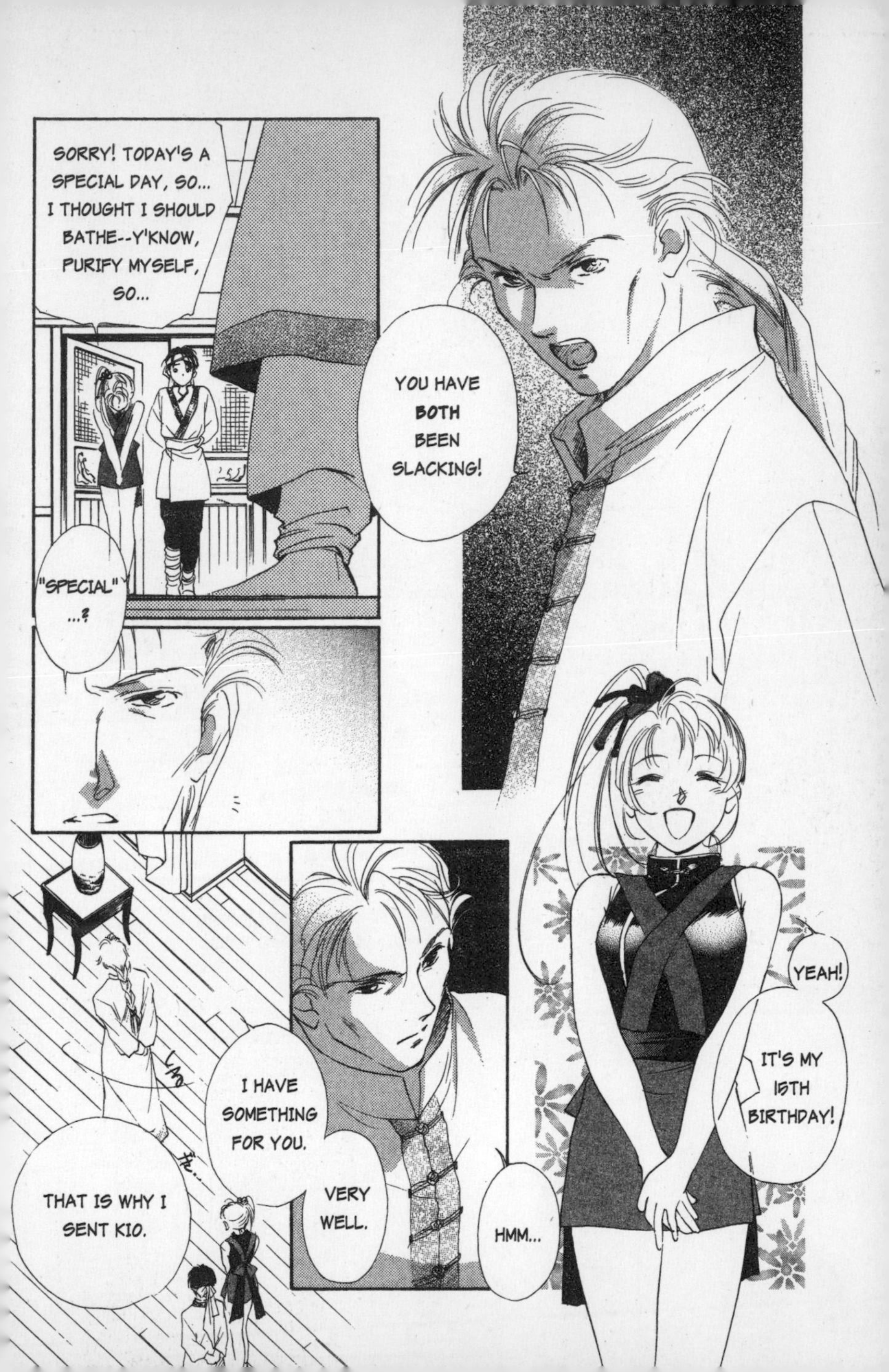

YOU HAVE BOTH BEEN SLACKING!
SORRY! TODAY'S A SPECIAL DAY, SO... I THOUGHT I SHOULD BATHE--Y'KNOW, PURIFY MYSELF, SO...
"SPECIAL" ...?
YEAH!
IT'S MY 15TH BIRTHDAY!
HMM...
VERY WELL.
I HAVE SOMETHING FOR YOU.
THAT IS WHY I SENT KIO.

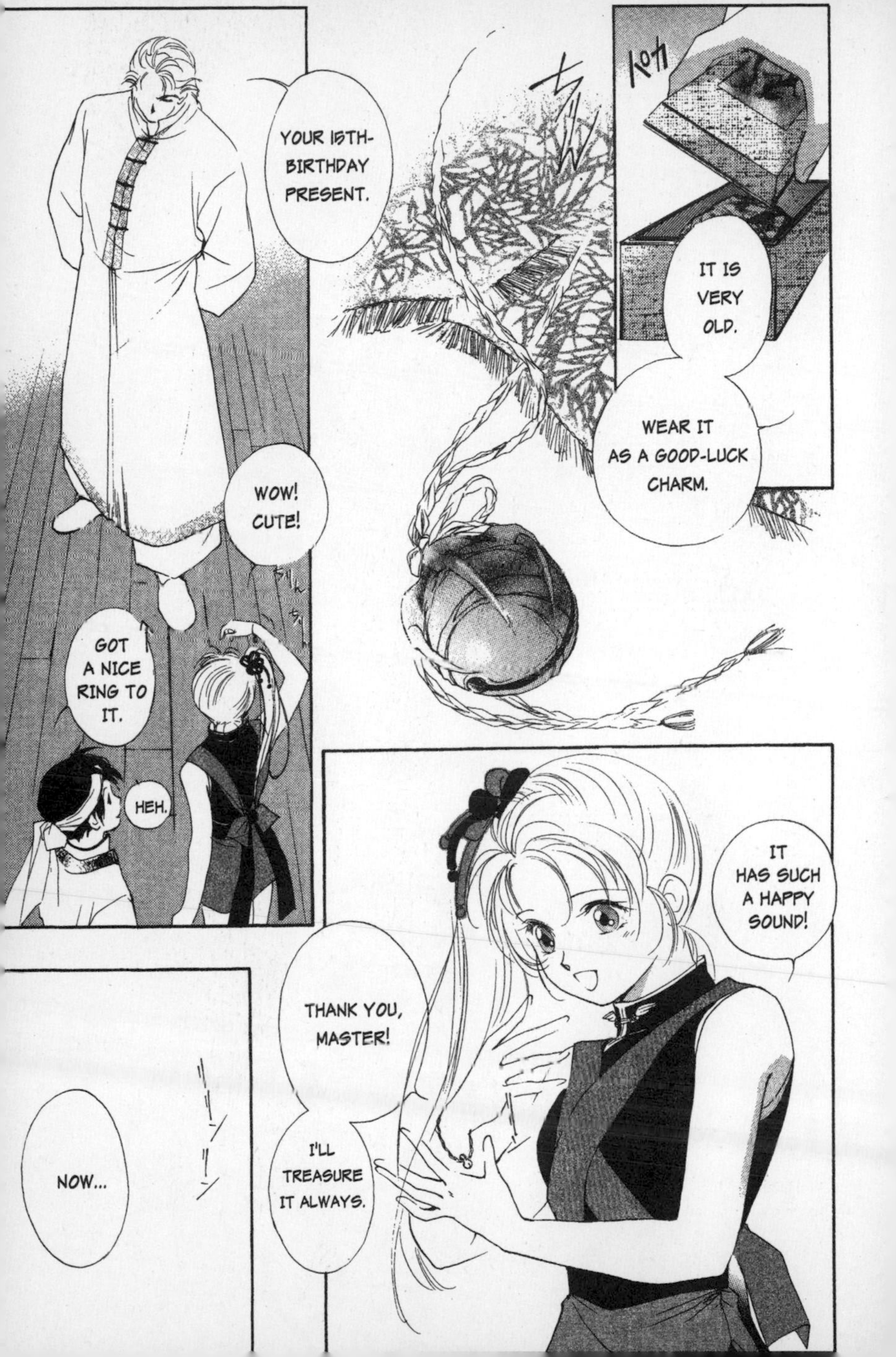
IT IS VERY OLD.
WEAR IT AS A GOOD-LUCK CHARM.
YOUR 15TH-BIRTHDAY PRESENT.
WOW! CUTE!
GOT A NICE RING TO IT.
HEH.
IT HAS SUCH A HAPPY SOUND!
THANK YOU, MASTER!
I'LL TREASURE IT ALWAYS.
NOW...

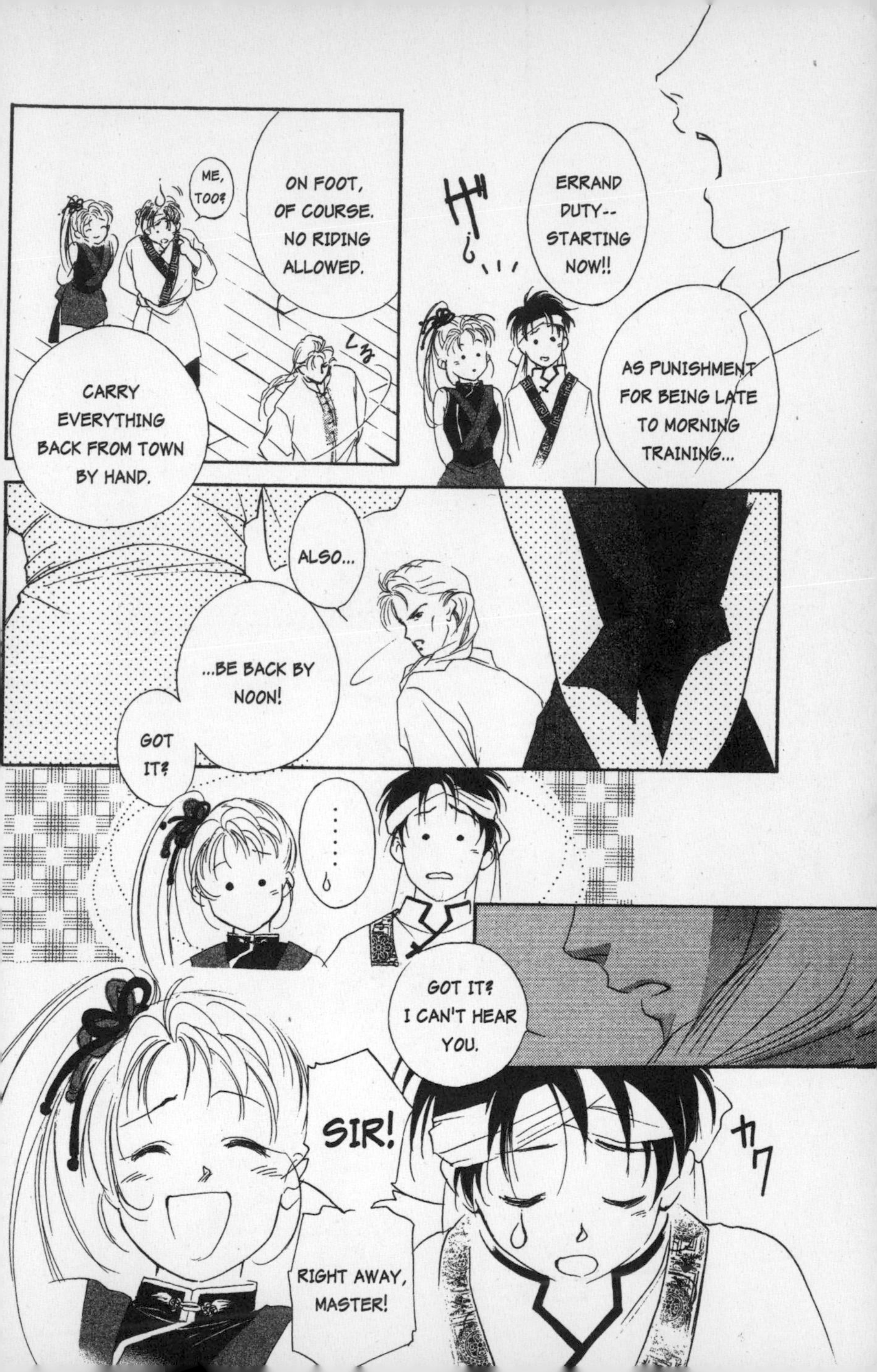
AS PUNISHMENT FOR BEING LATE TO MORNING TRAINING...
ERRAND DUTY-- STARTING NOW!!
ON FOOT, OF COURSE. NO RIDING ALLOWED.
ME, TOO?
CARRY EVERYTHING BACK FROM TOWN BY HAND.
ALSO...
...BE BACK BY NOON!
GOT IT?
......
GOT IT? I CAN'T HEAR YOU.
SIR!
RIGHT AWAY, MASTER!

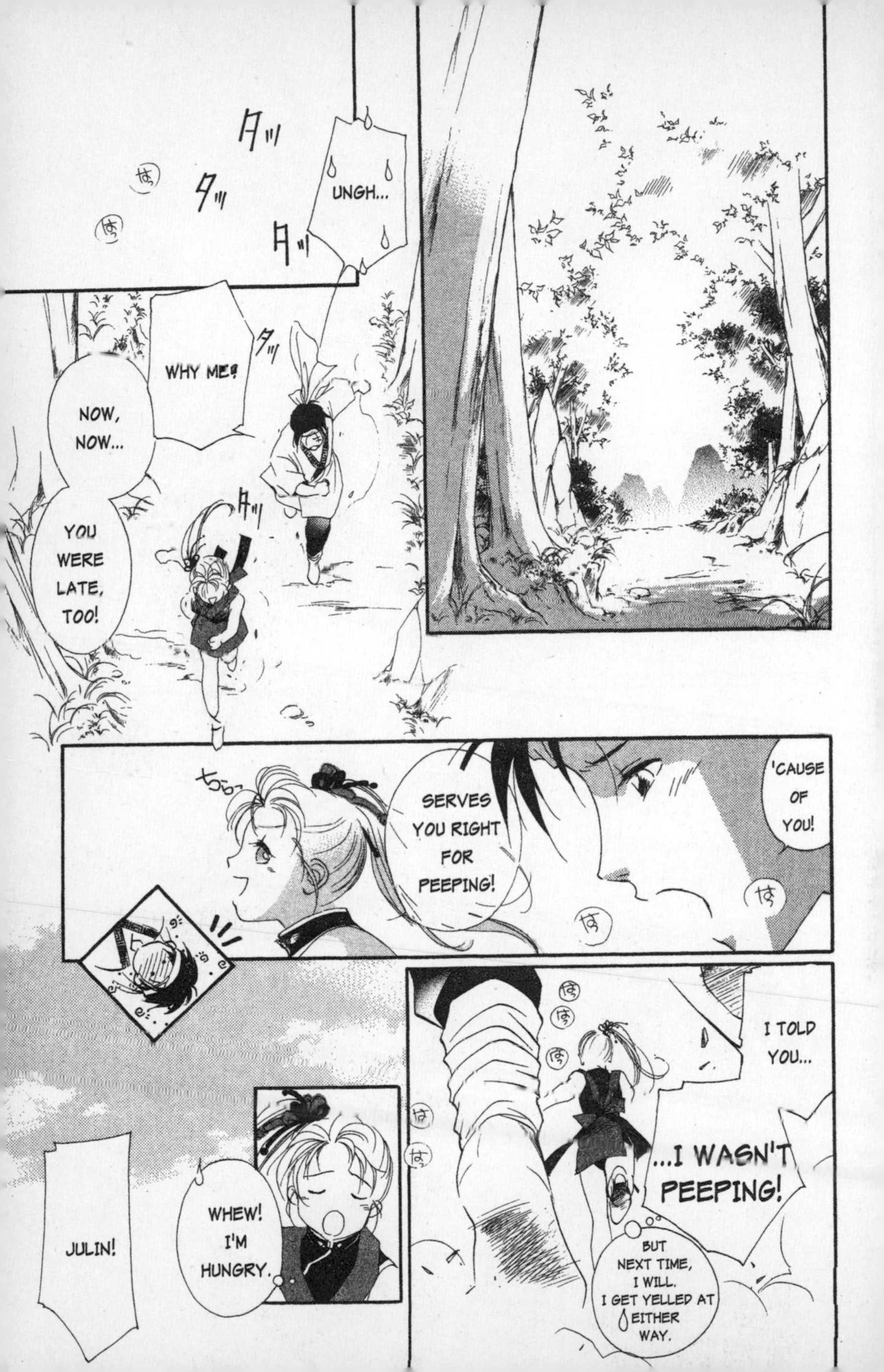
UNGH...
WHY ME!?
NOW, NOW...
YOU WERE LATE, TOO!
'CAUSE OF YOU!
SERVES YOU RIGHT FOR PEEPING!
I TOLD YOU...
...I WASN'T PEEPING!
BUT NEXT TIME, I WILL. I GET YELLED AT EITHER WAY.
WHEW! I'M HUNGRY.
JULIN!

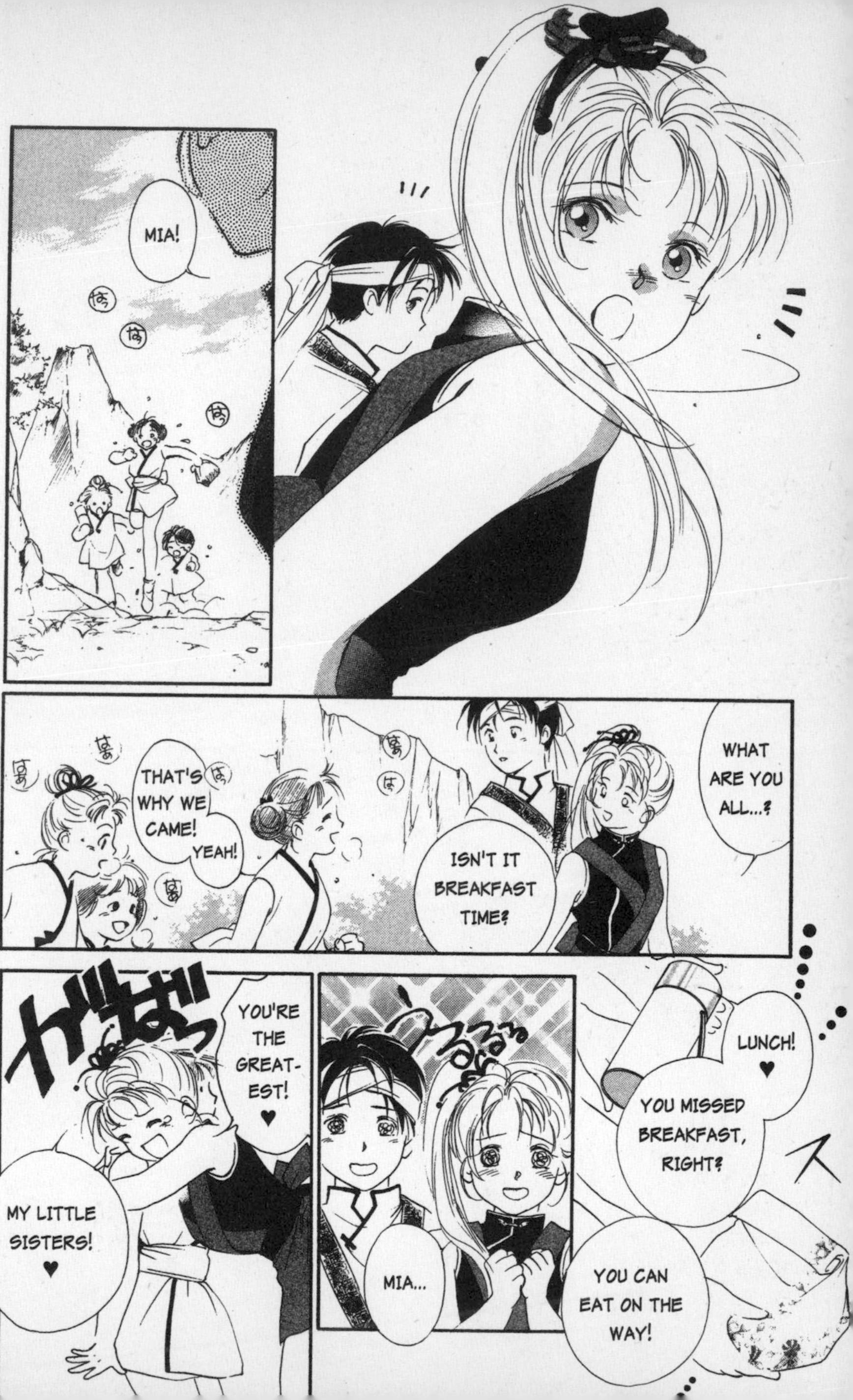
MIA!
WHAT ARE YOU ALL...?
ISN'T IT BREAKFAST TIME?
THAT'S WHY WE CAME!
YEAH!
LUNCH! ♥
YOU MISSED BREAKFAST, RIGHT?
YOU CAN EAT ON THE WAY!
MIA...
YOU'RE THE GREAT-EST! ♥
MY LITTLE SISTERS! ♥

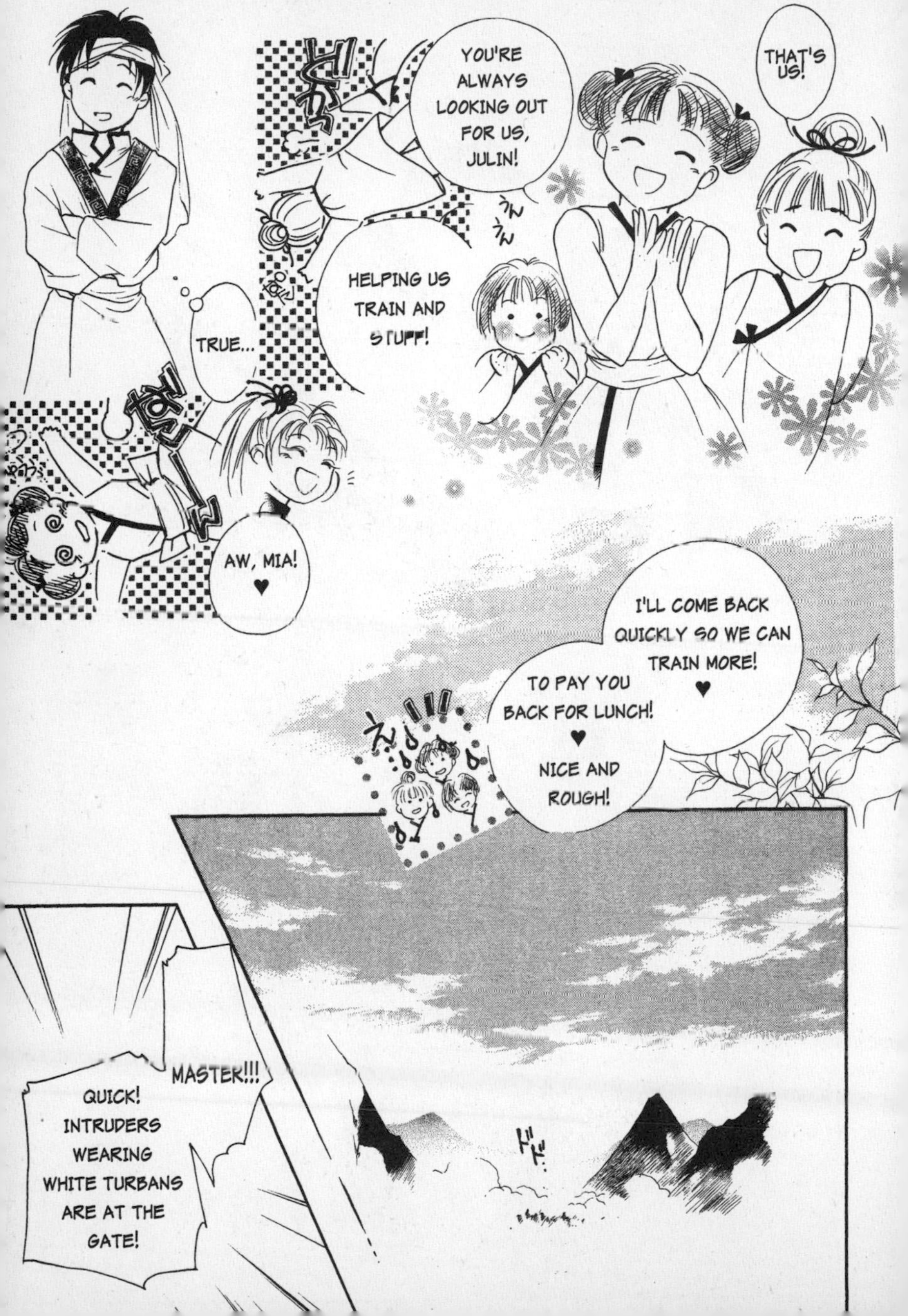
THAT'S US!
YOU'RE ALWAYS LOOKING OUT FOR US, JULIN!
HELPING US TRAIN AND STUFF!
TRUE...
AW, MIA! ♥
I'LL COME BACK QUICKLY SO WE CAN TRAIN MORE! ♥
TO PAY YOU BACK FOR LUNCH! ♥
NICE AND ROUGH!
MASTER!!!
QUICK! INTRUDERS WEARING WHITE TURBANS ARE AT THE GATE!

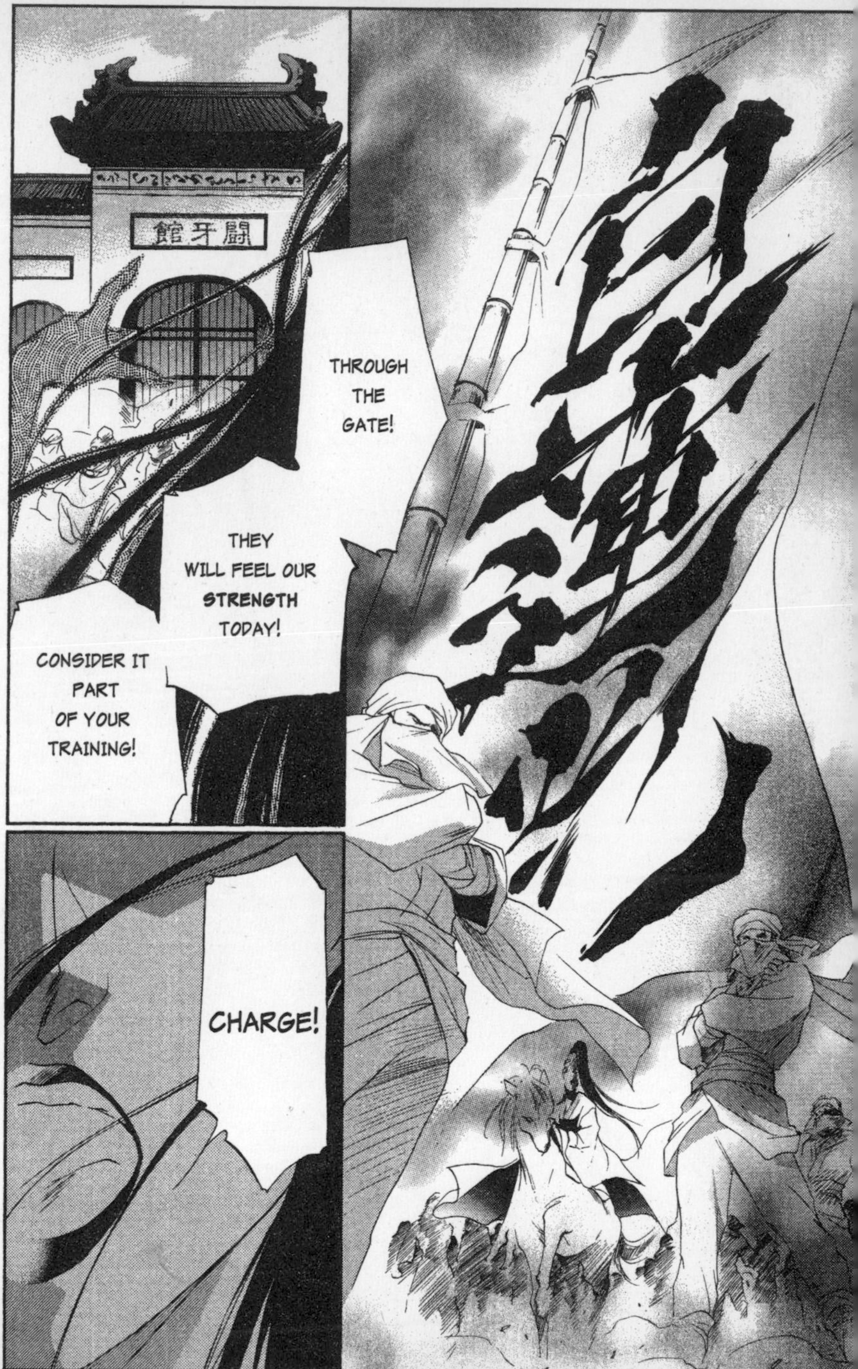
闘牙館
THROUGH THE GATE!
THEY WILL FEEL OUR STRENGTH TODAY!
CONSIDER IT PART OF YOUR TRAINING!
CHARGE!

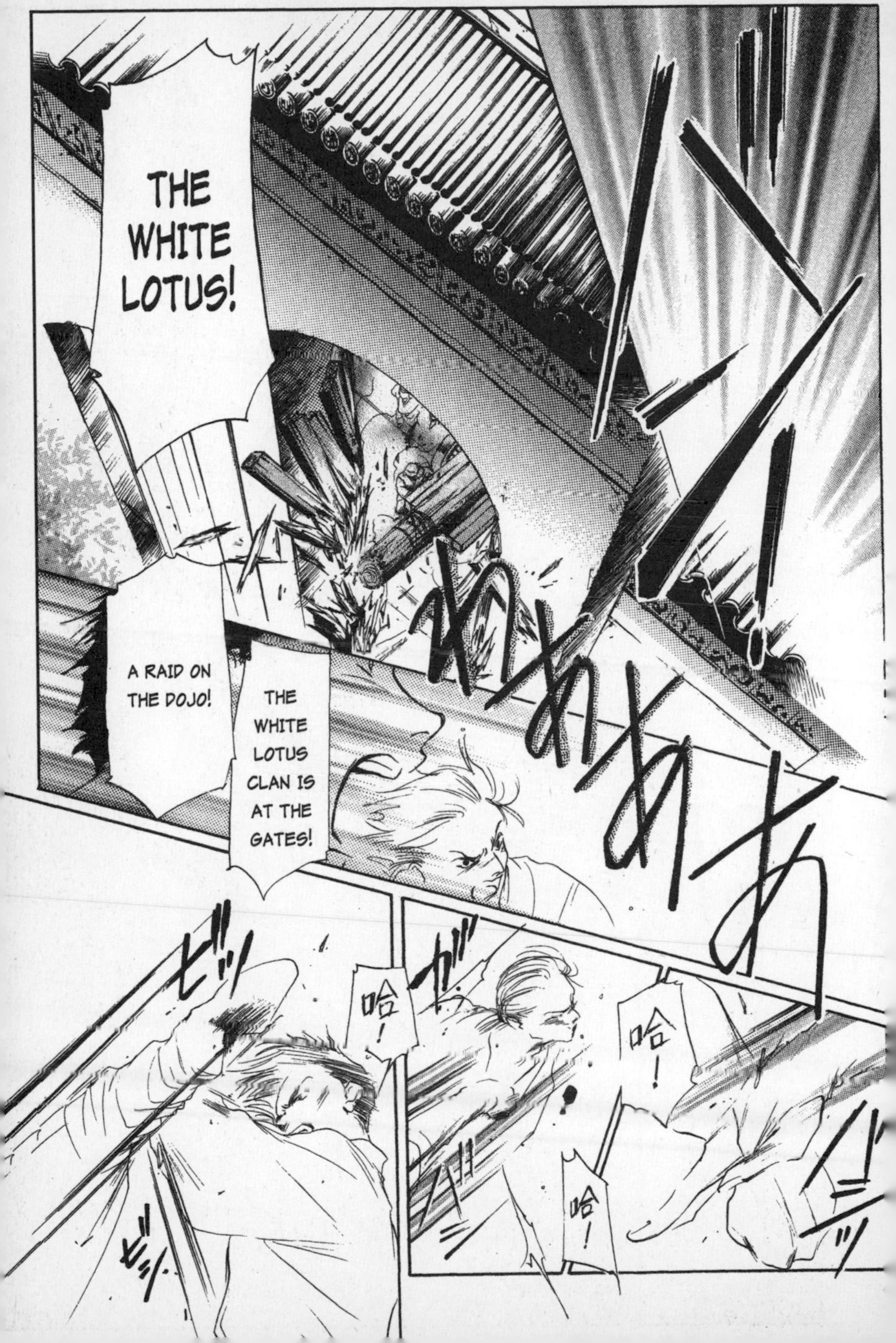
THE WHITE LOTUS!
THE WHITE LOTUS CLAN IS AT THE GATES!
A RAID ON THE DOJO!
わあああ
哈!
哈!
哈!

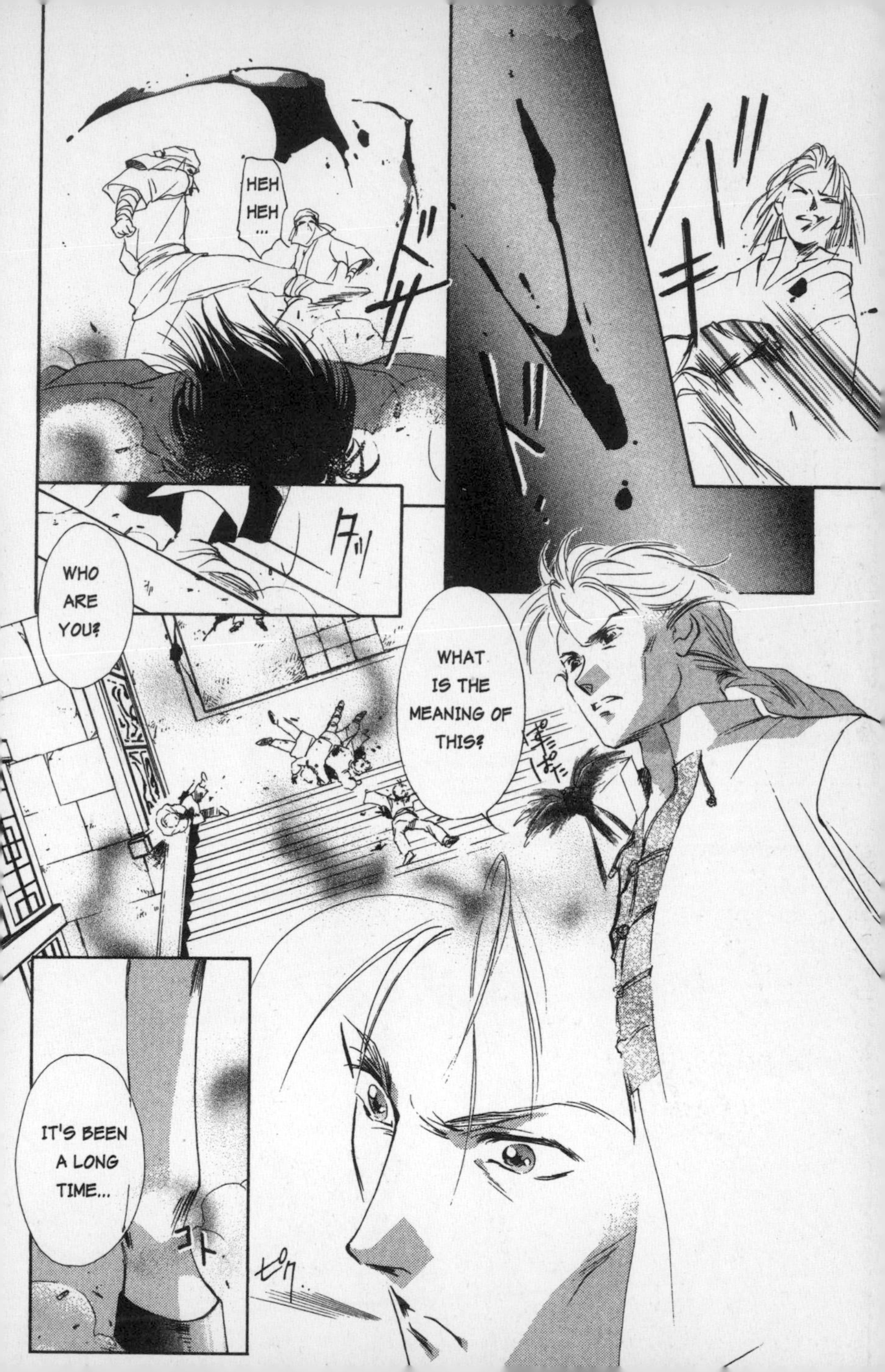
HEH HEH ...
WHAT IS THE MEANING OF THIS?
WHO ARE YOU?
IT'S BEEN A LONG TIME...

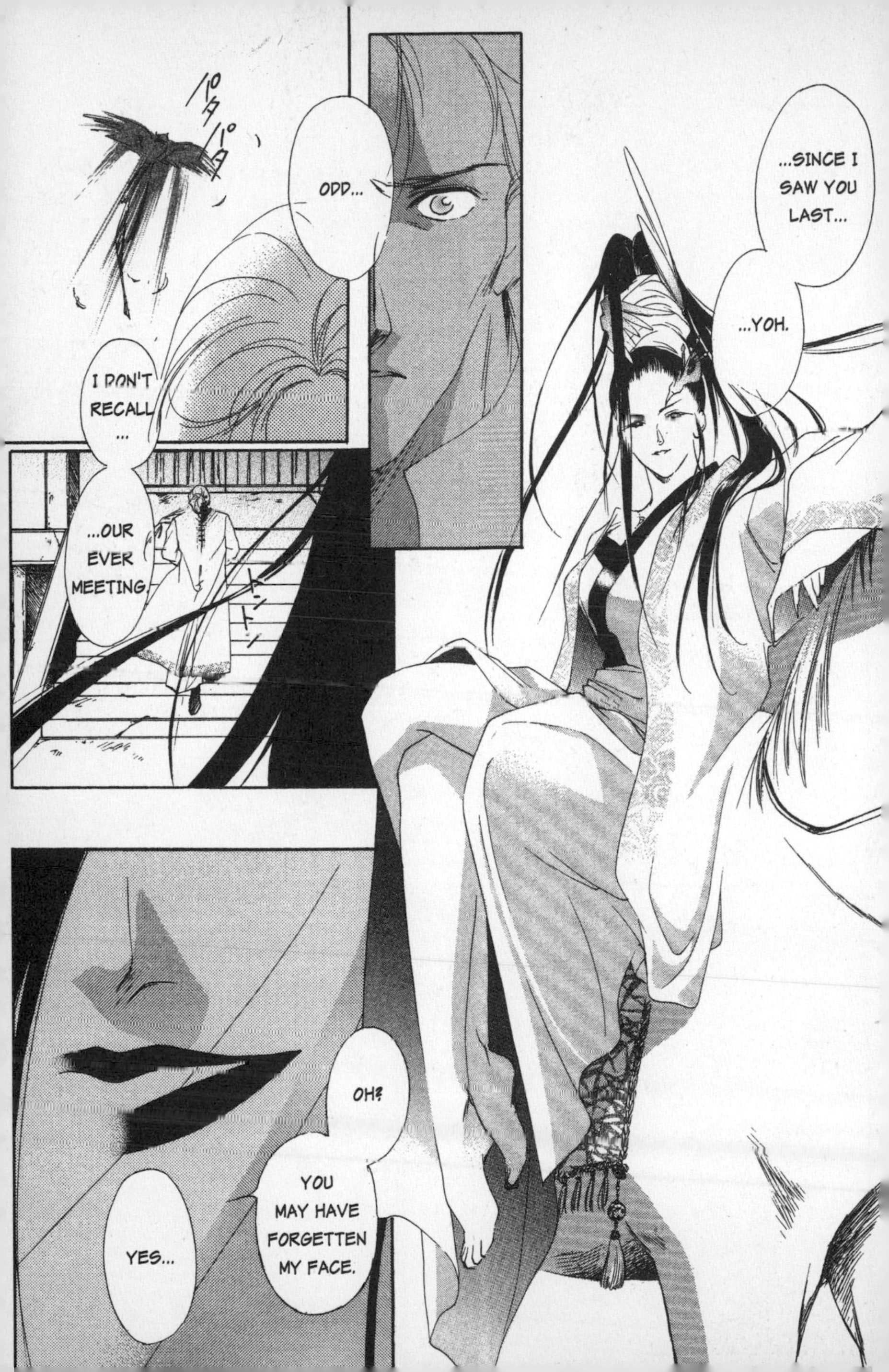
...SINCE I SAW YOU LAST...
...YOH.
ODD...
I DON'T RECALL ...
...OUR EVER MEETING.
OH?
YOU MAY HAVE FORGETTEN MY FACE.
YES...

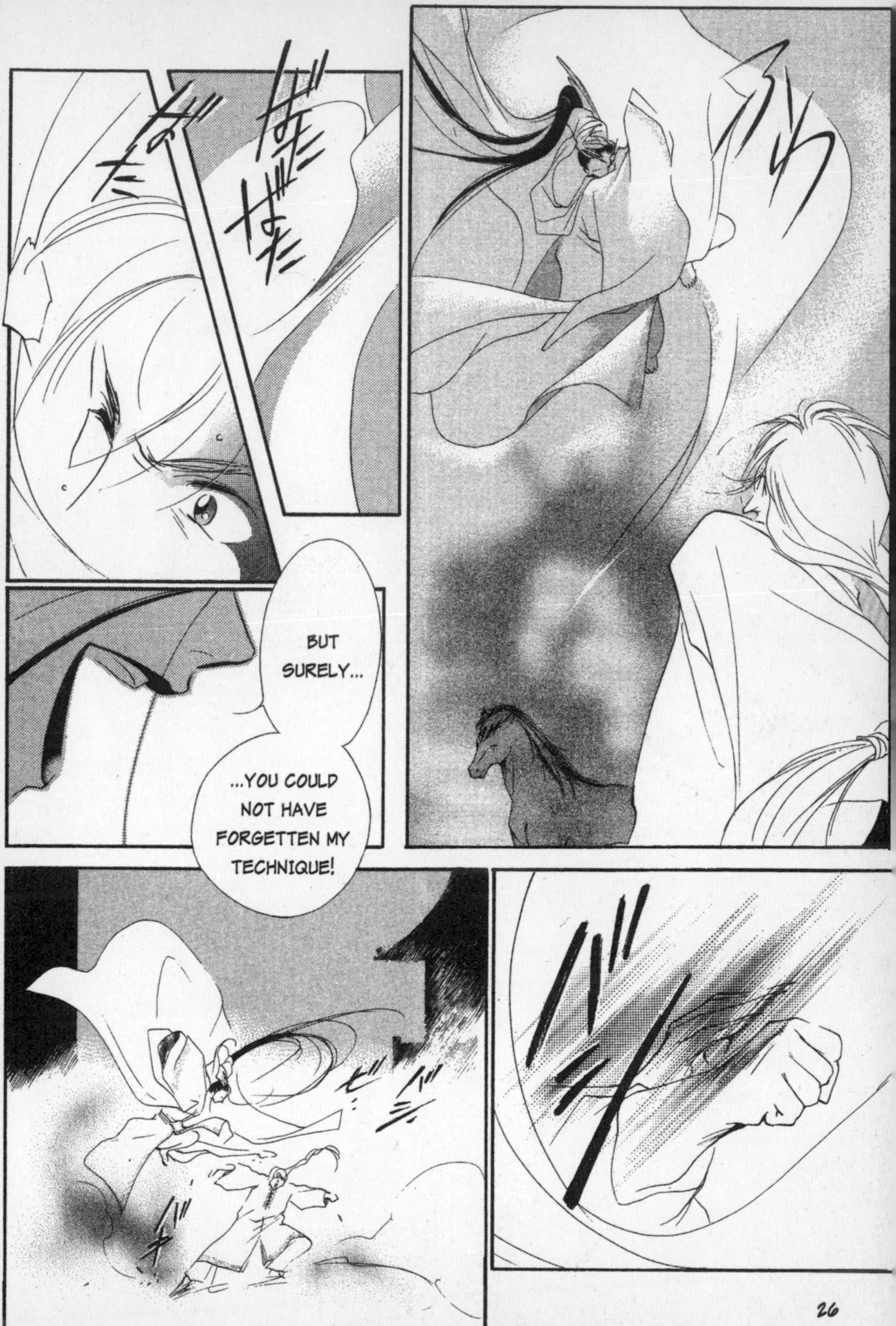
BUT SURELY...
...YOU COULD NOT HAVE FORGETTEN MY TECHNIQUE!

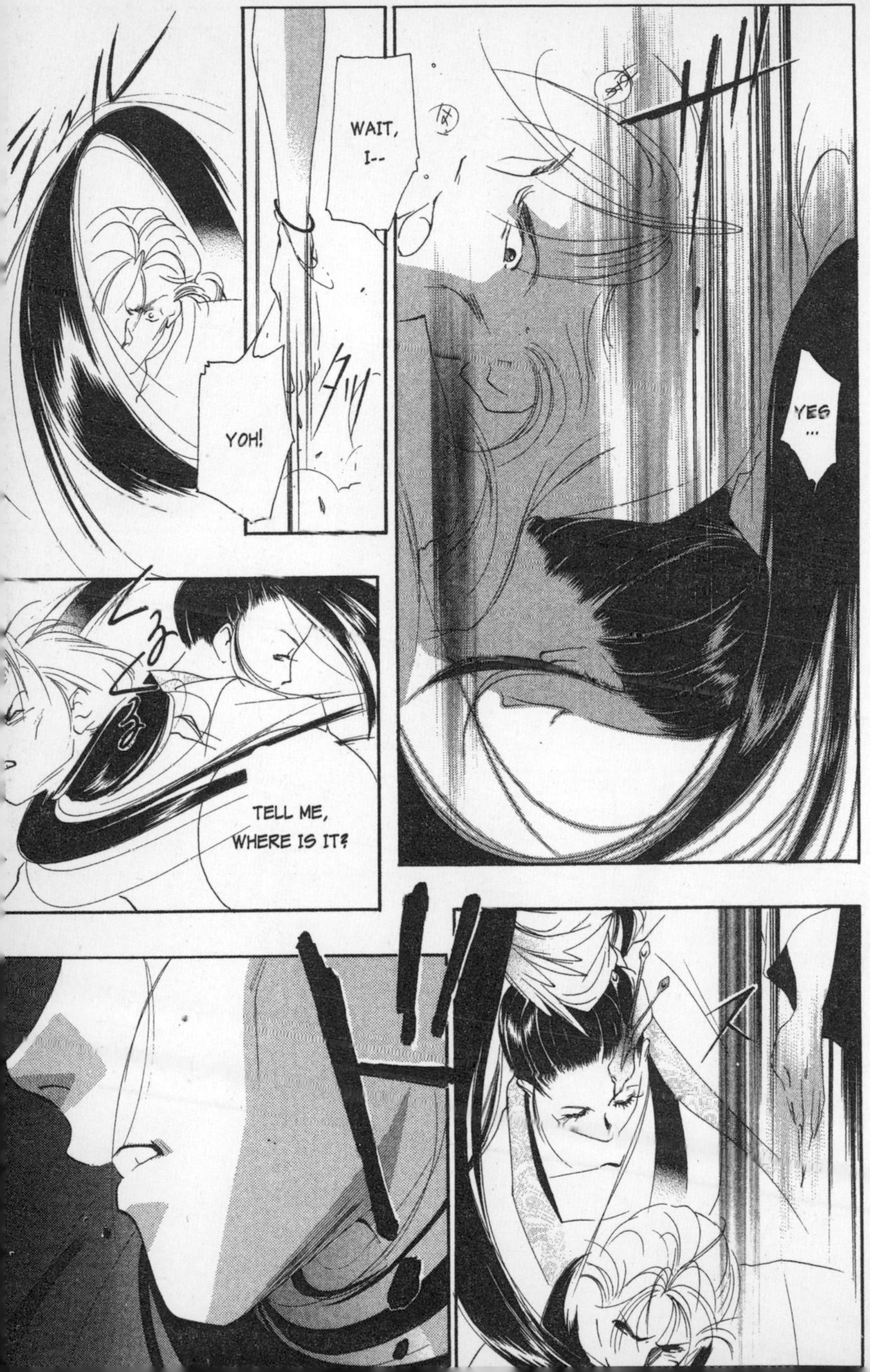
YES ...
WAIT, I--
YOH!
TELL ME, WHERE IS IT?

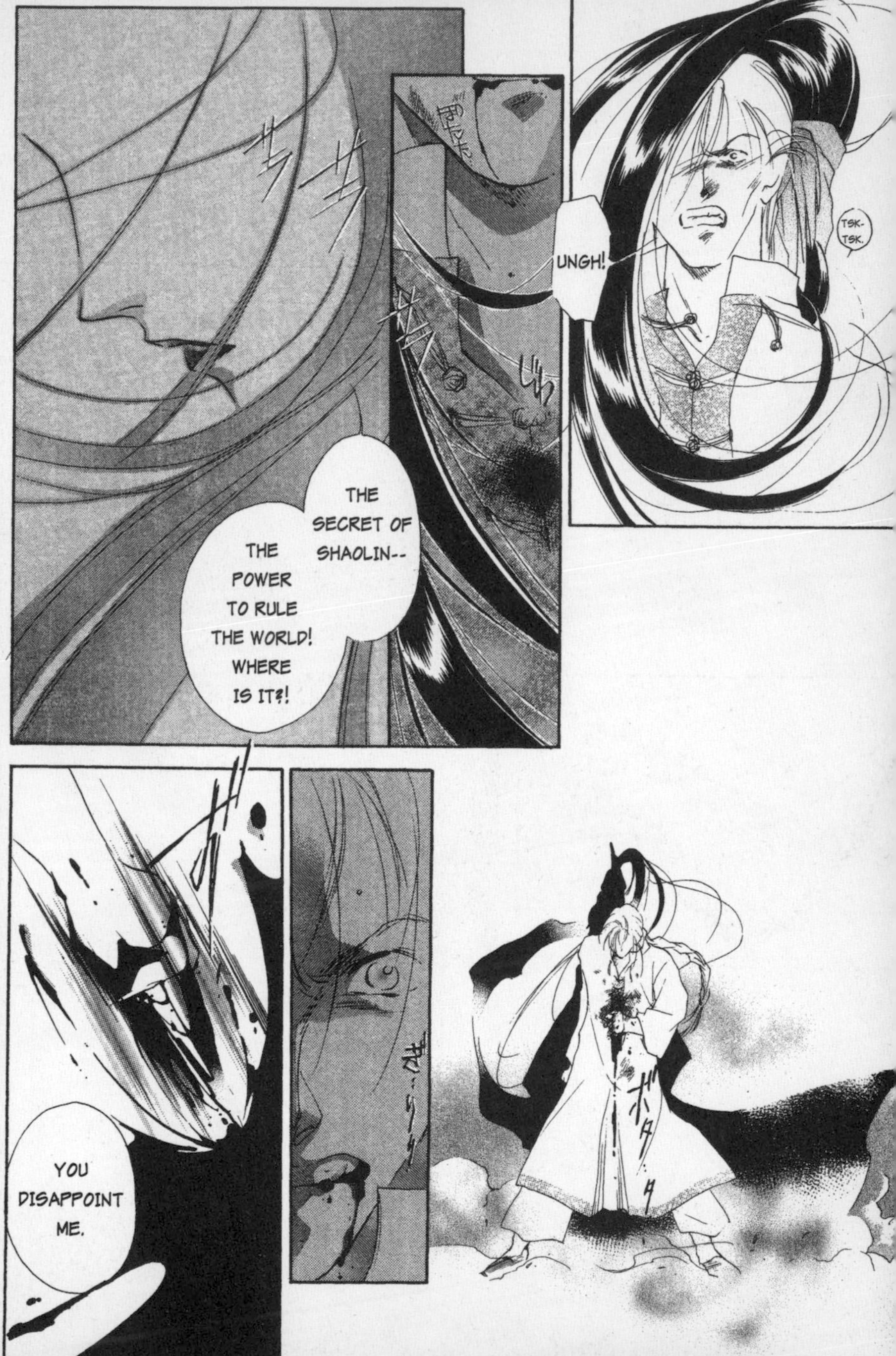
TSK-TSK.
UNGH!
THE SECRET OF SHAOLIN-- THE POWER TO RULE THE WORLD! WHERE IS IT?!
YOU DISAPPOINT ME.

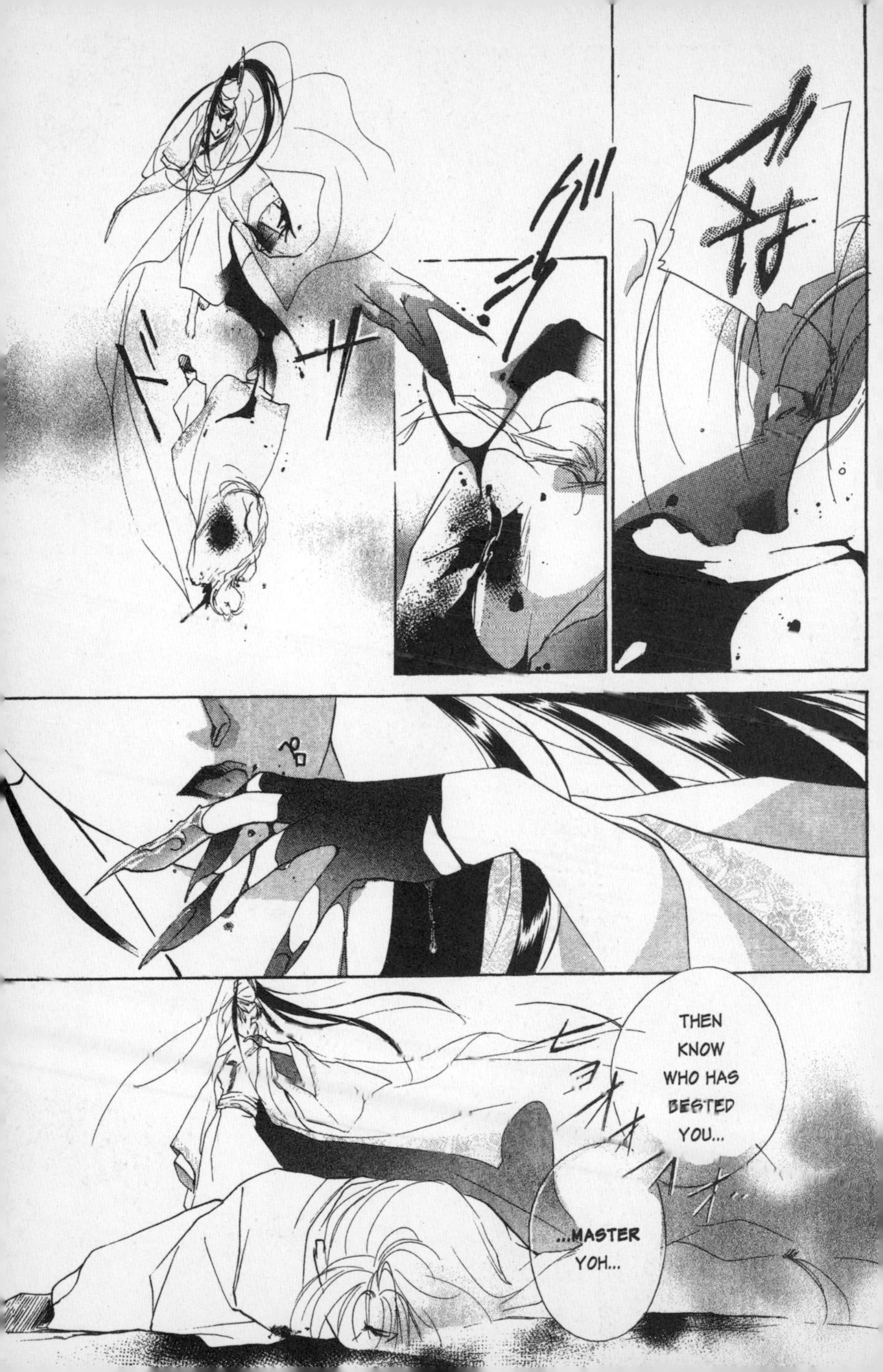
THEN KNOW WHO HAS BESTED YOU...
...MASTER YOH...

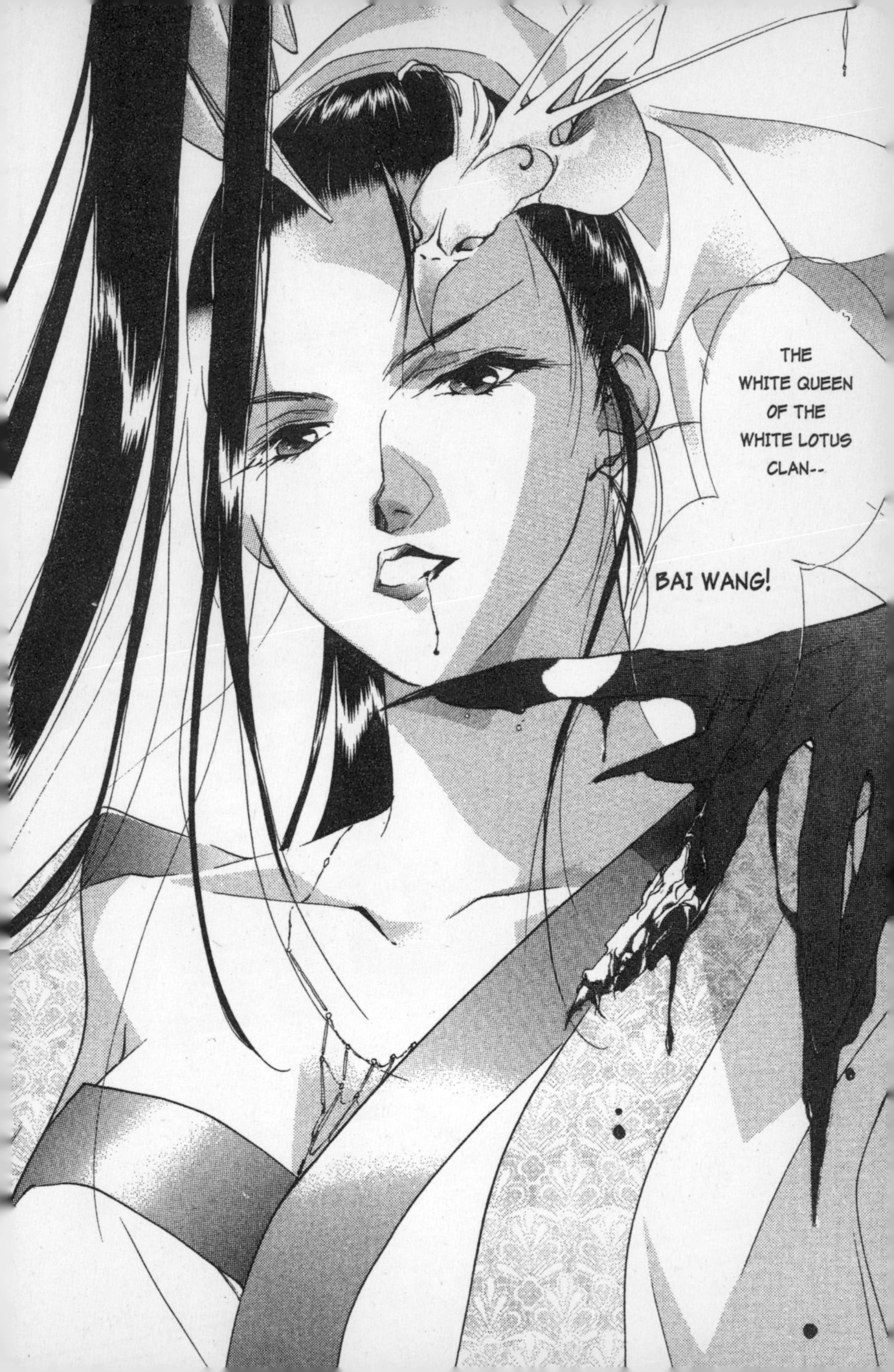
THE WHITE QUEEN OF THE WHITE LOTUS CLAN--
BAI WANG!

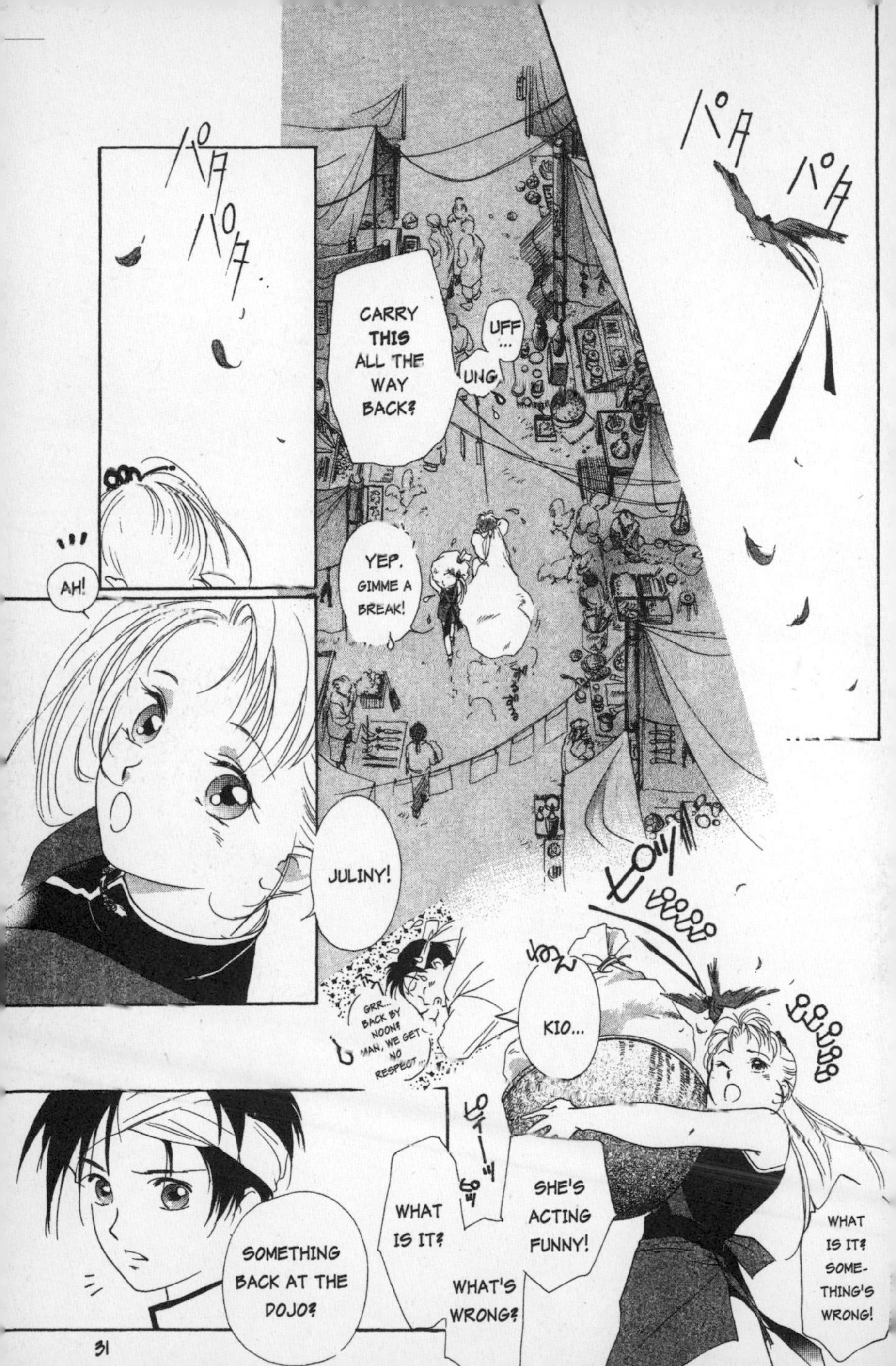
パタ パタ
UFF... UNG
CARRY THIS ALL THE WAY BACK?
YEP. GIMME A BREAK!
パタ パタ
AH!
JULINY!
KIO...
GRR... BACK BY NOON? MAN, WE GET NO RESPECT...
WHAT IS IT? SOMETHING'S WRONG!
SHE'S ACTING FUNNY!
WHAT IS IT?
WHAT'S WRONG?
SOMETHING BACK AT THE DOJO?

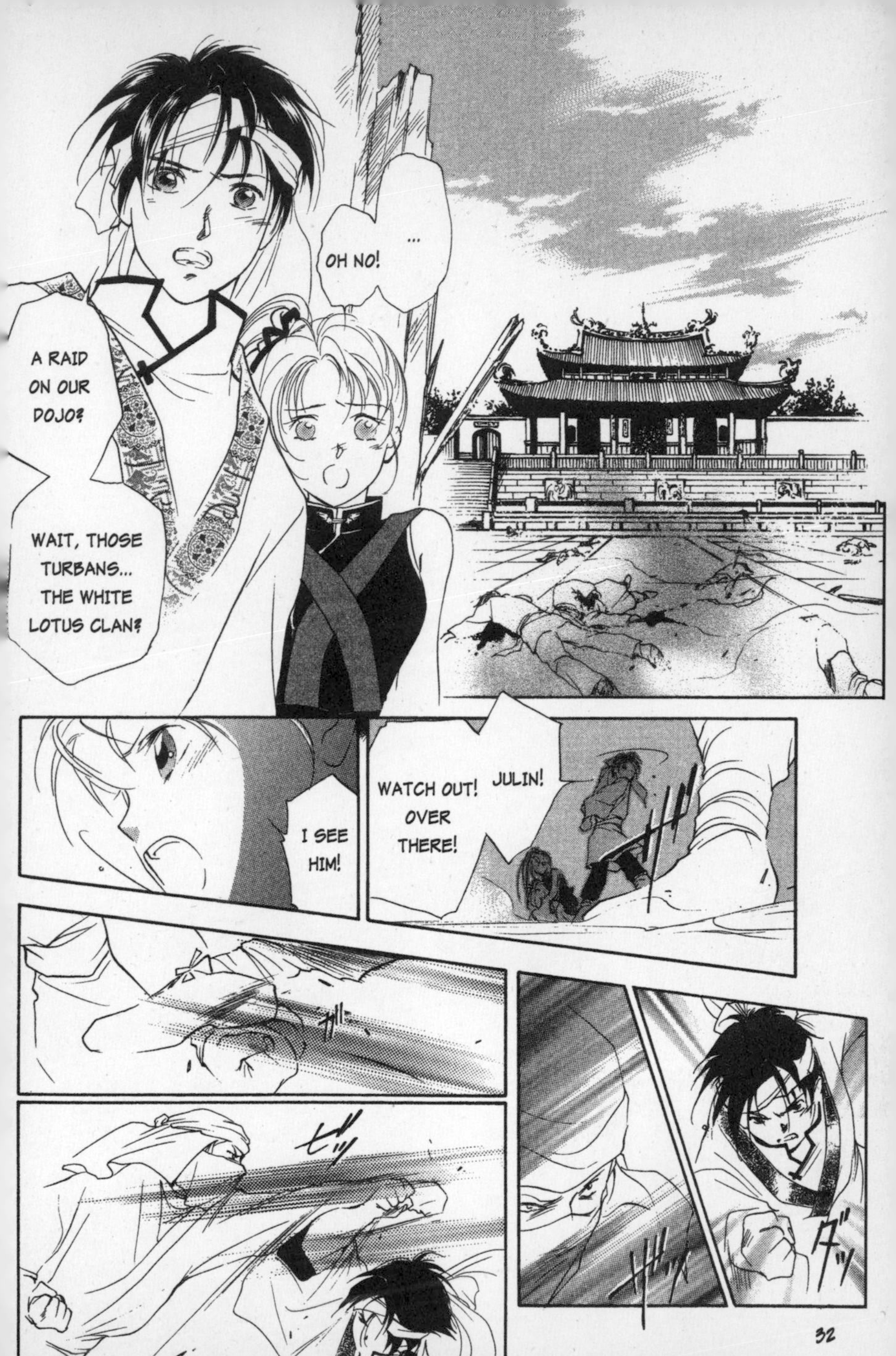

...
OH NO!
A RAID ON OUR DOJO?
WAIT, THOSE TURBANS... THE WHITE LOTUS CLAN?
JULIN!
WATCH OUT! OVER THERE!
I SEE HIM!

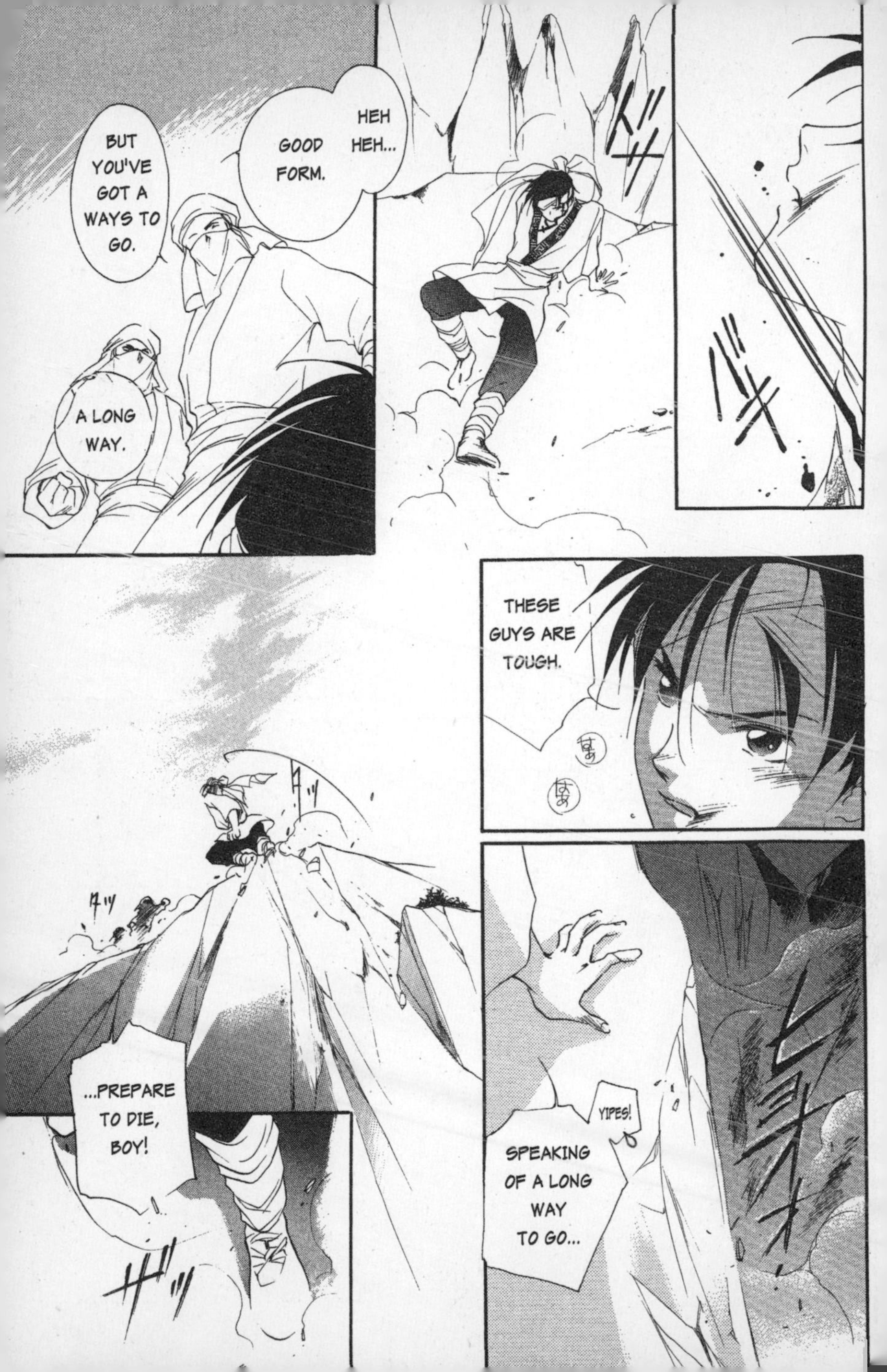
HEH HEH... GOOD FORM.
BUT YOU'VE GOT A WAYS TO GO.
A LONG WAY.
THESE GUYS ARE TOUGH.
YIPES!
SPEAKING OF A LONG WAY TO GO...
...PREPARE TO DIE, BOY!

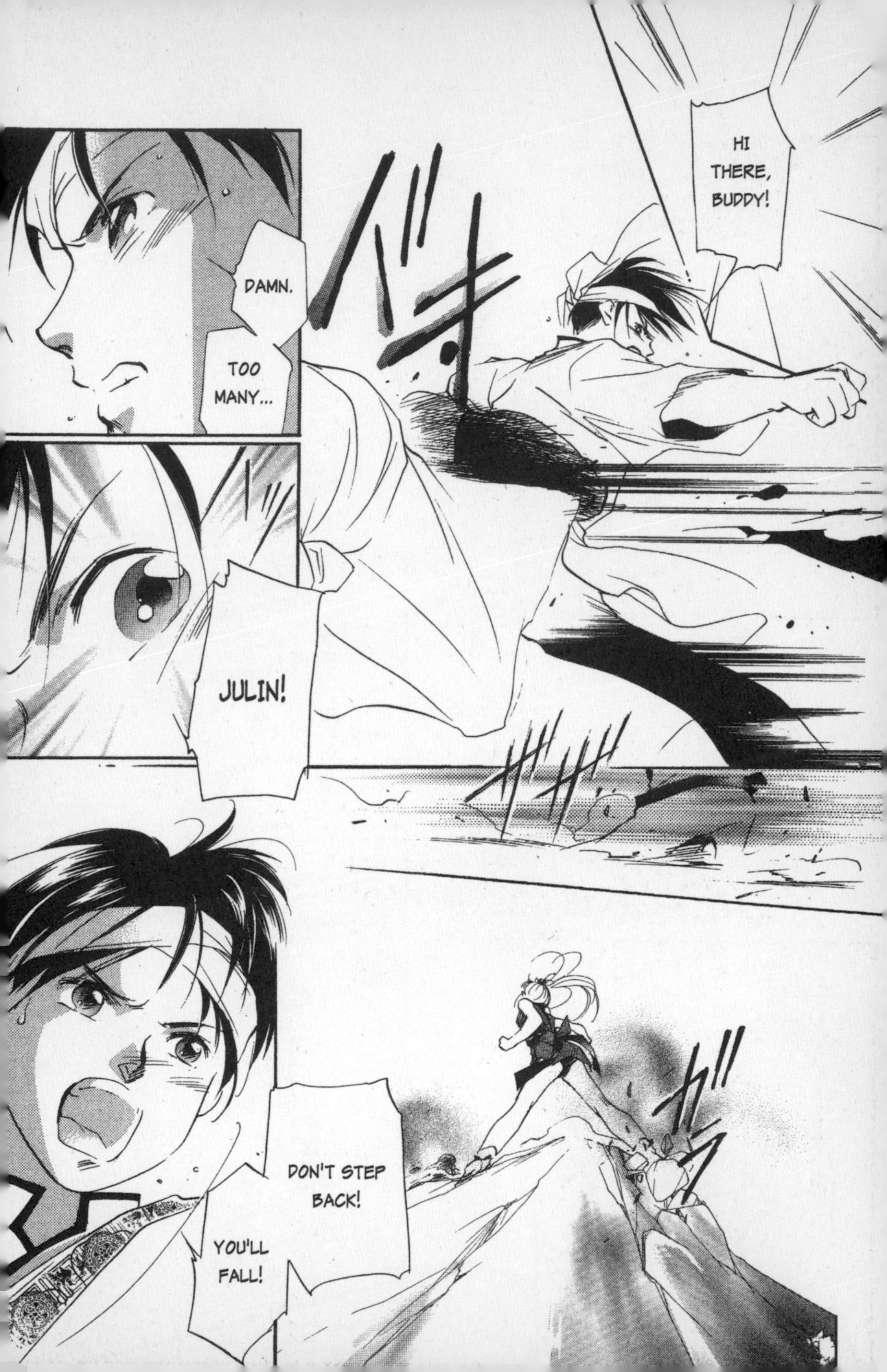
HI THERE, BUDDY!
DAMN.
TOO MANY...
JULIN!
DON'T STEP BACK!
YOU'LL FALL!

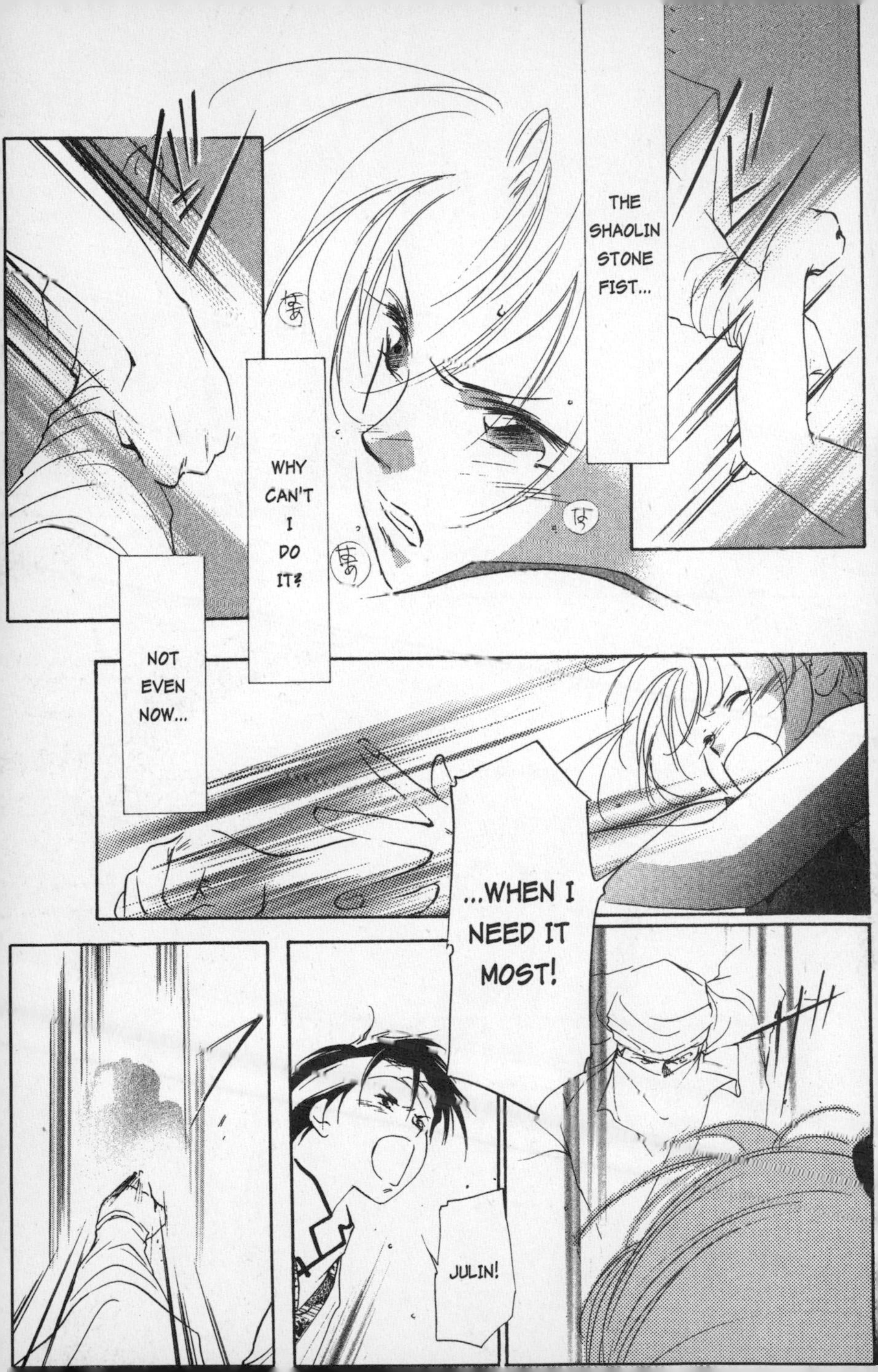
THE SHAOLIN STONE FIST...
WHY CAN'T I DO IT?
NOT EVEN NOW...
...WHEN I NEED IT MOST!
JULIN!

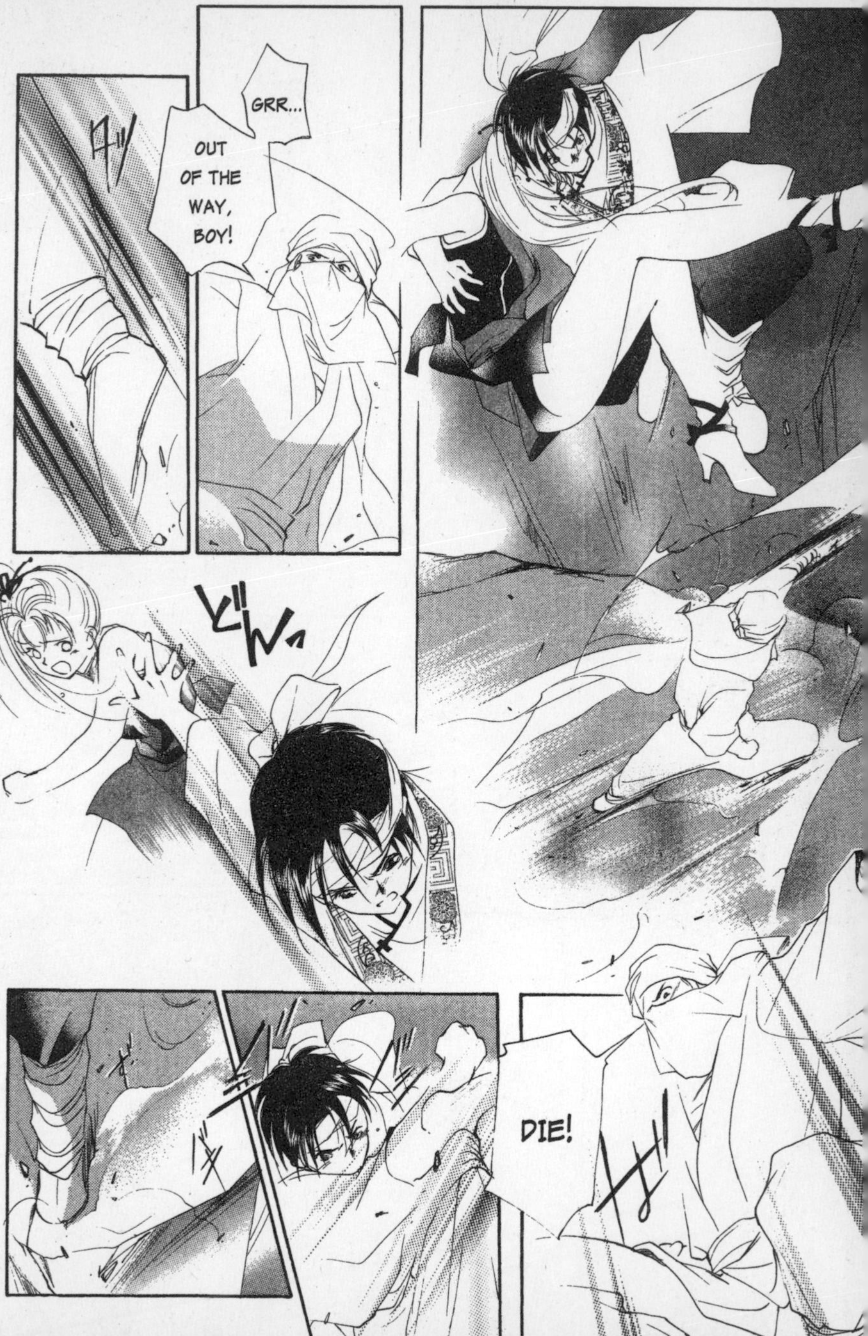
GRR...
OUT OF THE WAY, BOY!
DIE!

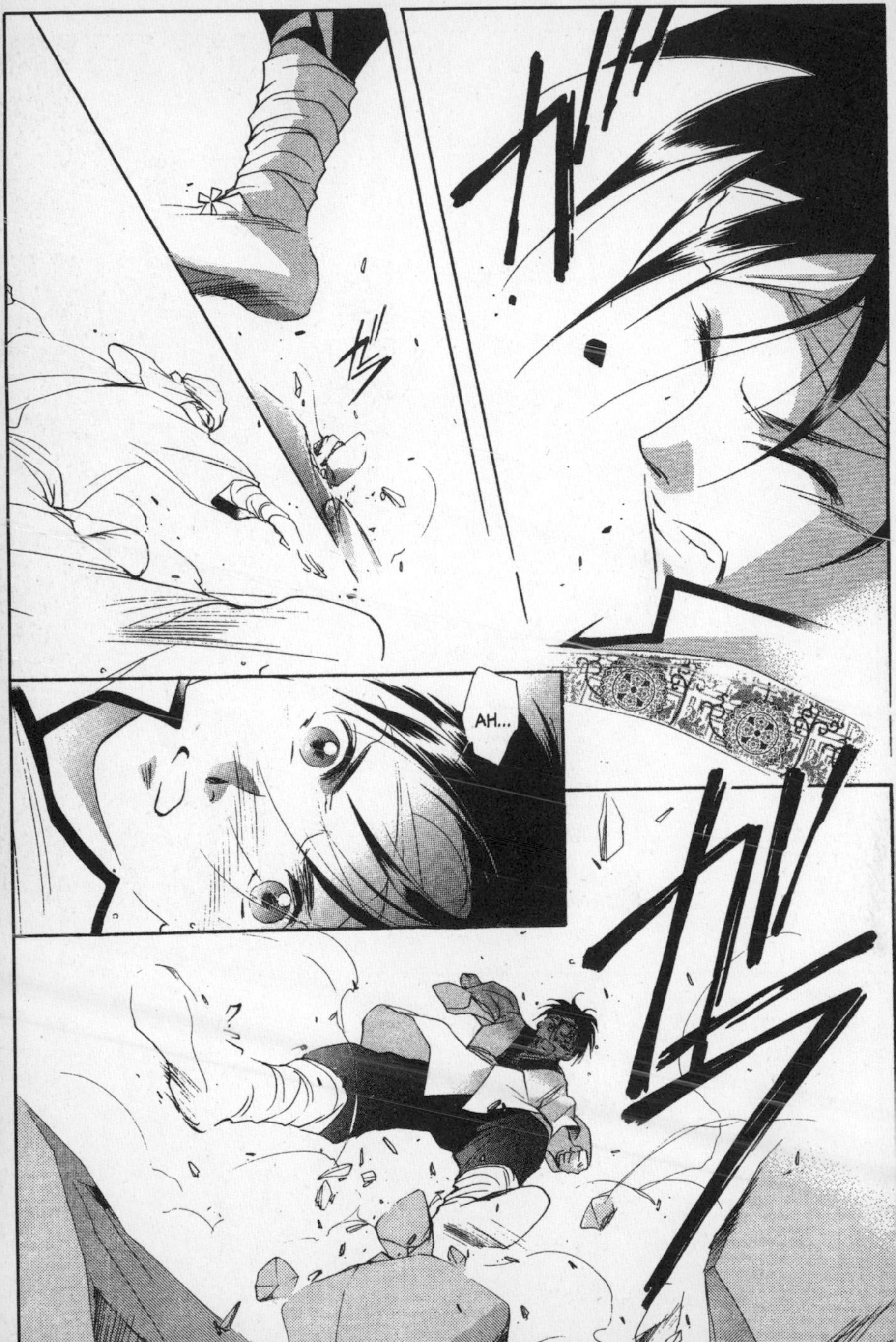
AH...

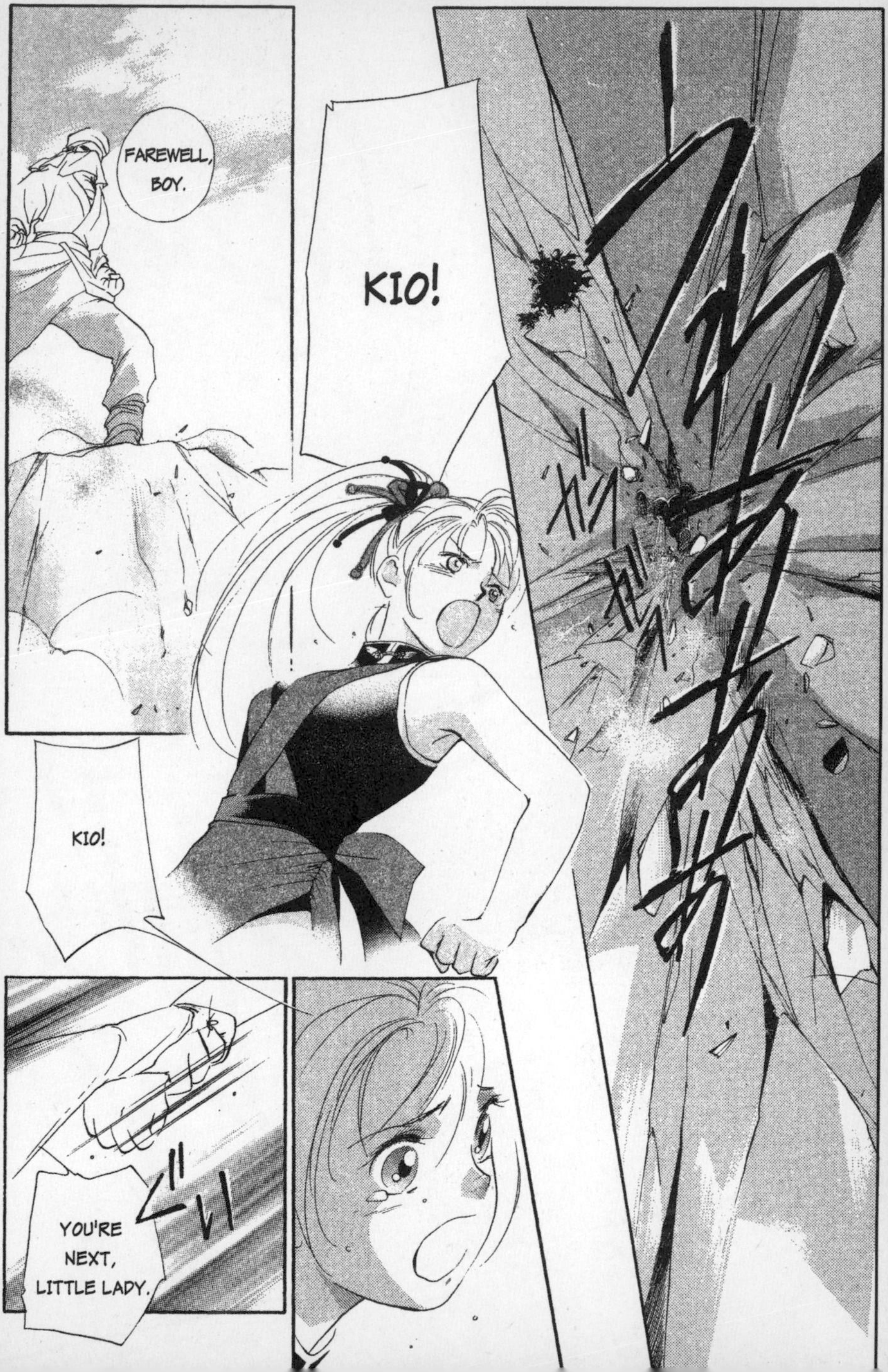
KIO!
FAREWELL, BOY.
KIO!
YOU'RE NEXT, LITTLE LADY.

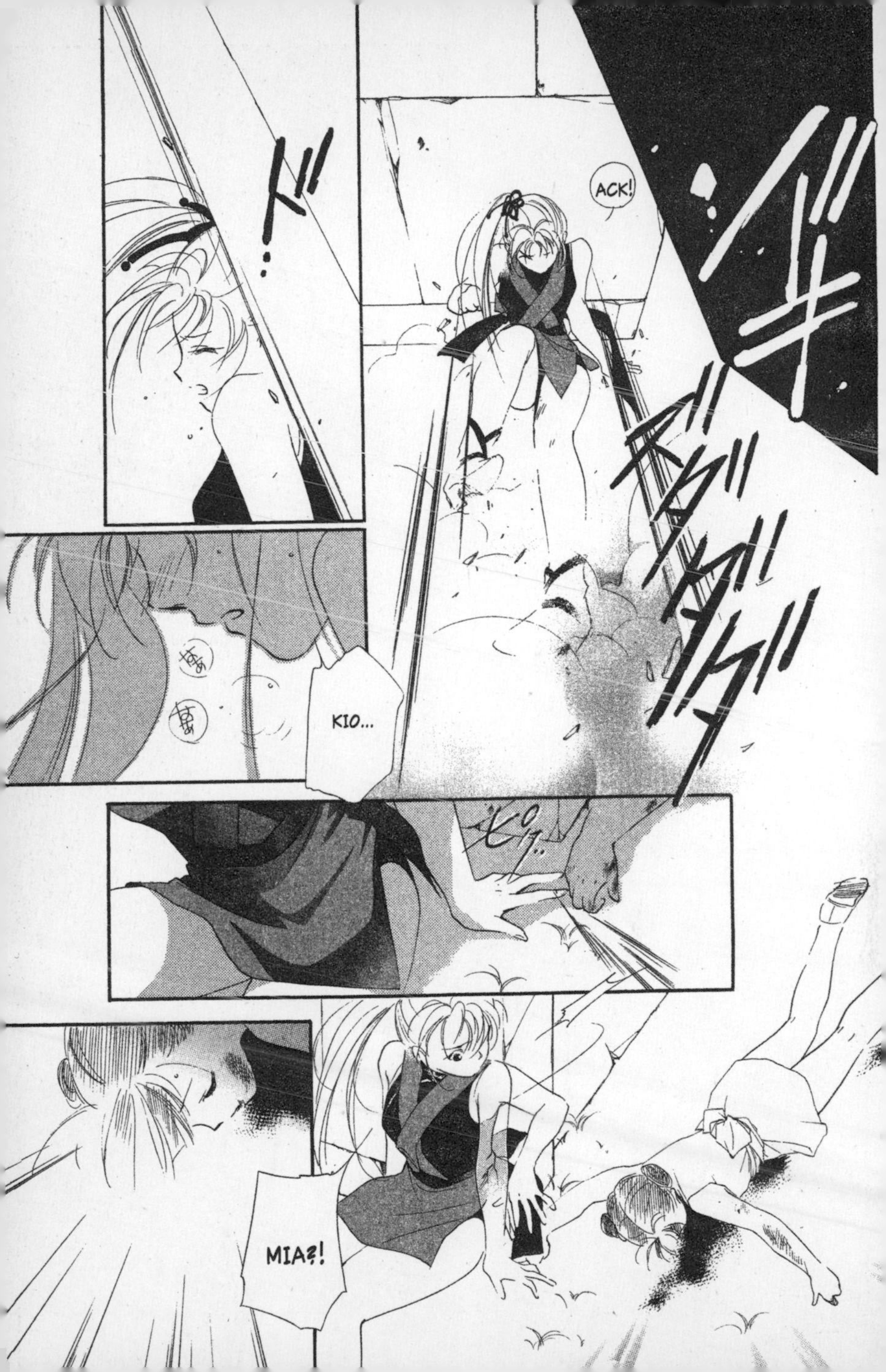
ACK!
KIO...
MIA?!

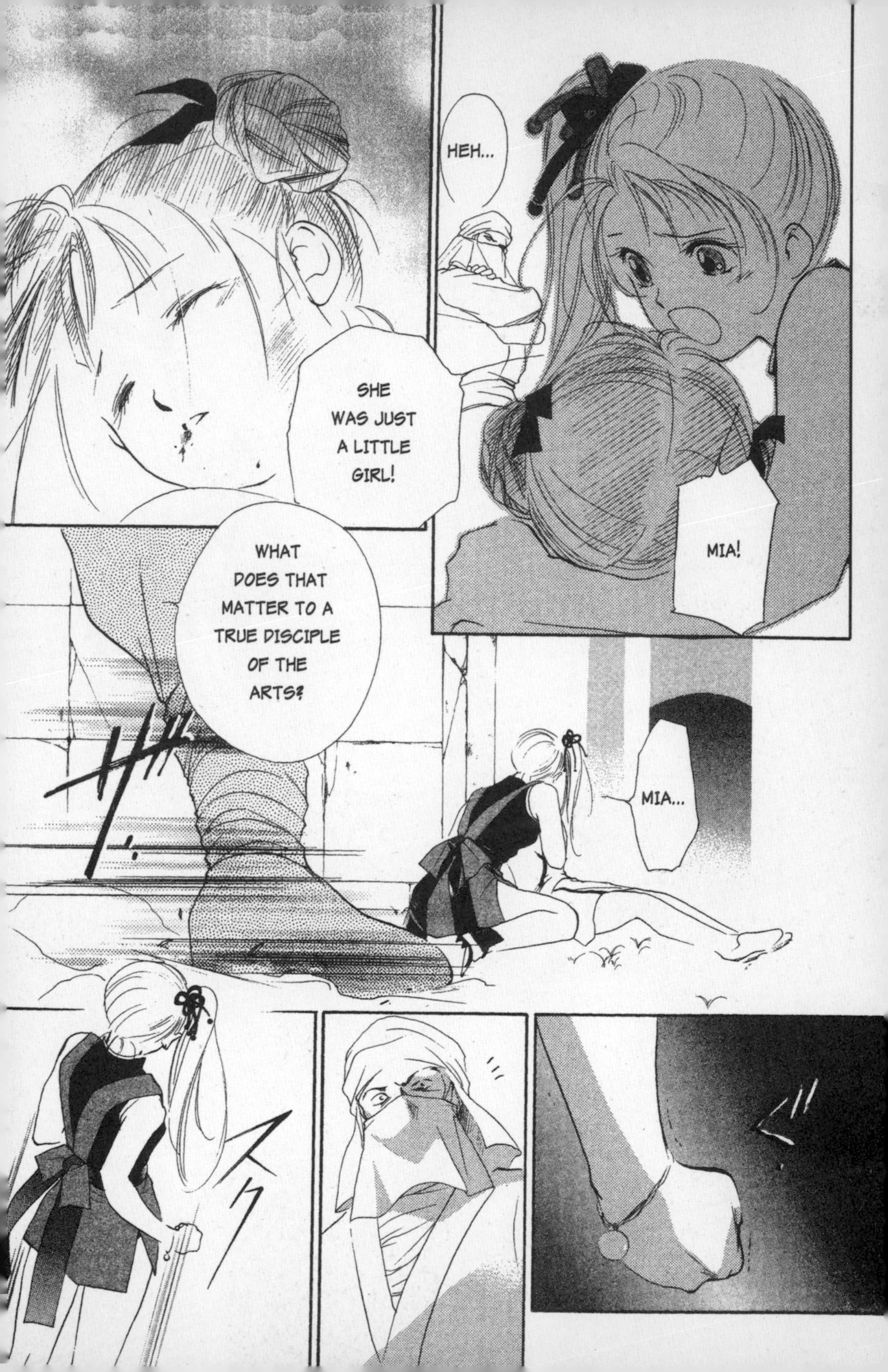
HEH...
MIA!
SHE WAS JUST A LITTLE GIRL!
WHAT DOES THAT MATTER TO A TRUE DISCIPLE OF THE ARTS?
MIA...

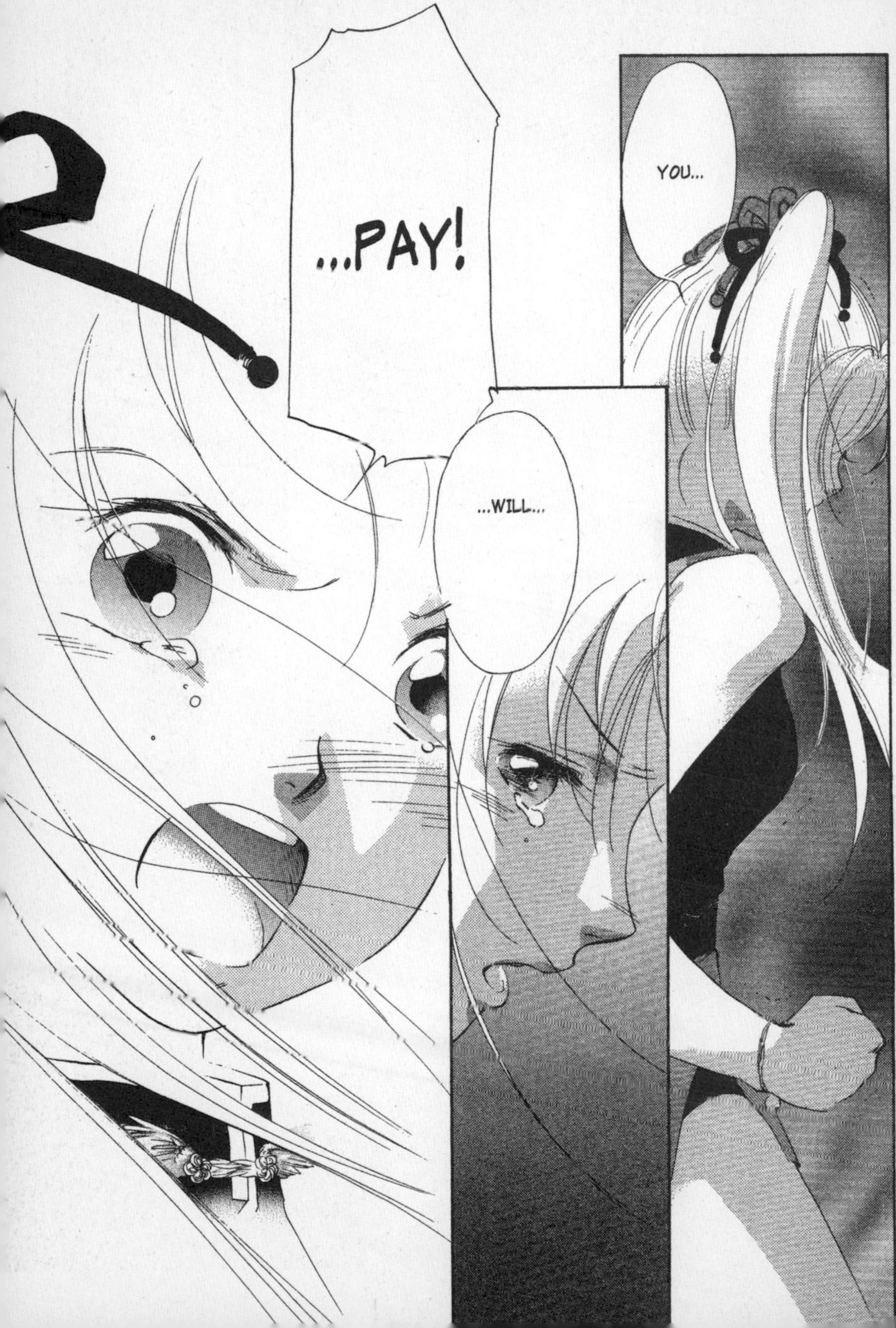
YOU...
...WILL...
...PAY!

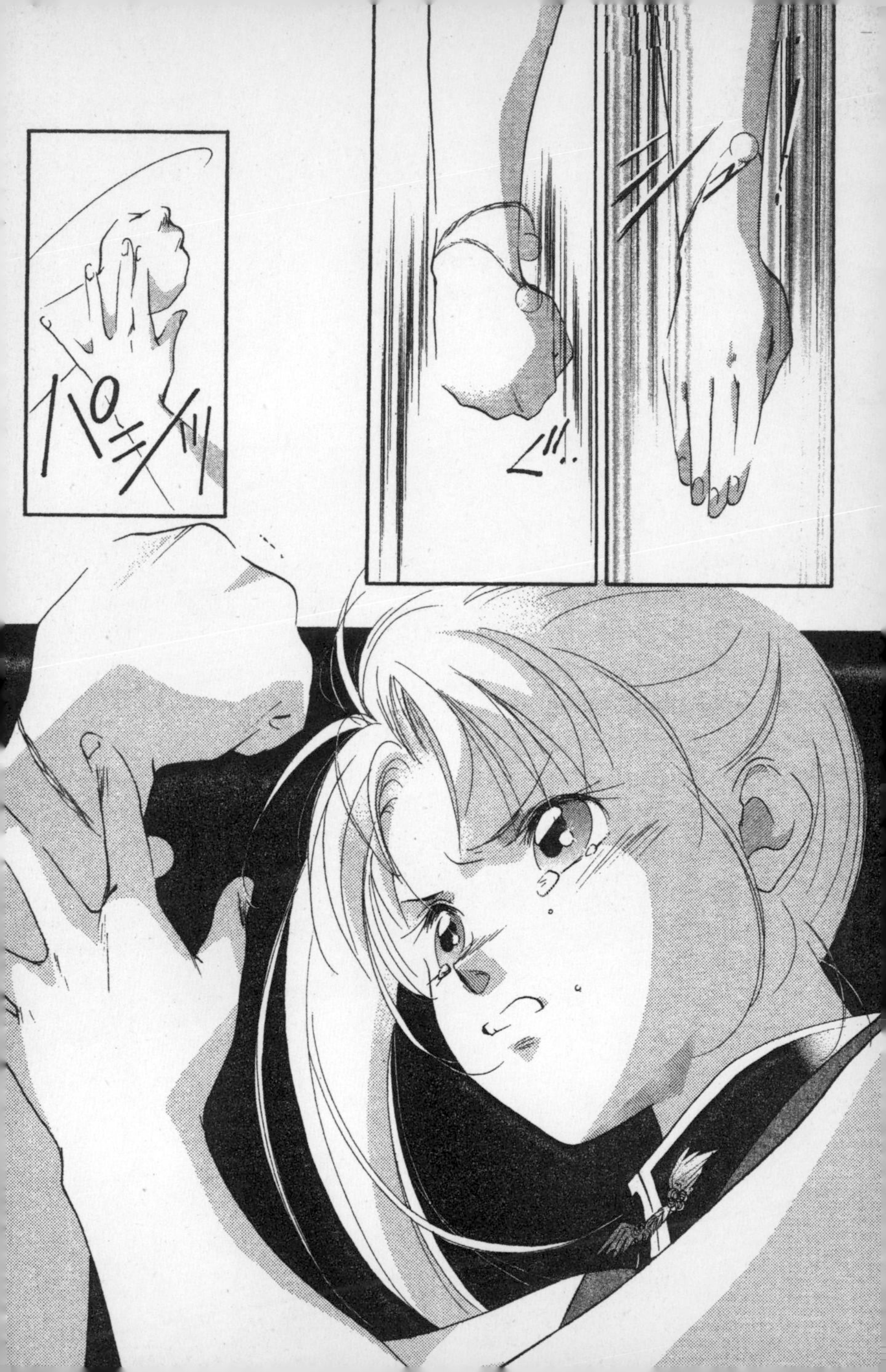
ぐ‥
パチッ

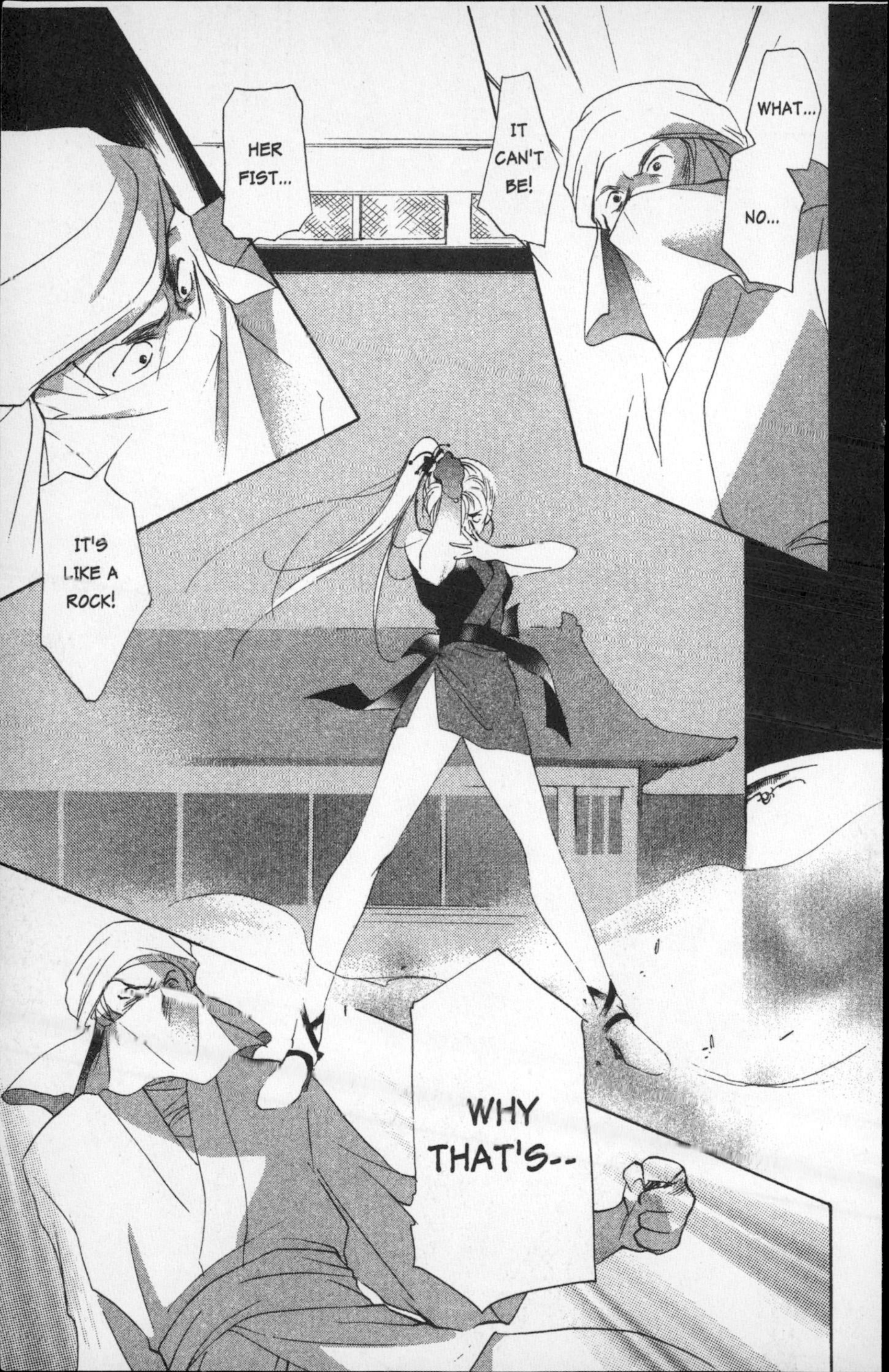
WHAT...
NO...
IT CAN'T BE!
HER FIST...
IT'S LIKE A ROCK!
WHY THAT'S--

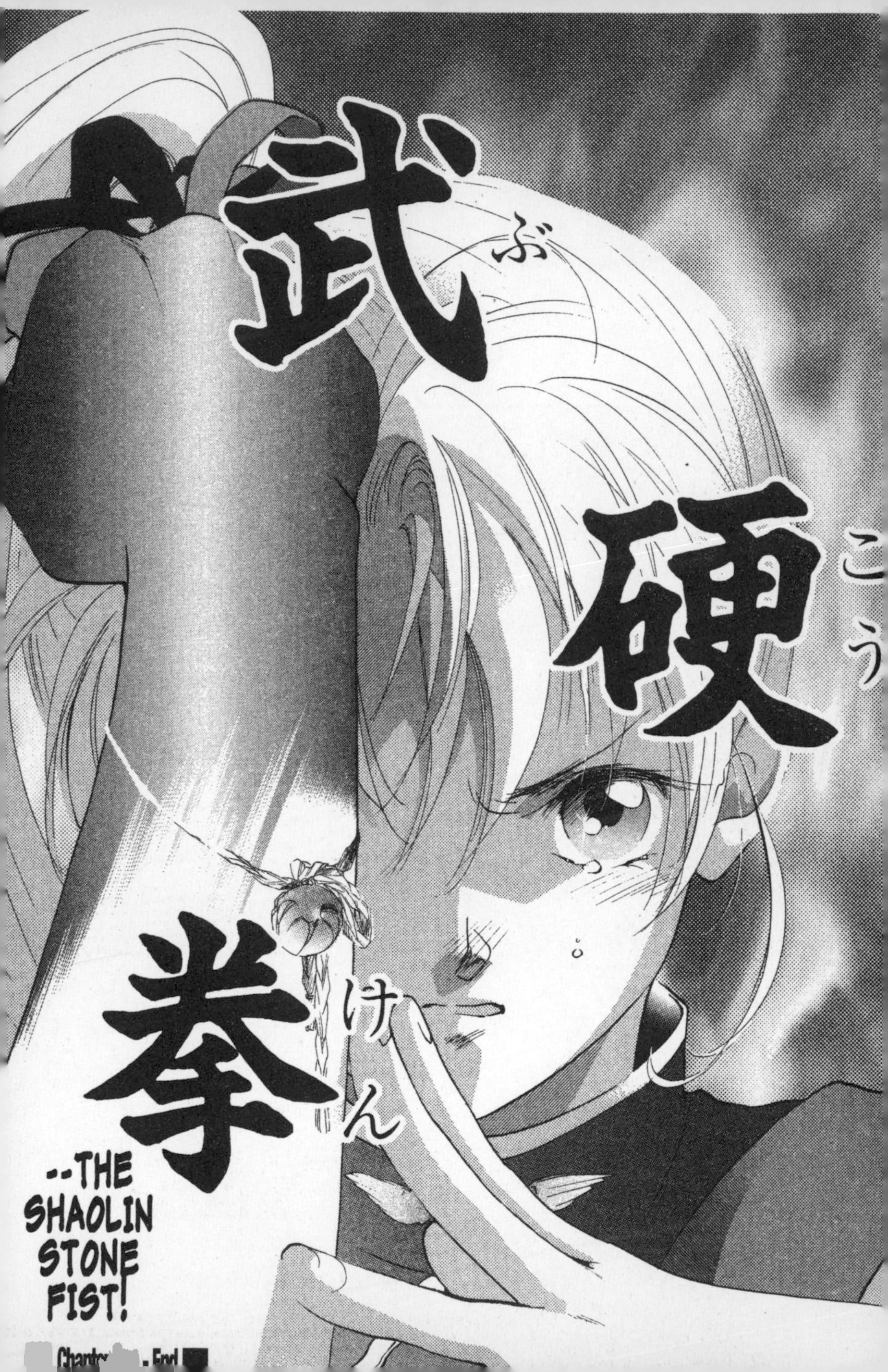
武硬拳
ぶこうけん
--THE SHAOLIN STONE FIST!
Chapter - End

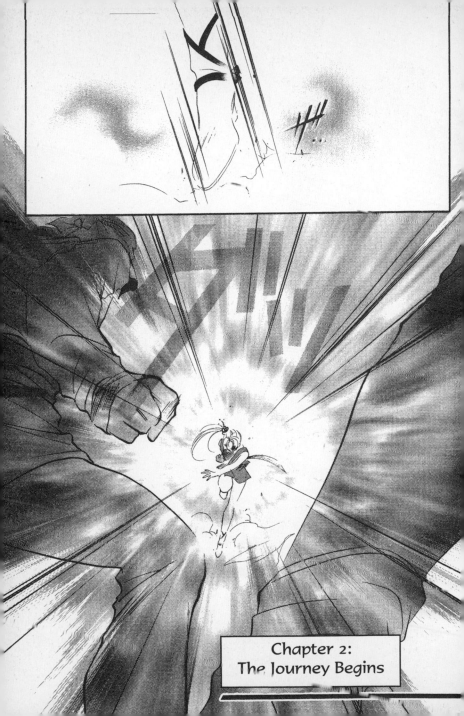

Chapter 2:
The Journey Begins

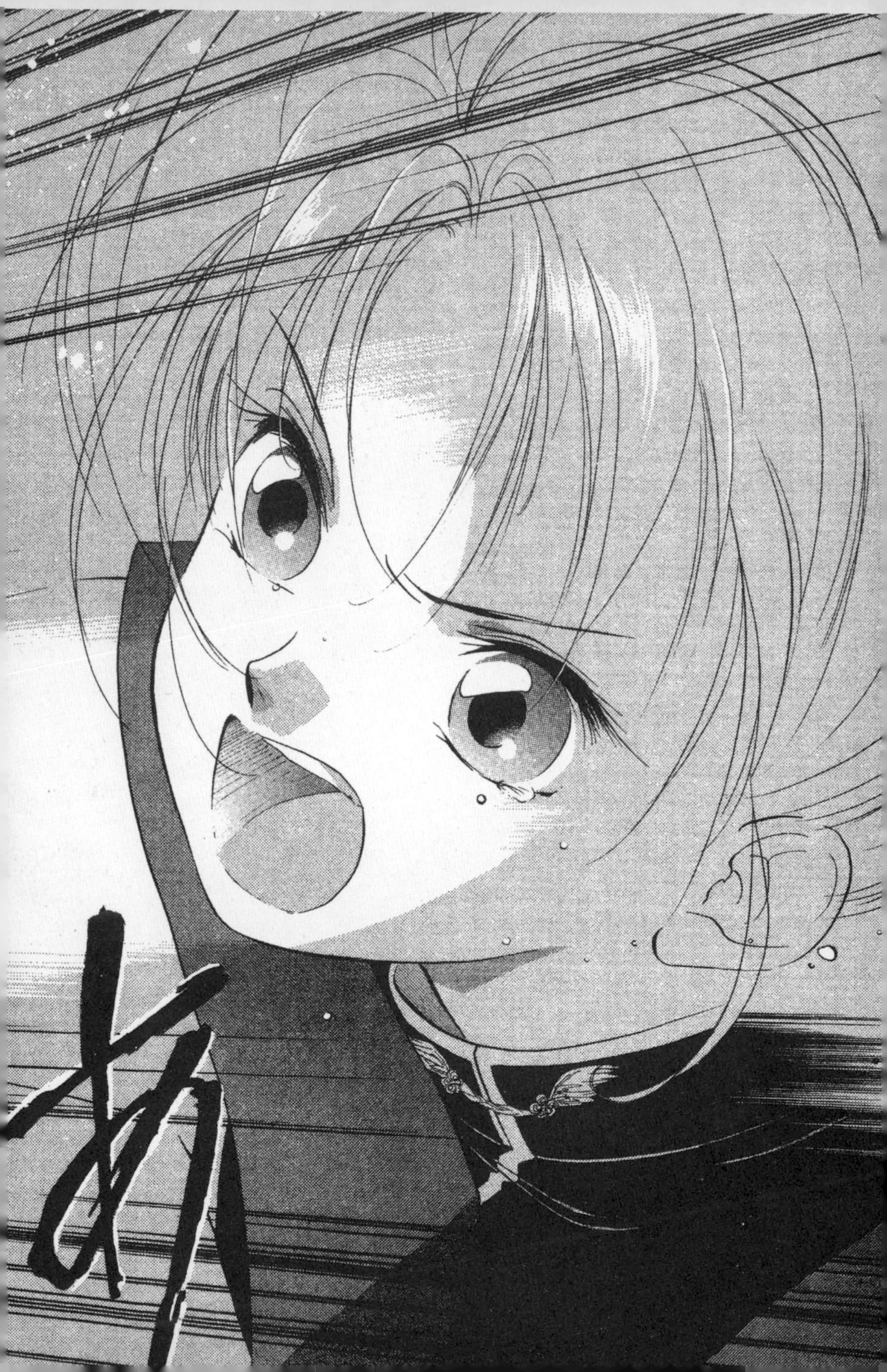

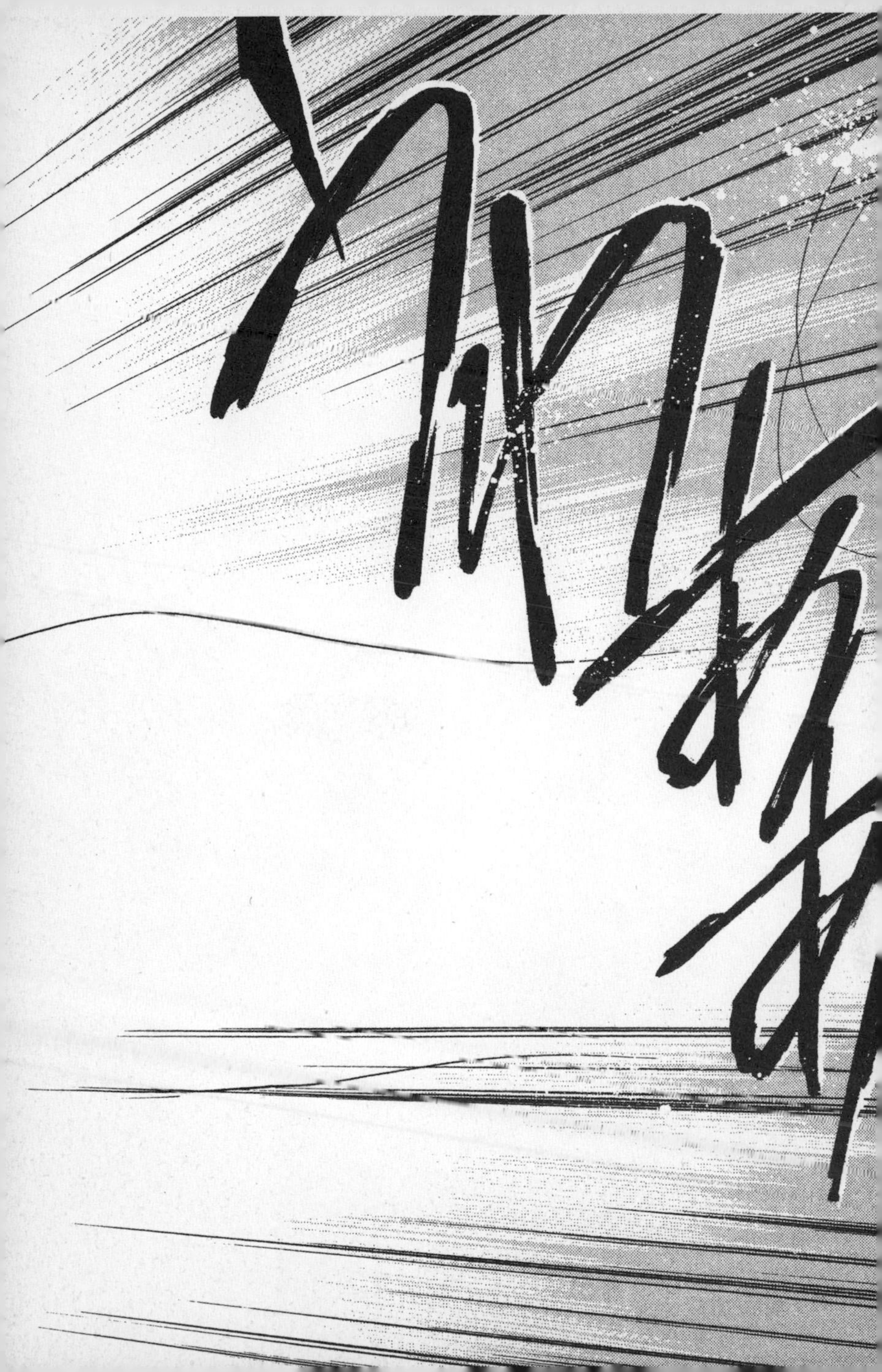

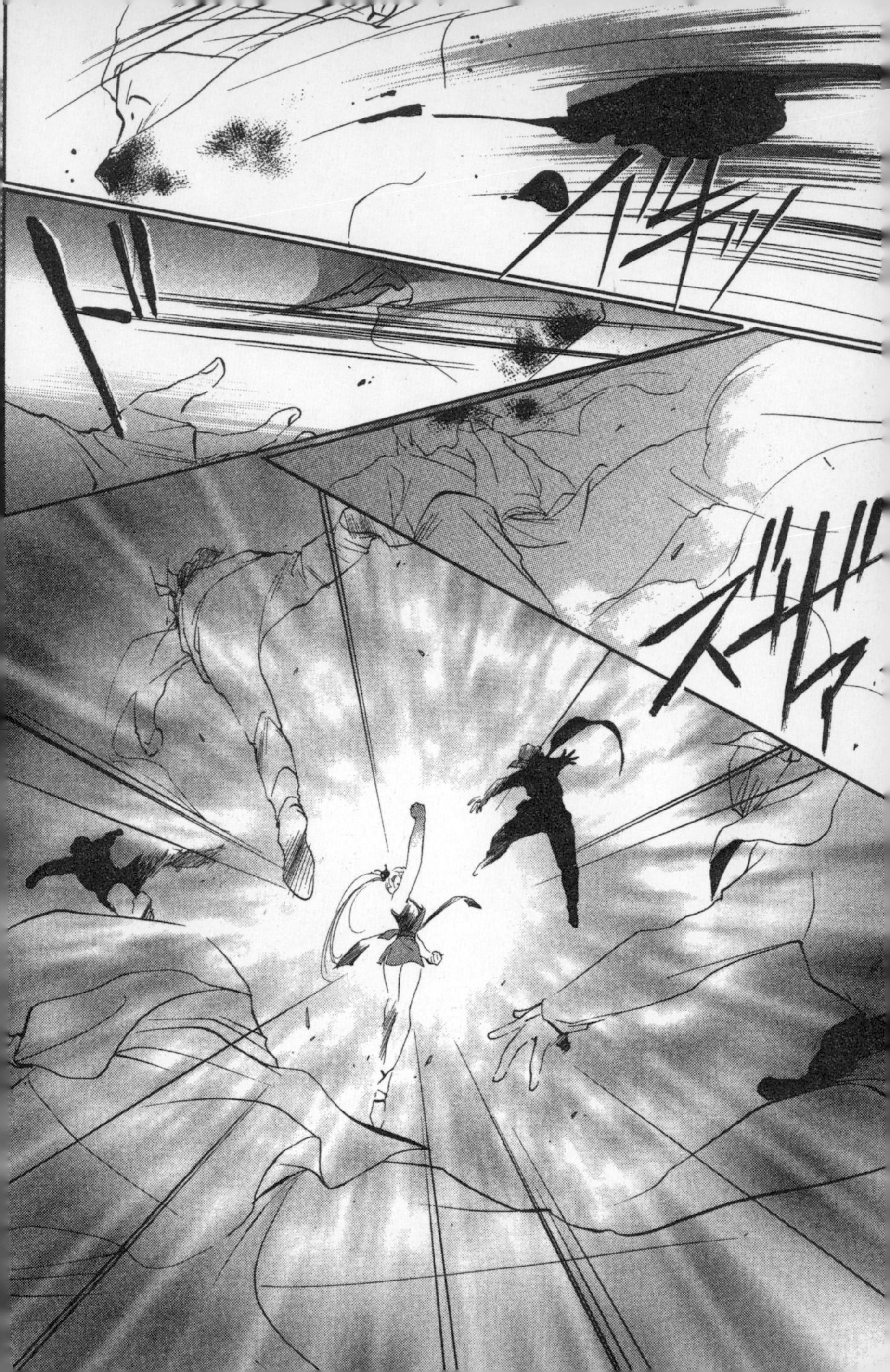
バキッ
ド
ズザァ

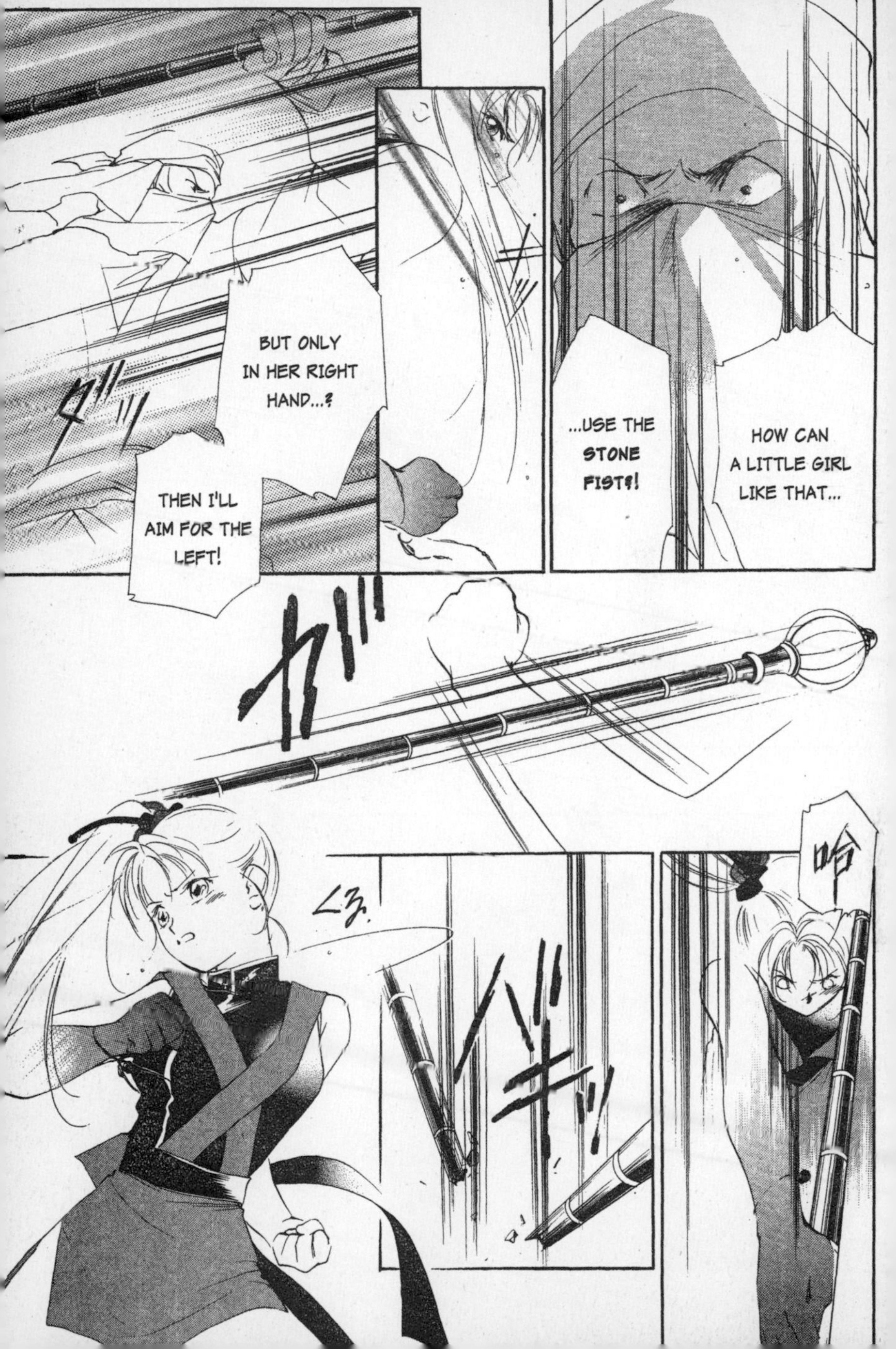
HOW CAN A LITTLE GIRL LIKE THAT...
...USE THE STONE FIST?!
BUT ONLY IN HER RIGHT HAND...?
THEN I'LL AIM FOR THE LEFT!
ガッ
バキッ

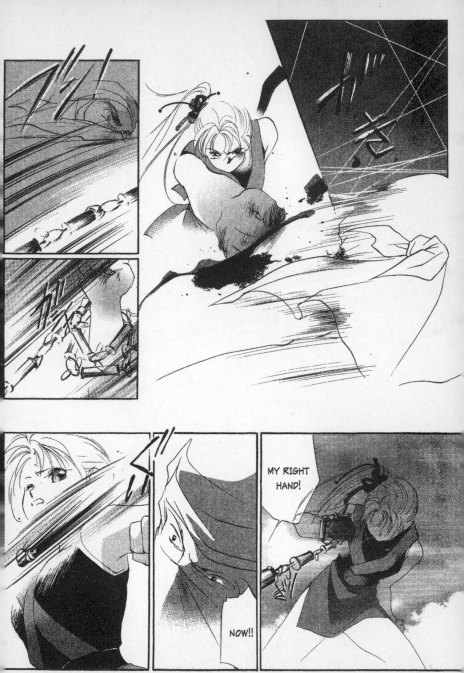

MY RIGHT
HAND!

NOW!!

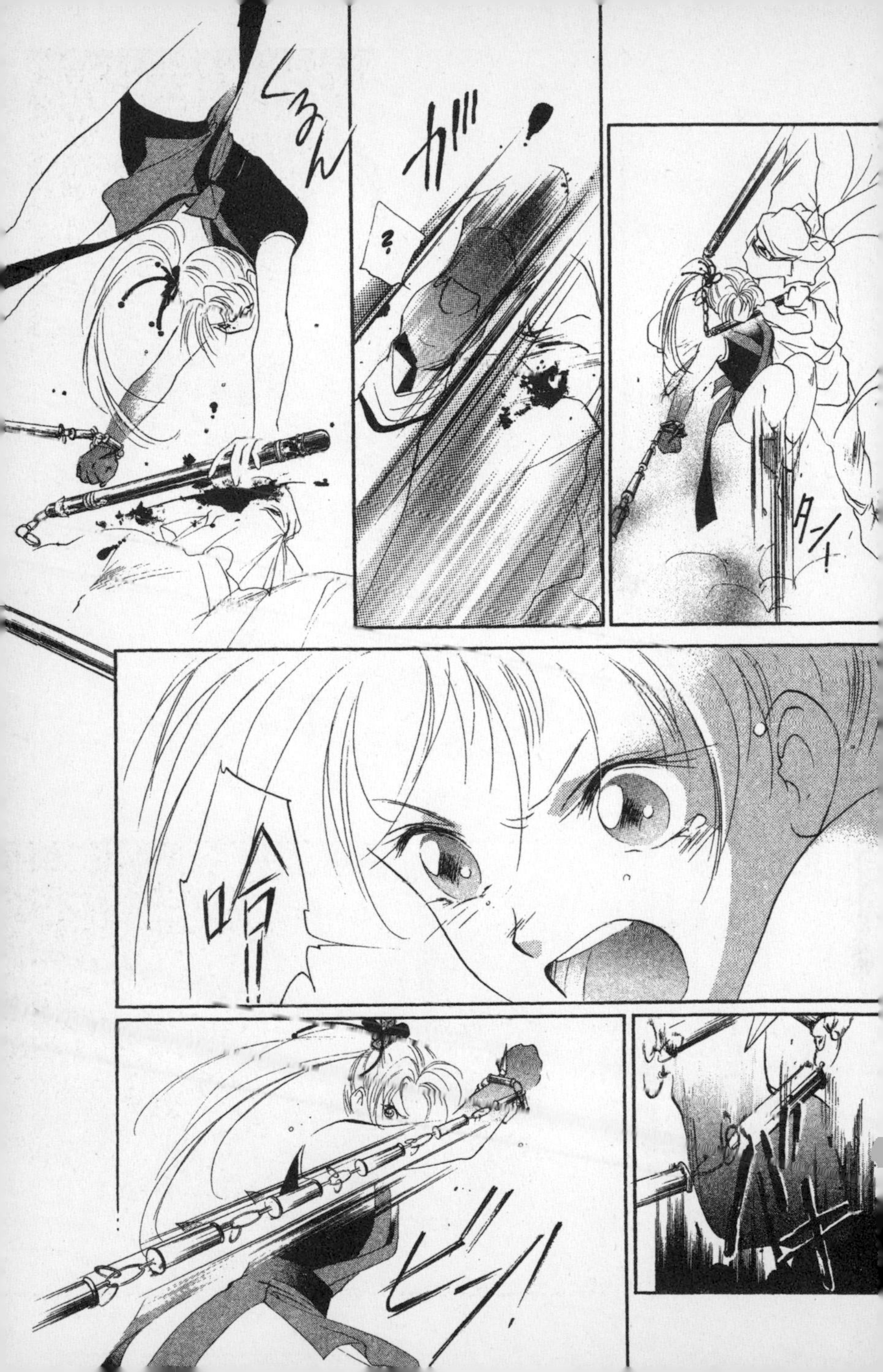
ダン!
ガッ!
?
くるん
哈!!

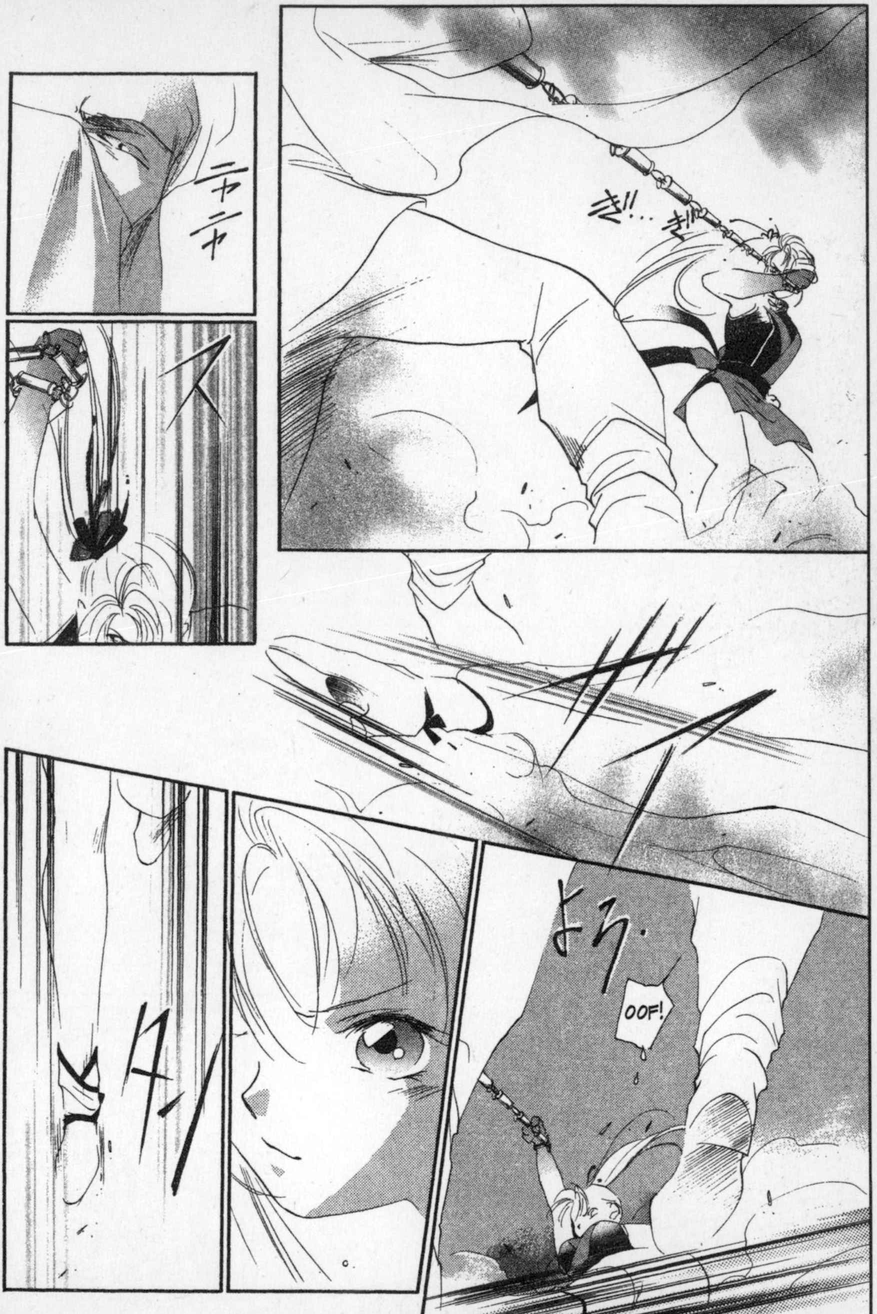
ぎ!!…ぎ!!
ニヤニヤ
ス
よろ
OOF!
タン

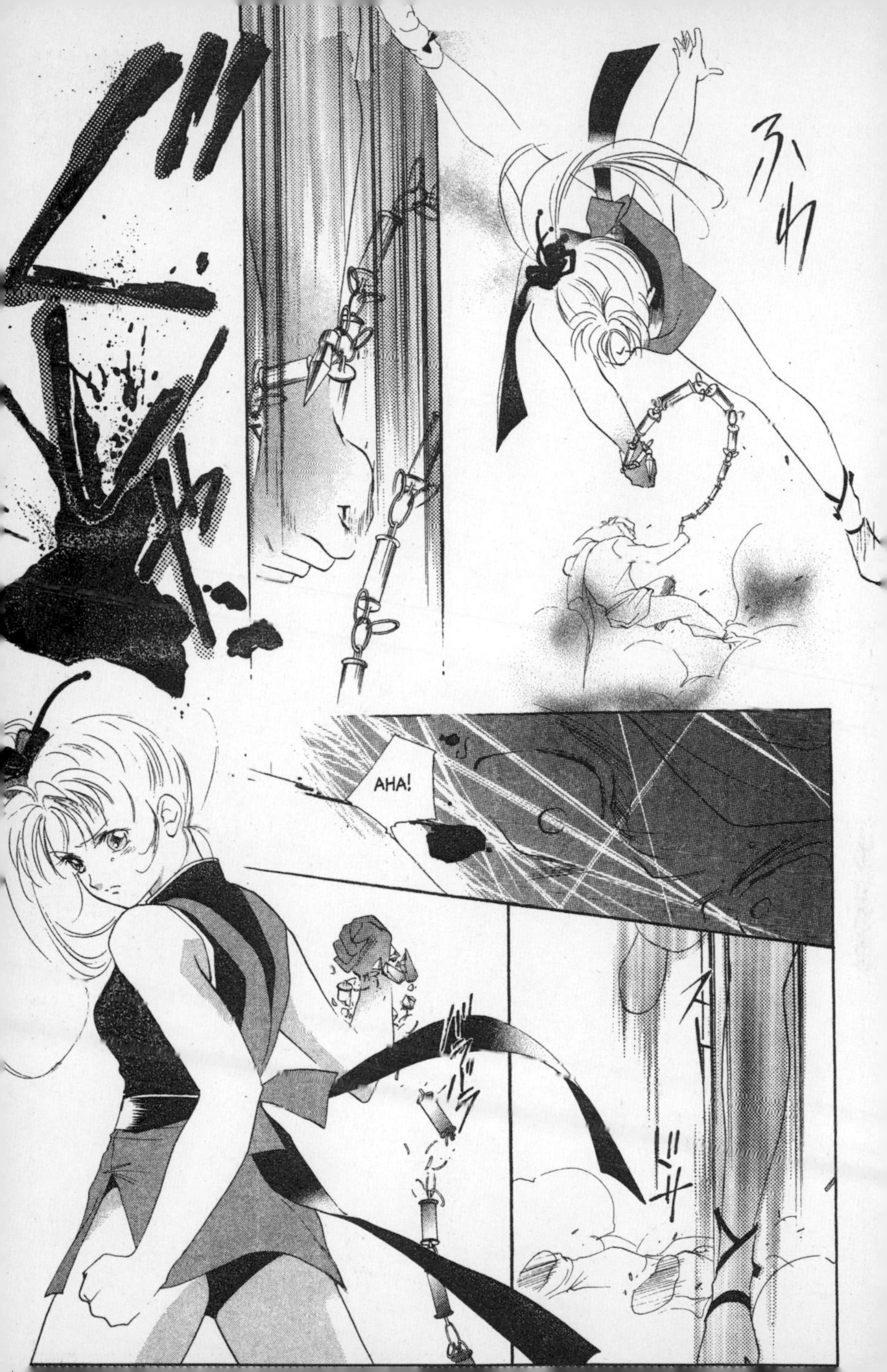
AHA!

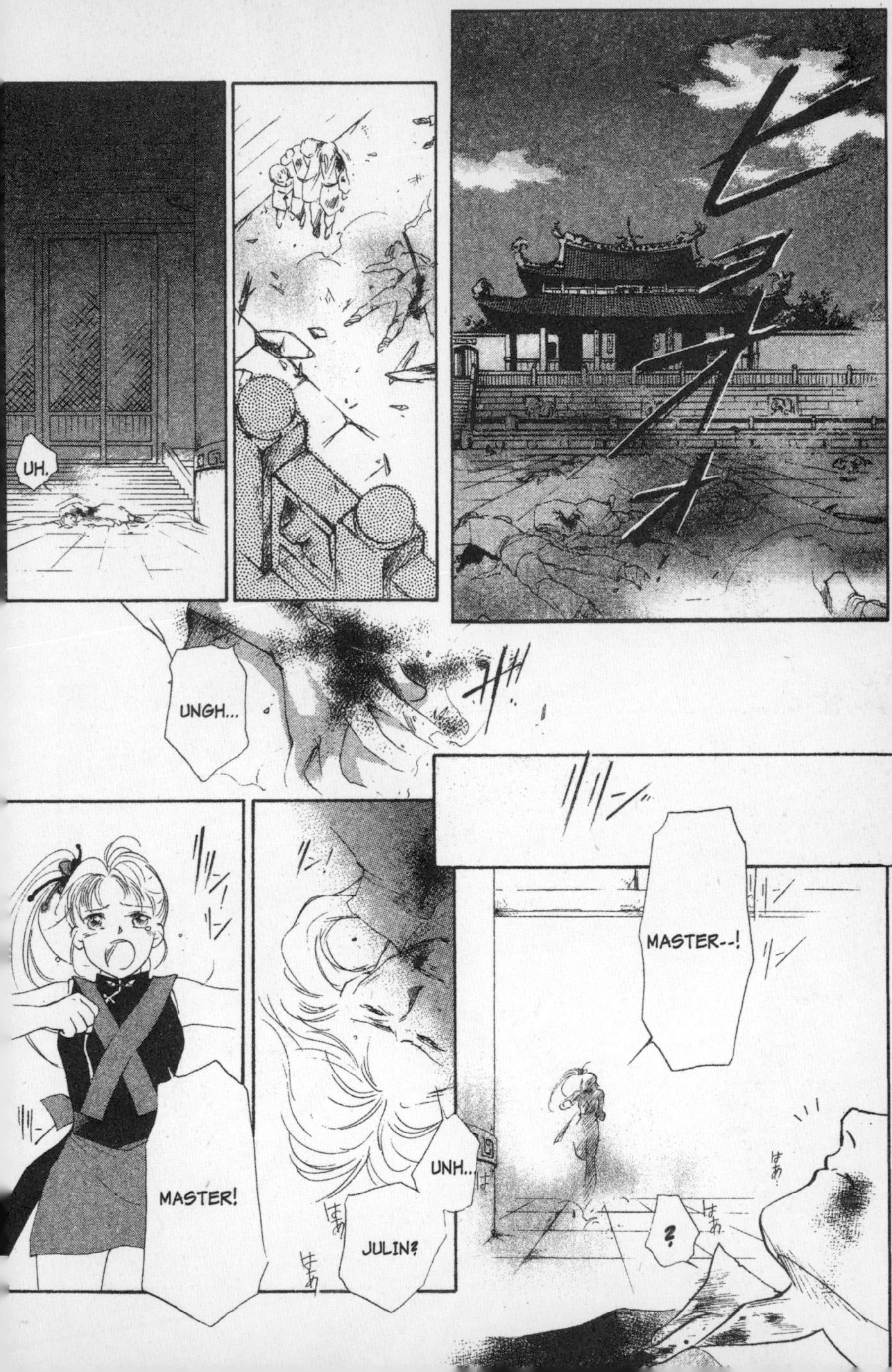
UH.
UNGH...
MASTER--!
?
UNH...
JULIN?
MASTER!

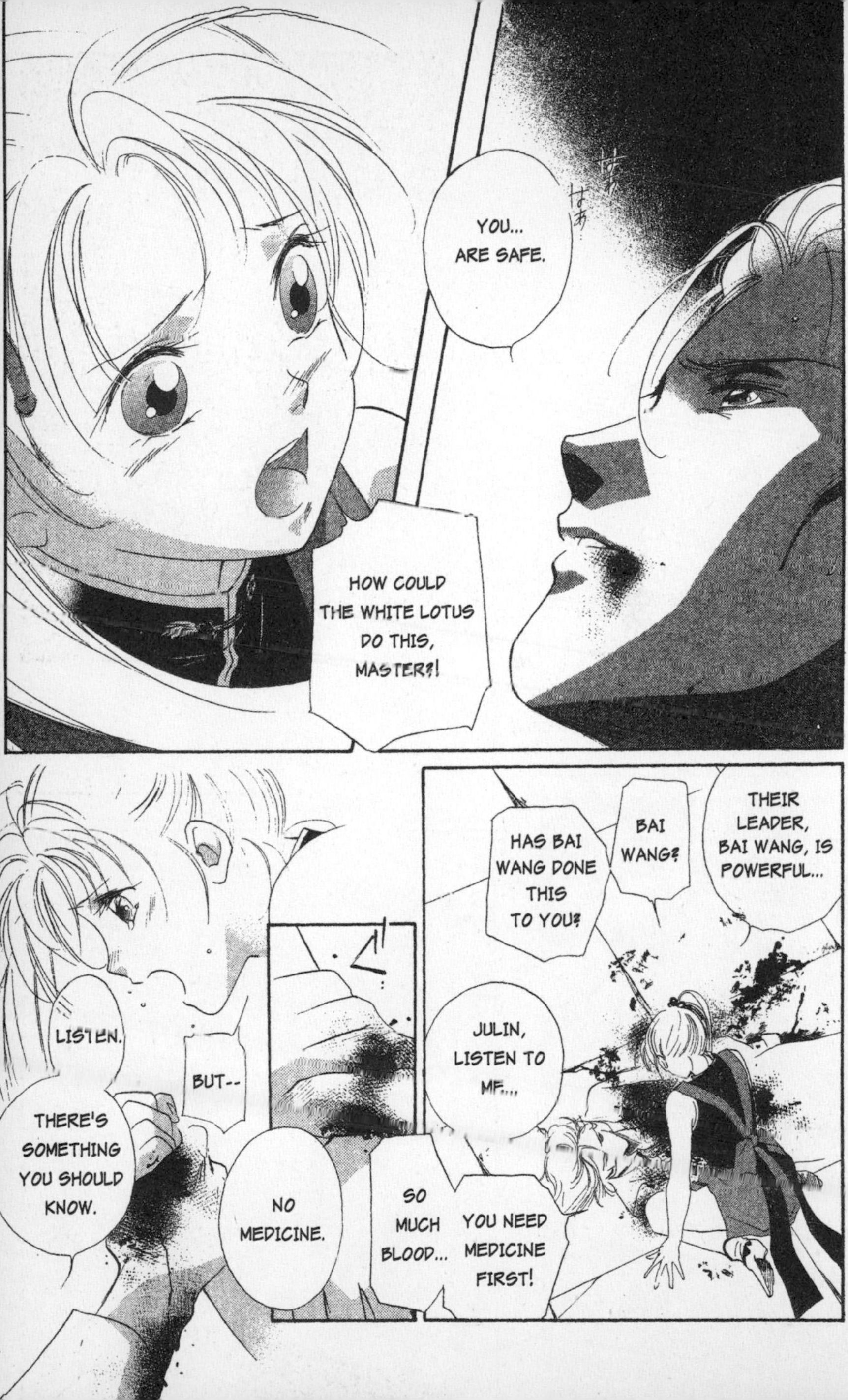
YOU... ARE SAFE.
HOW COULD THE WHITE LOTUS DO THIS, MASTER?!
THEIR LEADER, BAI WANG, IS POWERFUL...
BAI WANG?
HAS BAI WANG DONE THIS TO YOU?
JULIN, LISTEN TO ME...
YOU NEED MEDICINE FIRST!
SO MUCH BLOOD...
NO MEDICINE.
BUT--
LISTEN.
THERE'S SOMETHING YOU SHOULD KNOW.

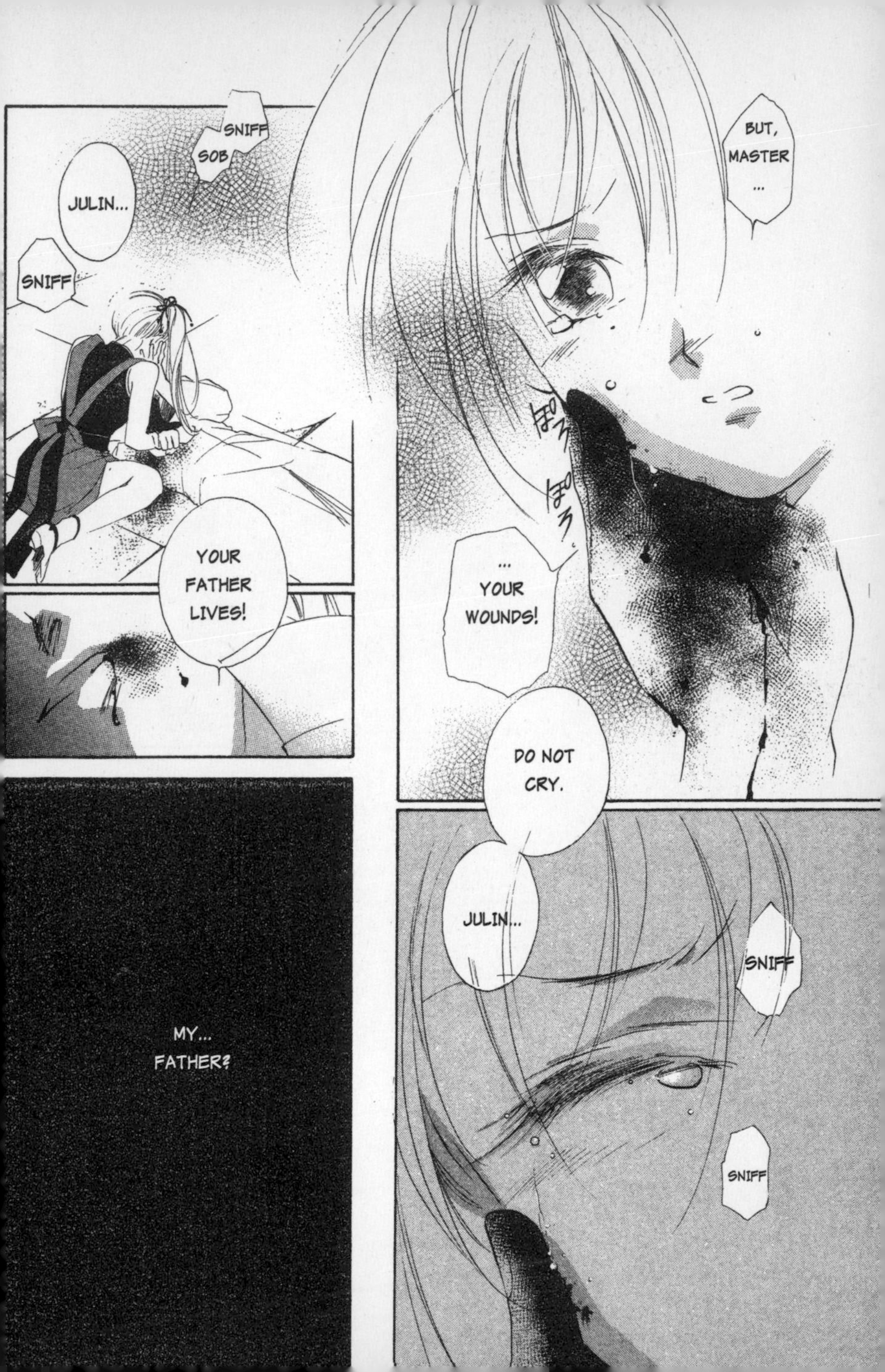
BUT, MASTER...
ぽろぽろ
... YOUR WOUNDS!
SNIFF
SOB
JULIN...
SNIFF
YOUR FATHER LIVES!
DO NOT CRY.
JULIN...
SNIFF
SNIFF
MY... FATHER?

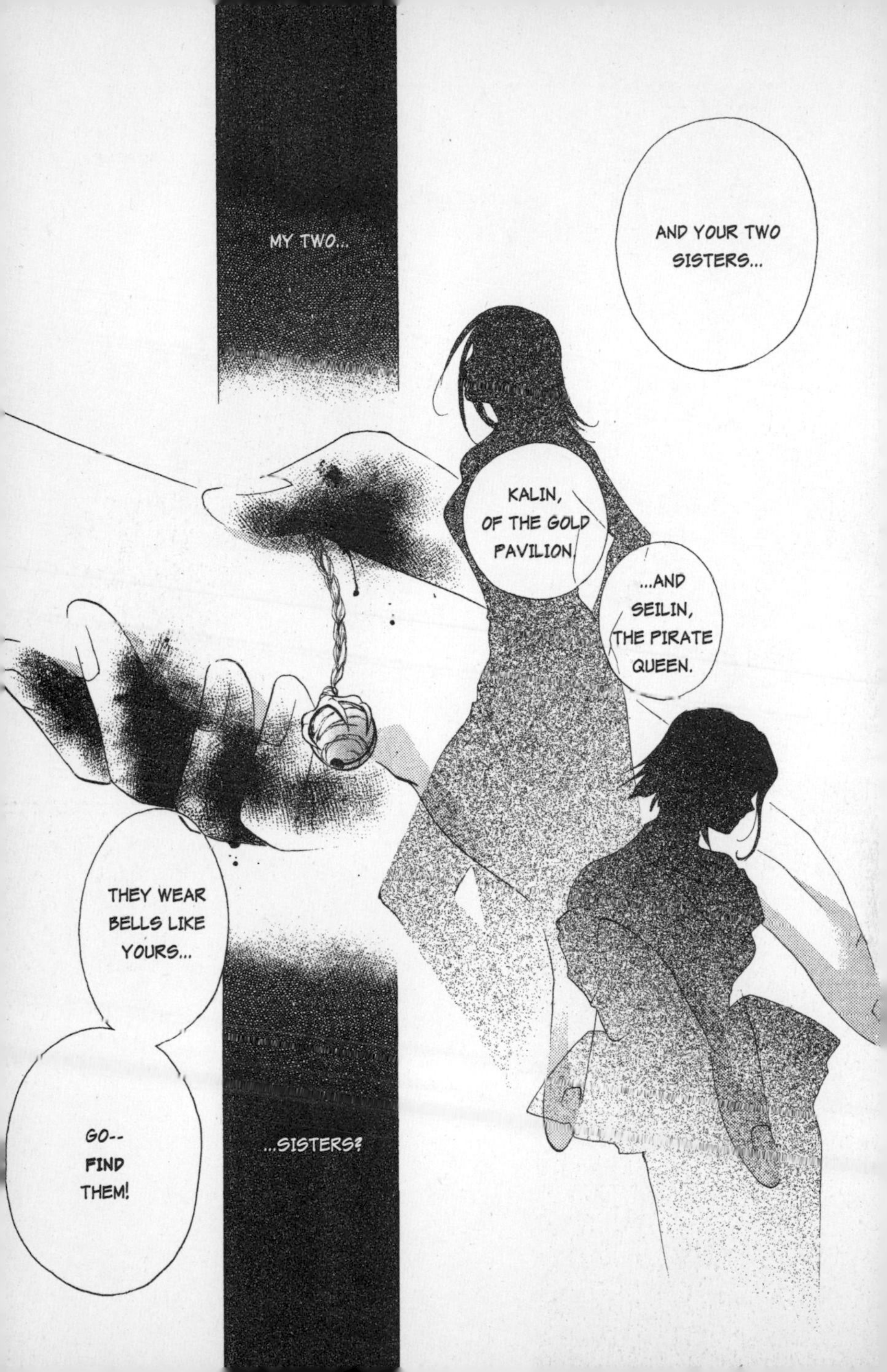
AND YOUR TWO SISTERS...
MY TWO...
KALIN, OF THE GOLD PAVILION.
...AND SEILIN, THE PIRATE QUEEN.
...SISTERS?
THEY WEAR BELLS LIKE YOURS...
GO-- FIND THEM!

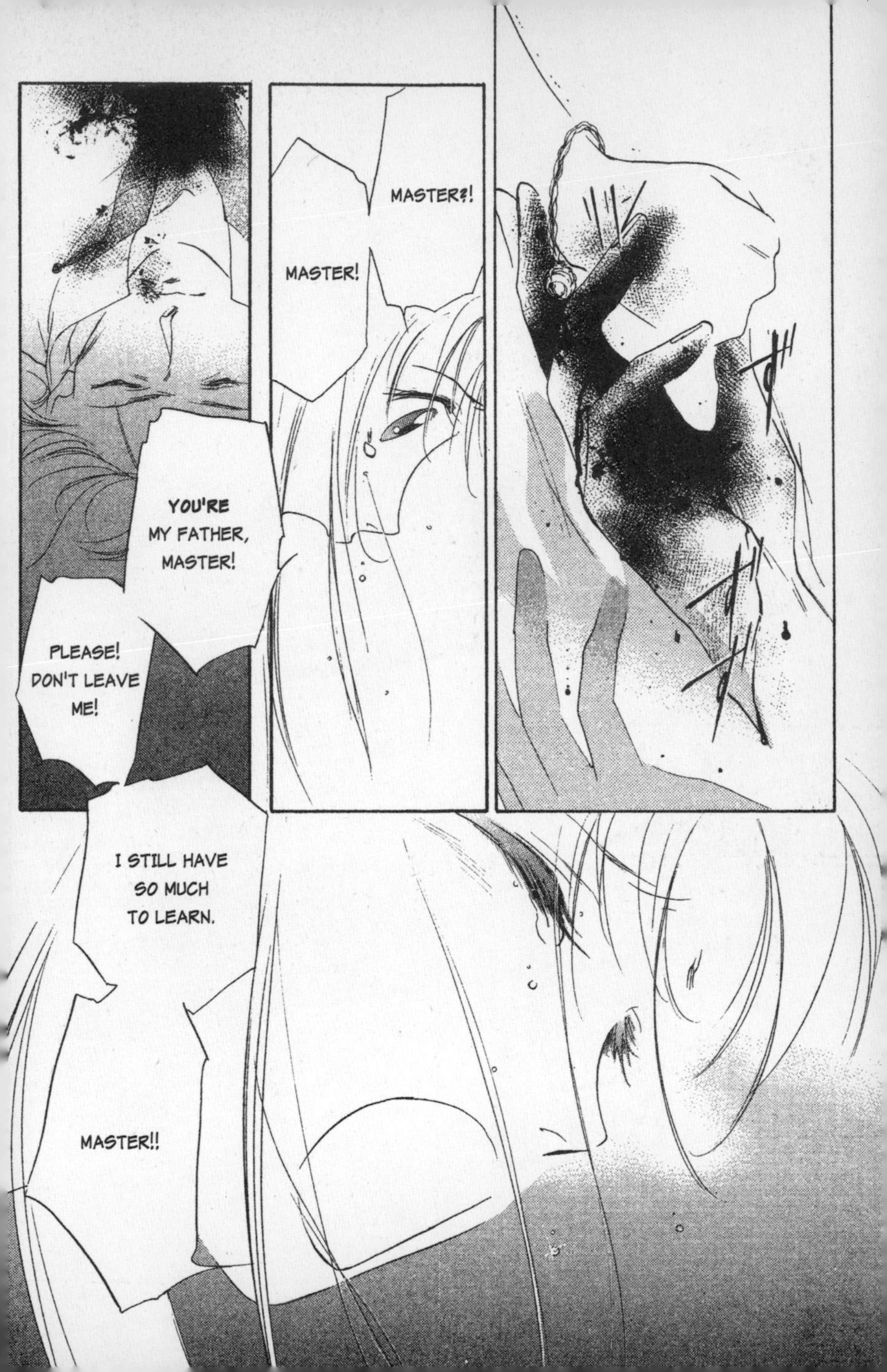
MASTER?!
MASTER!
YOU'RE MY FATHER, MASTER!
PLEASE! DON'T LEAVE ME!
I STILL HAVE SO MUCH TO LEARN.
MASTER!!

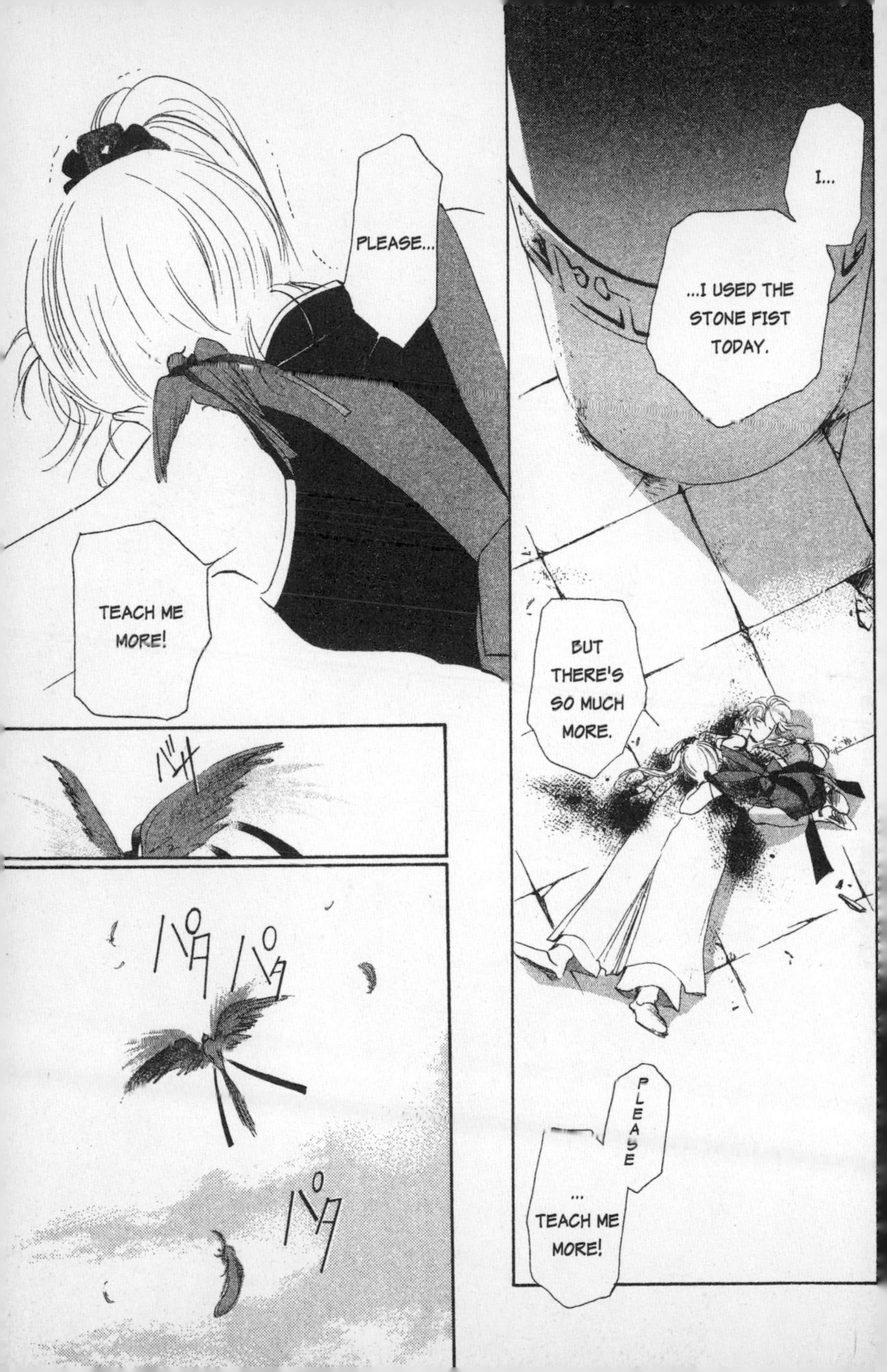
I...
...I USED THE STONE FIST TODAY.
BUT THERE'S SO MUCH MORE.
PLEASE
... TEACH ME MORE!
PLEASE...
TEACH ME MORE!
バサ
パタ パタ
パタ

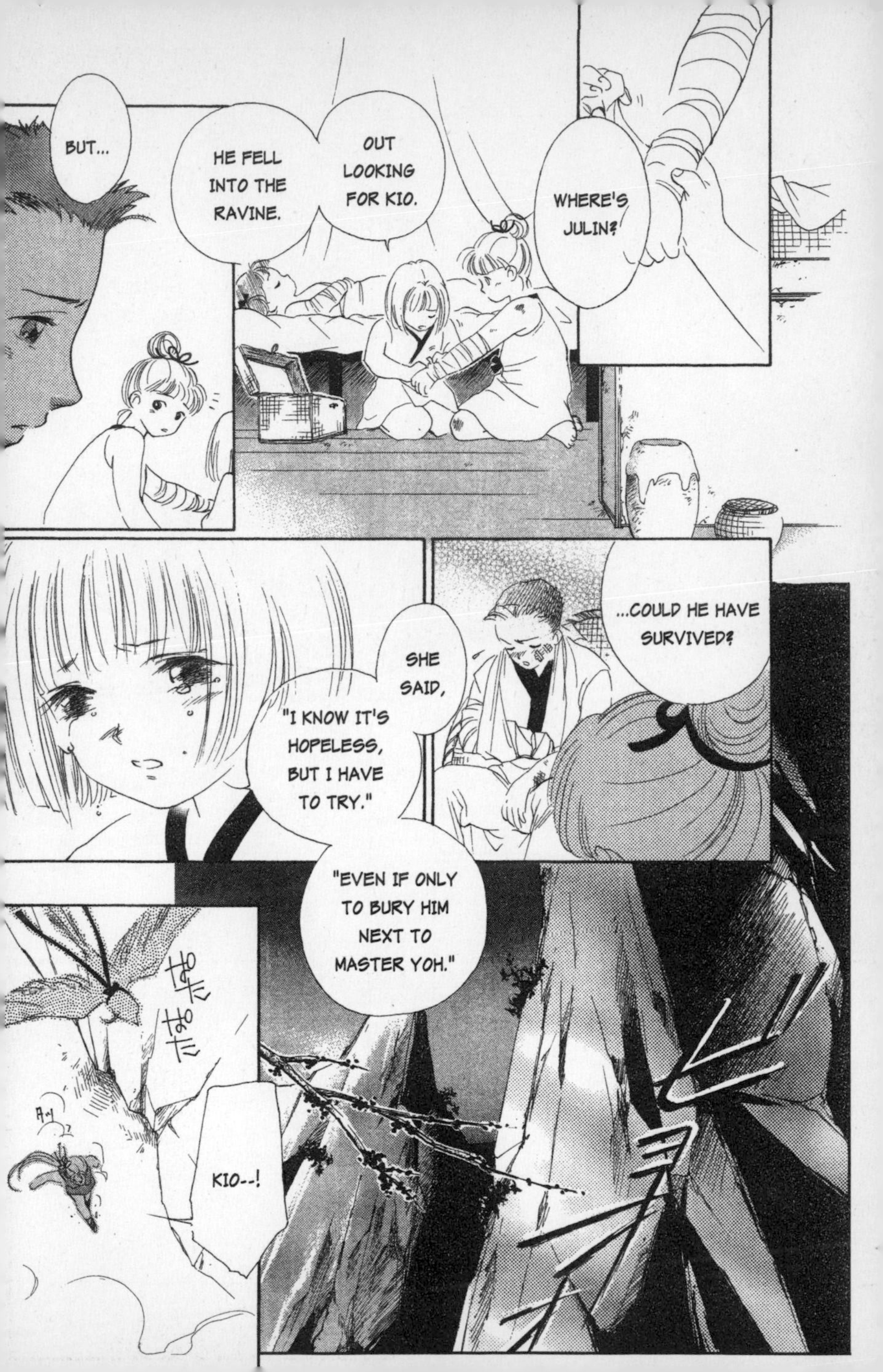
WHERE'S JULIN?
OUT LOOKING FOR KIO.
HE FELL INTO THE RAVINE.
BUT...
...COULD HE HAVE SURVIVED?
SHE SAID,
"I KNOW IT'S HOPELESS, BUT I HAVE TO TRY."
"EVEN IF ONLY TO BURY HIM NEXT TO MASTER YOH."
ぱた ぱた
KIO--!

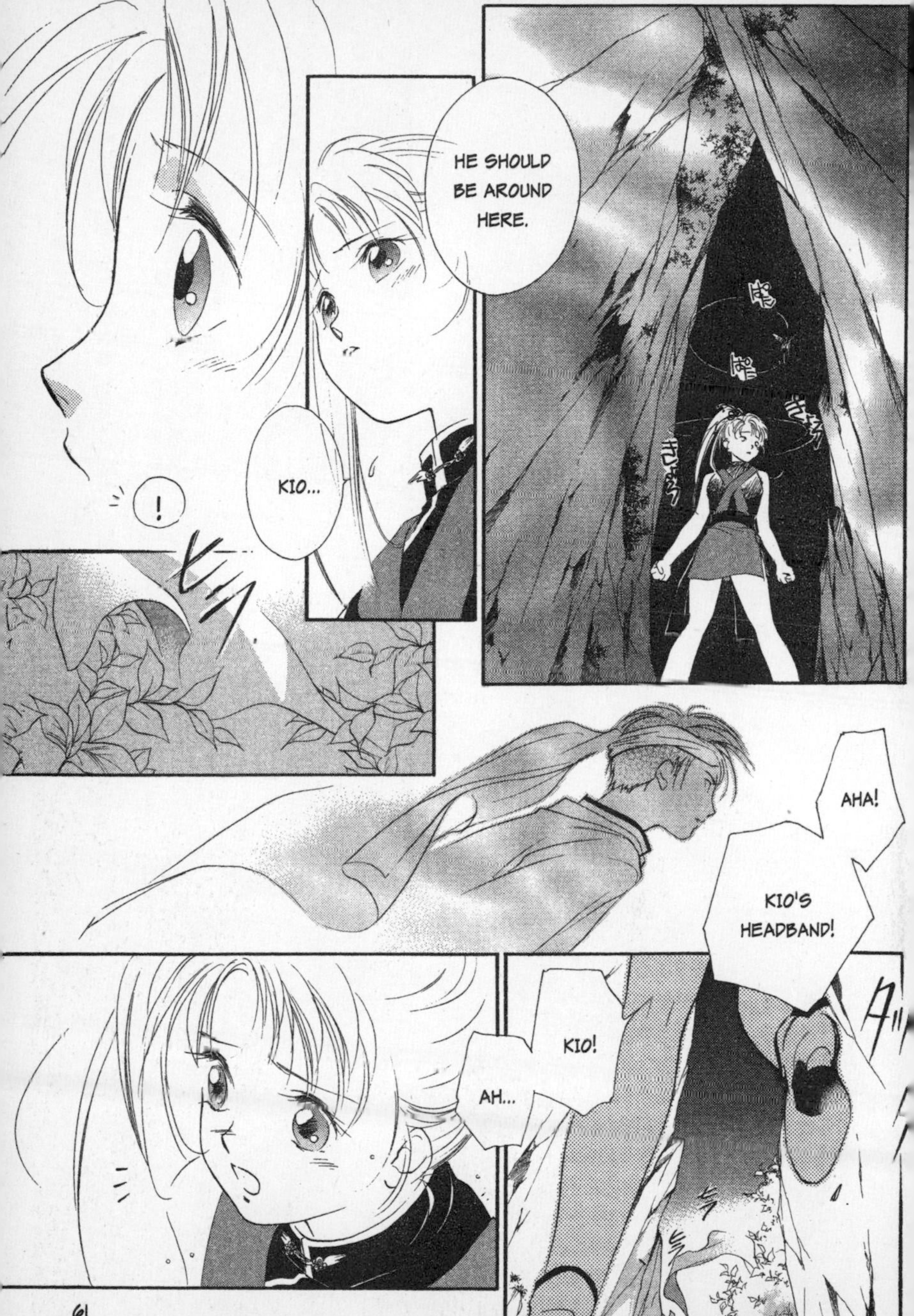
HE SHOULD BE AROUND HERE.
KIO...
!
AHA!
KIO'S HEADBAND!
KIO!
AH...

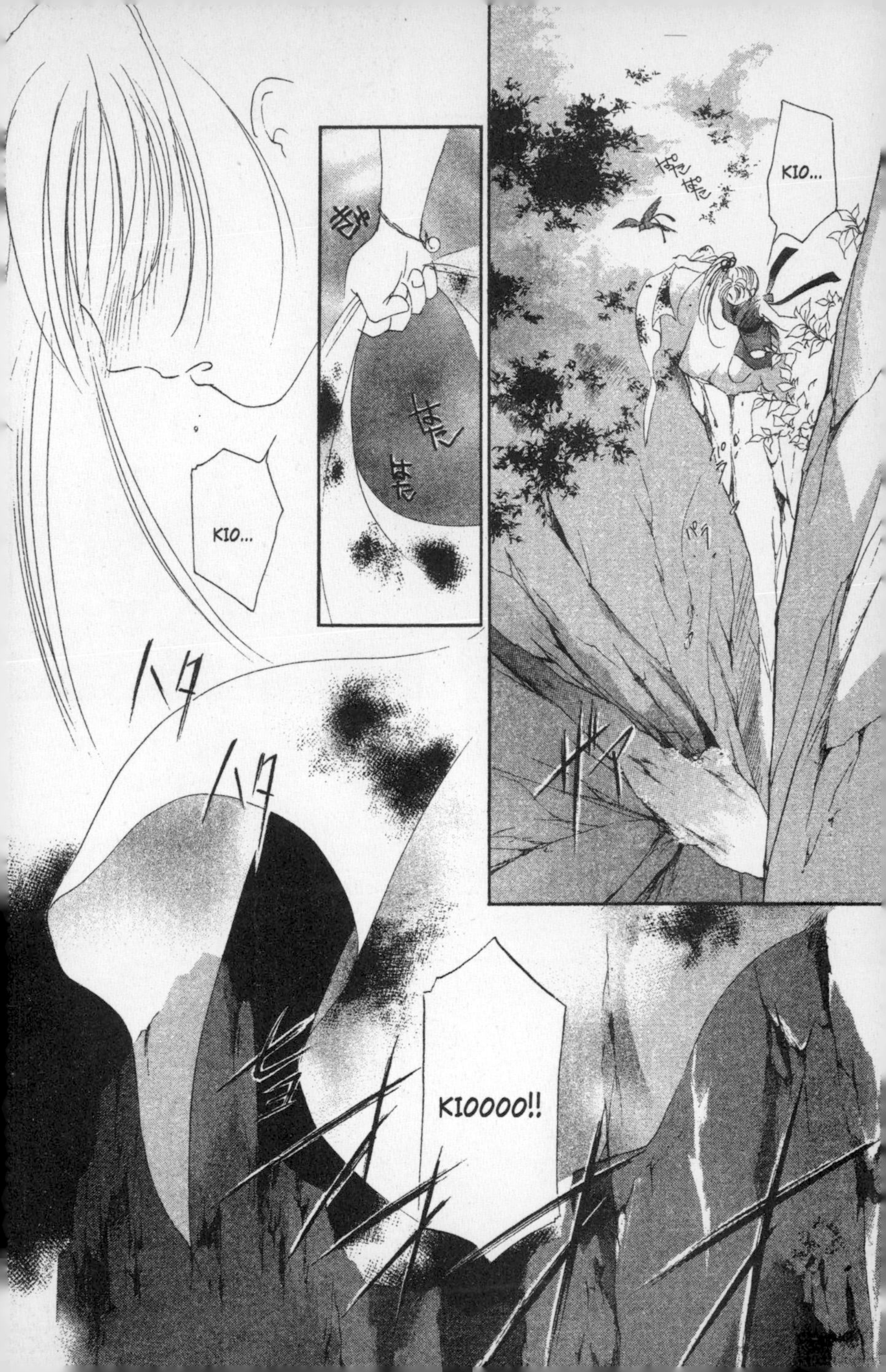
KIO...
KIO...
KIOOOO!!

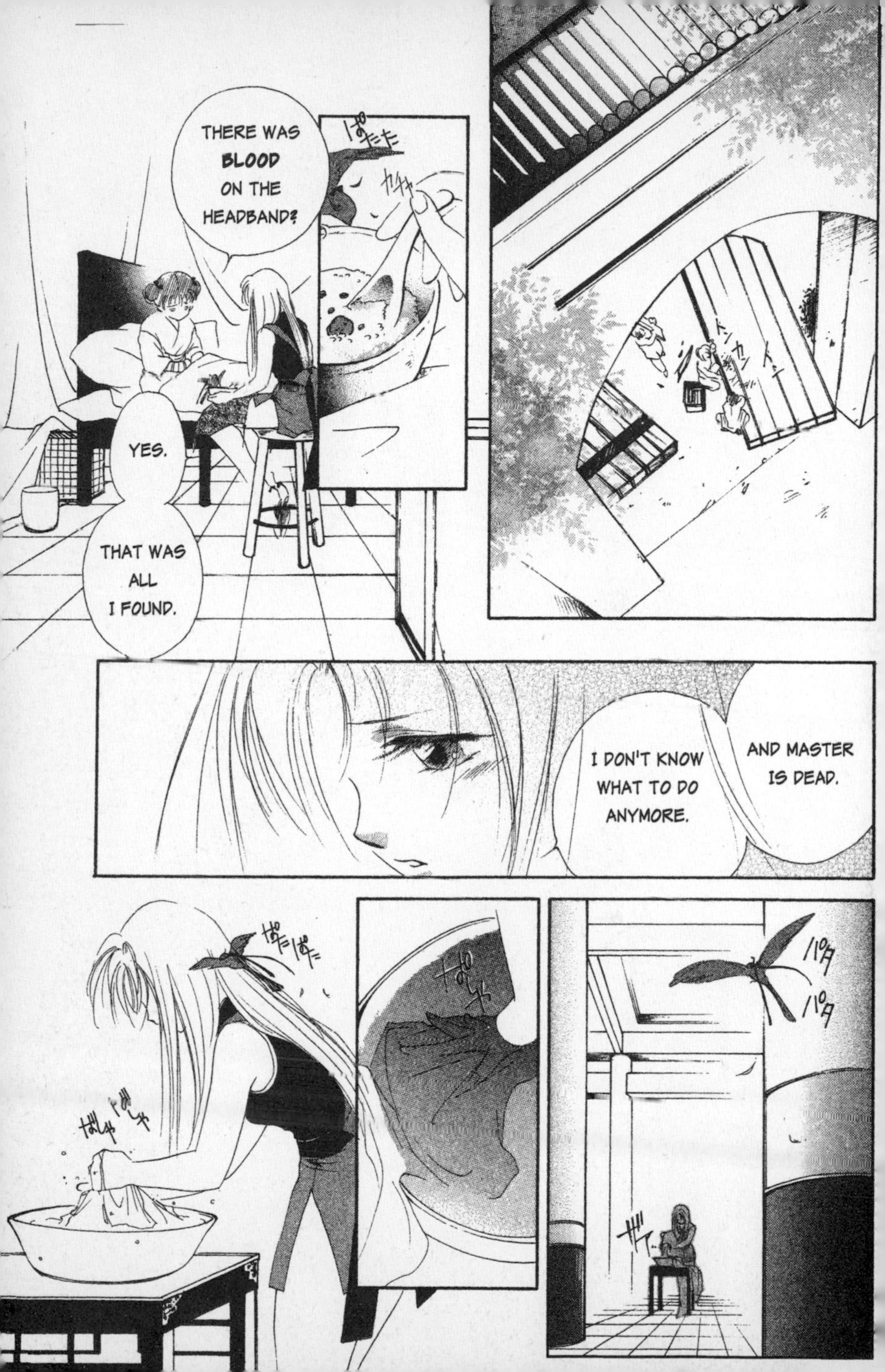
THERE WAS BLOOD ON THE HEADBAND?
YES.
THAT WAS ALL I FOUND.
AND MASTER IS DEAD.
I DON'T KNOW WHAT TO DO ANYMORE.
パタ
パタ

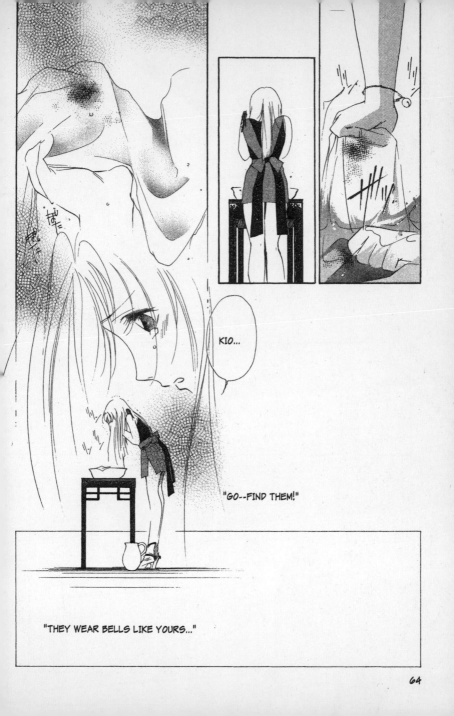

KIO...

"GO--FIND THEM!"

"THEY WEAR BELLS LIKE YOURS..."

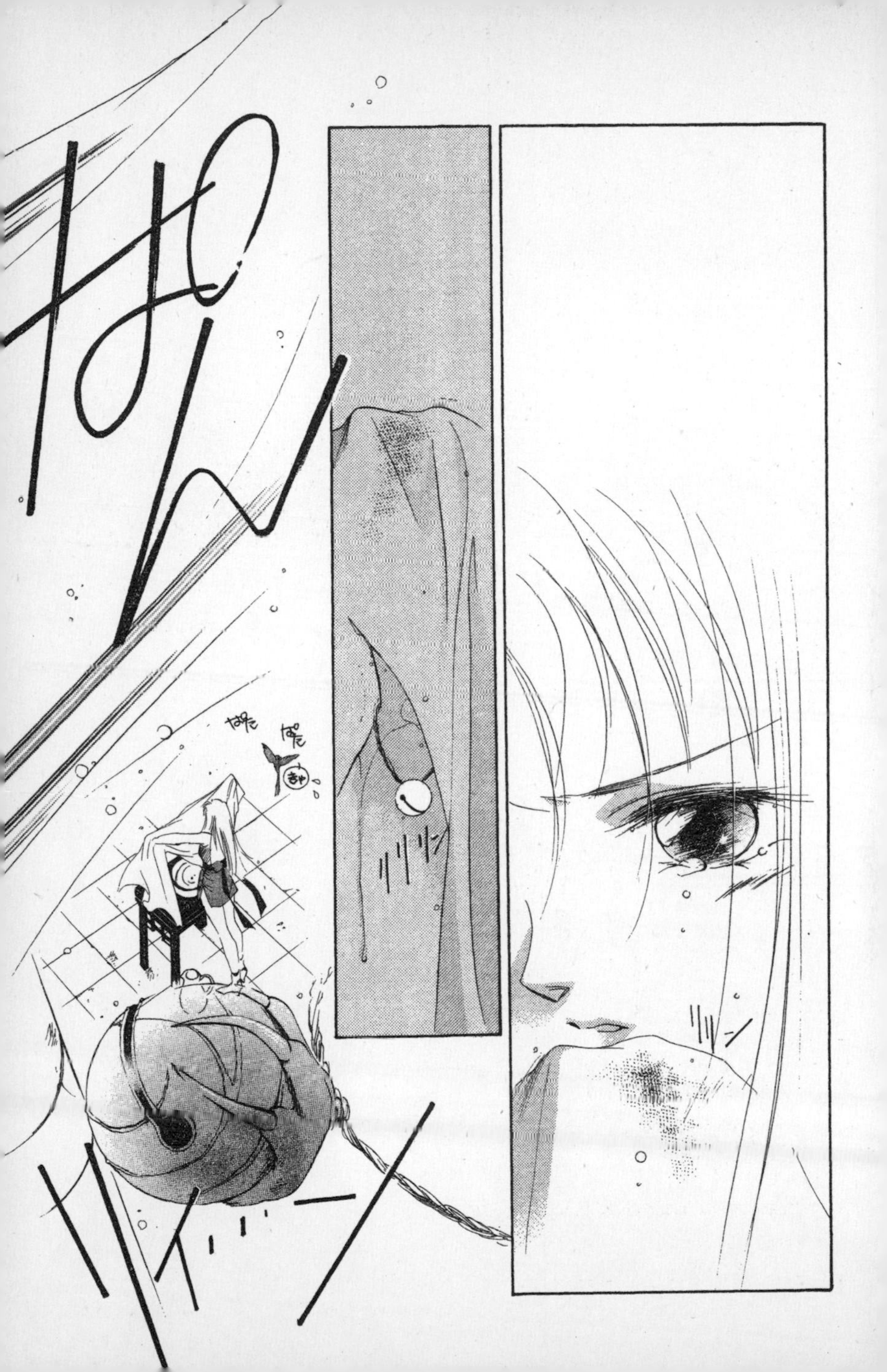
ぱた
ぱた
きゃ

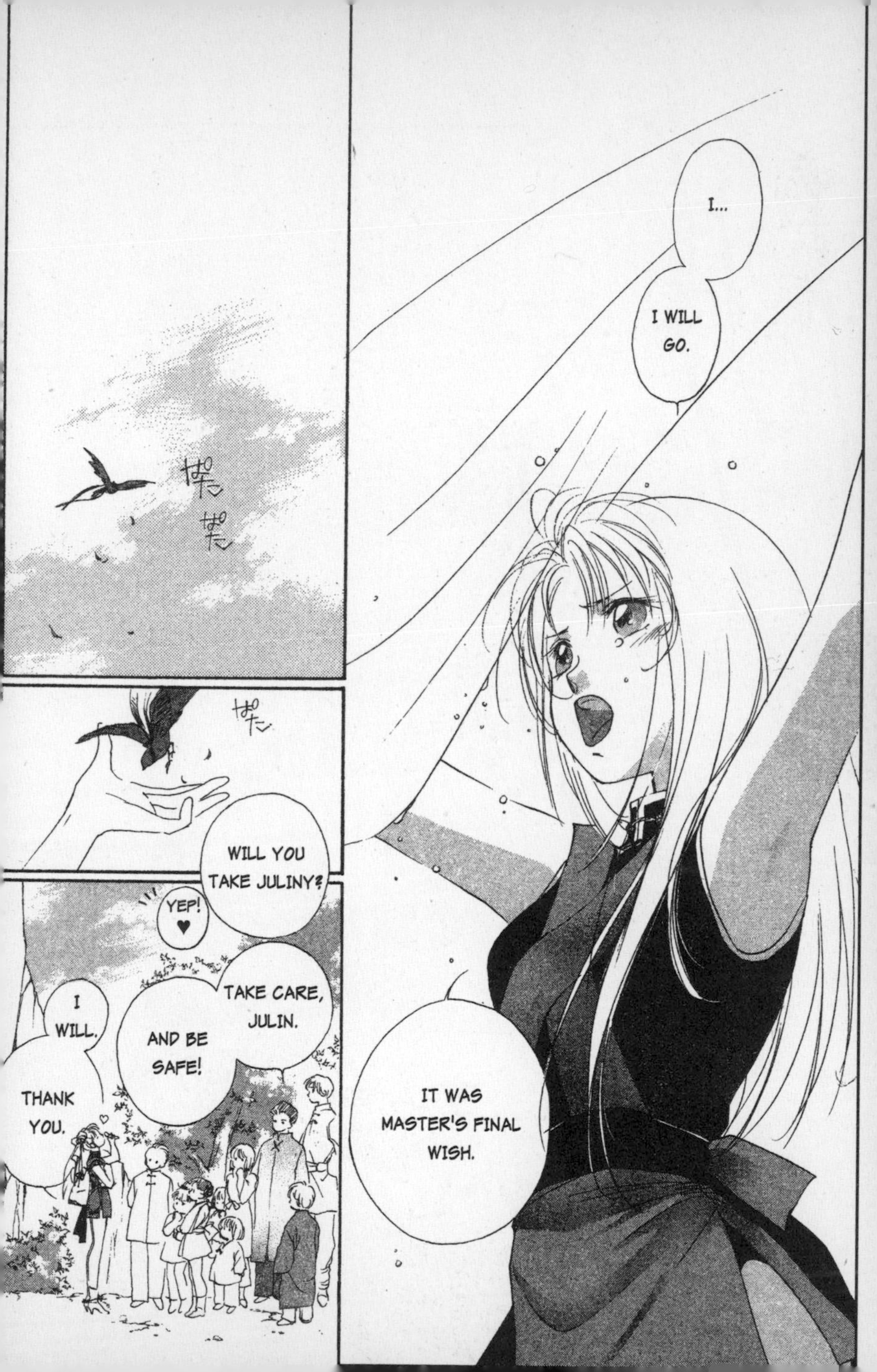
I...
I WILL GO.
IT WAS MASTER'S FINAL WISH.
ぱた ぱた
ぱた
WILL YOU TAKE JULINY?
YEP! ♥
TAKE CARE, JULIN.
AND BE SAFE!
I WILL.
THANK YOU.

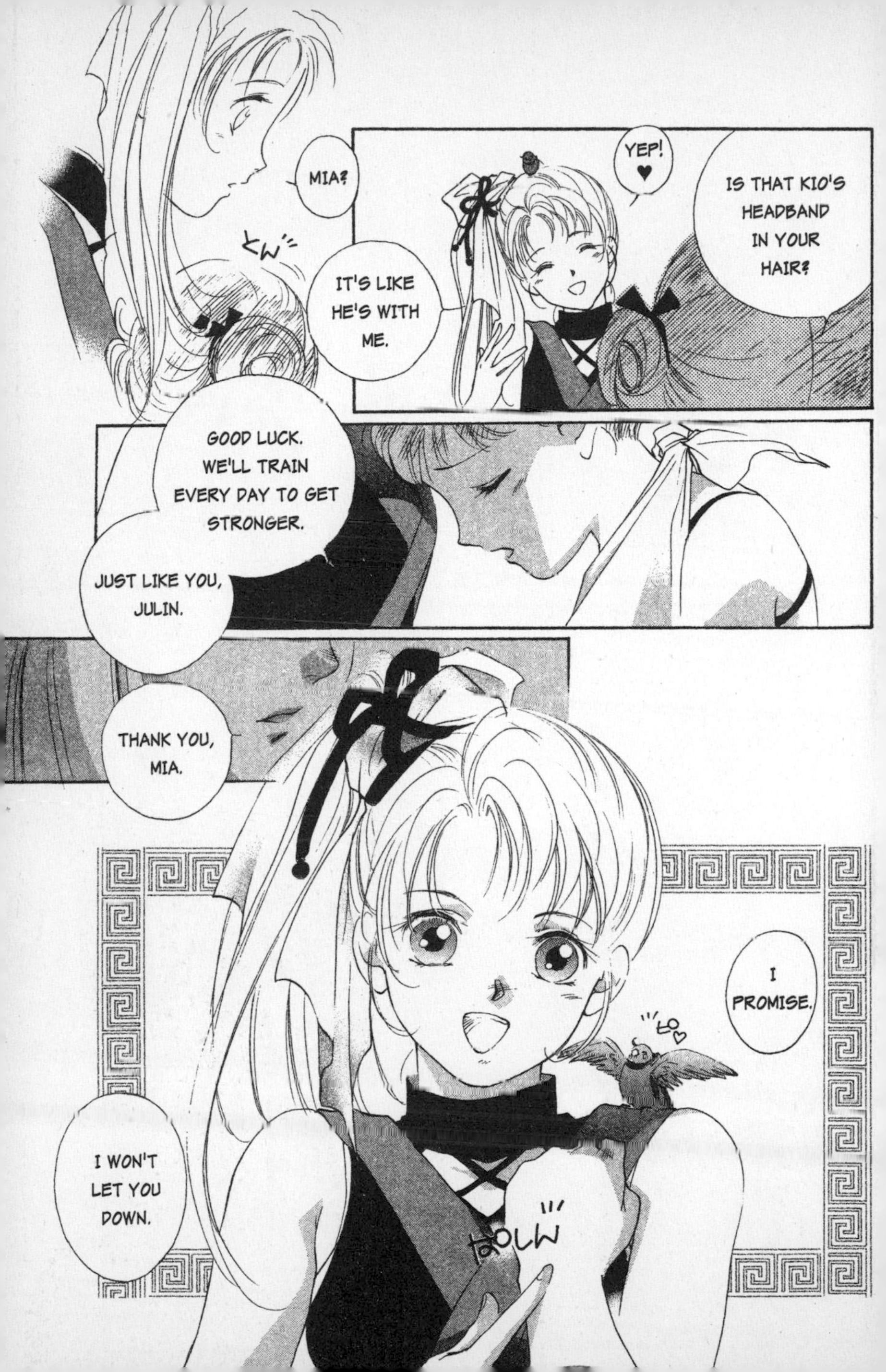
IS THAT KIO'S HEADBAND IN YOUR HAIR?
YEP! ♥
IT'S LIKE HE'S WITH ME.
MIA?
GOOD LUCK. WE'LL TRAIN EVERY DAY TO GET STRONGER.
JUST LIKE YOU, JULIN.
THANK YOU, MIA.
I PROMISE.
I WON'T LET YOU DOWN.

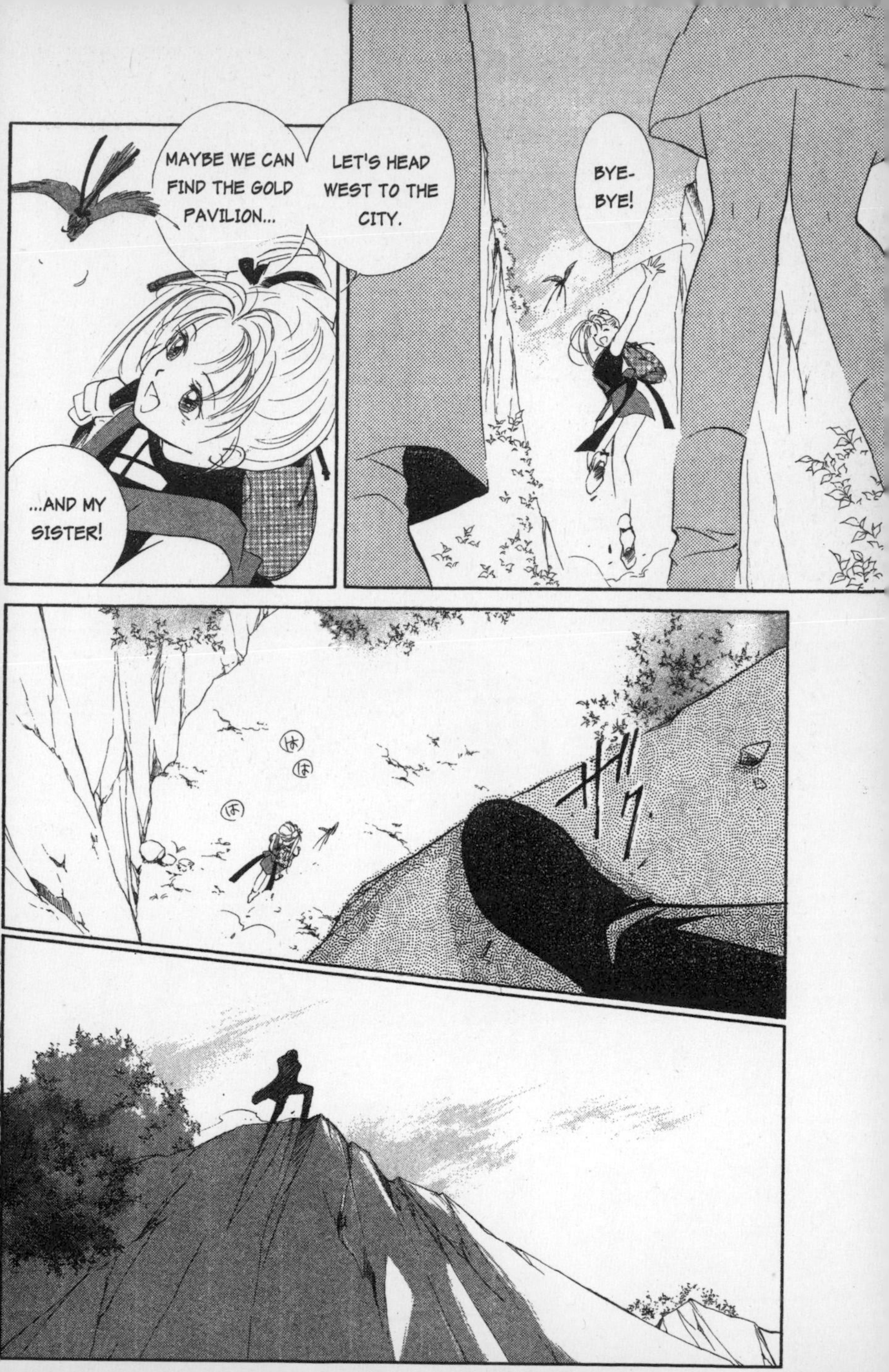
BYE-BYE!
LET'S HEAD WEST TO THE CITY.
MAYBE WE CAN FIND THE GOLD PAVILION...
...AND MY SISTER!
ザク
は
は
は

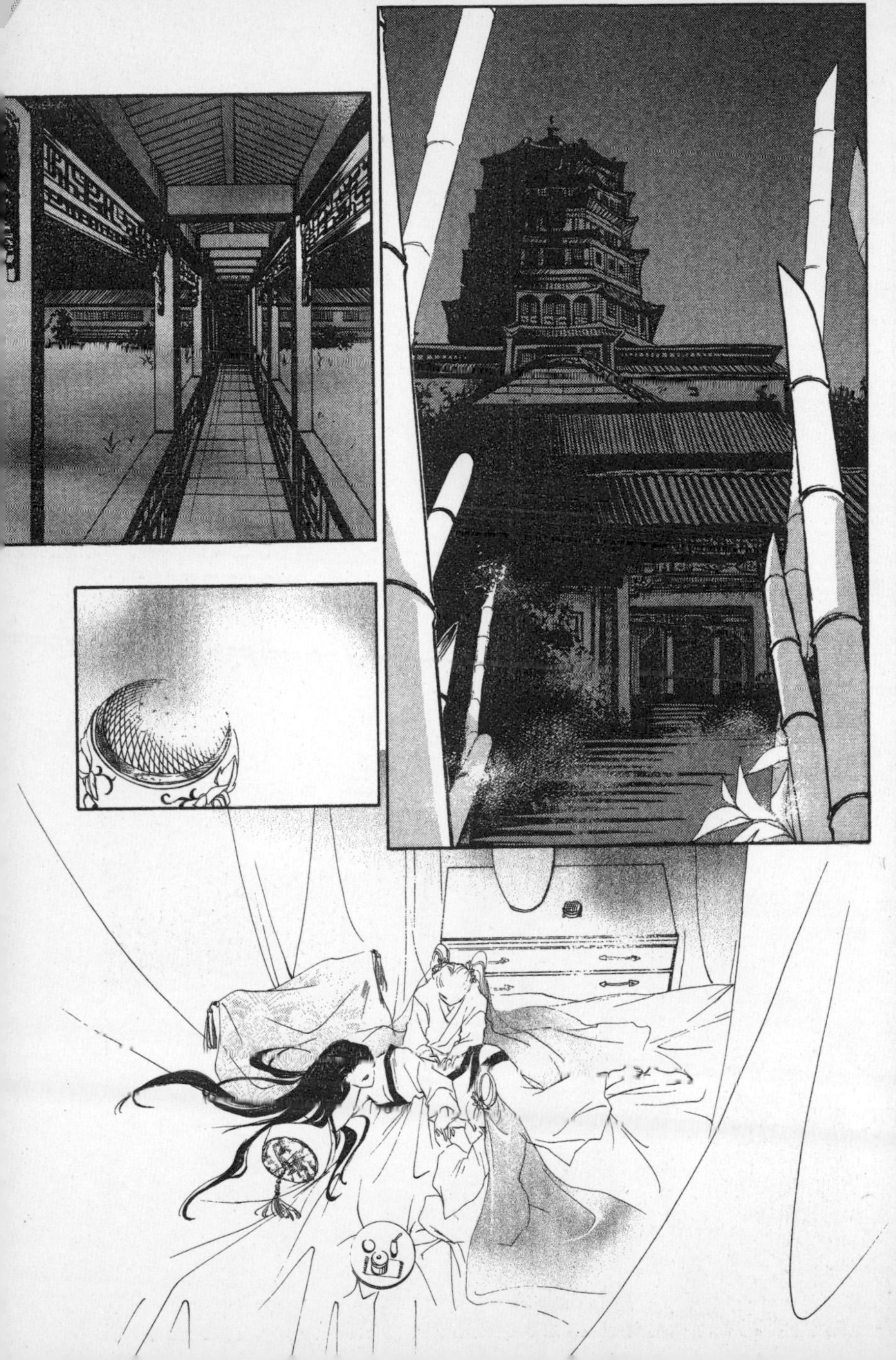

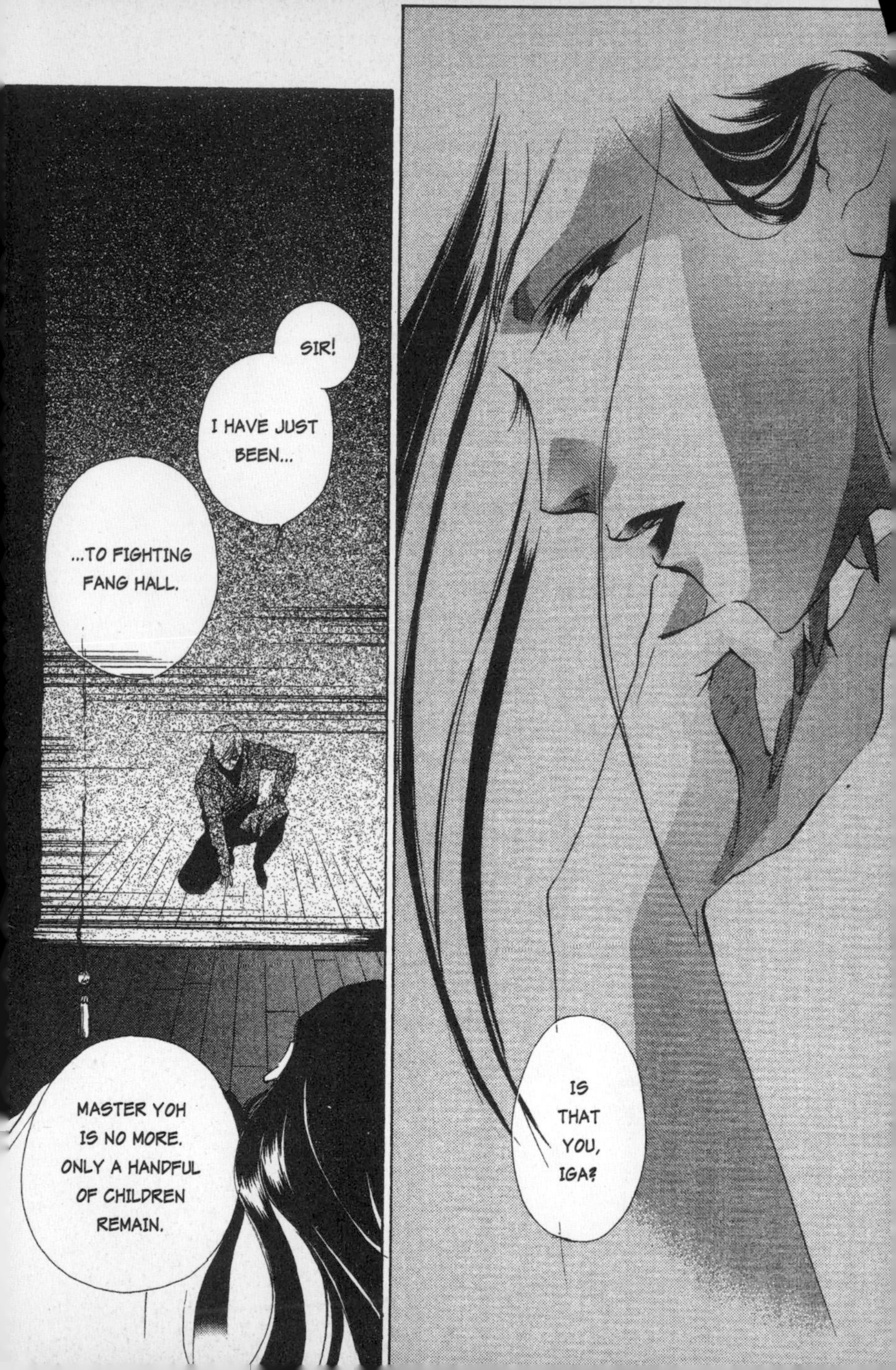
IS THAT YOU, IGA?
SIR!
I HAVE JUST BEEN...
...TO FIGHTING FANG HALL.
MASTER YOH IS NO MORE. ONLY A HANDFUL OF CHILDREN REMAIN.

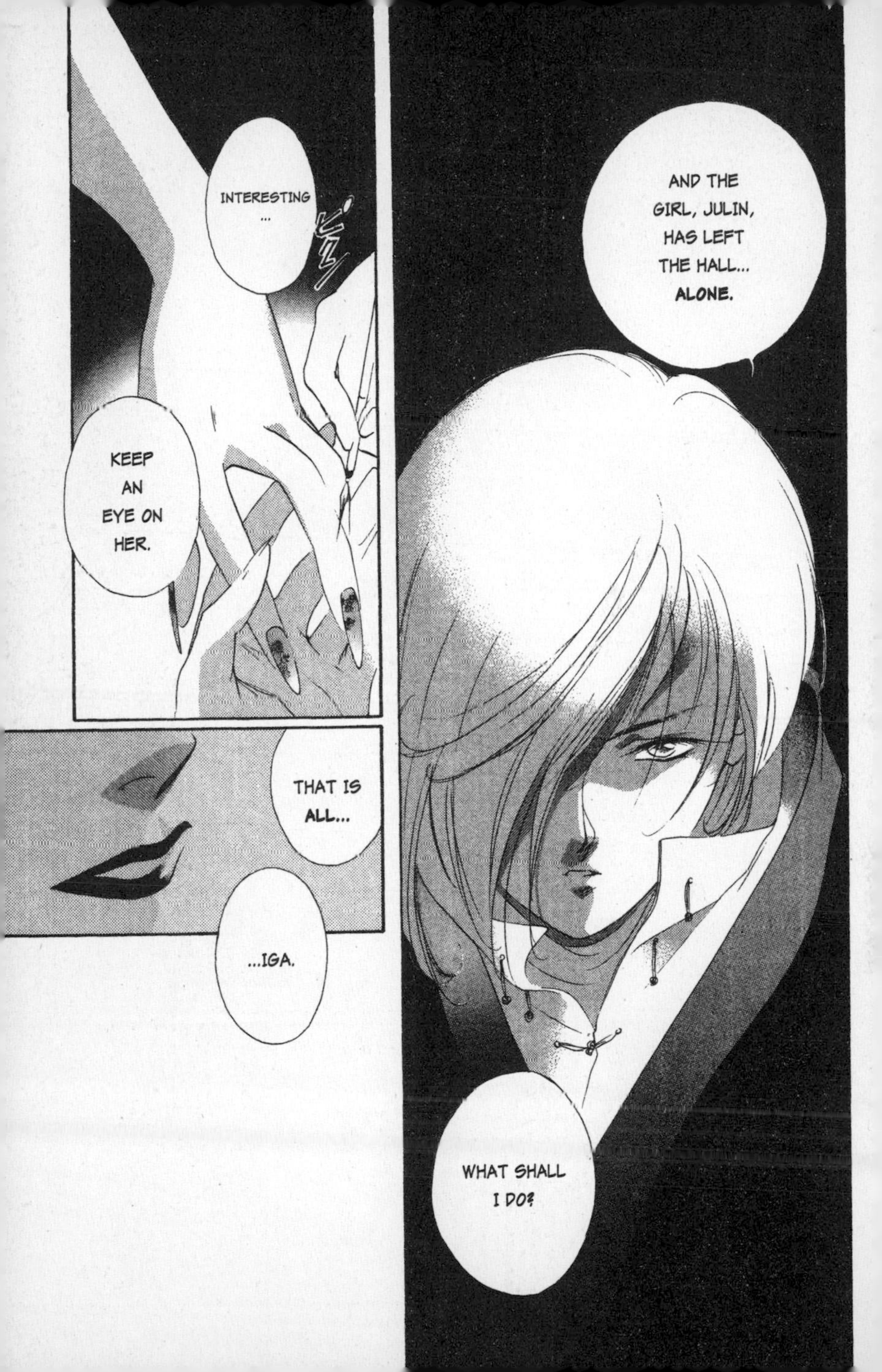
AND THE GIRL, JULIN, HAS LEFT THE HALL... ALONE.
WHAT SHALL I DO?
INTERESTING ...
KEEP AN EYE ON HER.
THAT IS ALL...
...IGA.

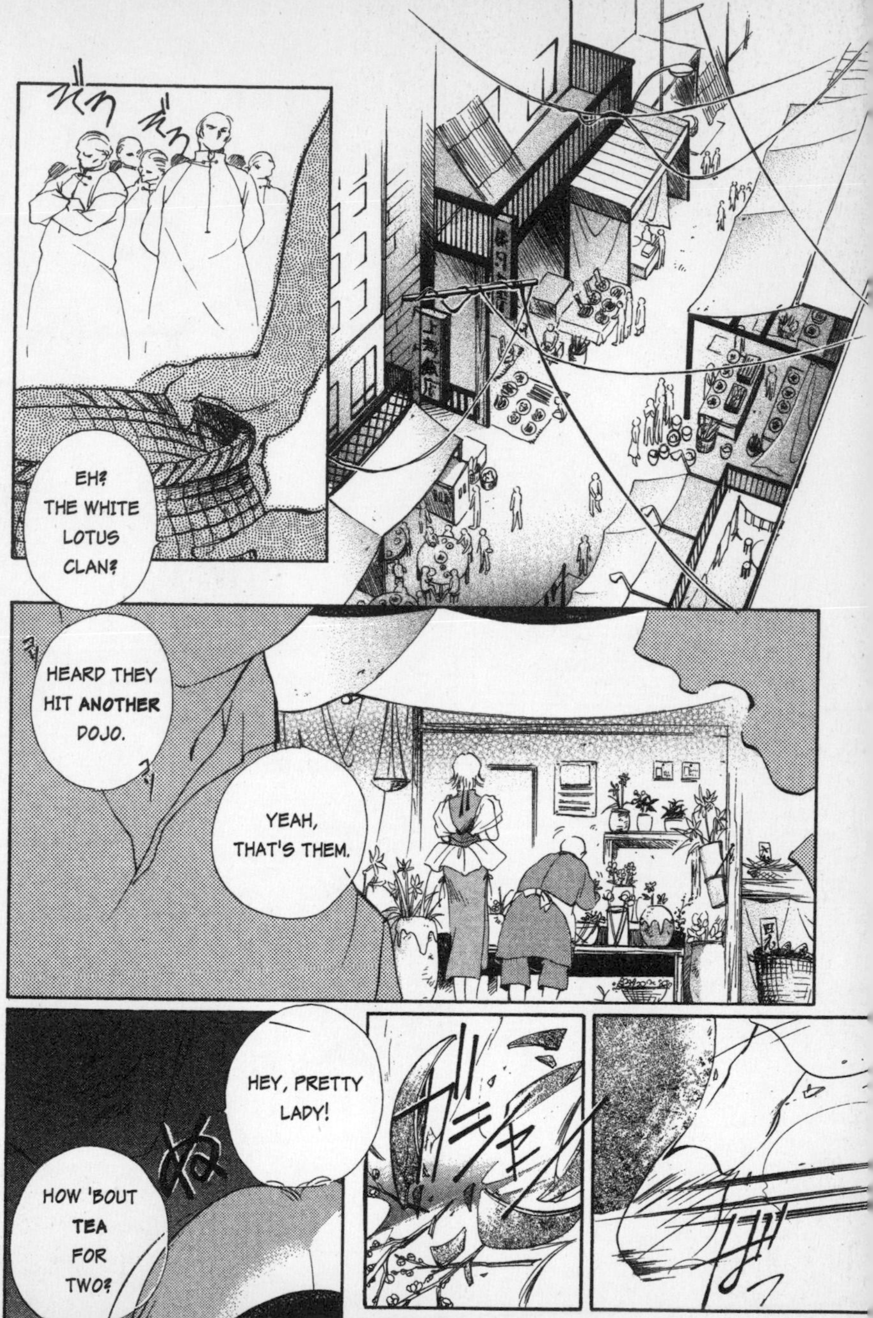
EH? THE WHITE LOTUS CLAN?
HEARD THEY HIT ANOTHER DOJO.
YEAH, THAT'S THEM.
HEY, PRETTY LADY!
HOW 'BOUT TEA FOR TWO?

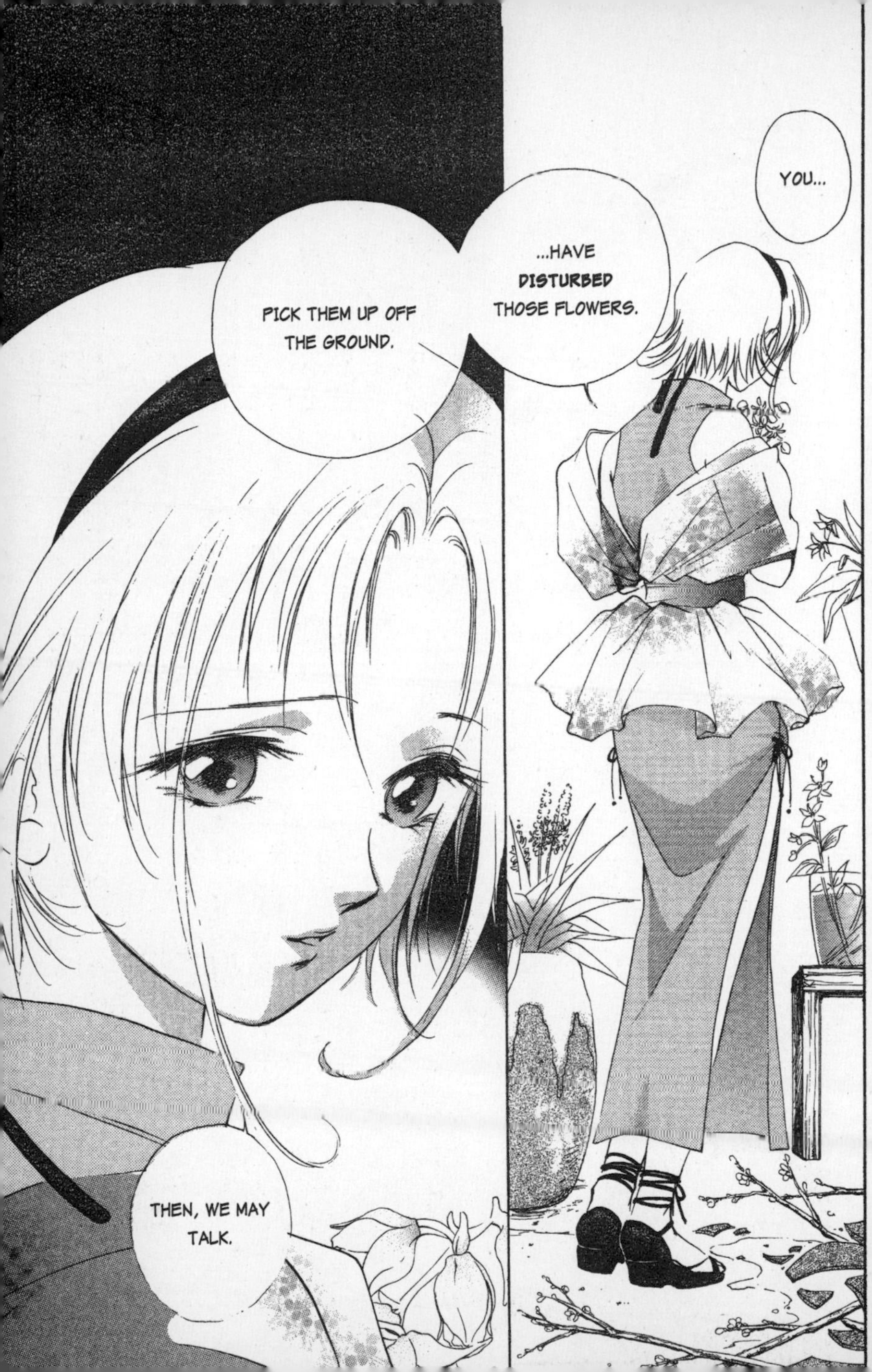
YOU...
...HAVE DISTURBED THOSE FLOWERS.
PICK THEM UP OFF THE GROUND.
THEN, WE MAY TALK.

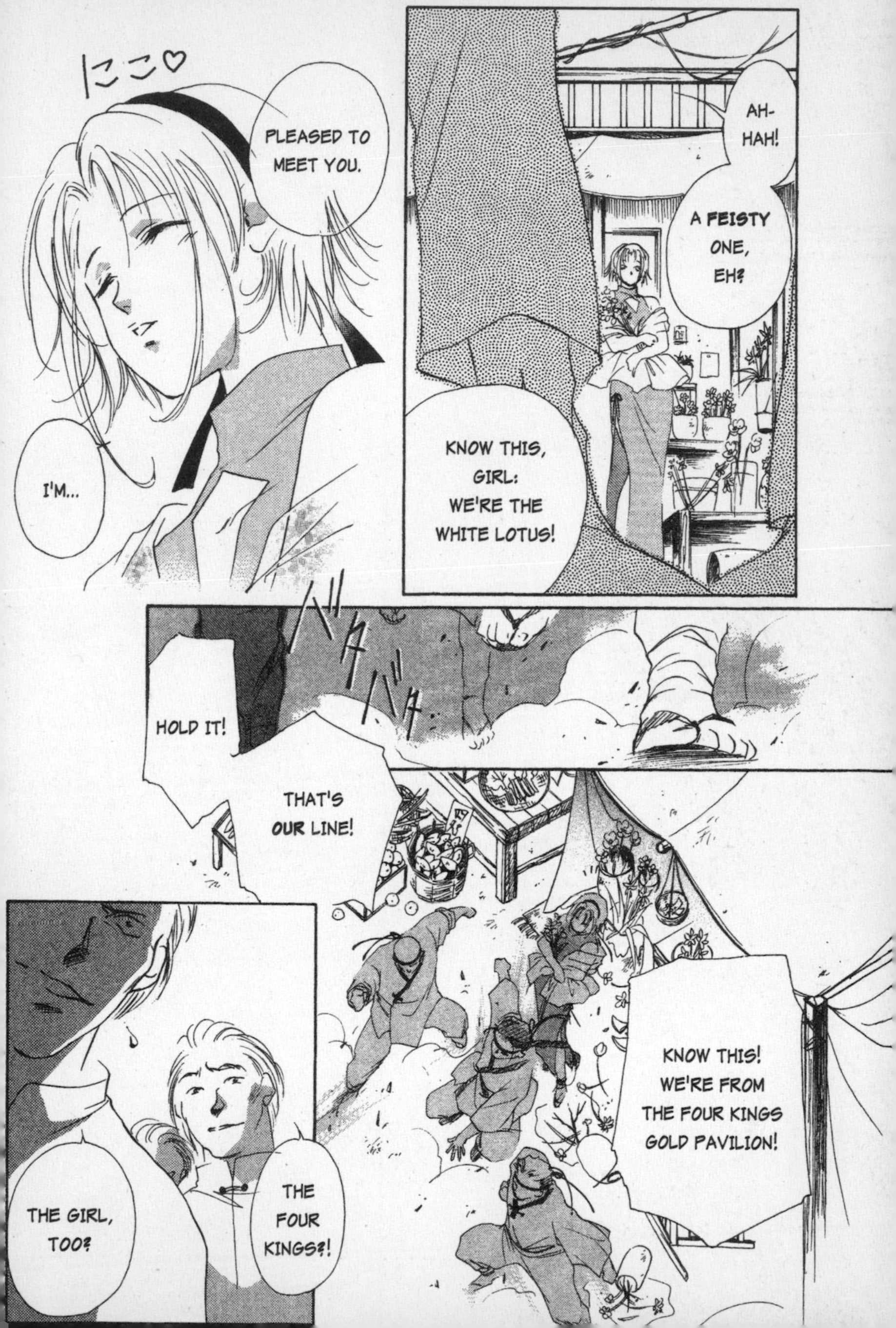
AH-HAH!
A FEISTY ONE, EH?
KNOW THIS, GIRL: WE'RE THE WHITE LOTUS!
にこ♡
PLEASED TO MEET YOU.
I'M...
バタバタ
HOLD IT!
THAT'S OUR LINE!
KNOW THIS! WE'RE FROM THE FOUR KINGS GOLD PAVILION!
THE FOUR KINGS?!
THE GIRL, TOO?

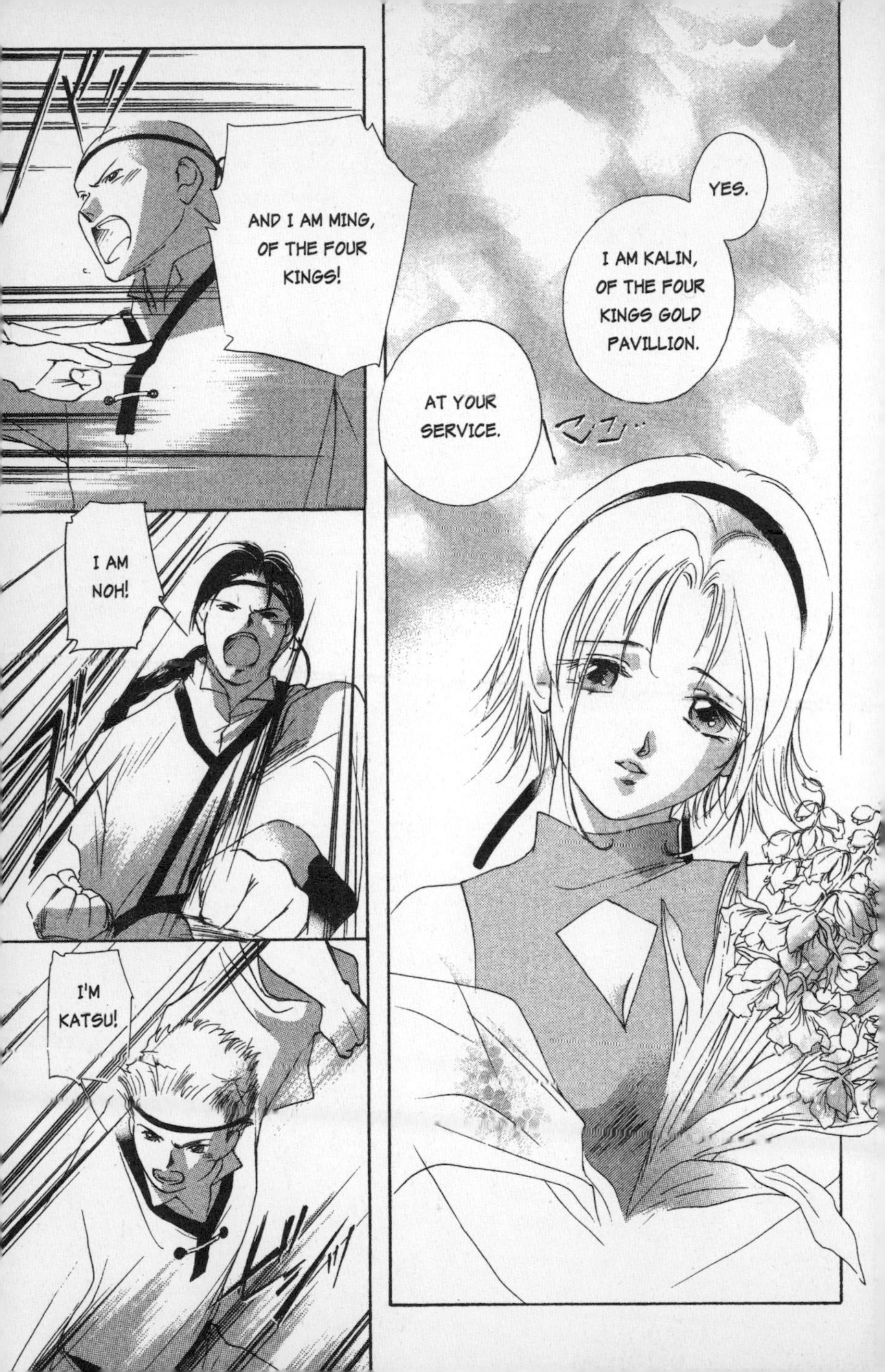
YES.
I AM KALIN, OF THE FOUR KINGS GOLD PAVILLION.
AT YOUR SERVICE.
AND I AM MING, OF THE FOUR KINGS!
I AM NOH!
I'M KATSU!

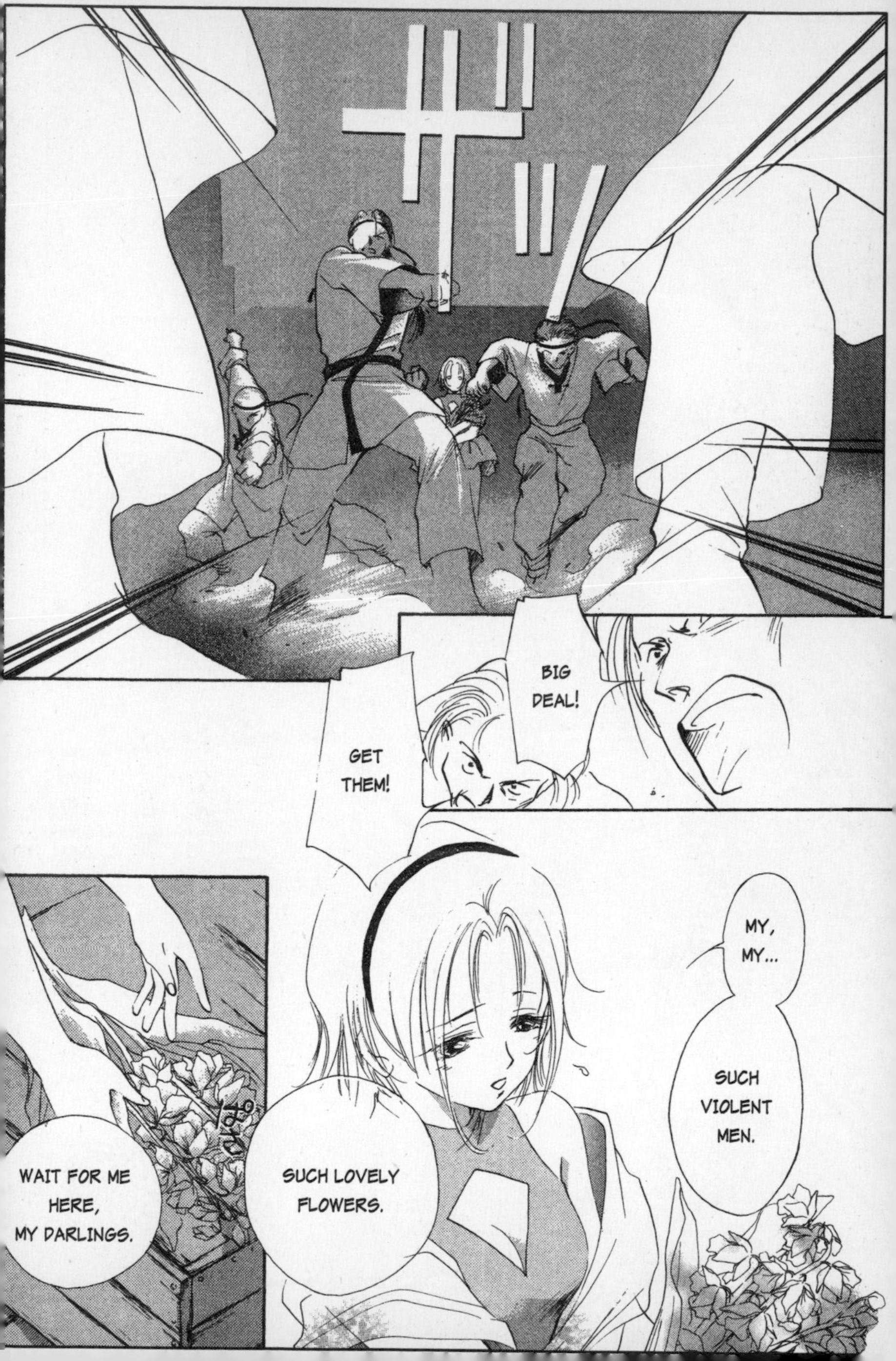
BIG DEAL!
GET THEM!
MY, MY...
SUCH VIOLENT MEN.
SUCH LOVELY FLOWERS.
WAIT FOR ME HERE, MY DARLINGS.

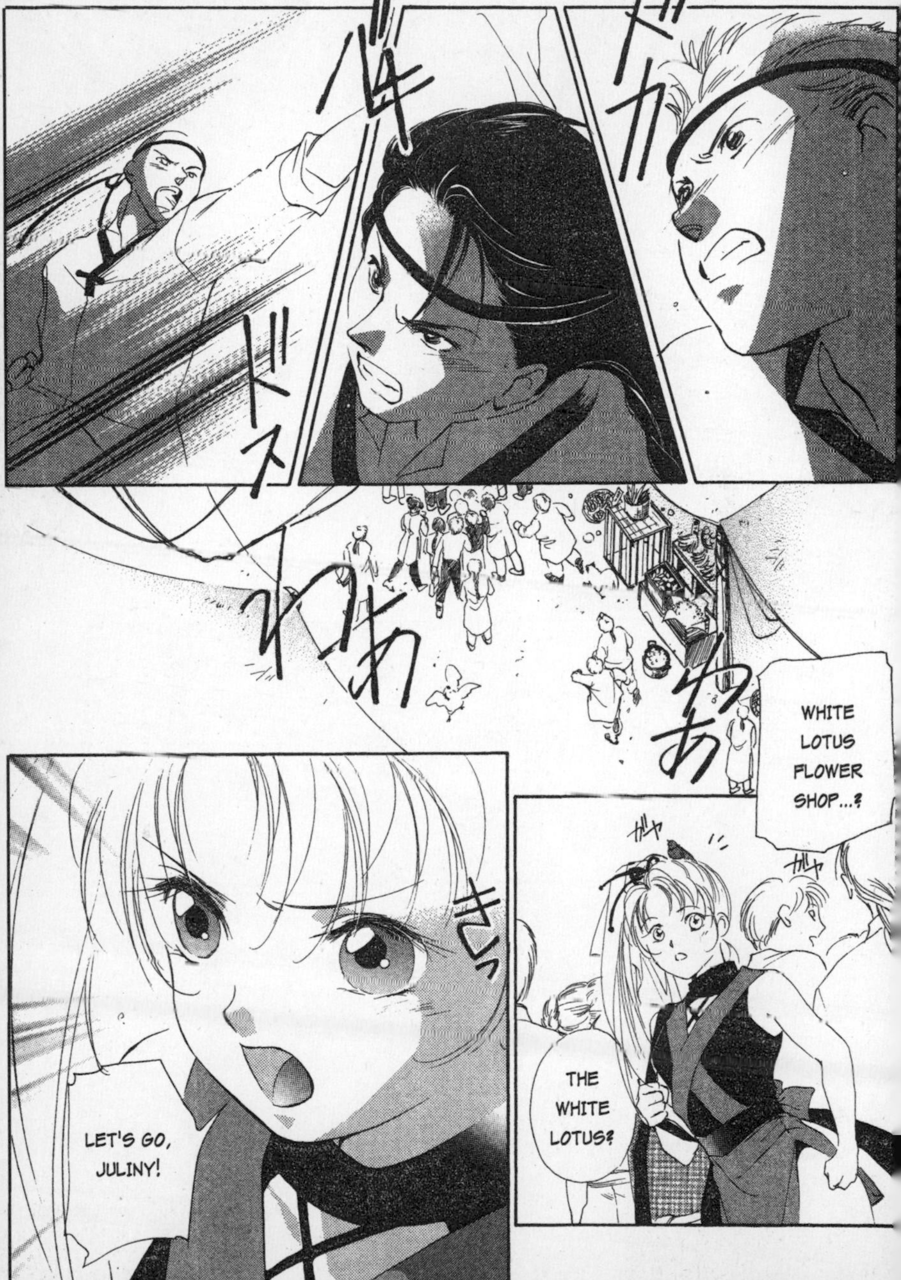

ドガ
バキ
ドス
わあ
わあ
WHITE LOTUS FLOWER SHOP...?
THE WHITE LOTUS?
LET'S GO, JULINY!

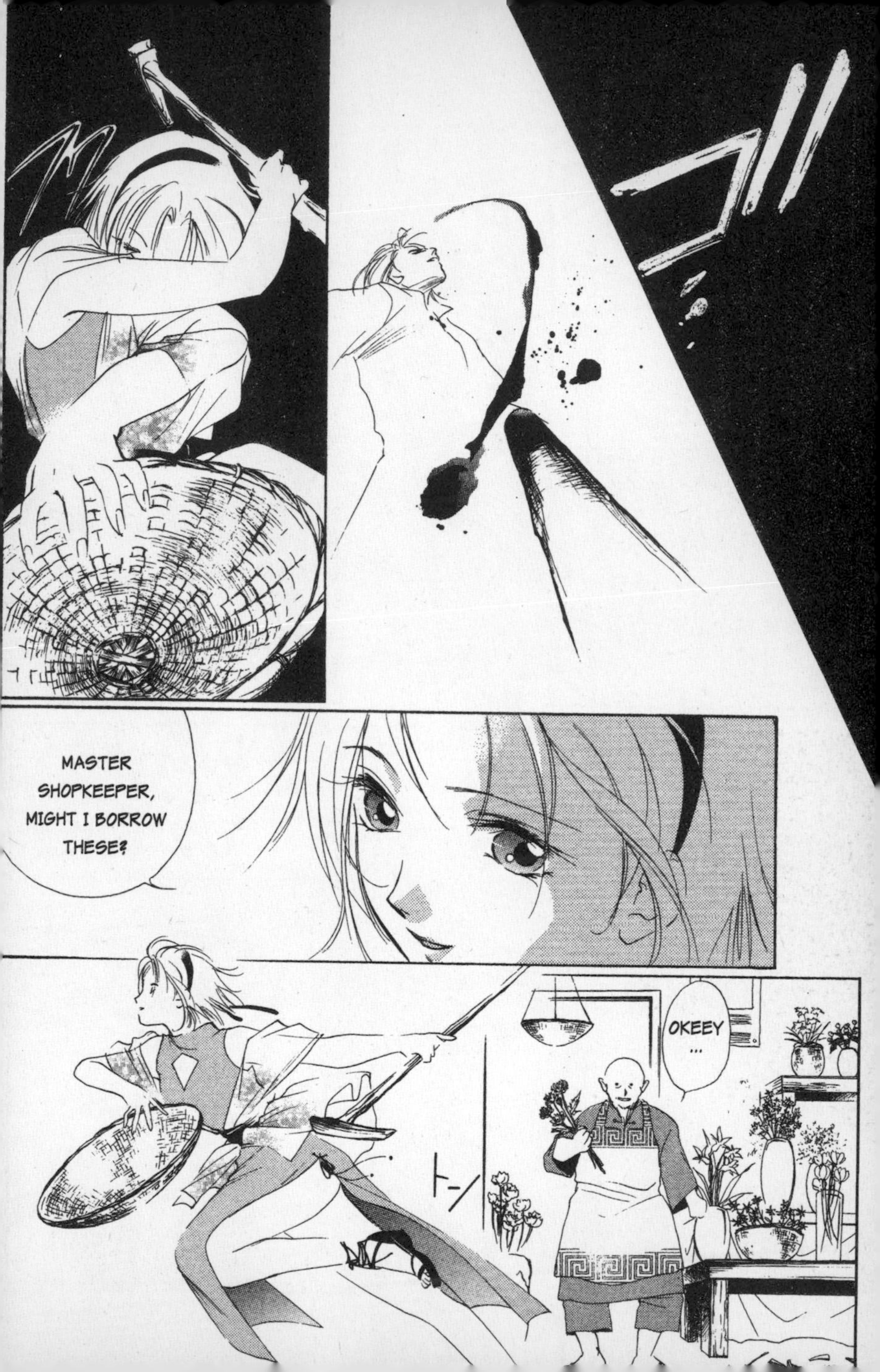
MASTER SHOPKEEPER, MIGHT I BORROW THESE?
OKEEY ...

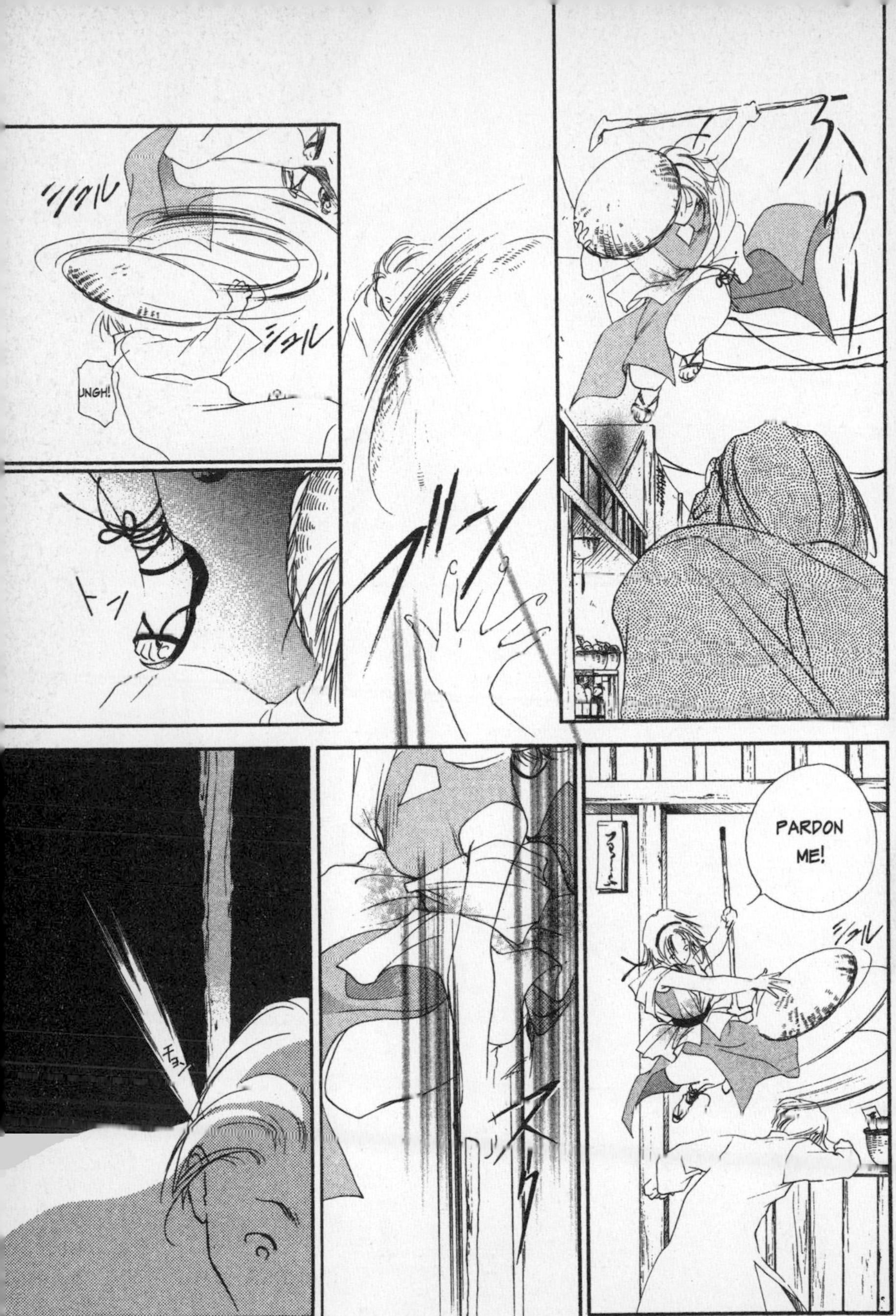
UNGH!
PARDON ME!

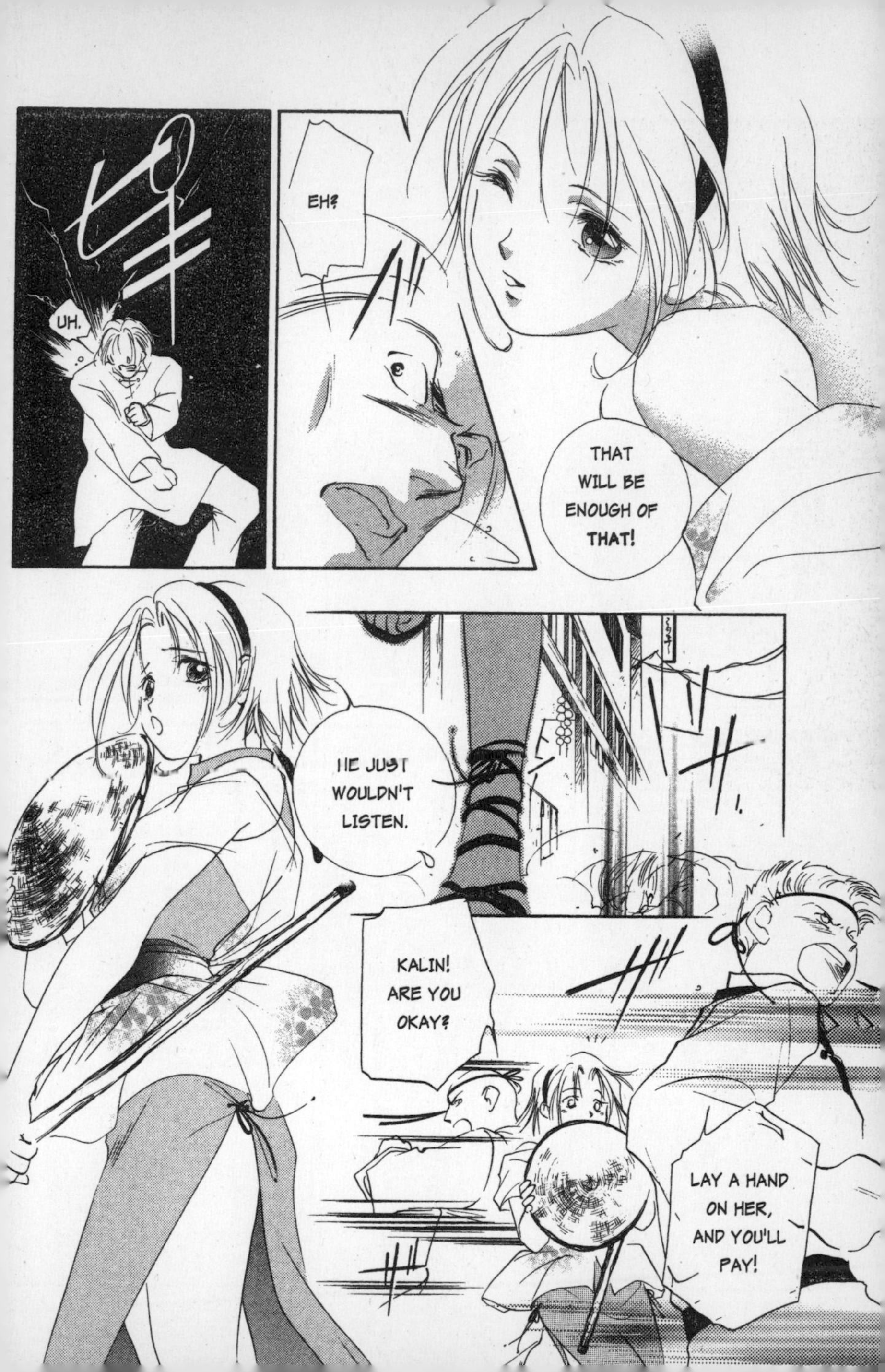
THAT WILL BE ENOUGH OF THAT!
EH?
UH.
KALIN! ARE YOU OKAY?
LAY A HAND ON HER, AND YOU'LL PAY!
HE JUST WOULDN'T LISTEN.

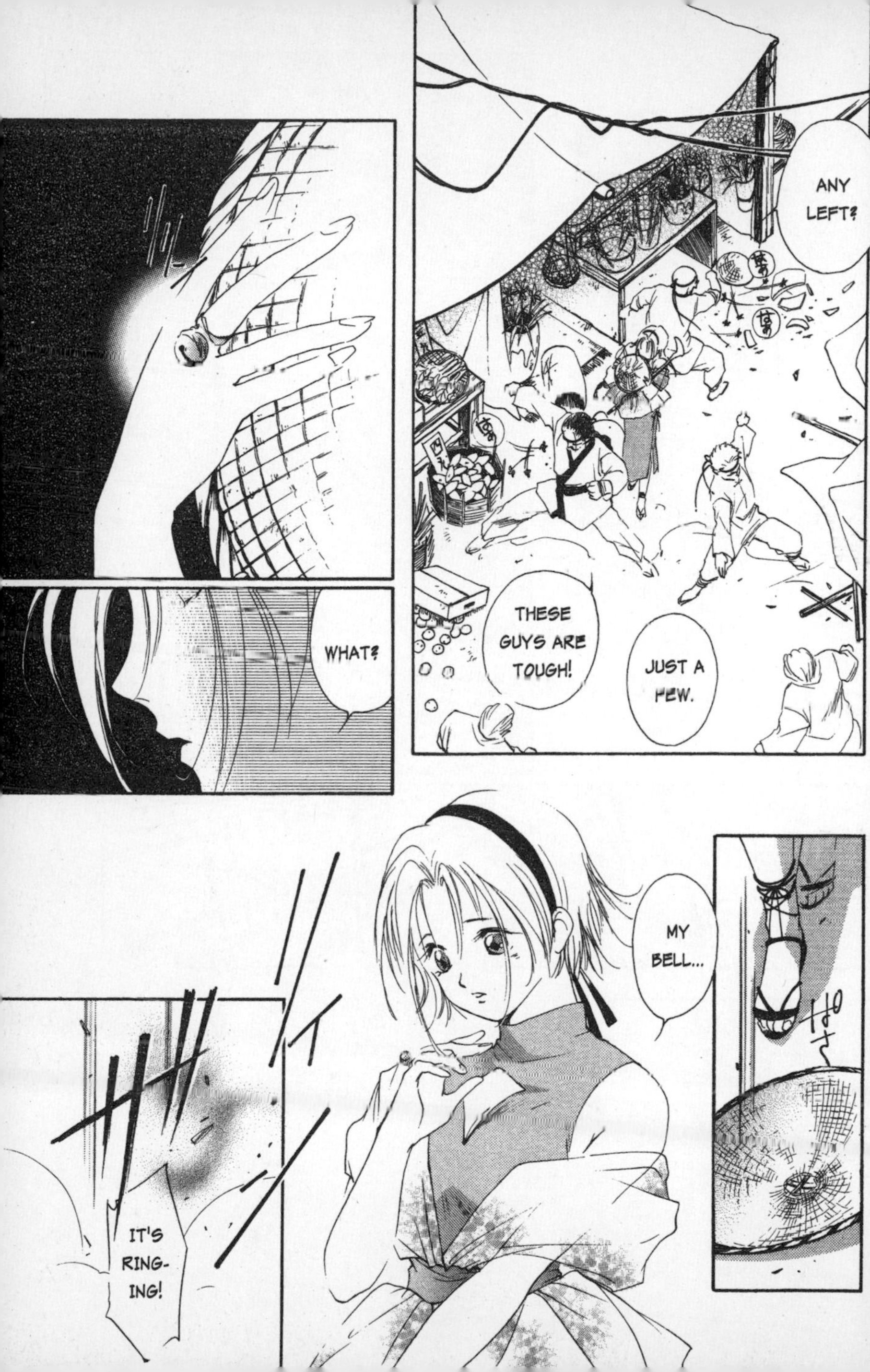
ANY LEFT?
JUST A FEW.
THESE GUYS ARE TOUGH!
WHAT?
MY BELL...
IT'S RING-ING!

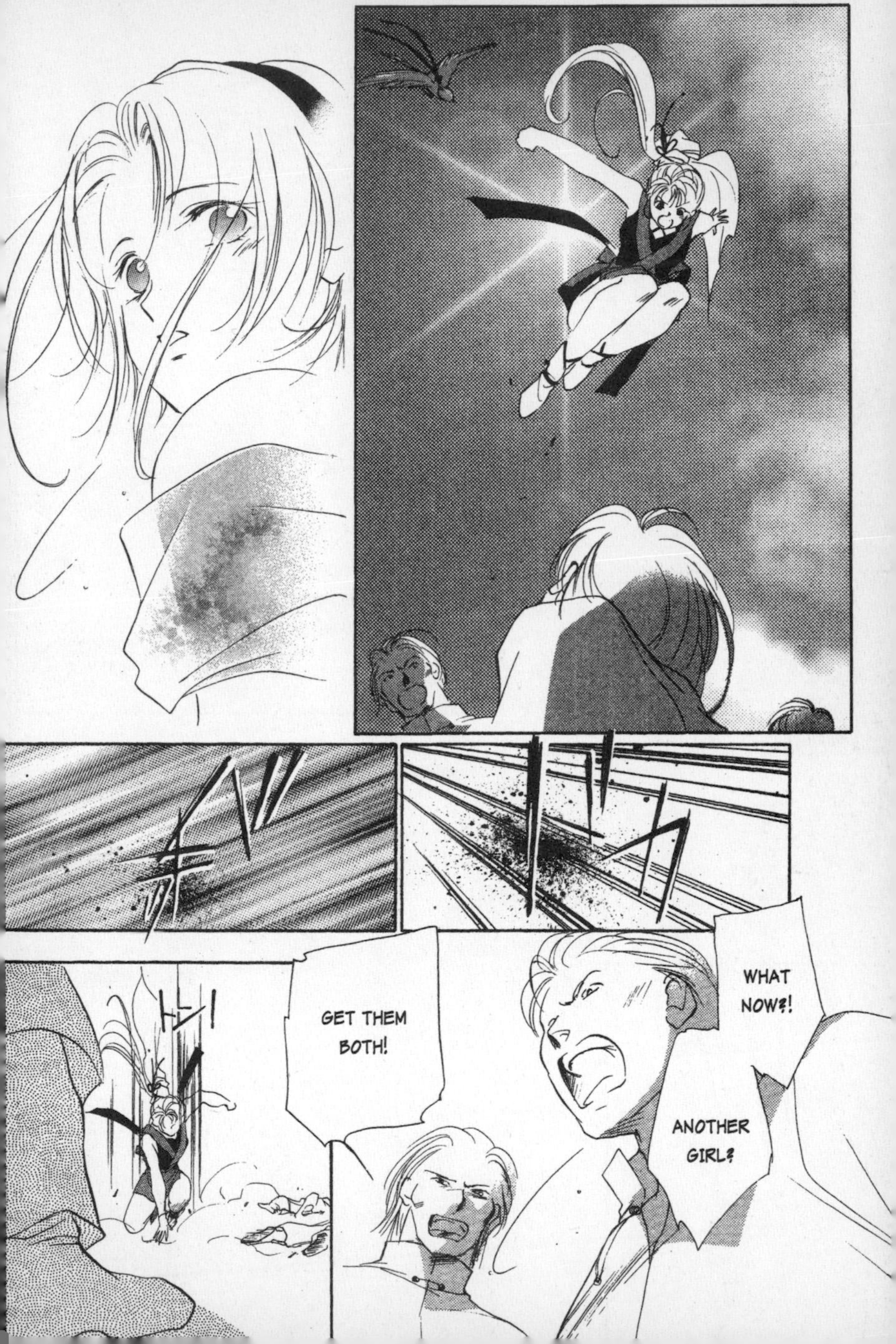
WHAT NOW?!
ANOTHER GIRL?
GET THEM BOTH!

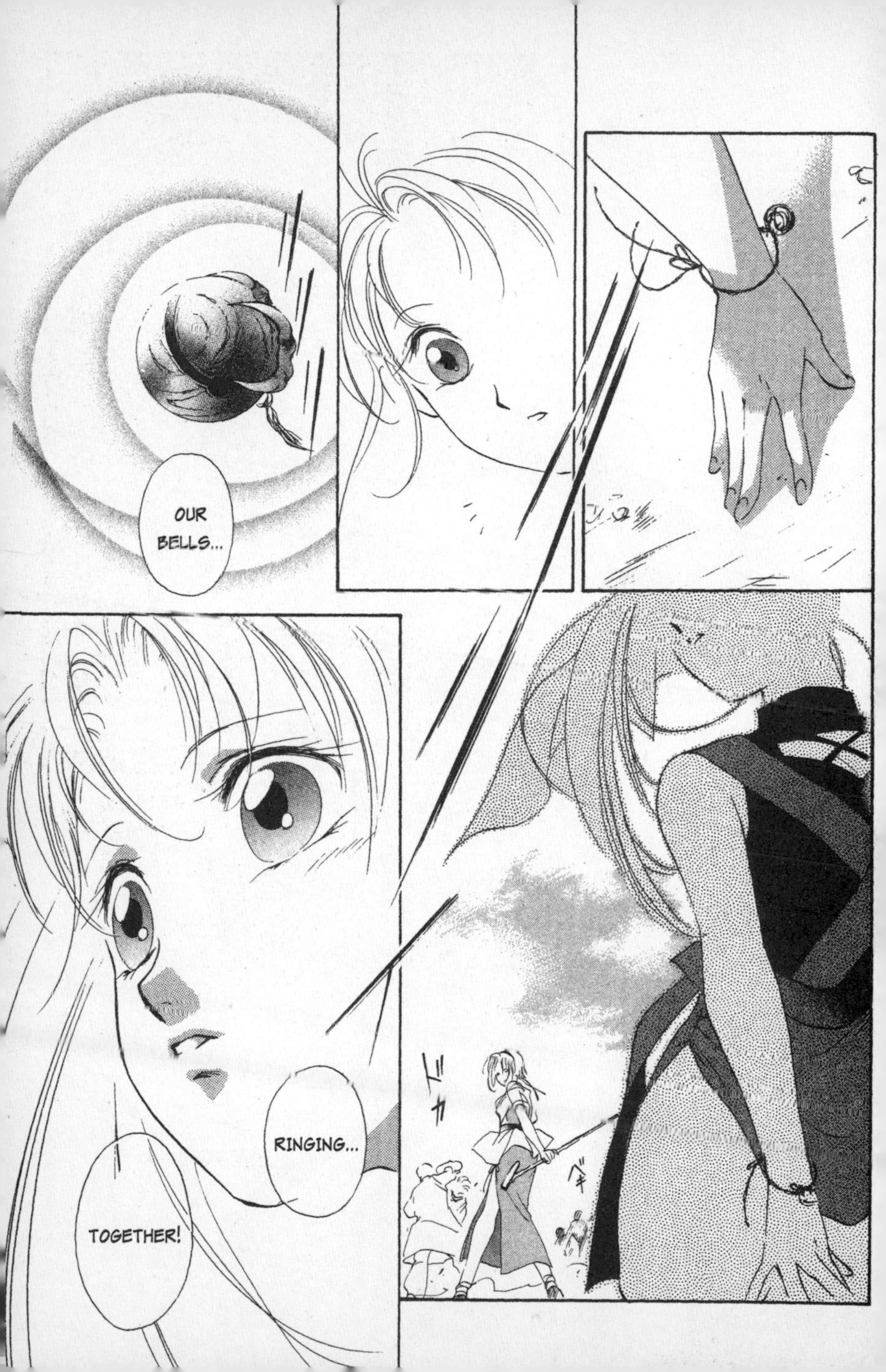
OUR BELLS...
RINGING...
TOGETHER!

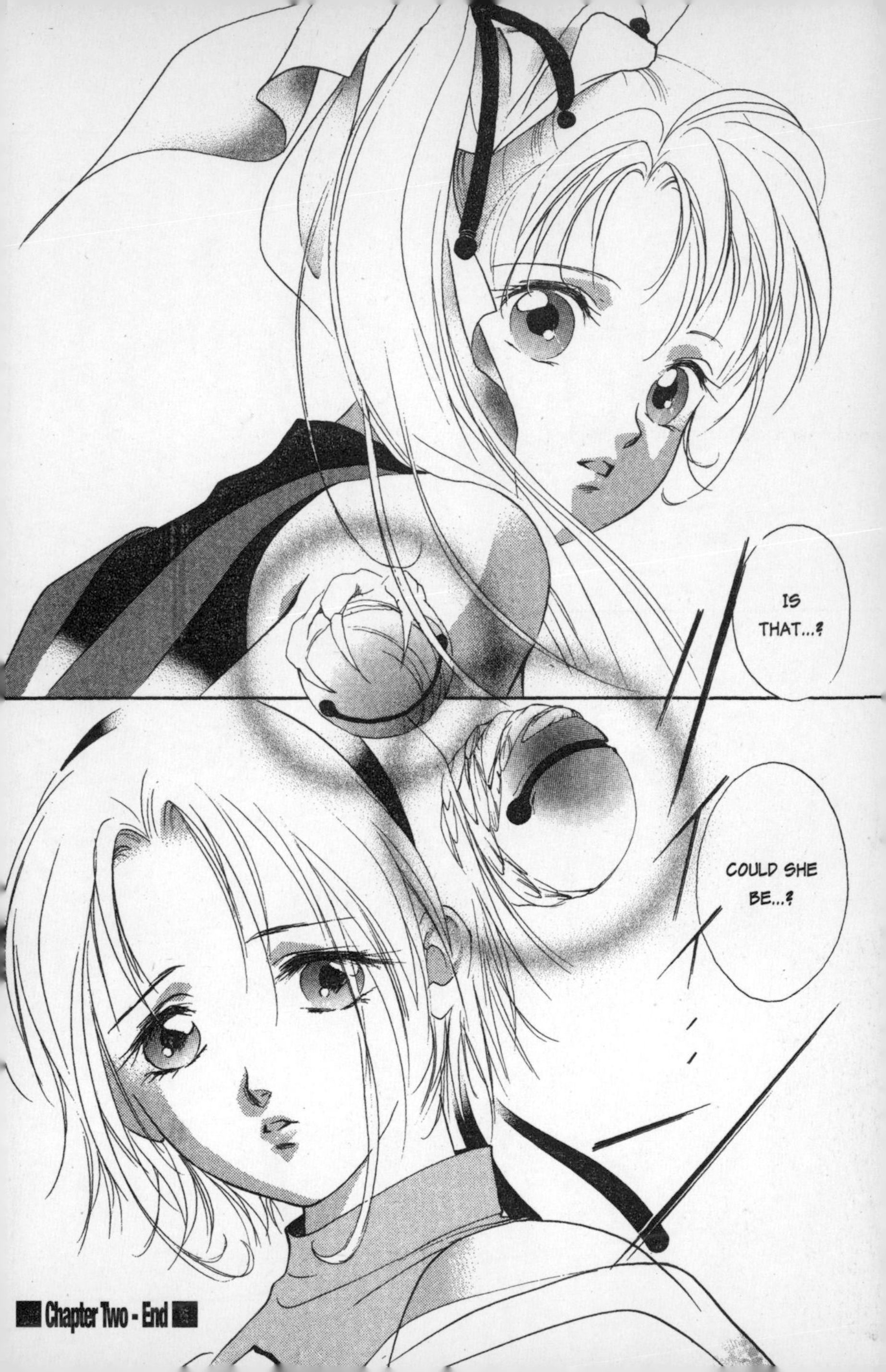
IS THAT...?
COULD SHE BE...?
Chapter Two - End

Chapter 3: The Secret of the Bells

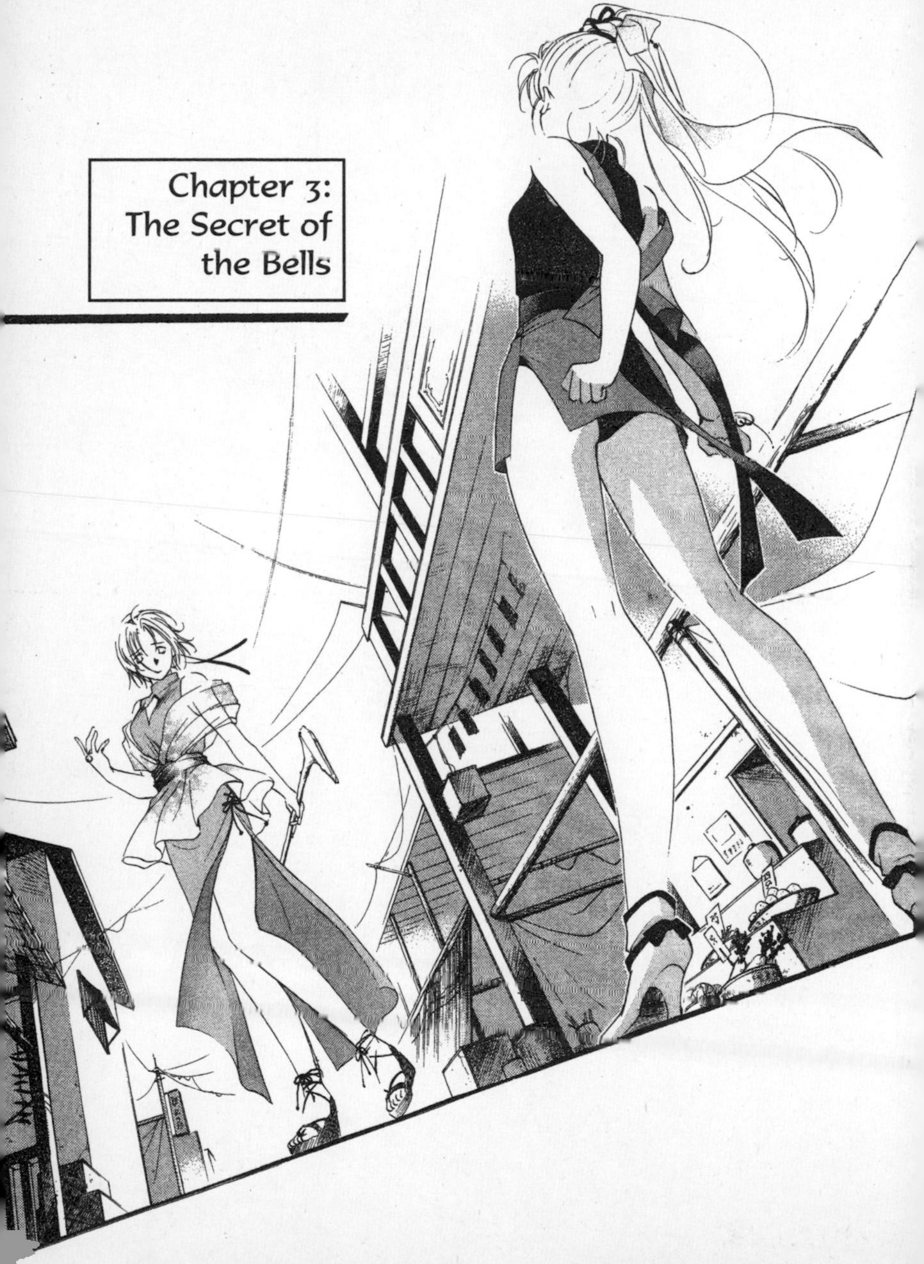

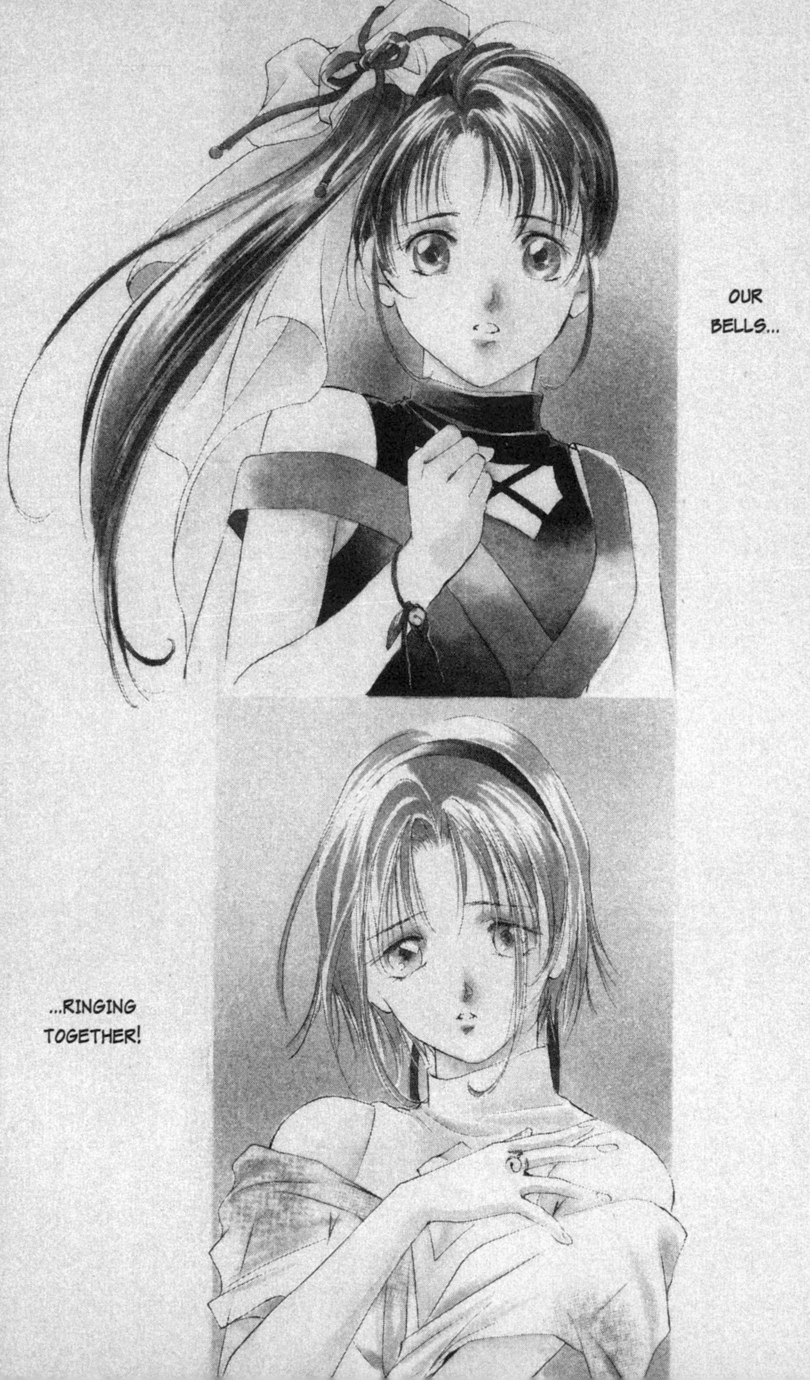
OUR BELLS...
...RINGING TOGETHER!

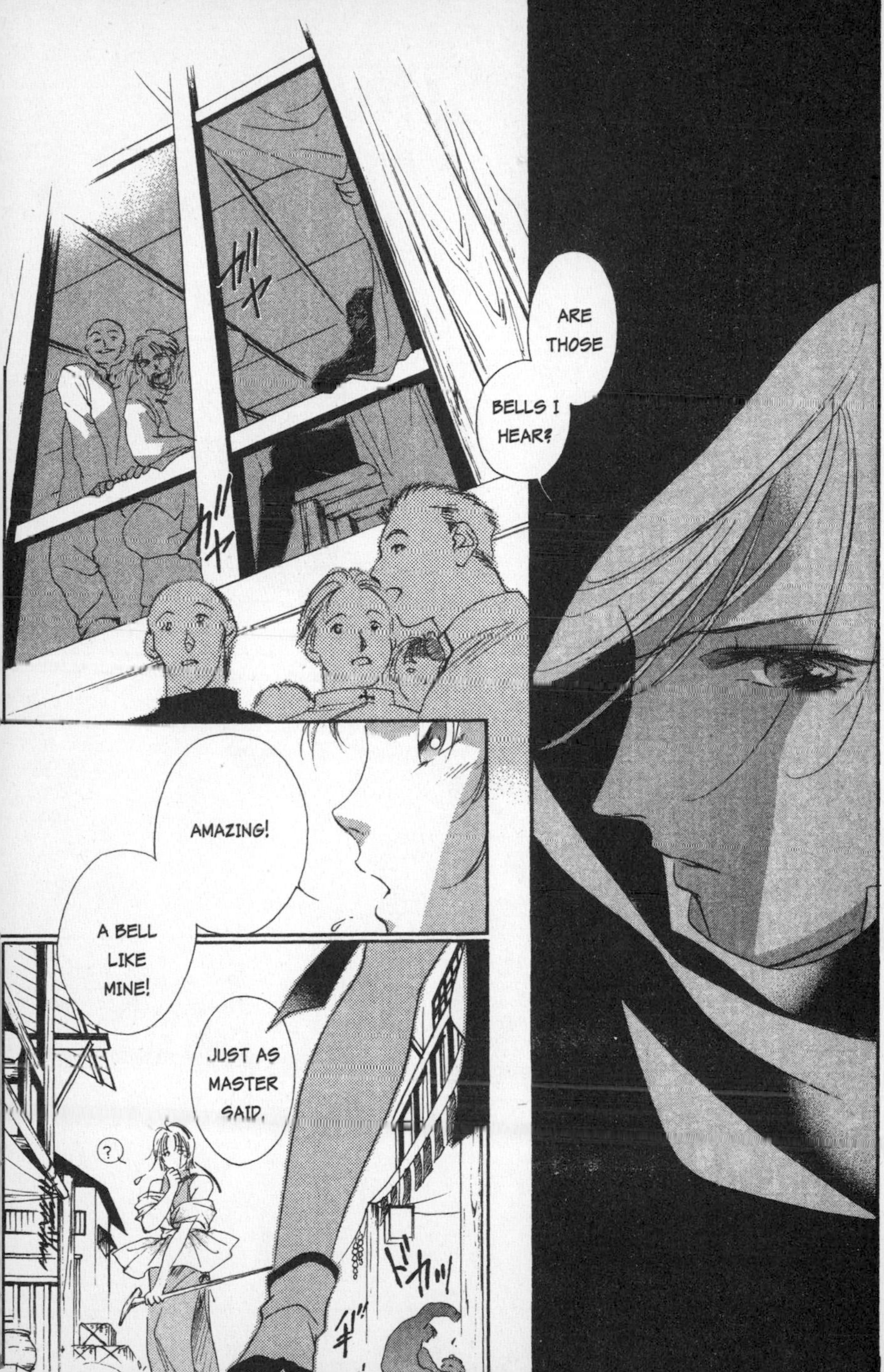
ARE THOSE
BELLS I HEAR?
AMAZING!
A BELL LIKE MINE!
JUST AS MASTER SAID.
?

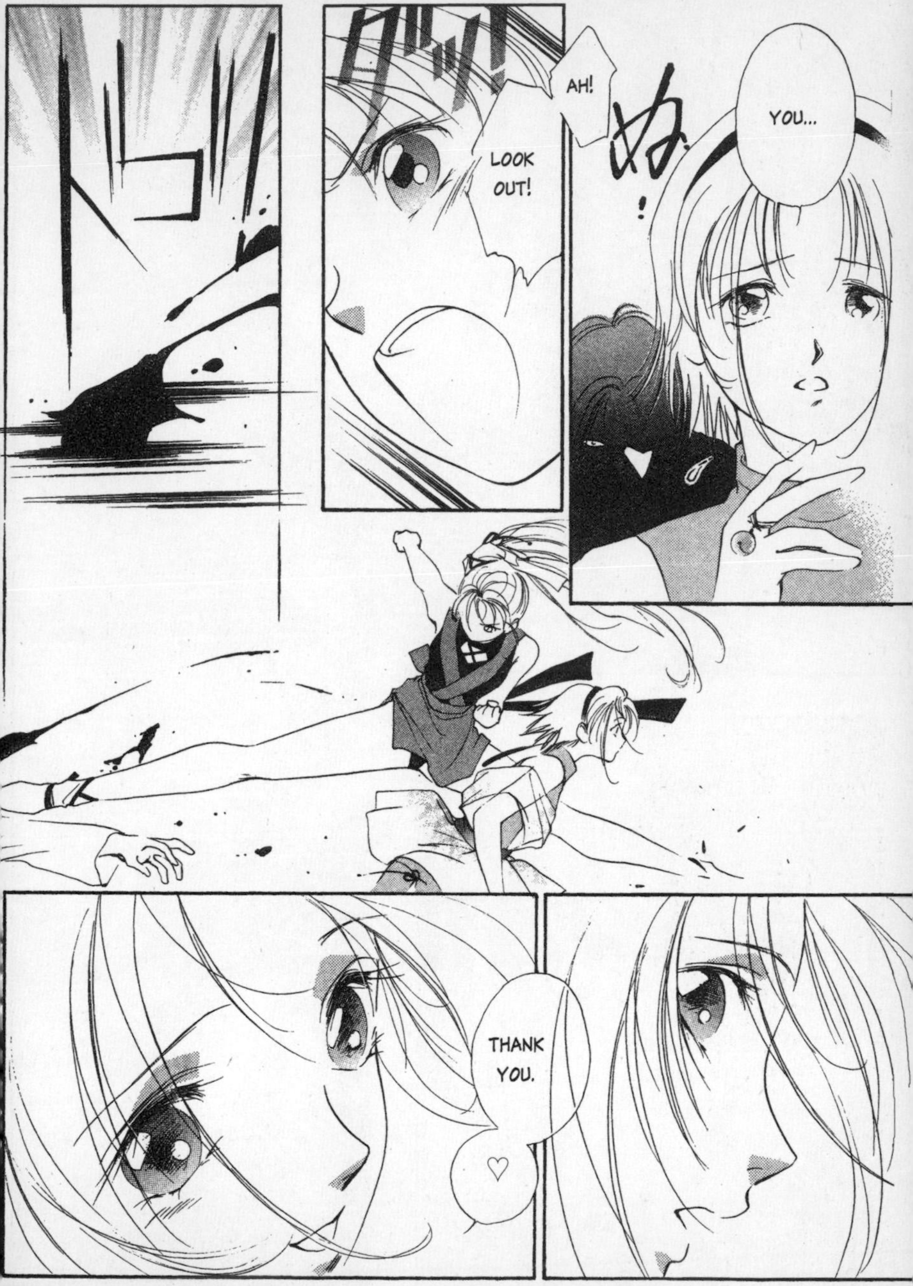
YOU...
AH!
LOOK OUT!
THANK YOU.
♡

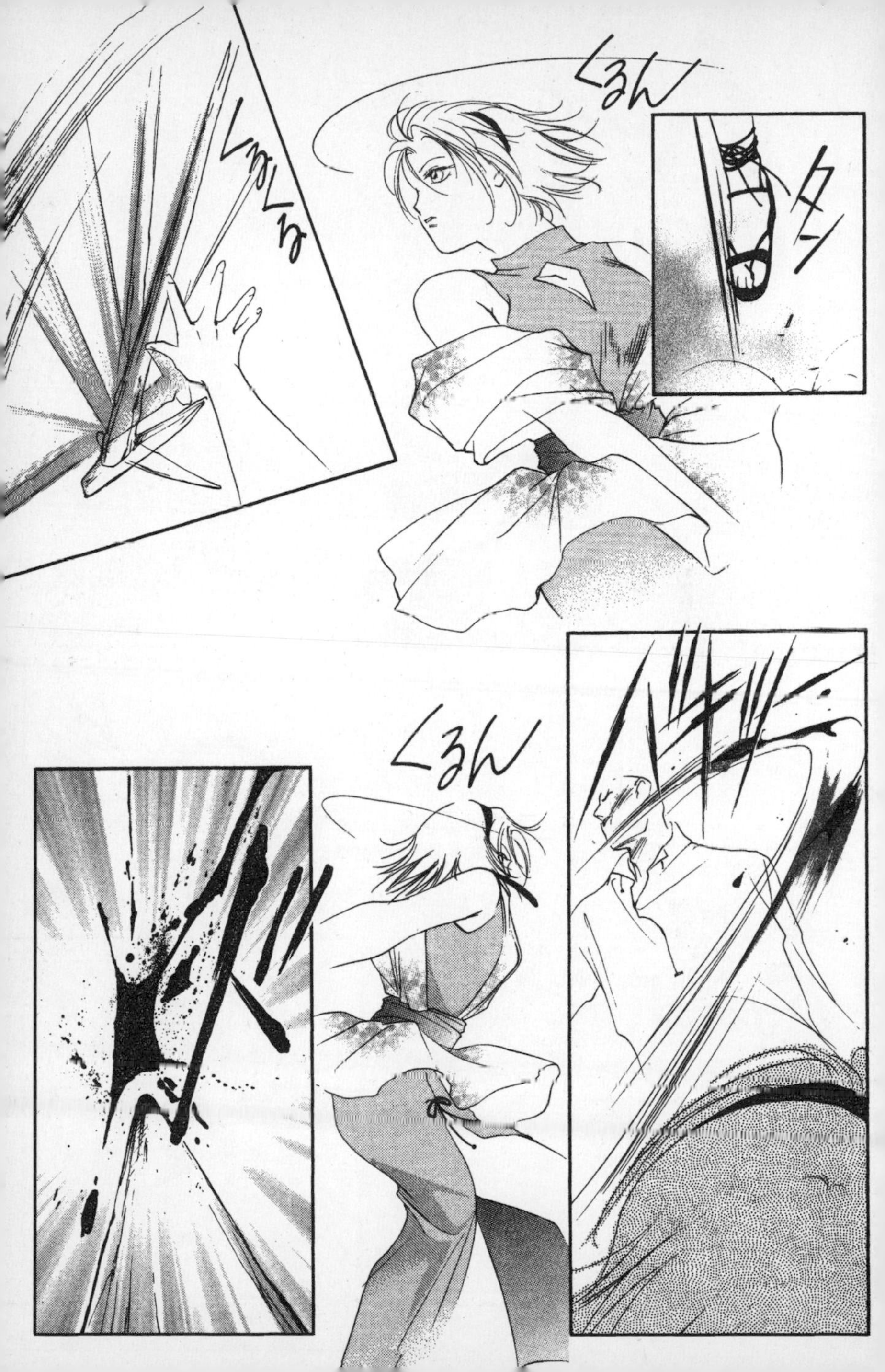
くるん
タン
しゅるしゅる
くるん

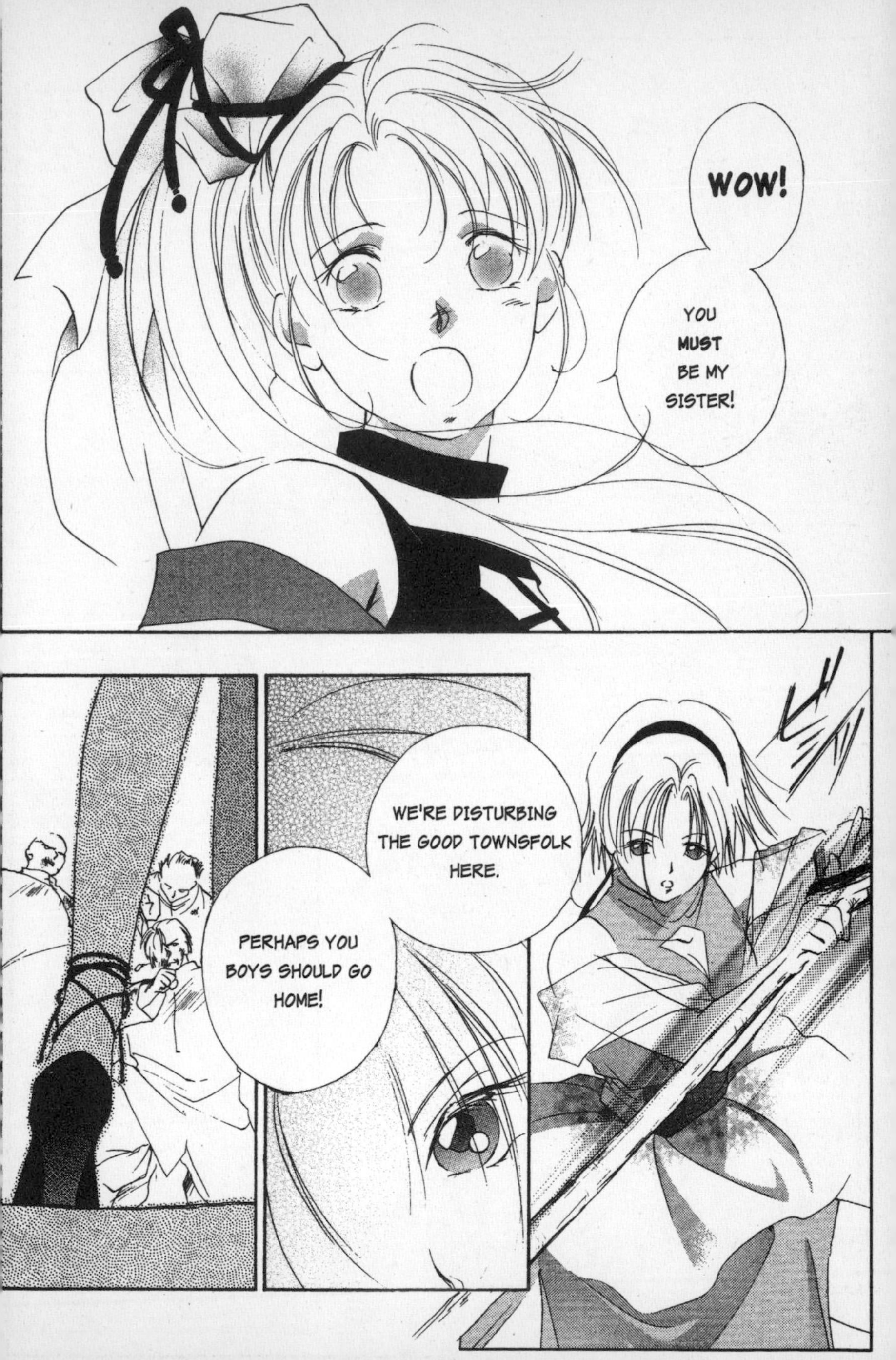
WOW!
YOU MUST BE MY SISTER!
WE'RE DISTURBING THE GOOD TOWNSFOLK HERE.
PERHAPS YOU BOYS SHOULD GO HOME!

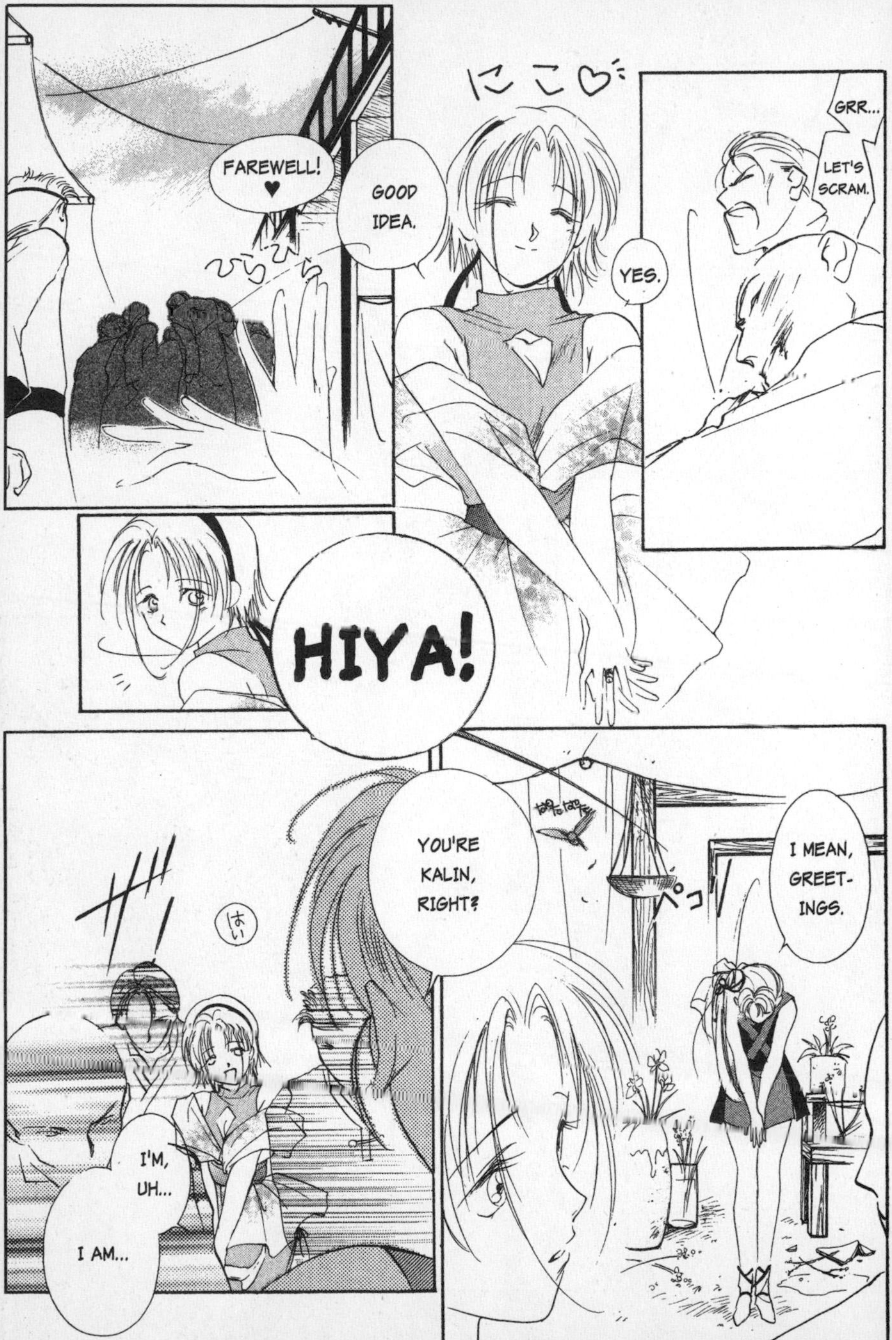
GRR...
LET'S SCRAM.
にこ♡
YES.
FAREWELL! ♥
GOOD IDEA.
ひらひら
HIYA!
I MEAN, GREET-INGS.
ペコ
YOU'RE KALIN, RIGHT?
はい
I'M, UH...
I AM...

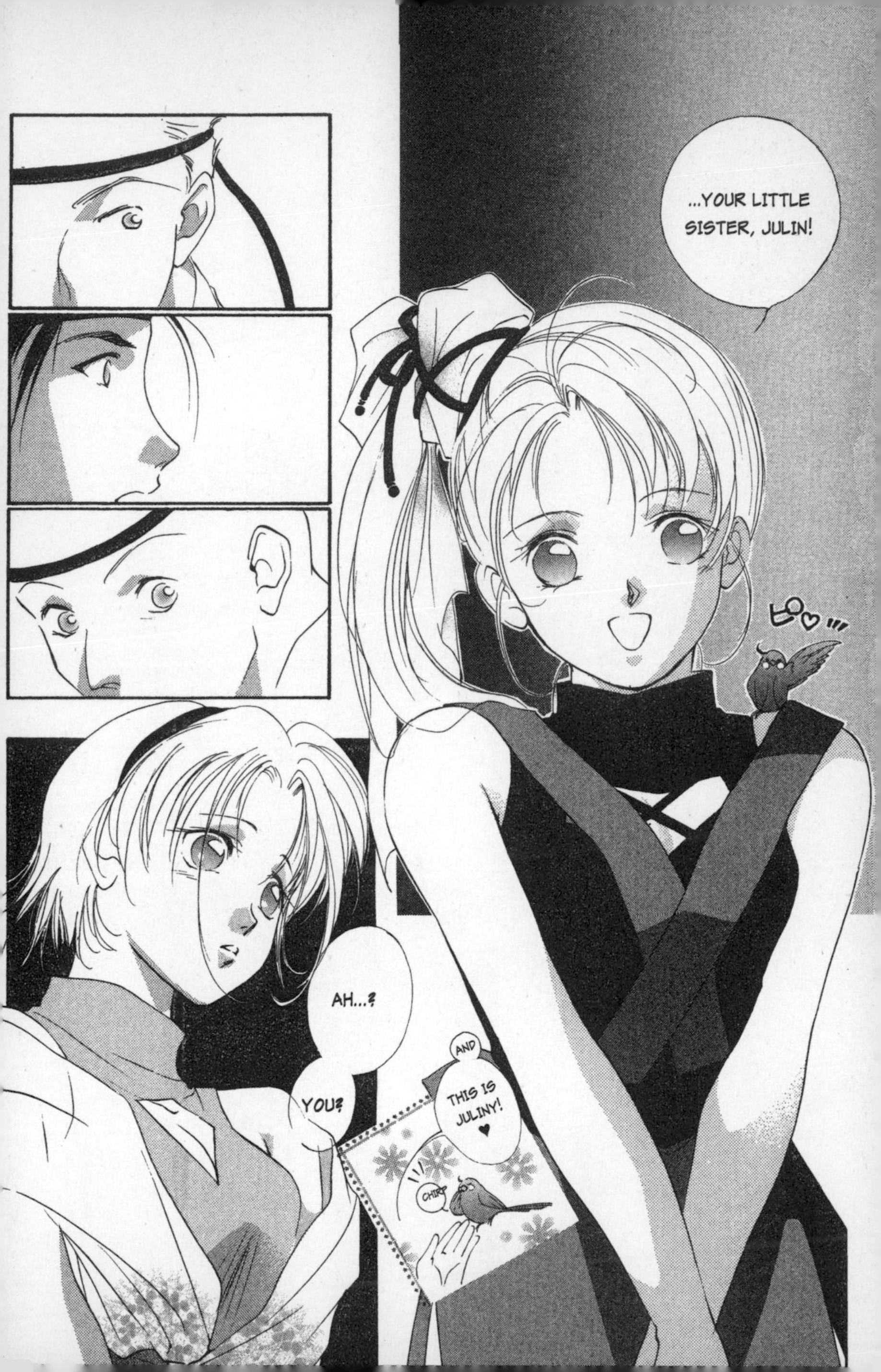
...YOUR LITTLE SISTER, JULIN!
ピ♡
AND
THIS IS JULINY! ♥
CHIRP
AH...?
YOU?

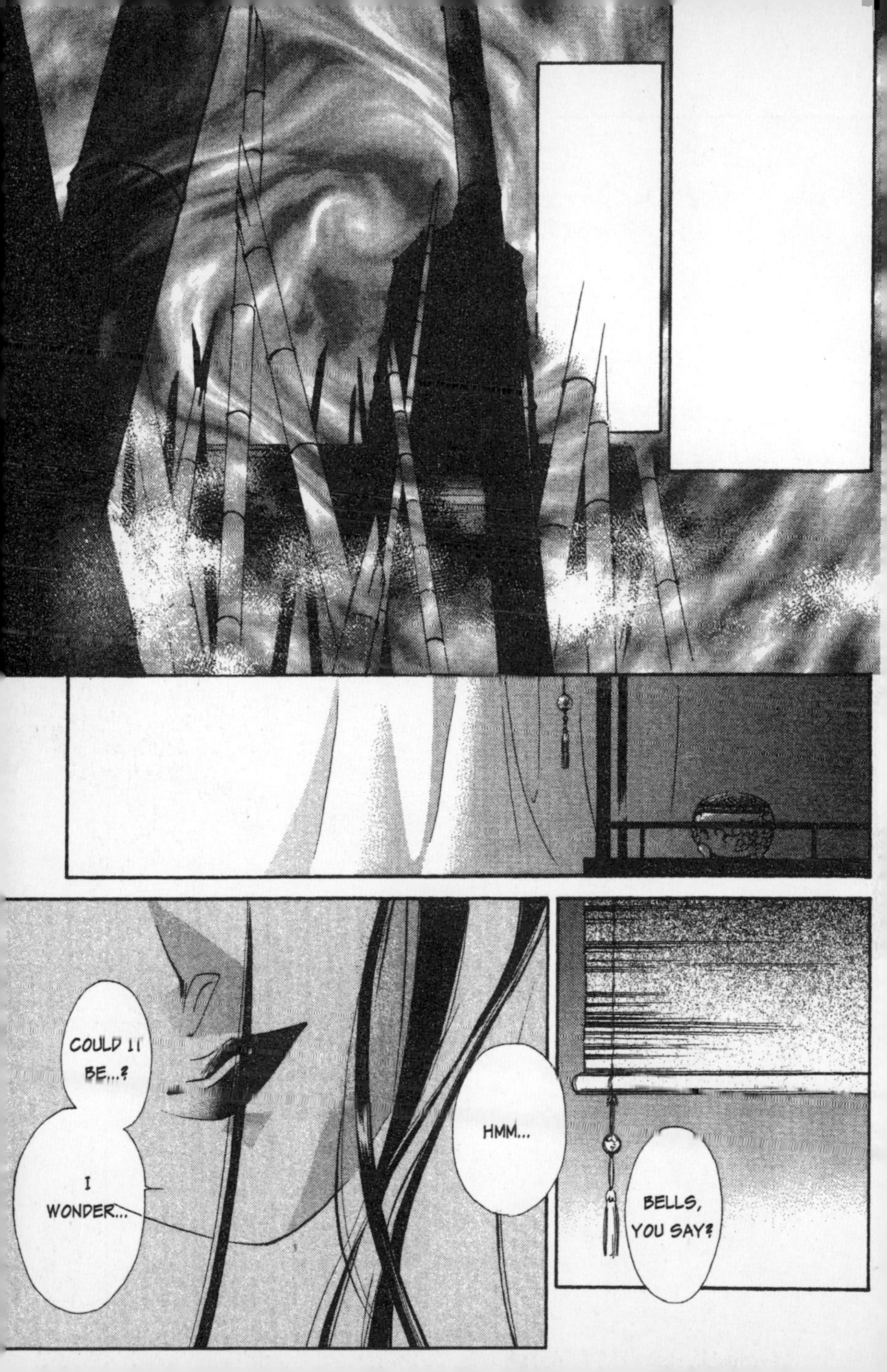
BELLS, YOU SAY?
HMM...
COULD IT BE...?
I WONDER...

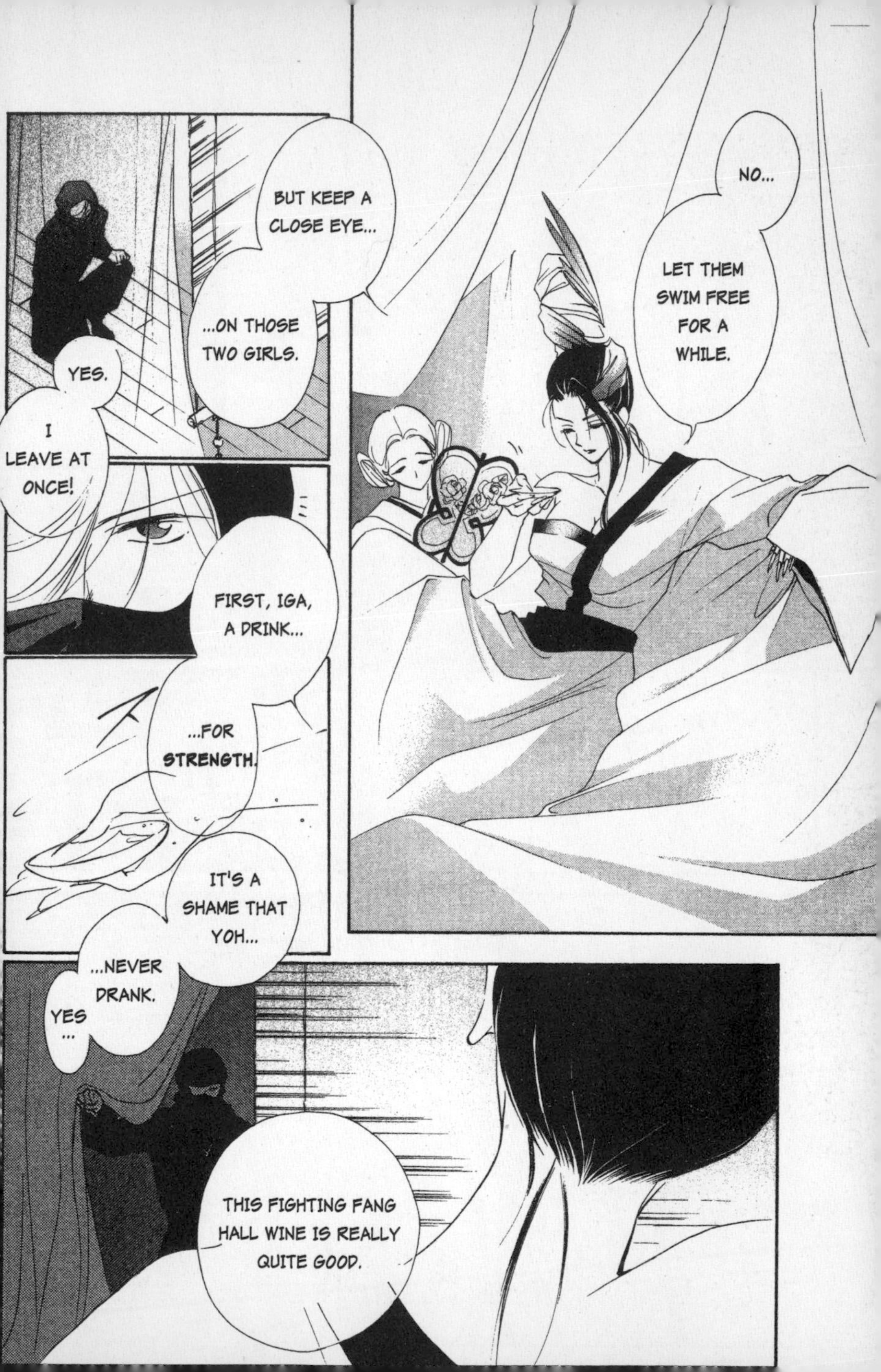
NO...
LET THEM SWIM FREE FOR A WHILE.
BUT KEEP A CLOSE EYE...
...ON THOSE TWO GIRLS.
YES.
I LEAVE AT ONCE!
FIRST, IGA, A DRINK...
...FOR STRENGTH.
IT'S A SHAME THAT YOH...
...NEVER DRANK.
YES...
THIS FIGHTING FANG HALL WINE IS REALLY QUITE GOOD.

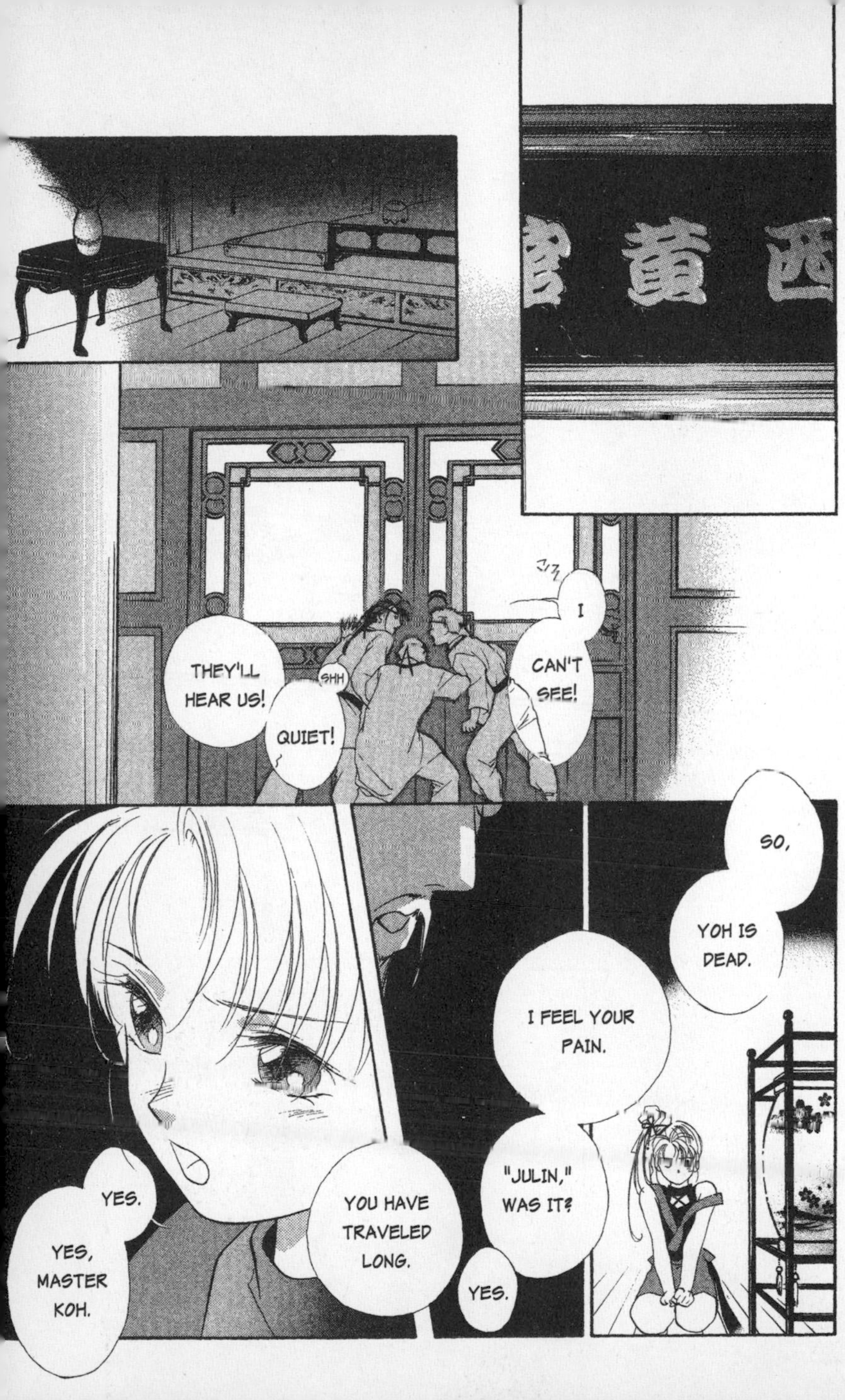

I CAN'T SEE!
THEY'LL HEAR US!
SHH
QUIET!
SO, YOH IS DEAD.
I FEEL YOUR PAIN.
"JULIN," WAS IT?
YES.
YOU HAVE TRAVELED LONG.
YES.
YES, MASTER KOH.

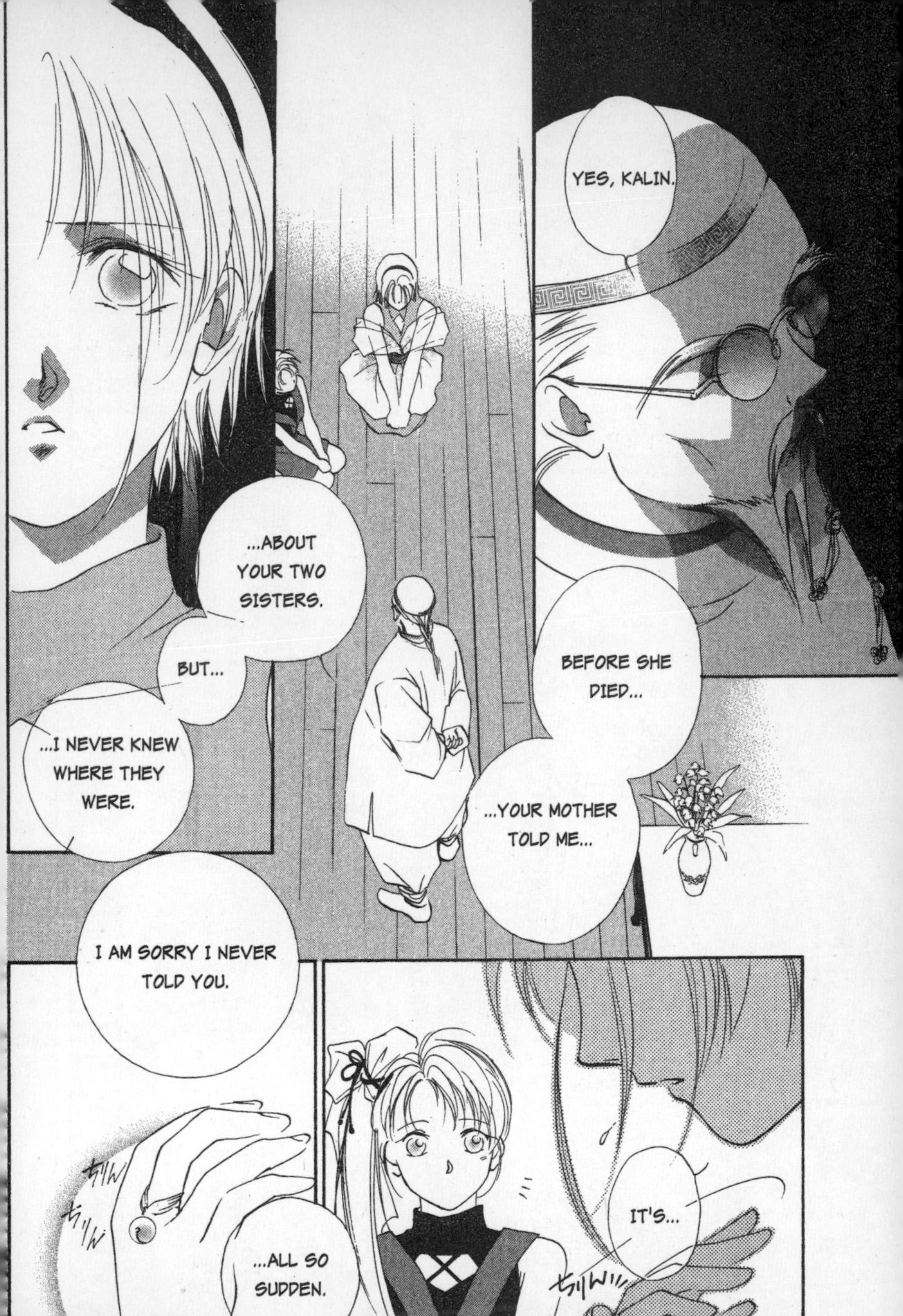
YES, KALIN.
BEFORE SHE DIED...
...YOUR MOTHER TOLD ME...
...ABOUT YOUR TWO SISTERS.
BUT...
...I NEVER KNEW WHERE THEY WERE.
I AM SORRY I NEVER TOLD YOU.
IT'S...
...ALL SO SUDDEN.

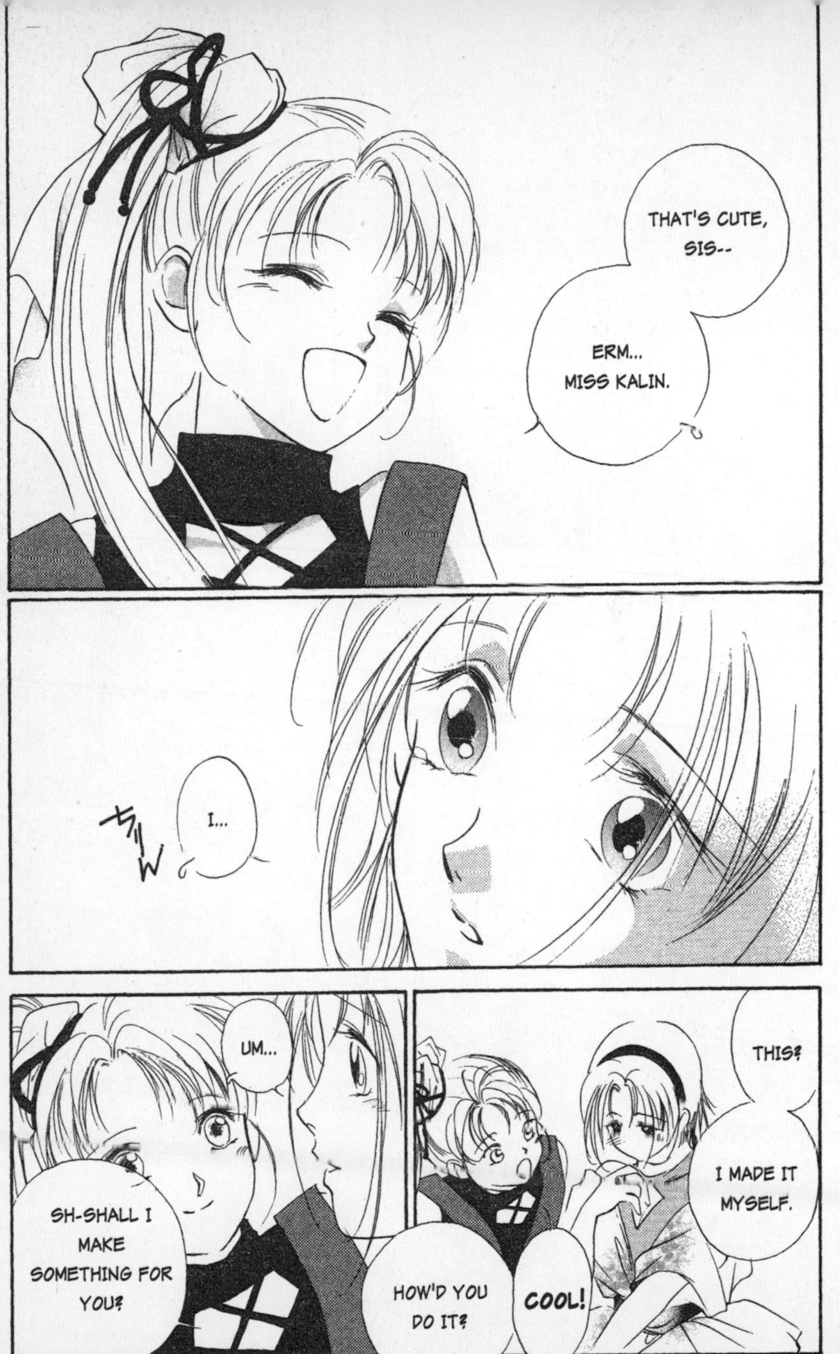
THAT'S CUTE, SIS--
ERM... MISS KALIN.
I...
THIS?
I MADE IT MYSELF.
COOL!
HOW'D YOU DO IT?
UM...
SH-SHALL I MAKE SOMETHING FOR YOU?

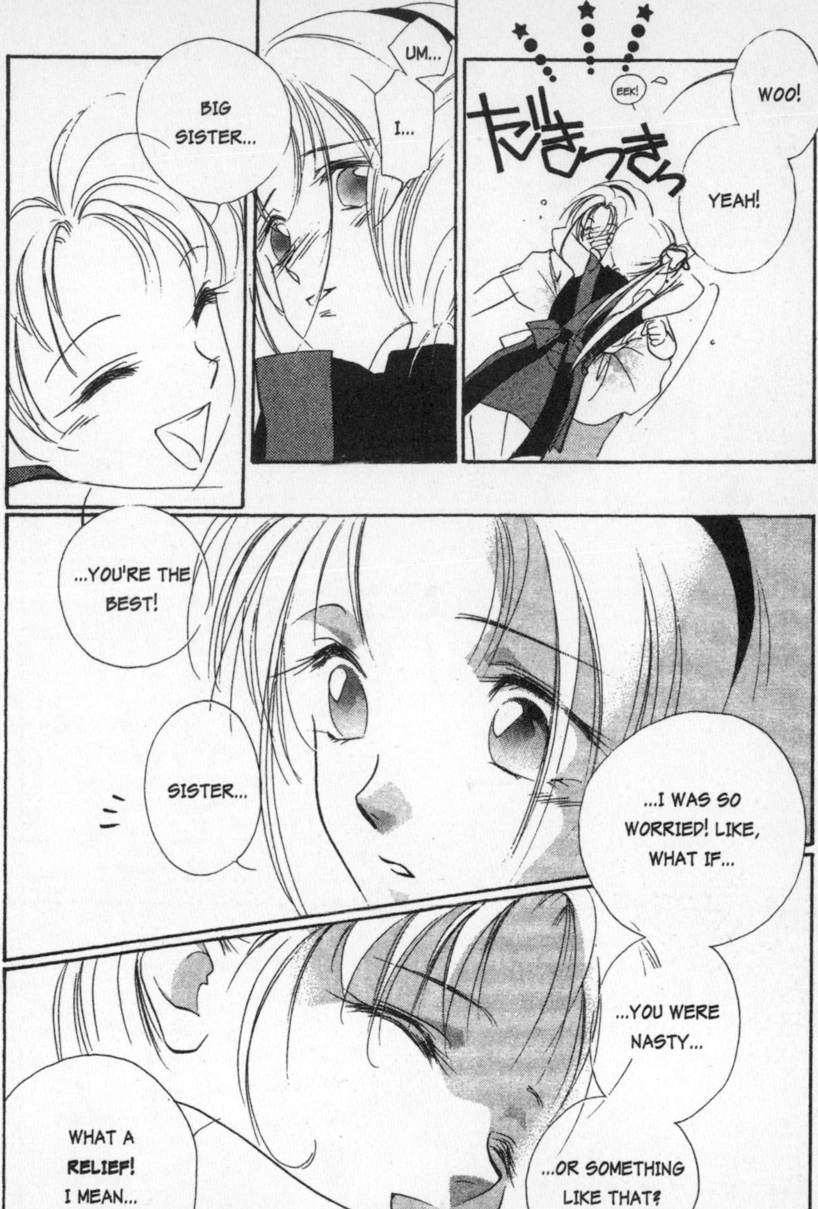
WOO!
YEAH!
EEK!
だきっきっ
UM...
I...
BIG SISTER...
...YOU'RE THE BEST!
SISTER...
...I WAS SO WORRIED! LIKE, WHAT IF...
...YOU WERE NASTY...
...OR SOMETHING LIKE THAT?
WHAT A **RELIEF!** I MEAN...

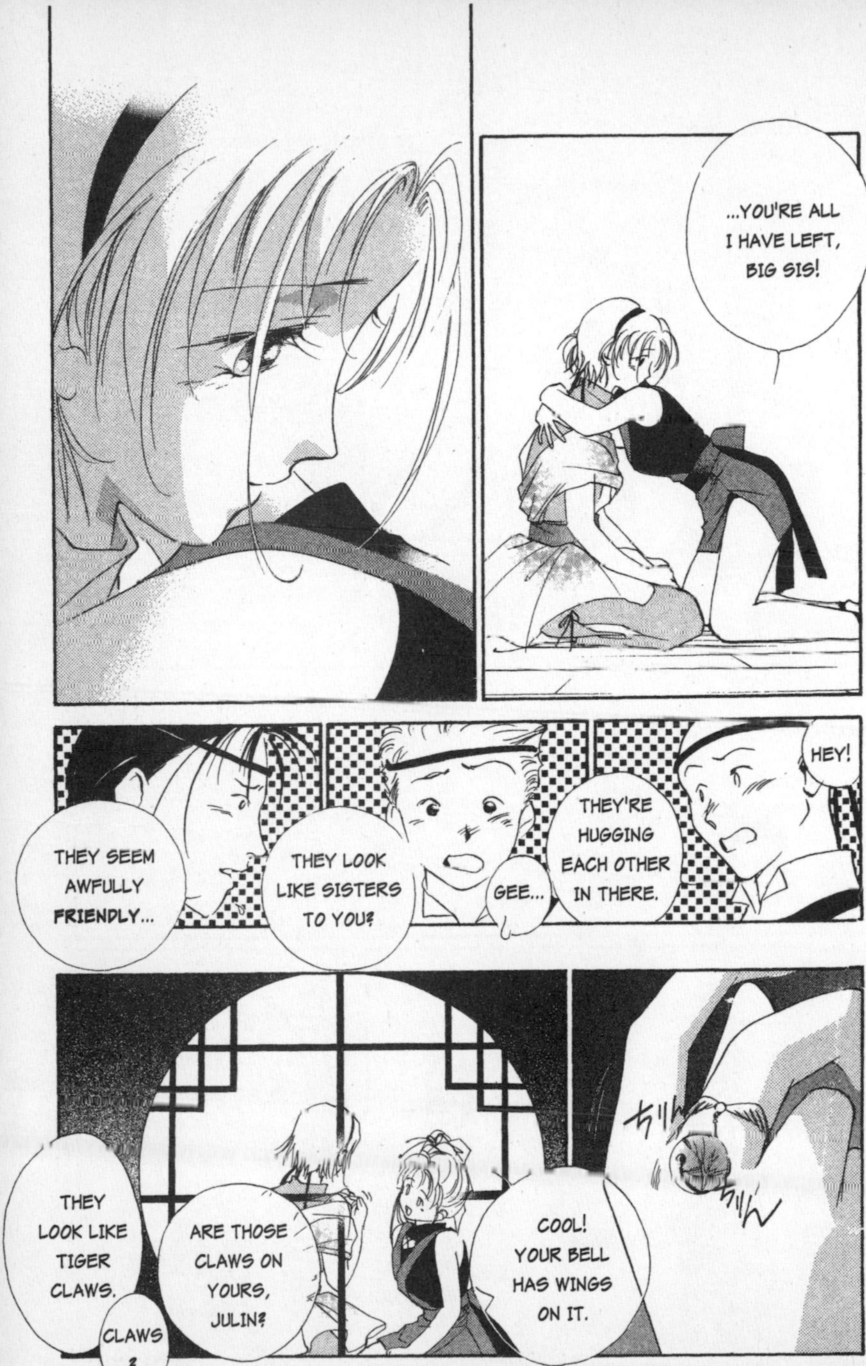
...YOU'RE ALL I HAVE LEFT, BIG SIS!
HEY!
THEY'RE HUGGING EACH OTHER IN THERE.
GEE...
THEY LOOK LIKE SISTERS TO YOU?
THEY SEEM AWFULLY FRIENDLY...
ちりん
ちりん
COOL! YOUR BELL HAS WINGS ON IT.
ARE THOSE CLAWS ON YOURS, JULIN?
THEY LOOK LIKE TIGER CLAWS.
CLAWS?

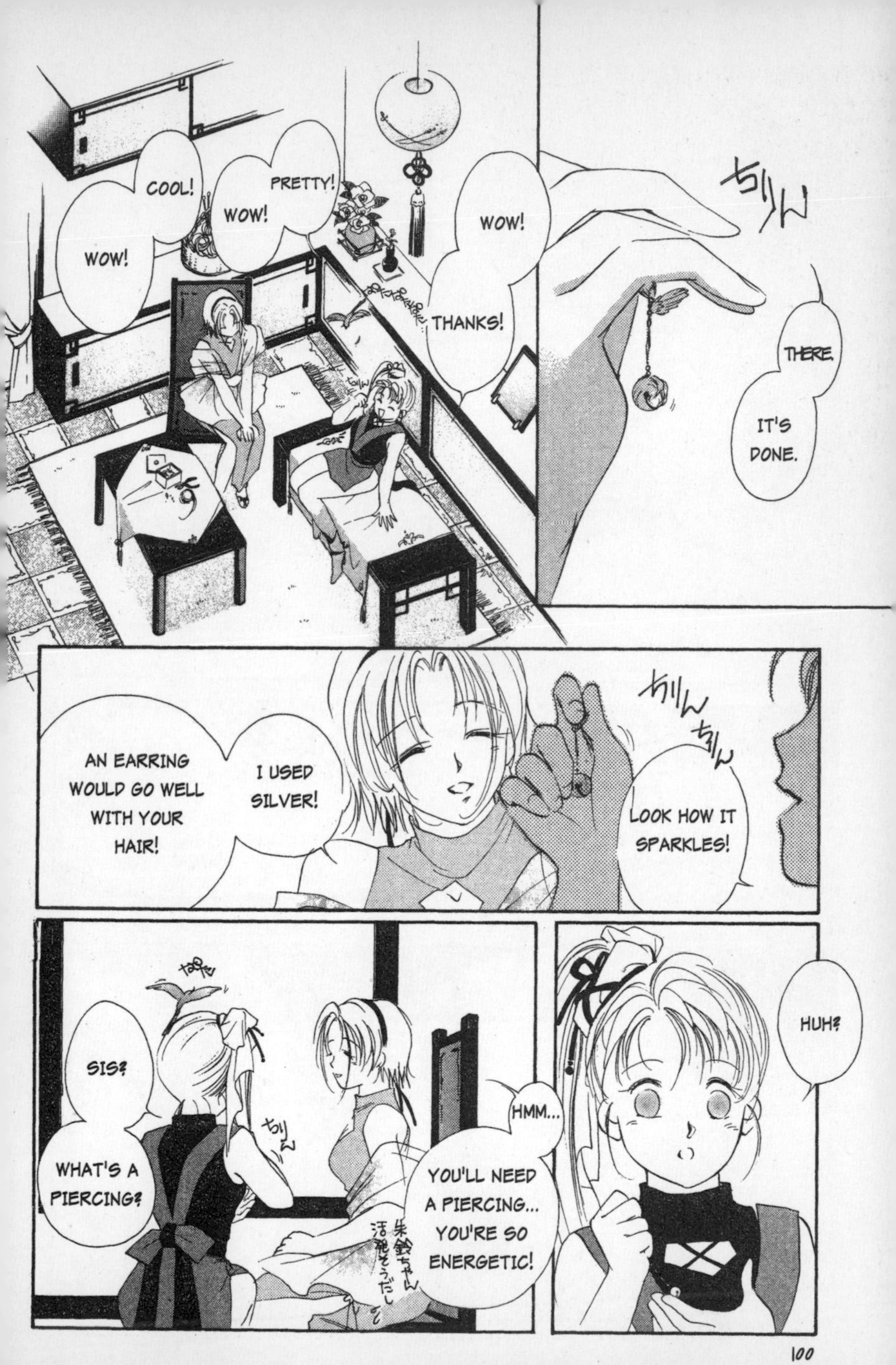
ちりん
THERE.
IT'S DONE.
WOW!
THANKS!
PRETTY!
WOW!
COOL!
WOW!
ちりん
ちりん ちりん
LOOK HOW IT SPARKLES!
I USED SILVER!
AN EARRING WOULD GO WELL WITH YOUR HAIR!
HUH?
HMM...
YOU'LL NEED A PIERCING... YOU'RE SO ENERGETIC!
朱鈴ちゃん活発そうだし
ちりん
SIS?
WHAT'S A PIERCING?

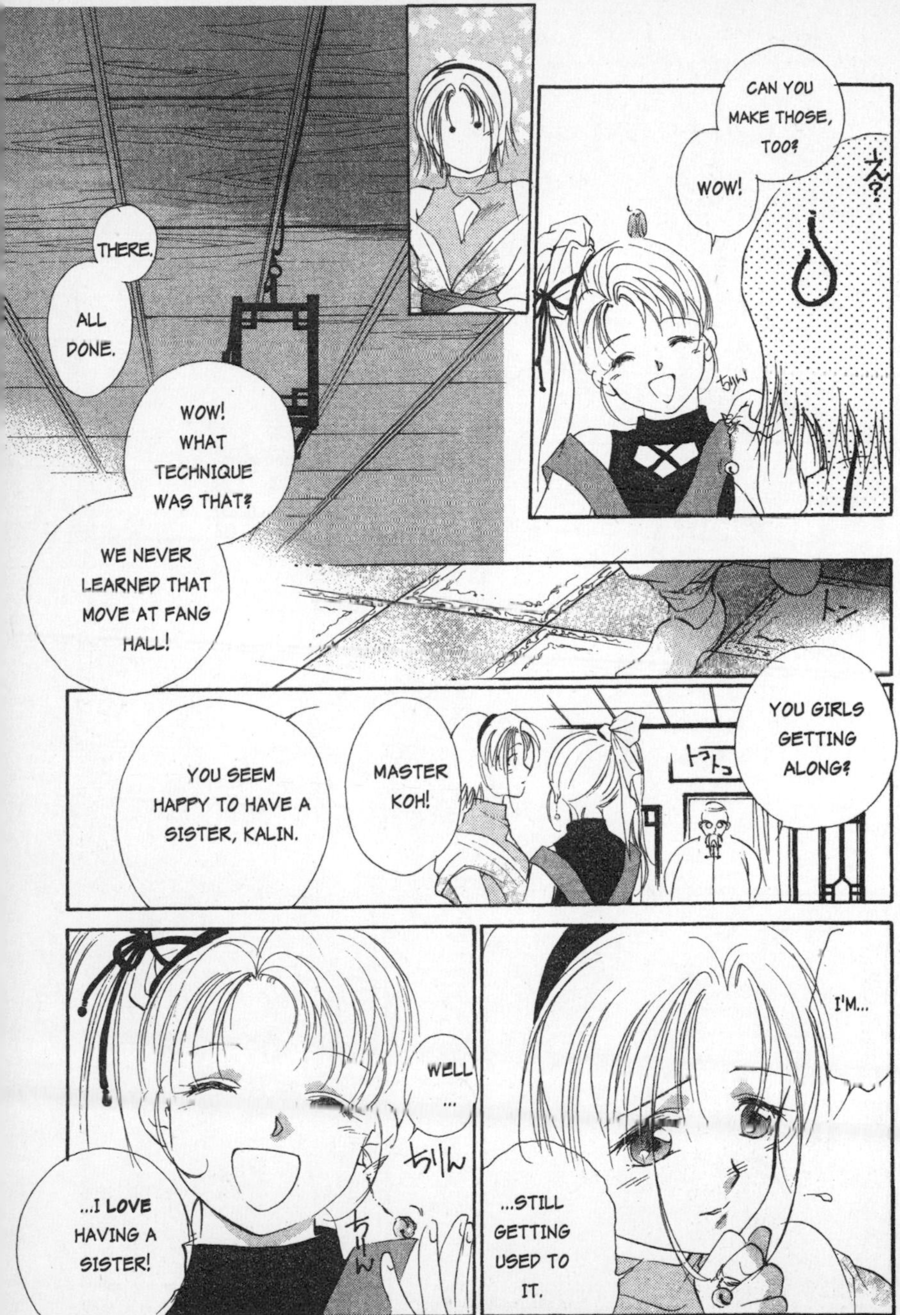
えっ?
CAN YOU MAKE THOSE, TOO?
WOW!
ちりん
THERE.
ALL DONE.
WOW! WHAT TECHNIQUE WAS THAT?
WE NEVER LEARNED THAT MOVE AT FANG HALL!
トン
YOU GIRLS GETTING ALONG?
トコトコ
MASTER KOH!
YOU SEEM HAPPY TO HAVE A SISTER, KALIN.
I'M...
...STILL GETTING USED TO IT.
WELL ...
ちりん
ちりん
...I LOVE HAVING A SISTER!

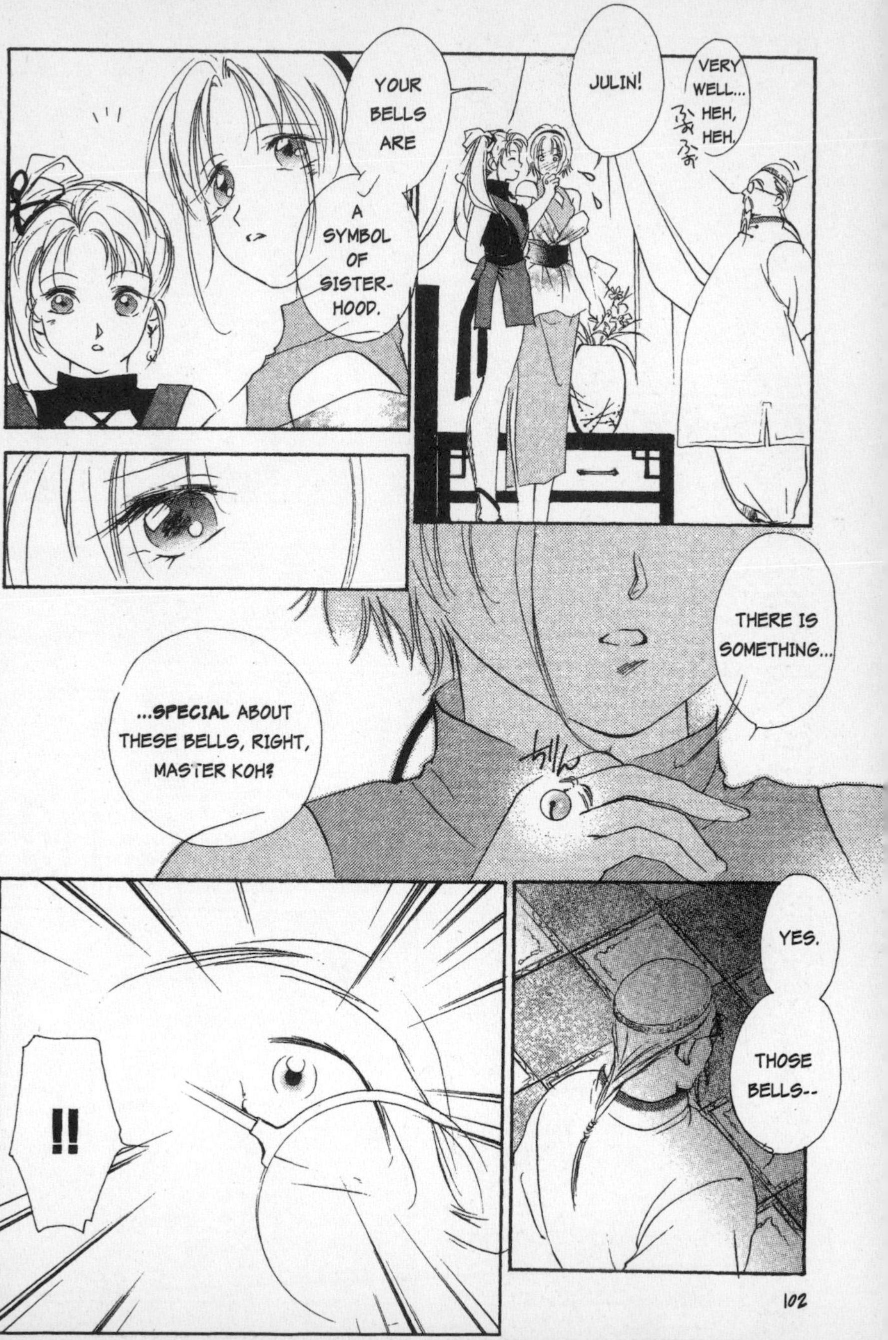
JULIN!
VERY WELL... HEH, HEH.
YOUR BELLS ARE
A SYMBOL OF SISTER-HOOD.
THERE IS SOMETHING...
...SPECIAL ABOUT THESE BELLS, RIGHT, MASTER KOH?
YES.
THOSE BELLS--
!!

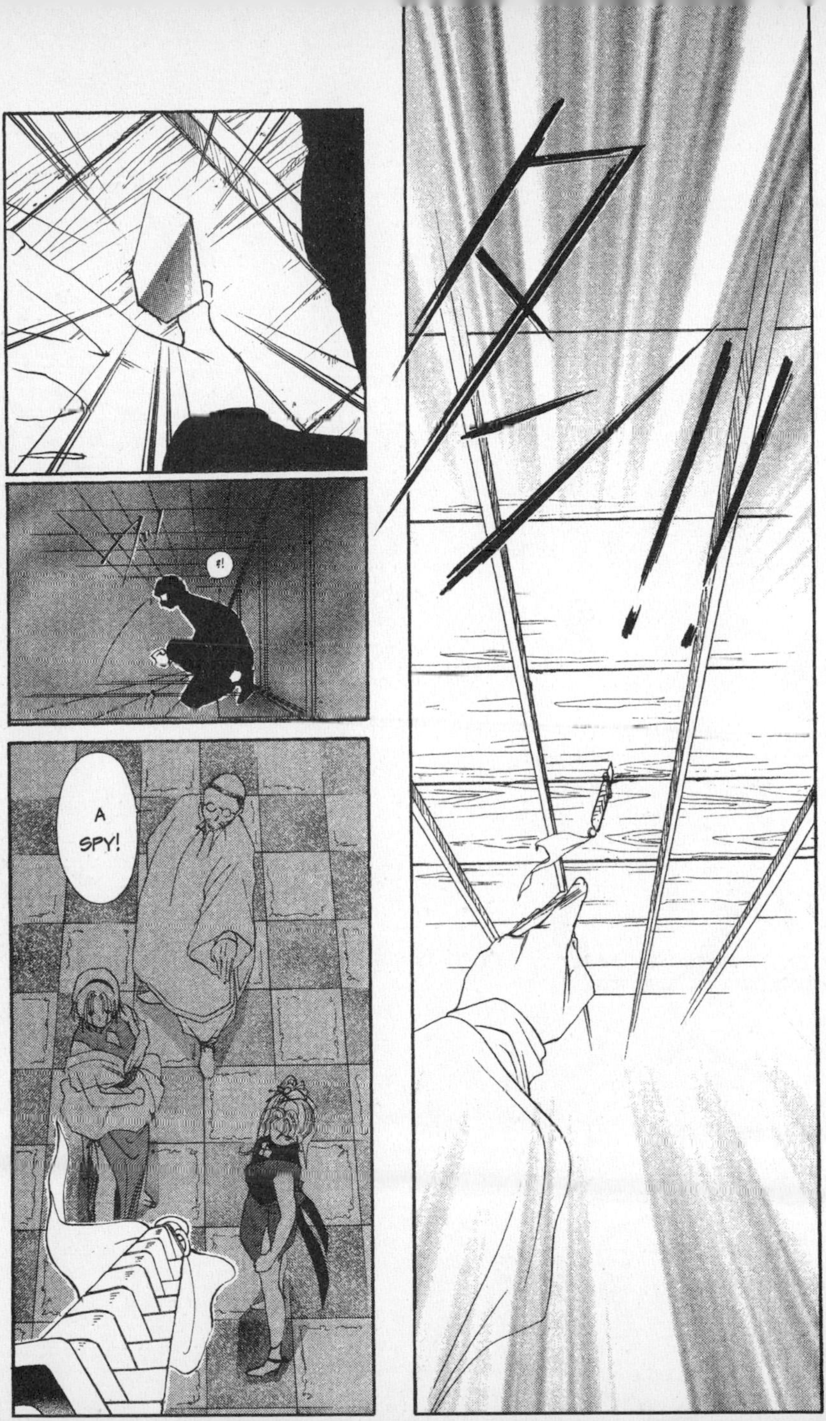
?!
A SPY!

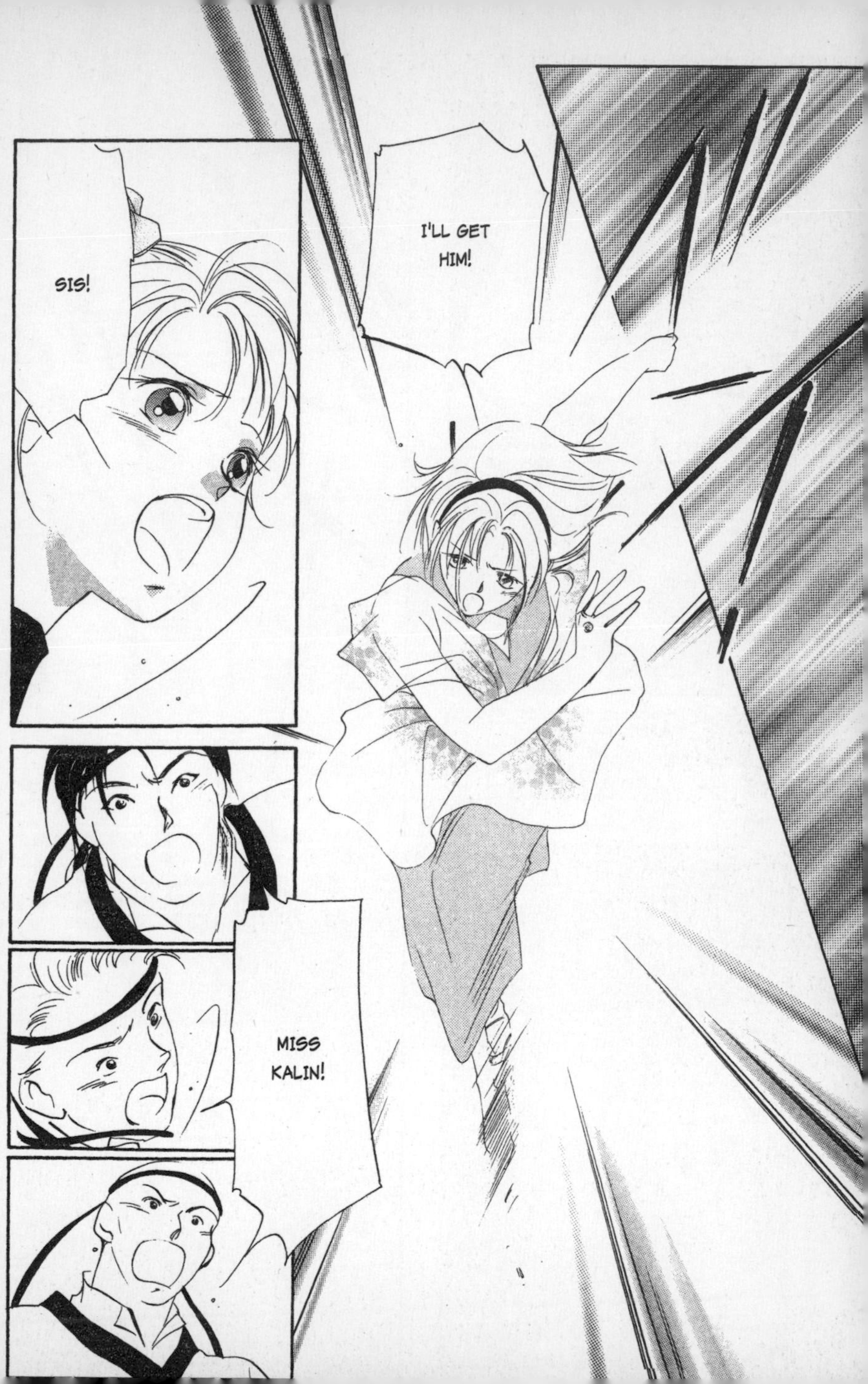
I'LL GET HIM!
SIS!
MISS KALIN!

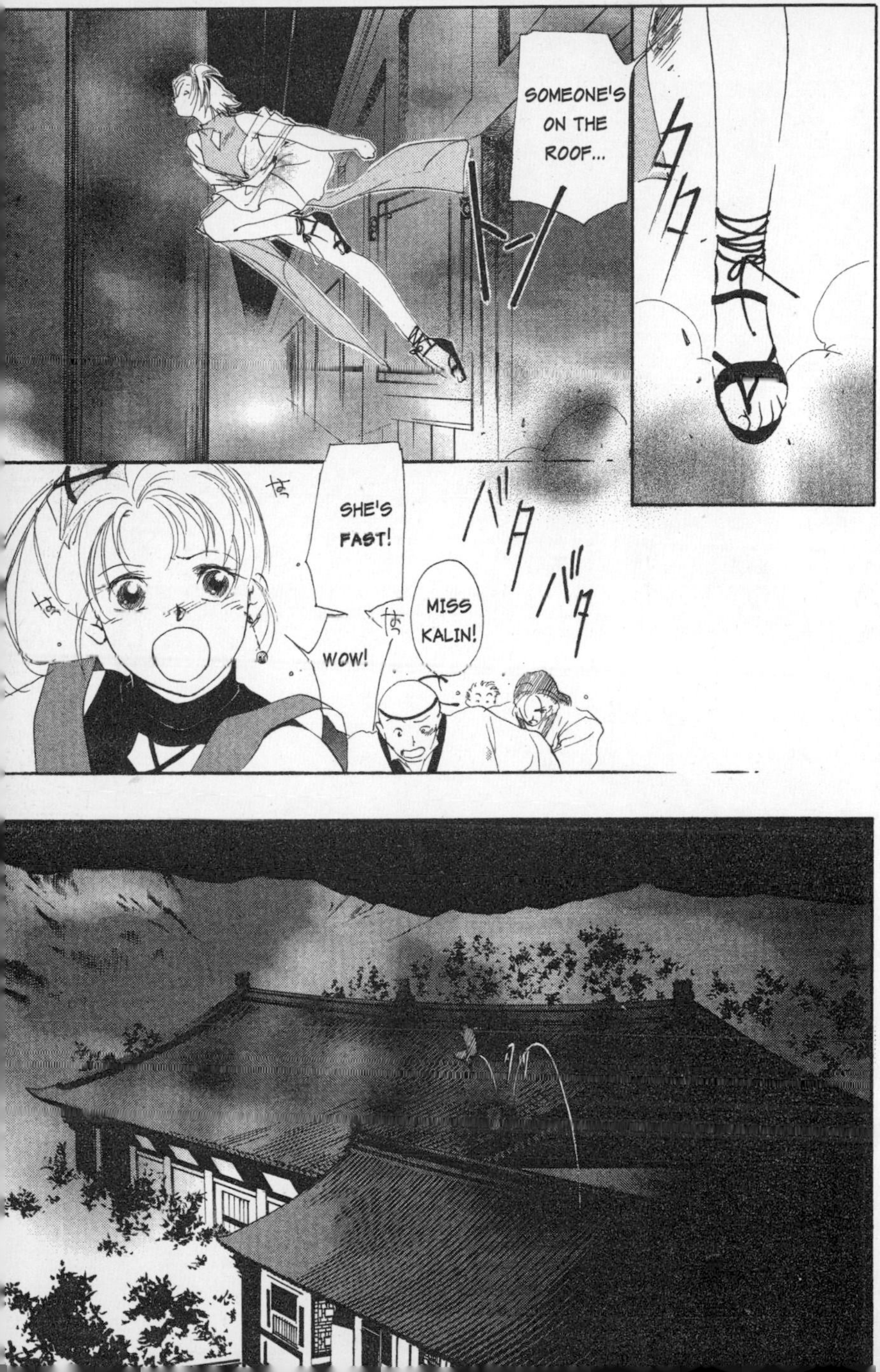
タタ
SOMEONE'S ON THE ROOF...
トン
バタ バタ
MISS KALIN!
SHE'S FAST!
WOW!

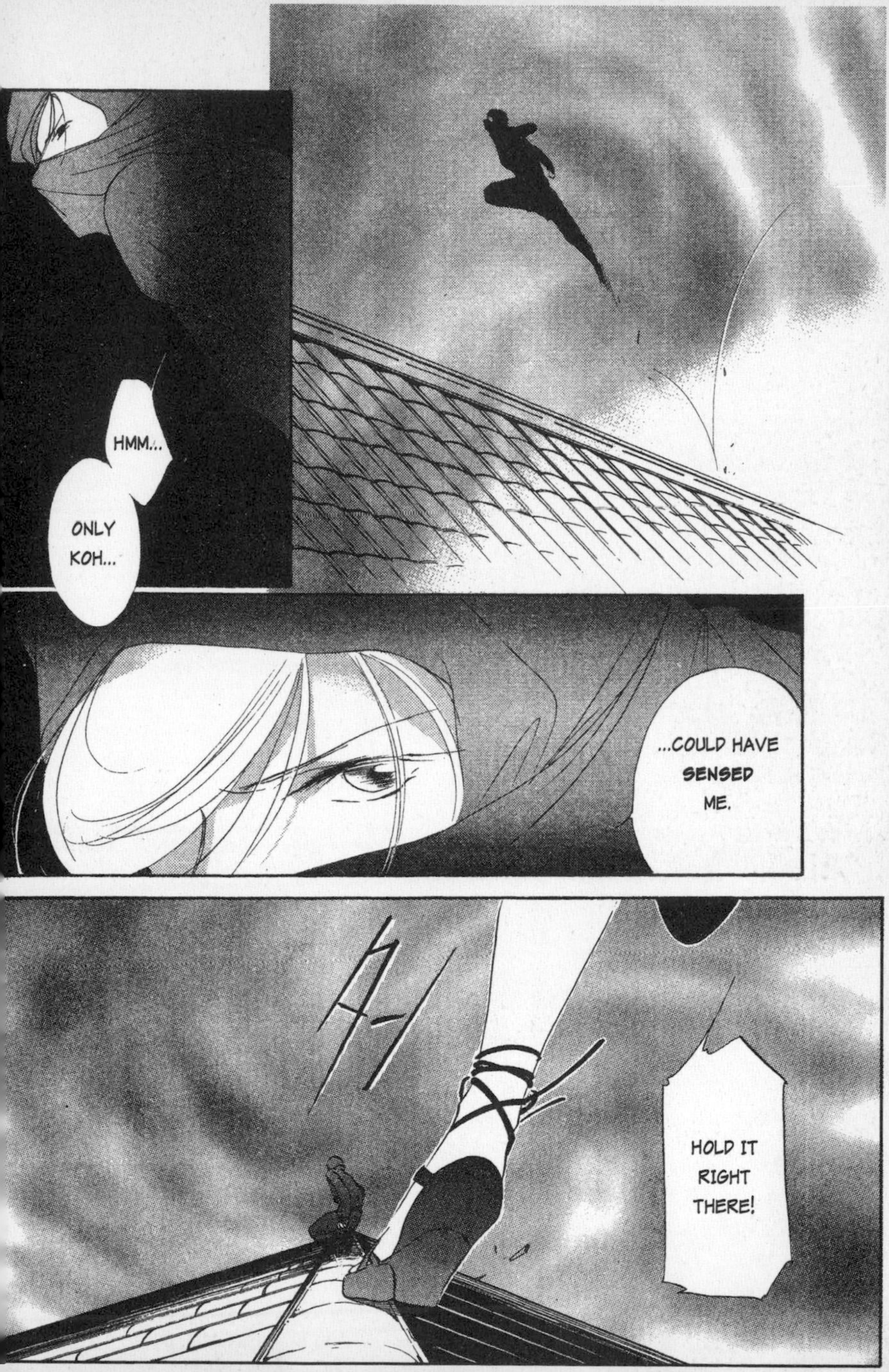
HMM...
ONLY KOH...
...COULD HAVE SENSED ME.
HOLD IT RIGHT THERE!

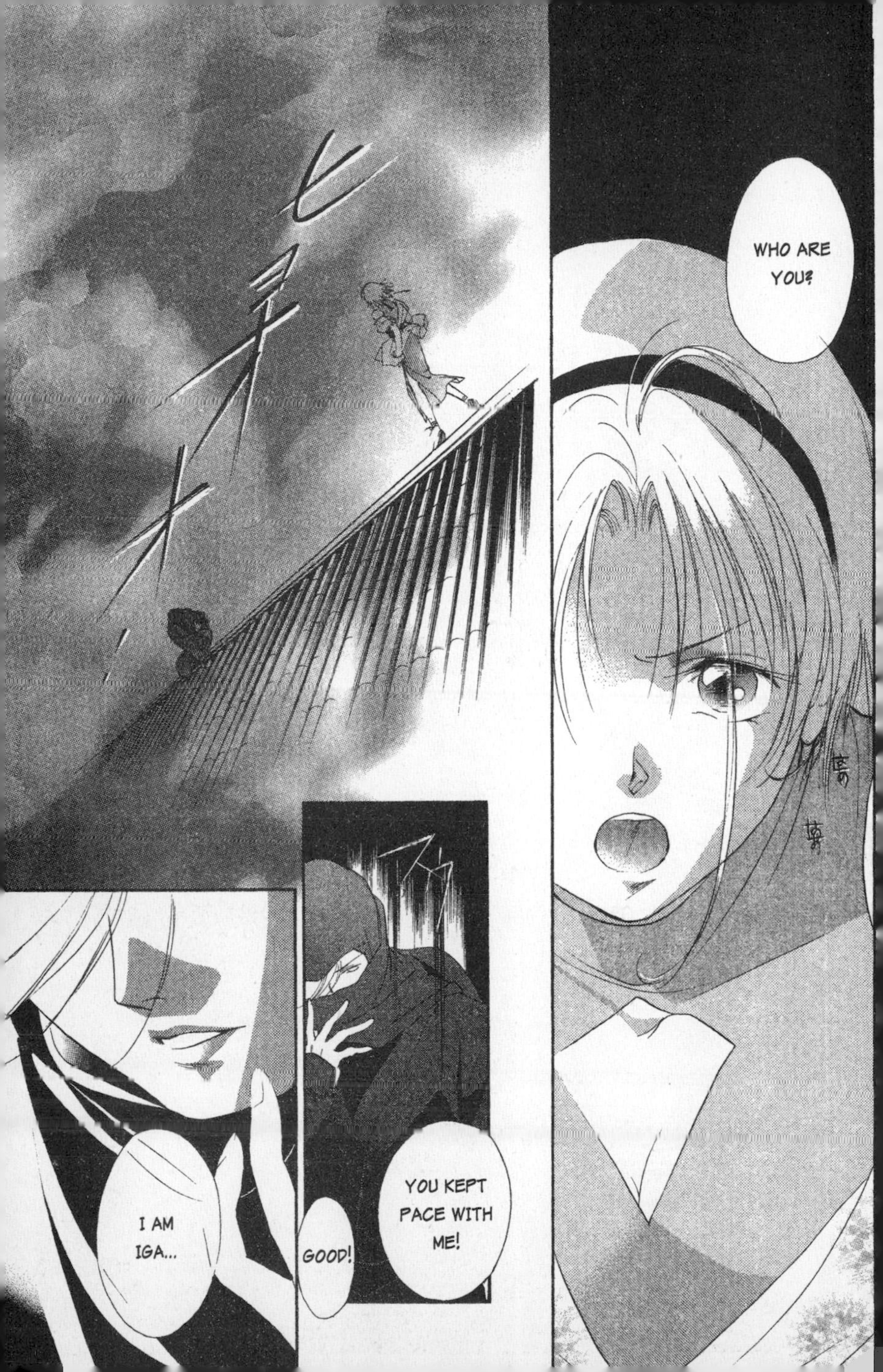
WHO ARE YOU?
YOU KEPT PACE WITH ME!
GOOD!
I AM IGA...

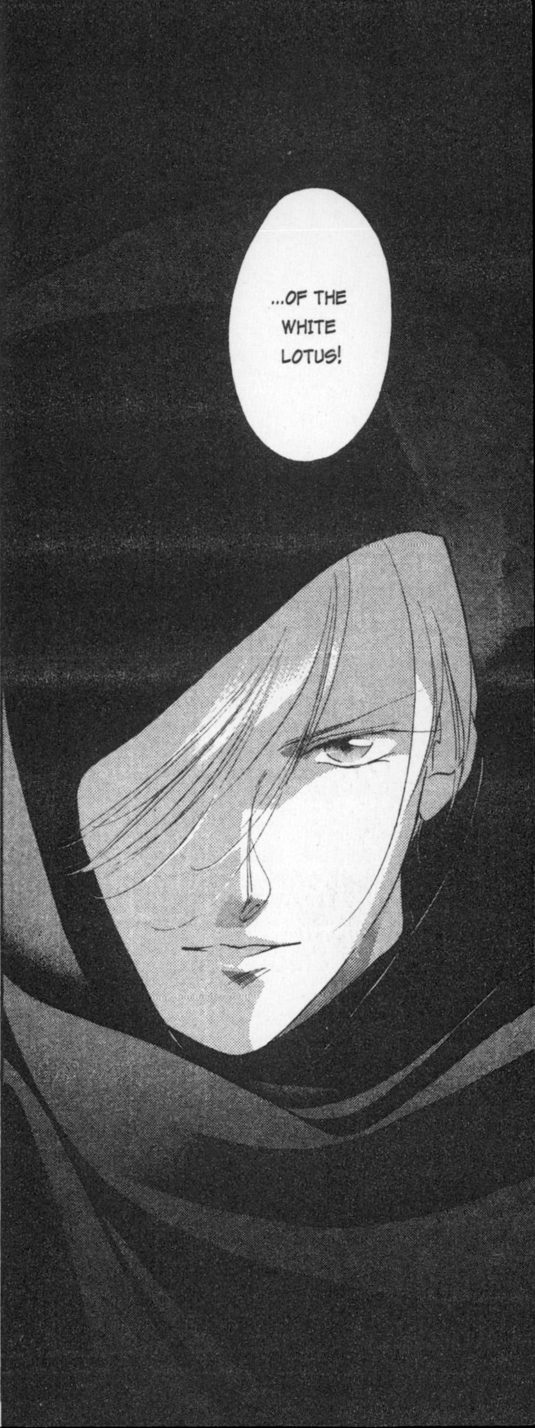
...OF THE WHITE LOTUS!
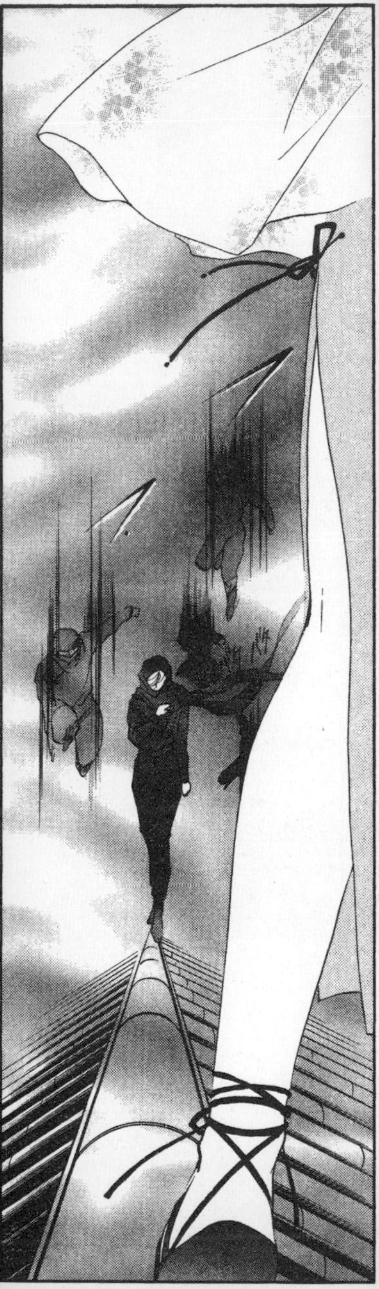

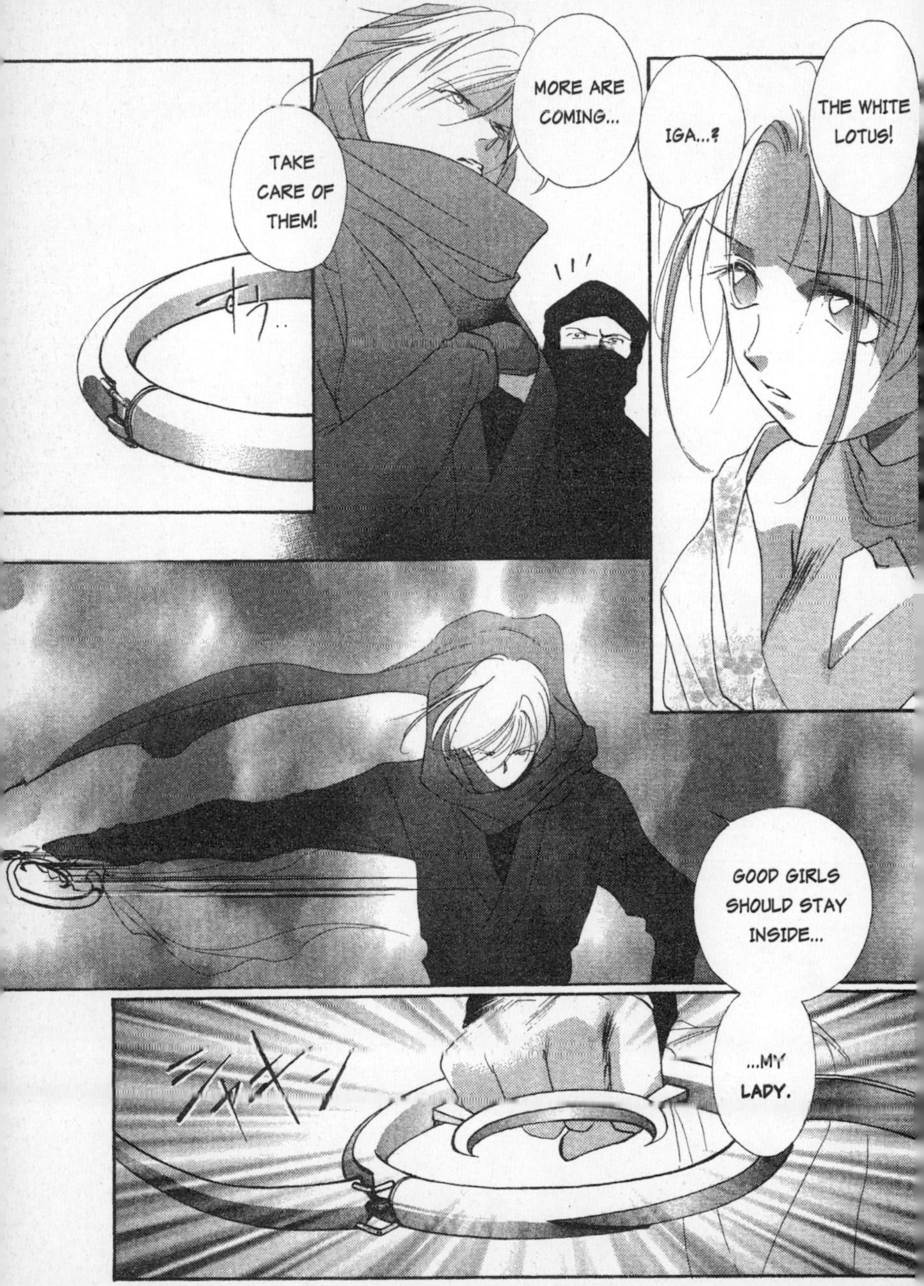
THE WHITE LOTUS!
IGA...?
MORE ARE COMING...
TAKE CARE OF THEM!
GOOD GIRLS SHOULD STAY INSIDE...
...MY LADY.

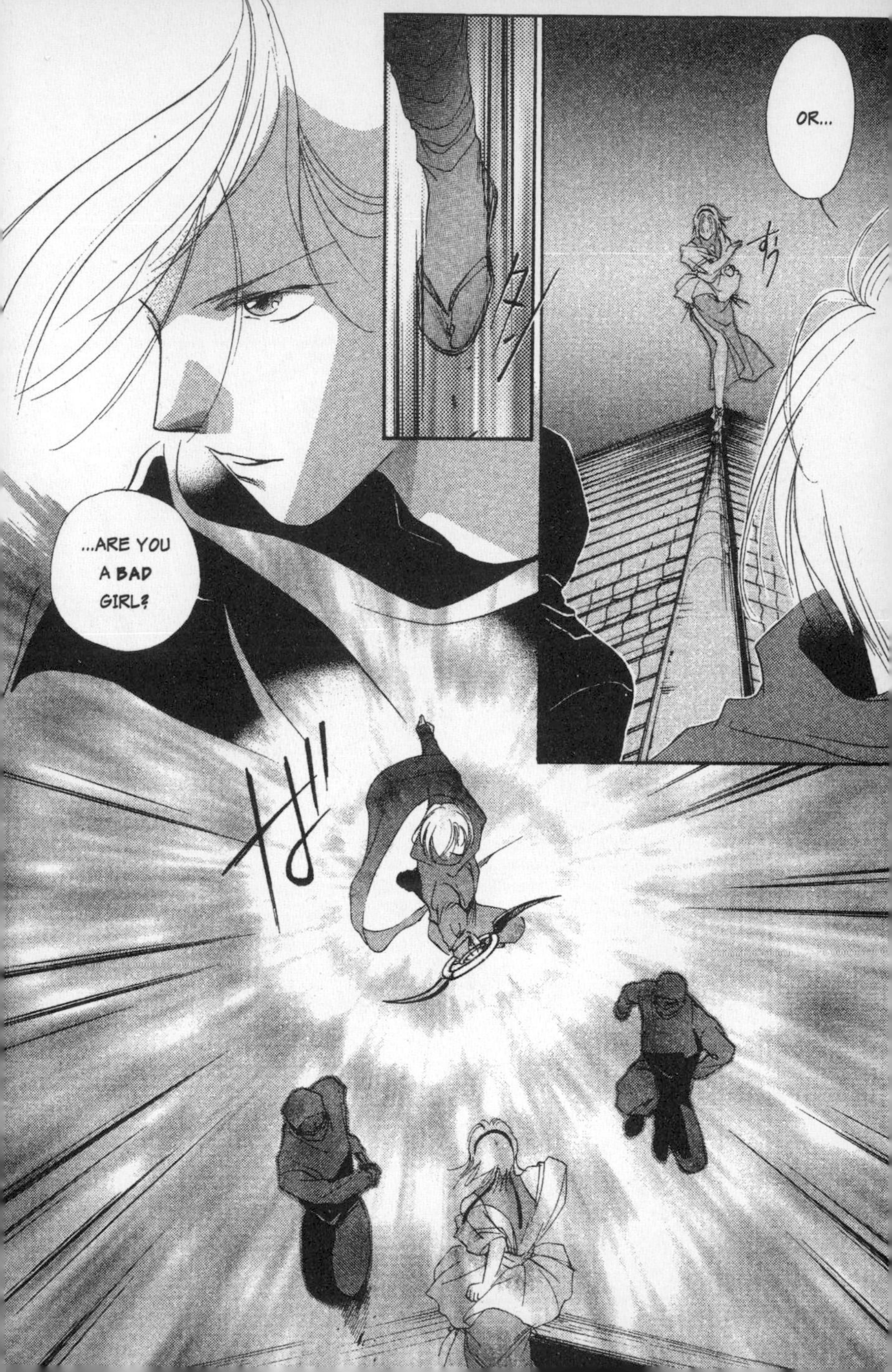
OR...
...ARE YOU A BAD GIRL?

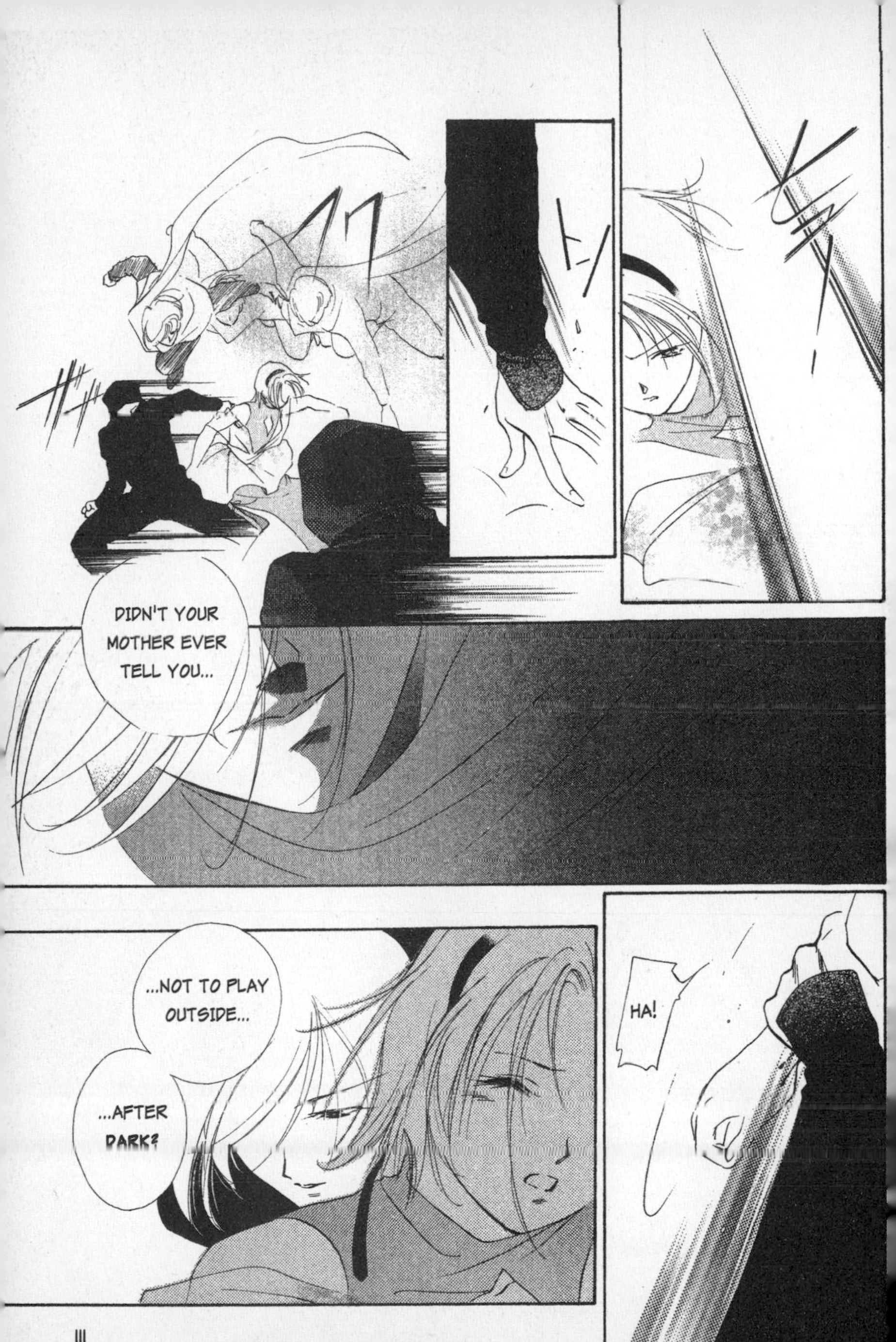
DIDN'T YOUR MOTHER EVER TELL YOU...
HA!
...NOT TO PLAY OUTSIDE...
...AFTER DARK?

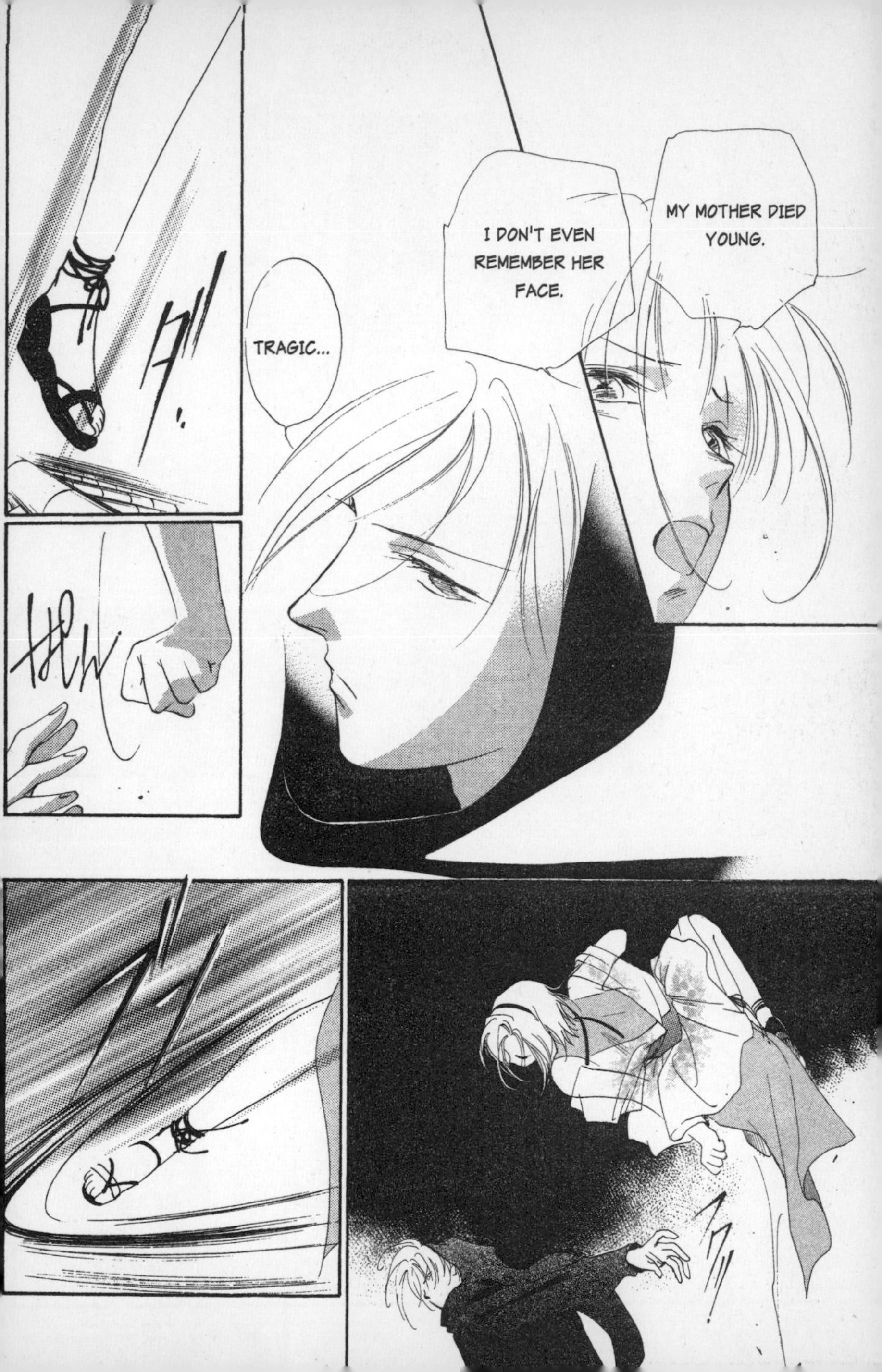
MY MOTHER DIED YOUNG.
I DON'T EVEN REMEMBER HER FACE.
TRAGIC...

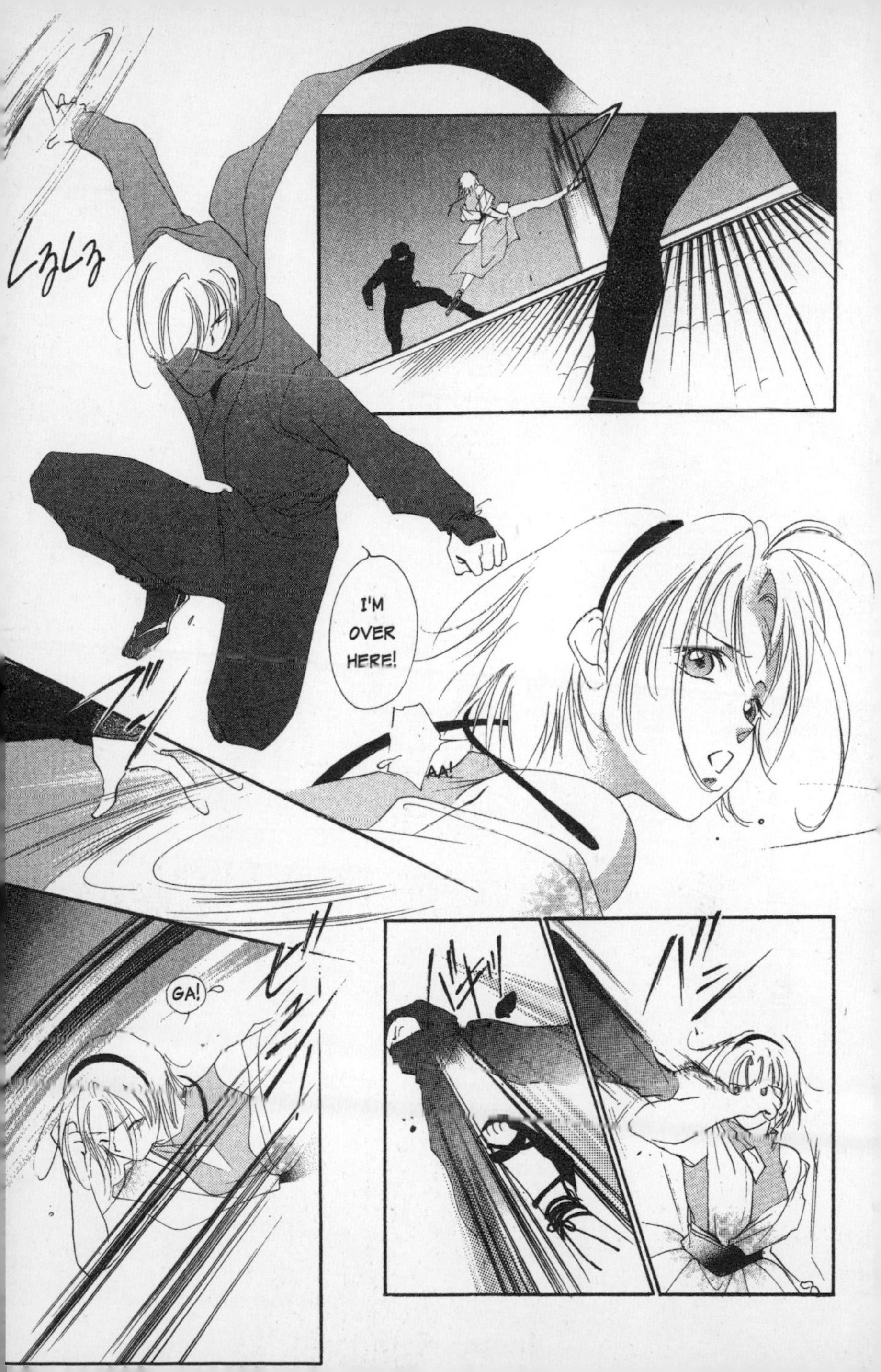
I'M OVER HERE!
AA!
GA!

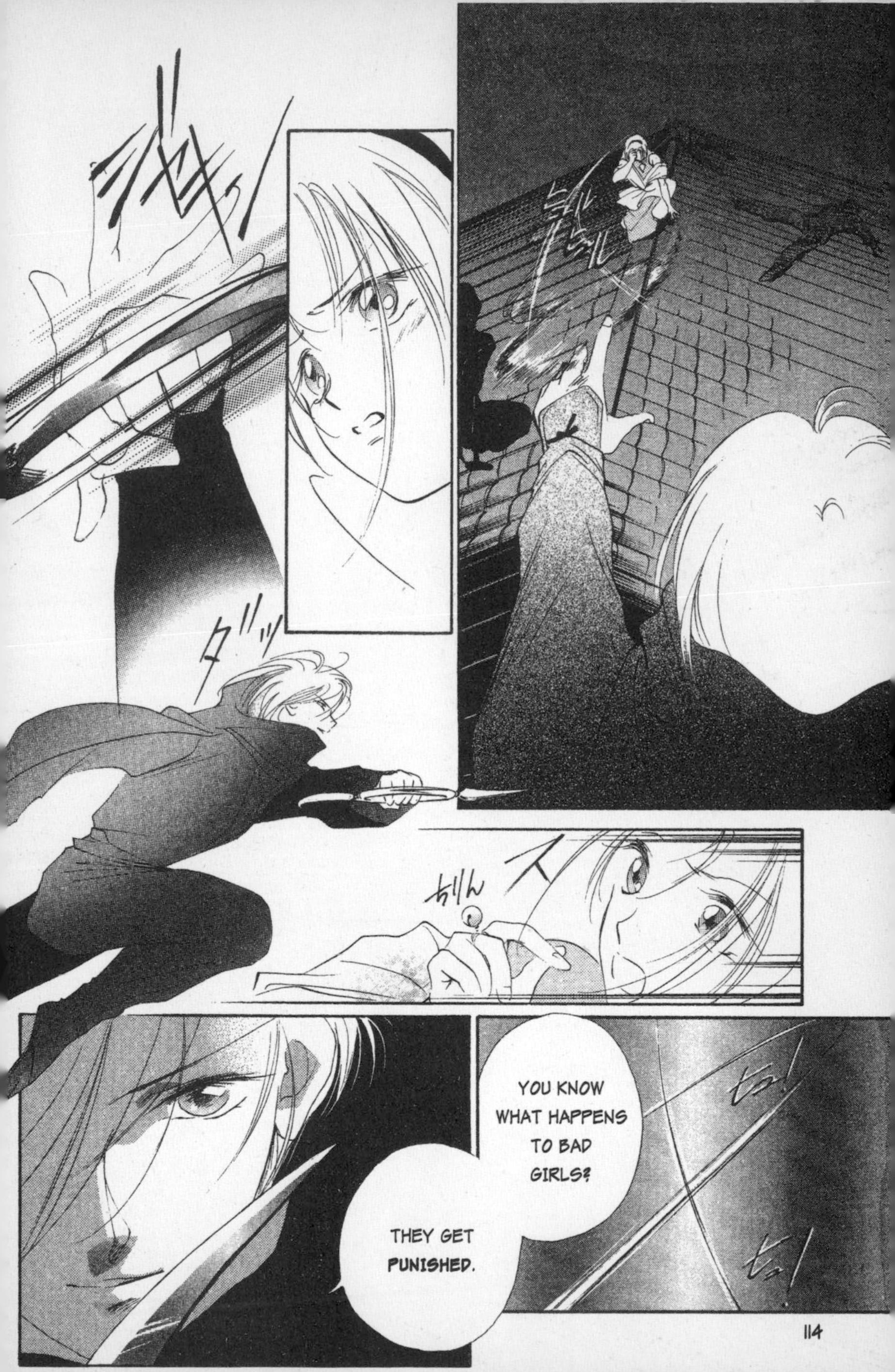
YOU KNOW WHAT HAPPENS TO BAD GIRLS?
THEY GET PUNISHED.

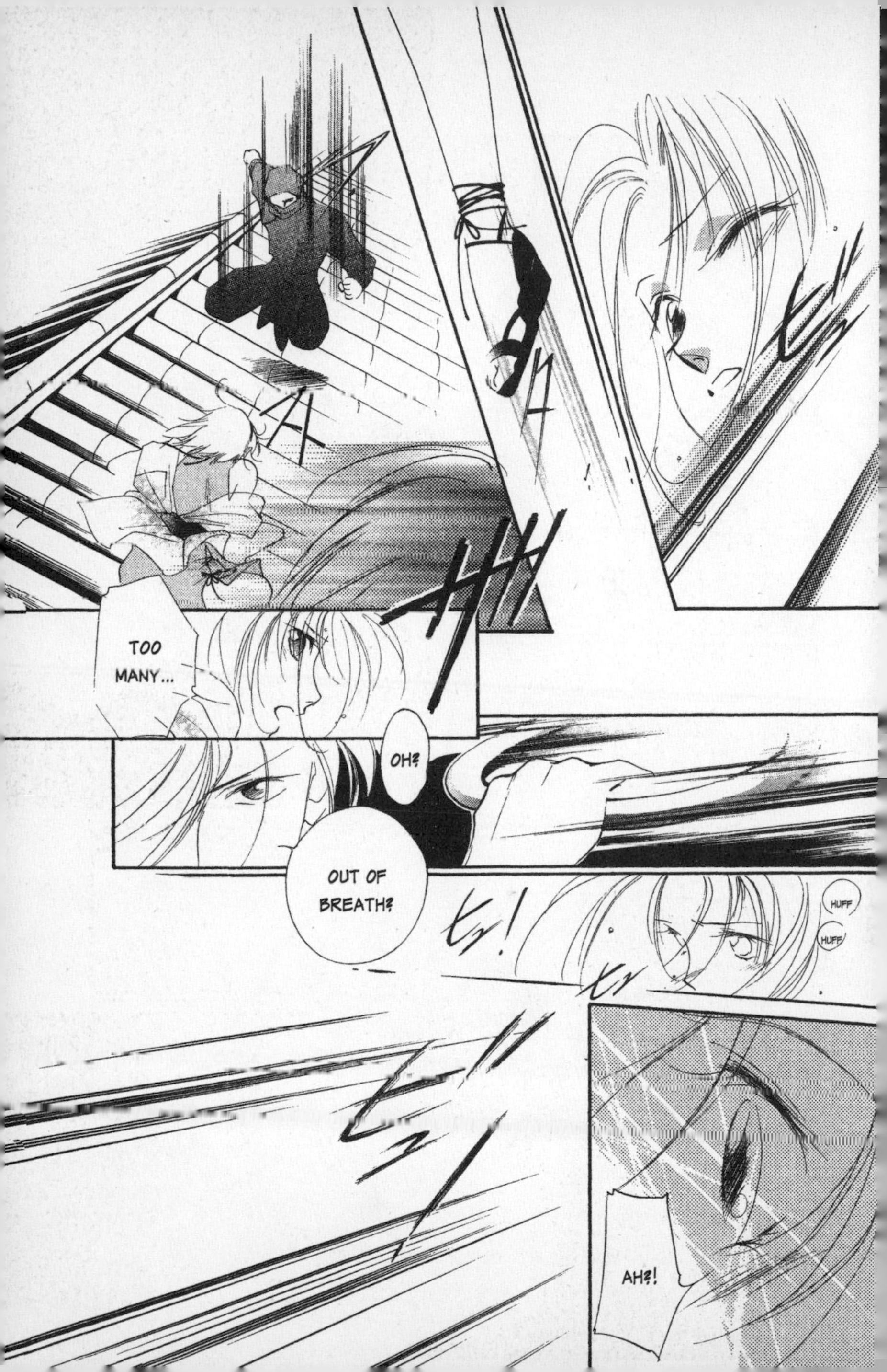

TOO MANY...
OH?
OUT OF BREATH?
HUFF
HUFF
AH?!

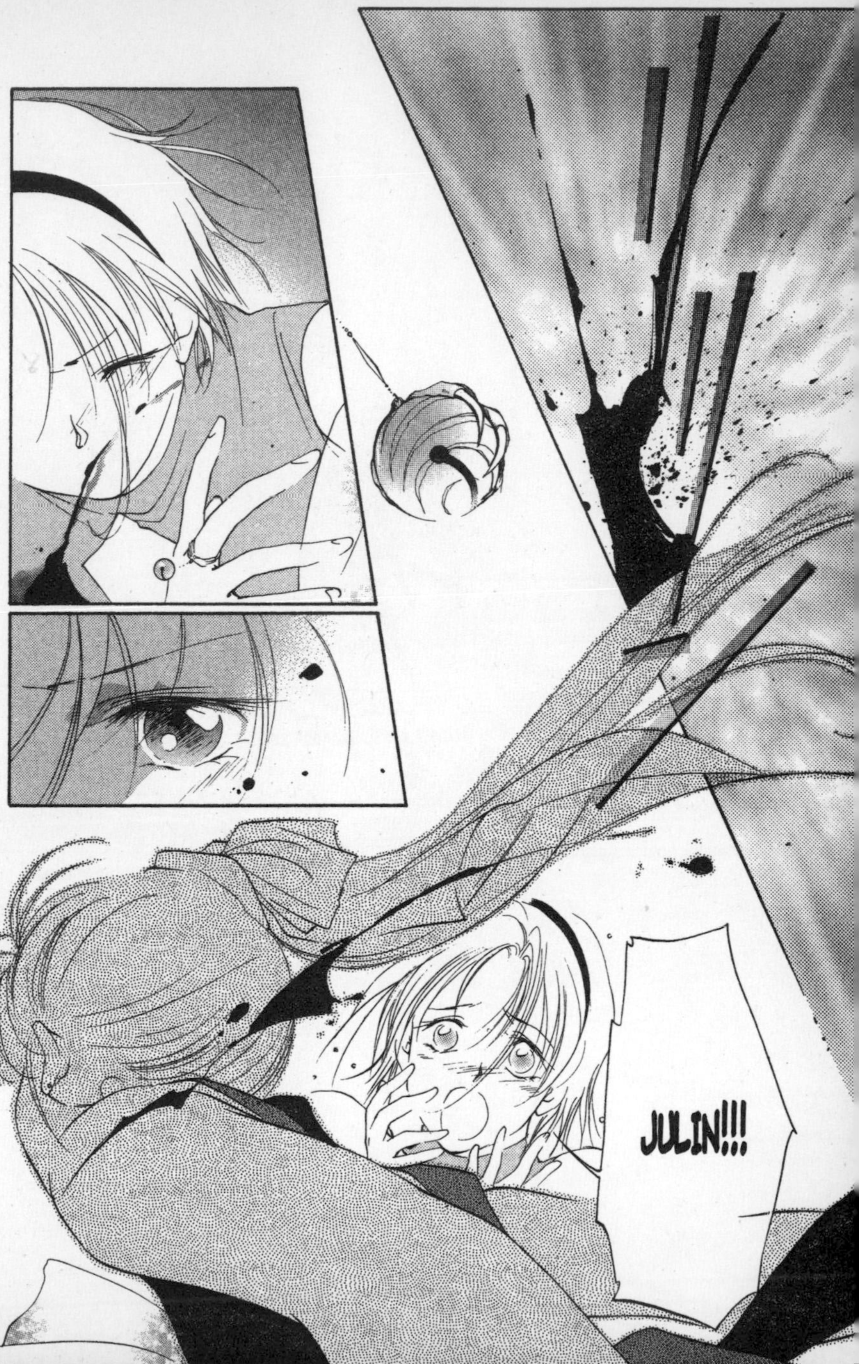
JULIN!!!

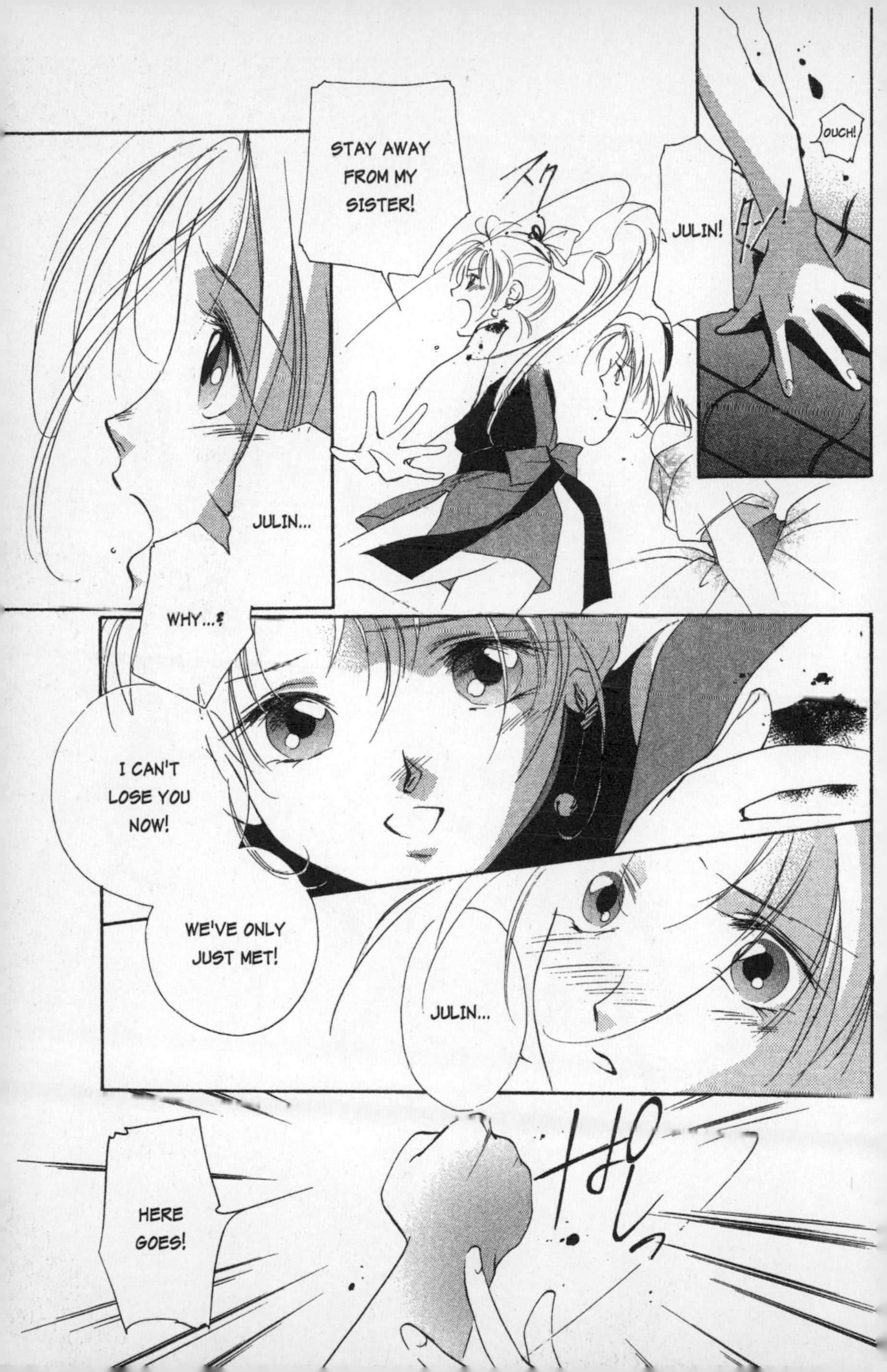
OUCH!
STAY AWAY FROM MY SISTER!
JULIN!
JULIN...
WHY...?
I CAN'T LOSE YOU NOW!
WE'VE ONLY JUST MET!
JULIN...
HERE GOES!

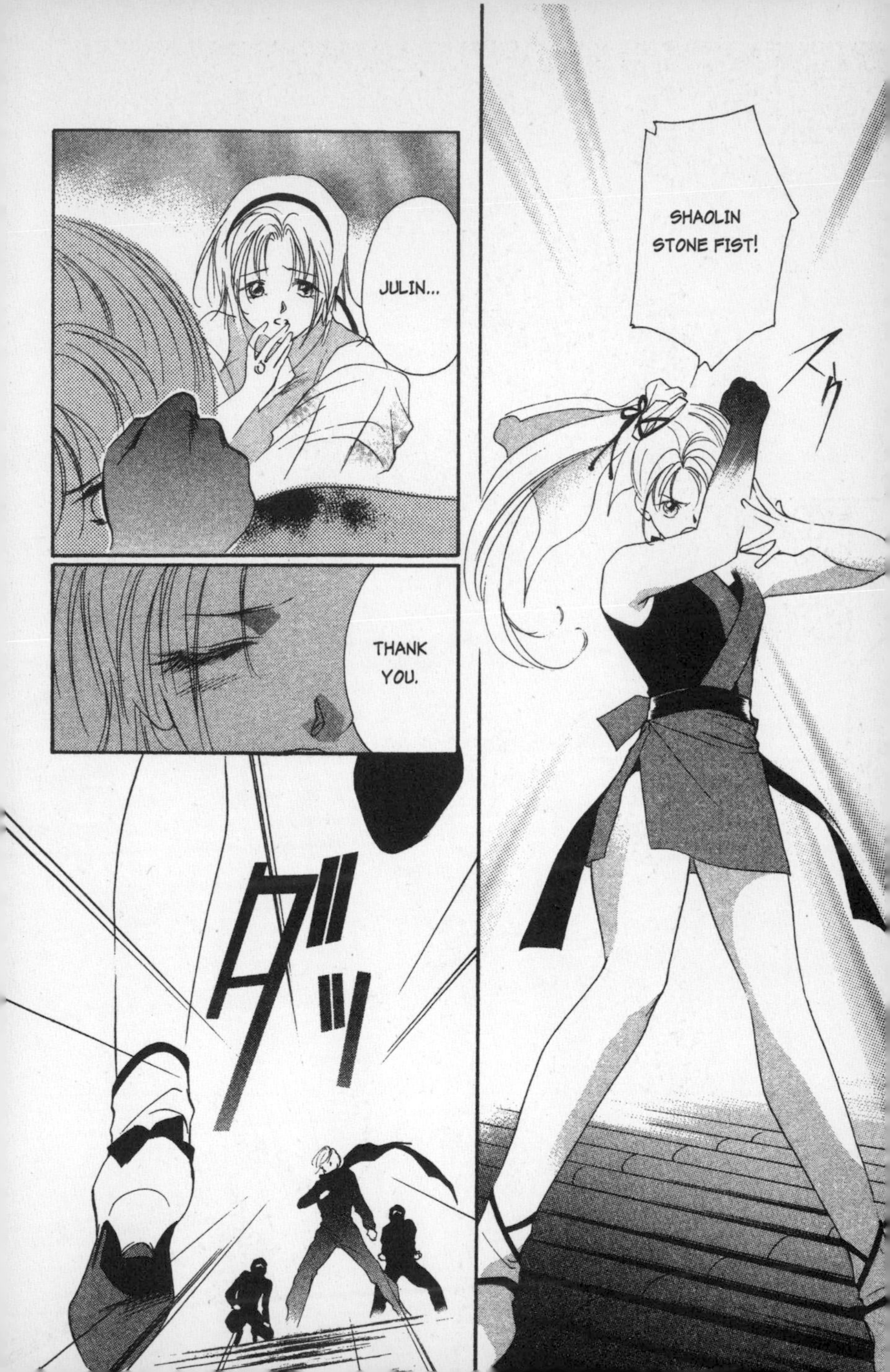
SHAOLIN STONE FIST!
JULIN...
THANK YOU.
ダッ

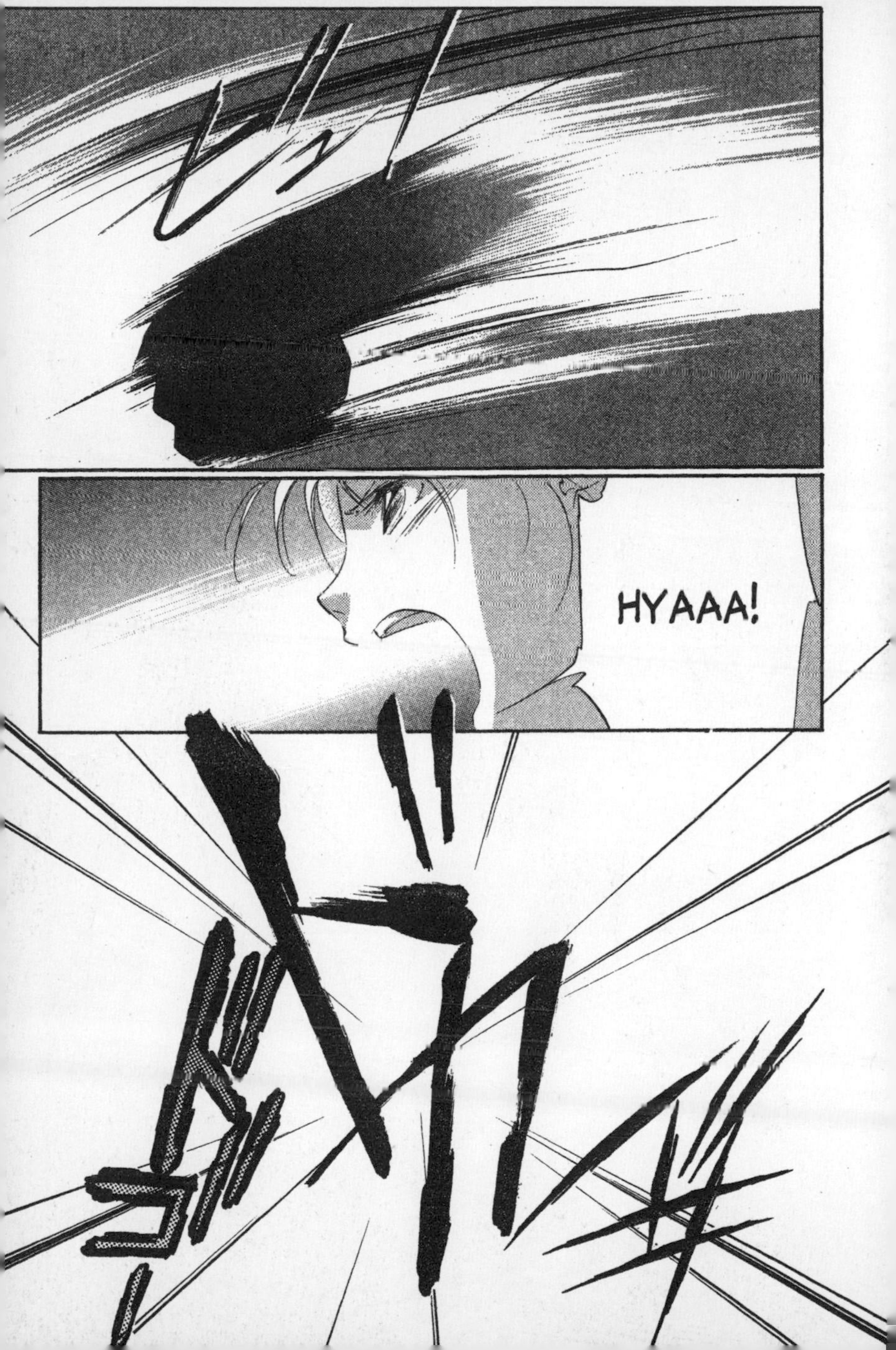
HYAAA!

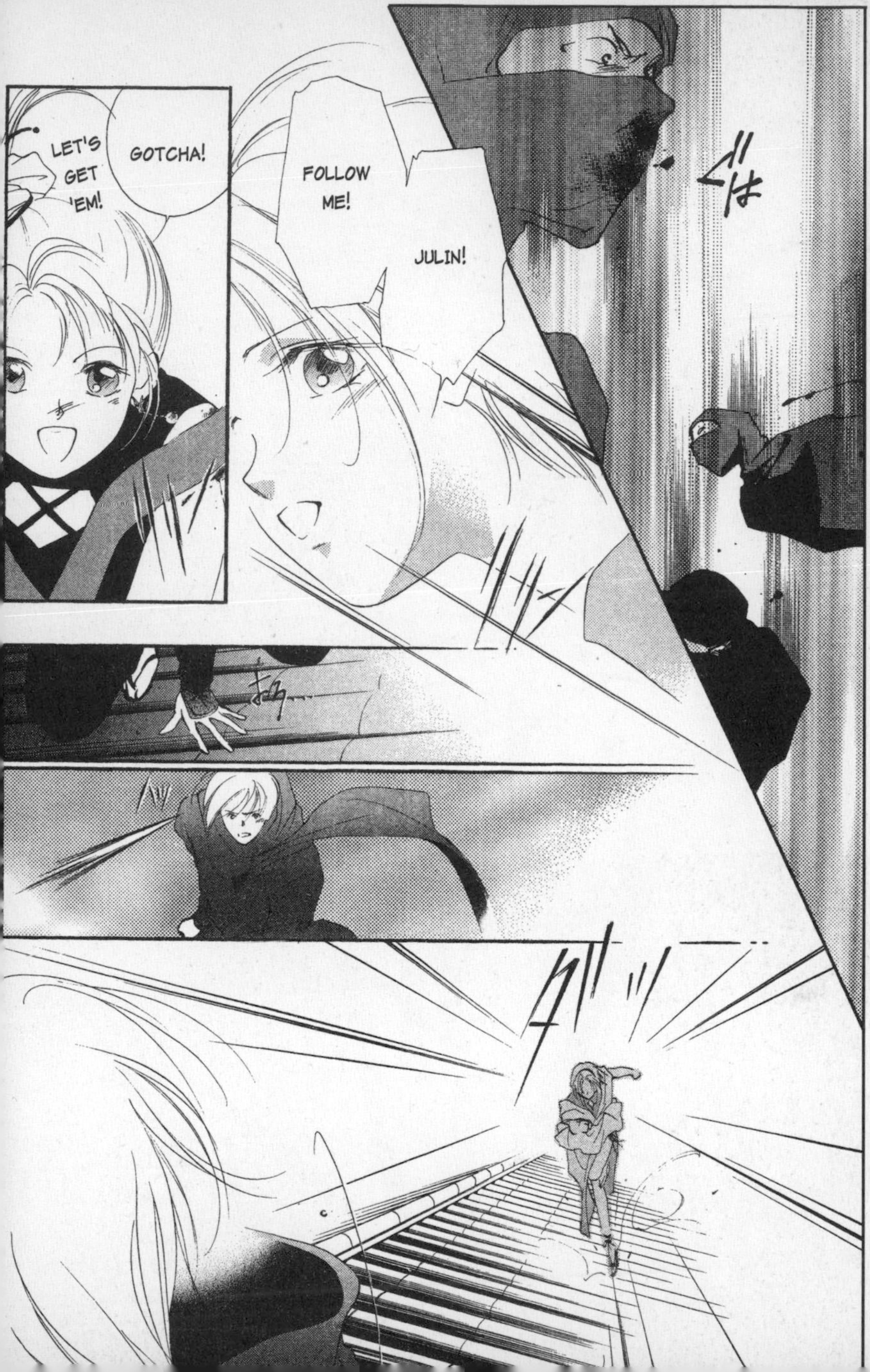
ぐは
FOLLOW ME!
JULIN!
GOTCHA!
LET'S GET 'EM!

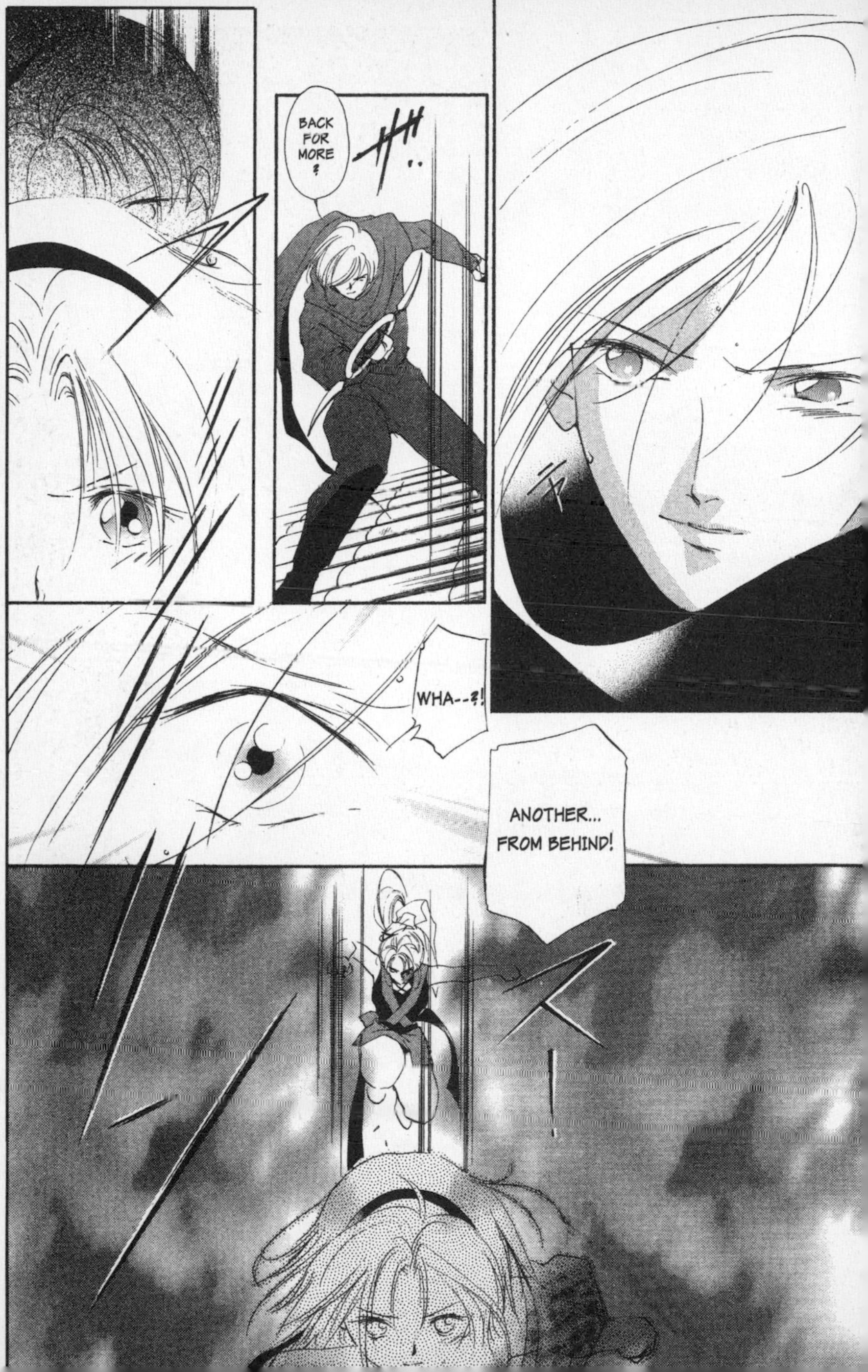
BACK FOR MORE?
WHA--?!
ANOTHER... FROM BEHIND!

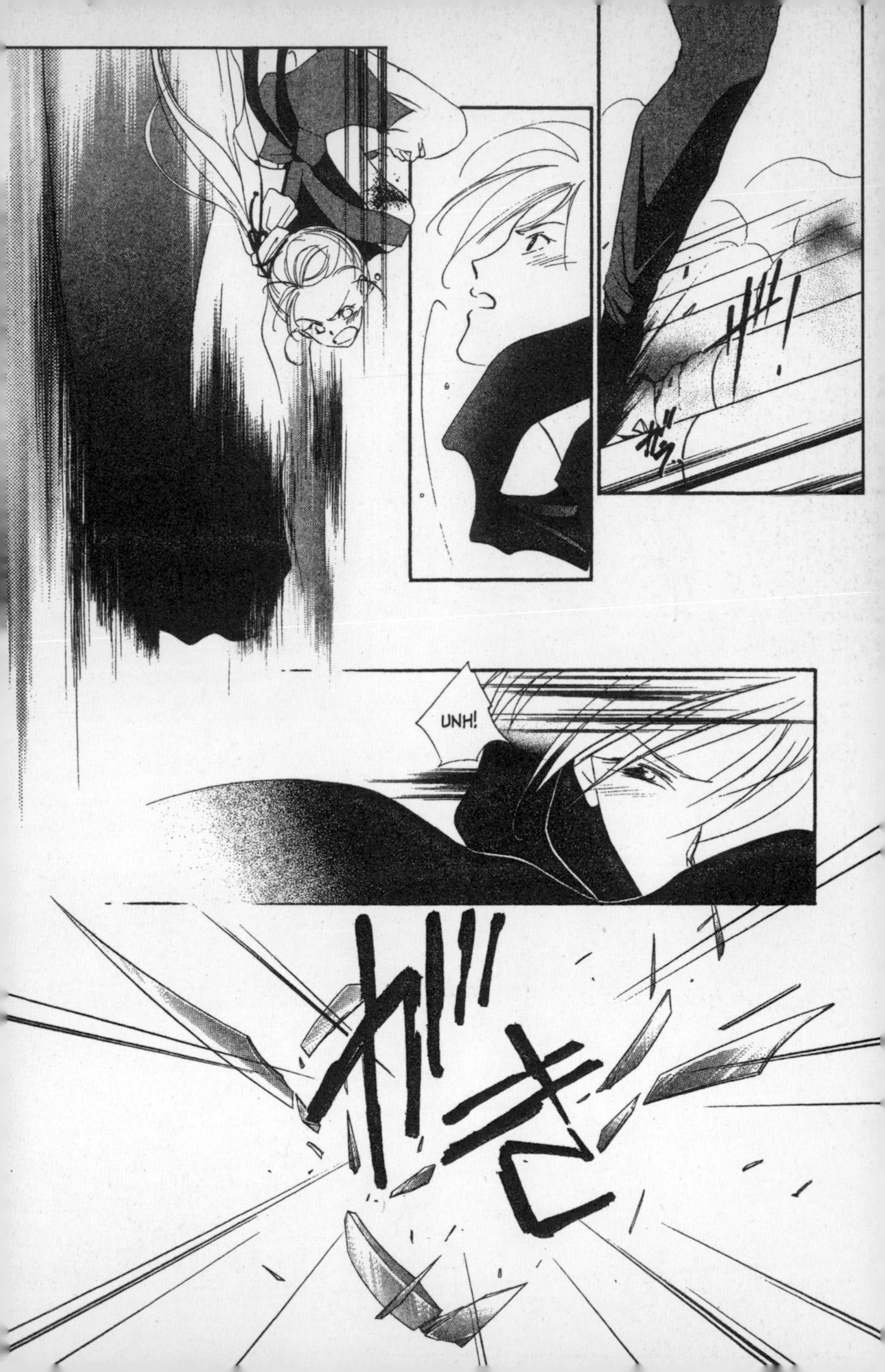
UNH!

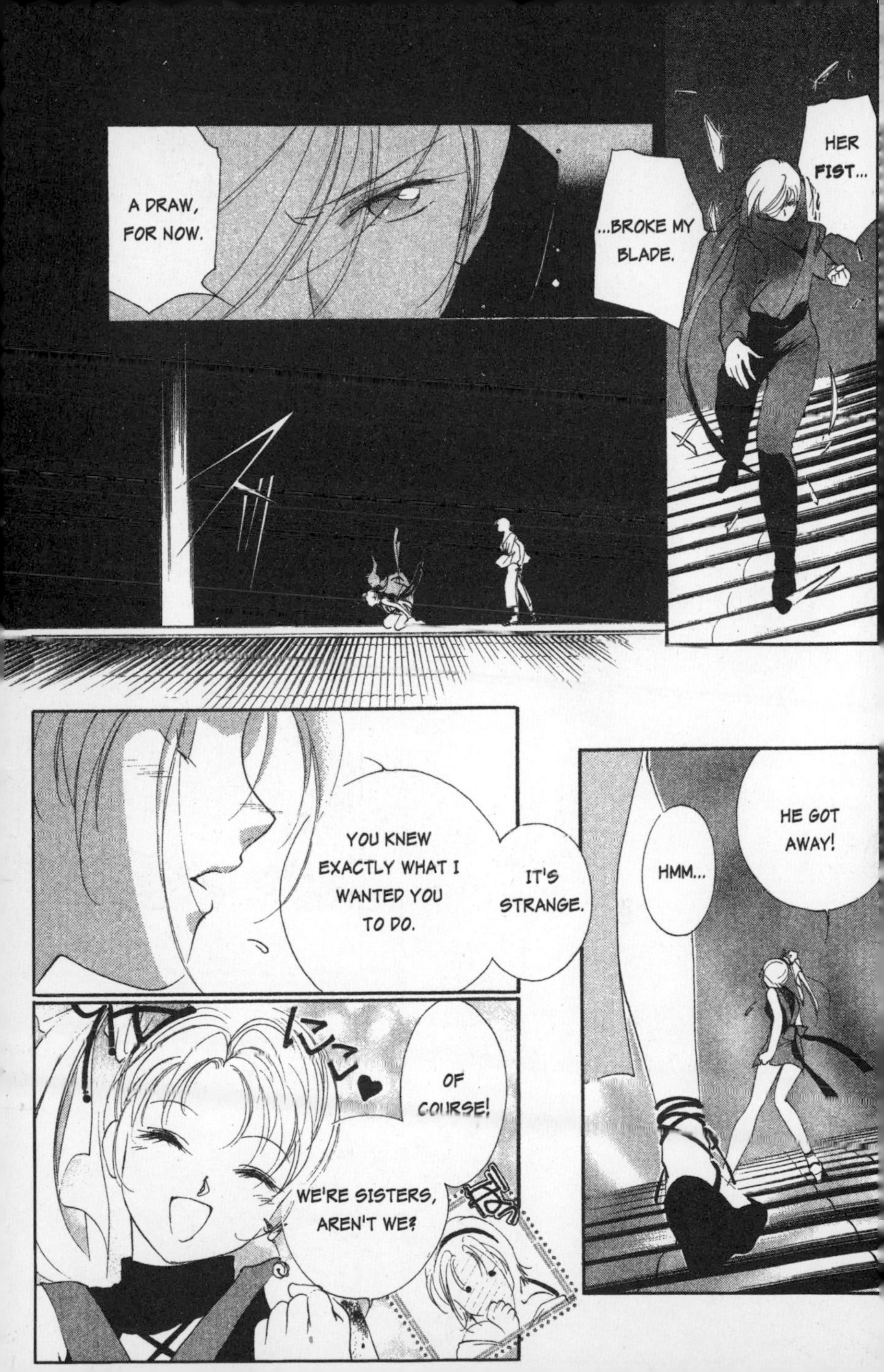
HER FIST...
...BROKE MY BLADE.
A DRAW, FOR NOW.
HE GOT AWAY!
HMM...
IT'S STRANGE.
YOU KNEW EXACTLY WHAT I WANTED YOU TO DO.
OF COURSE!
WE'RE SISTERS, AREN'T WE?

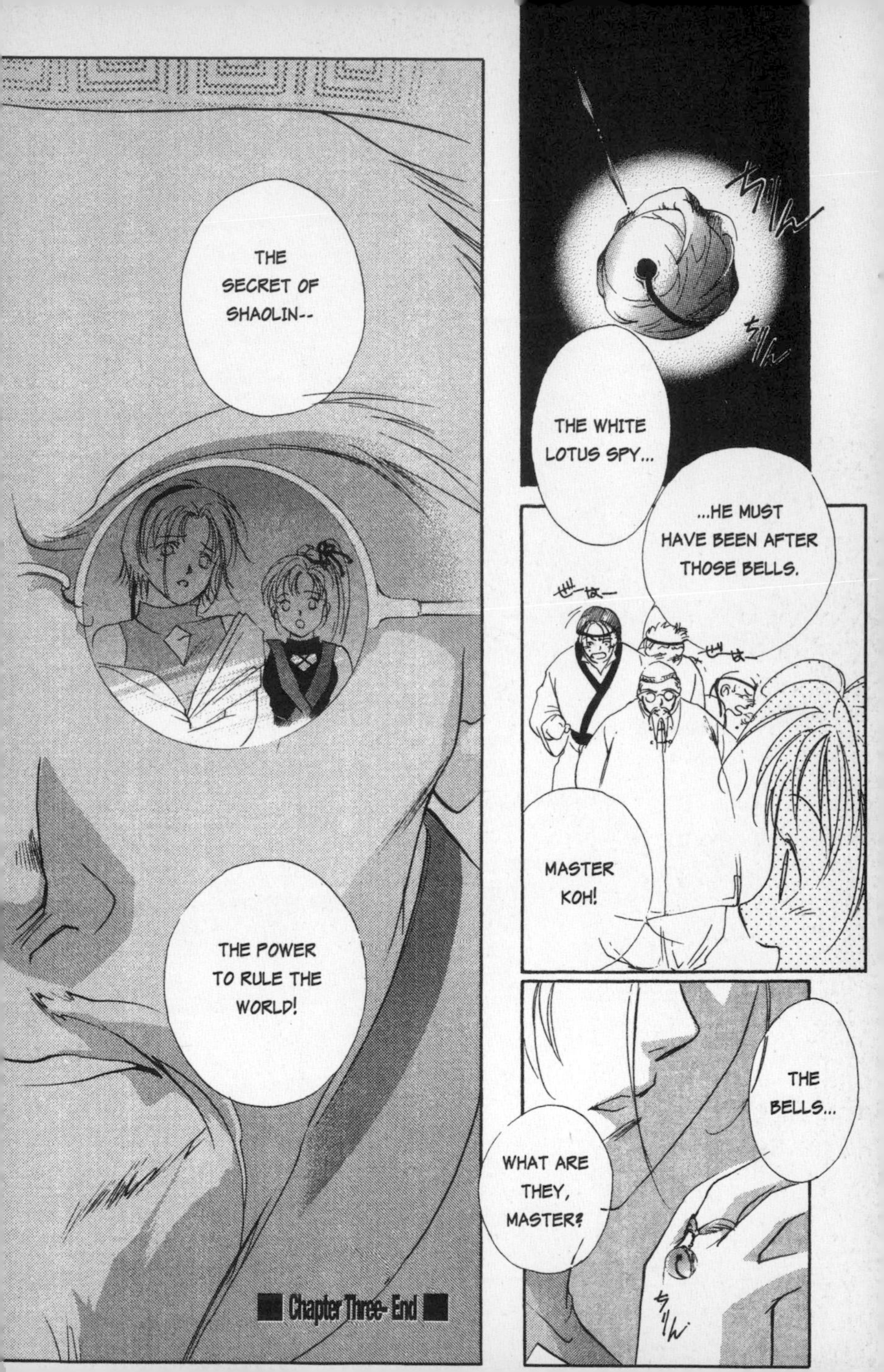
THE WHITE LOTUS SPY...
...HE MUST HAVE BEEN AFTER THOSE BELLS.
MASTER KOH!
THE BELLS...
WHAT ARE THEY, MASTER?
THE SECRET OF SHAOLIN--
THE POWER TO RULE THE WORLD!

Chapter Three- End

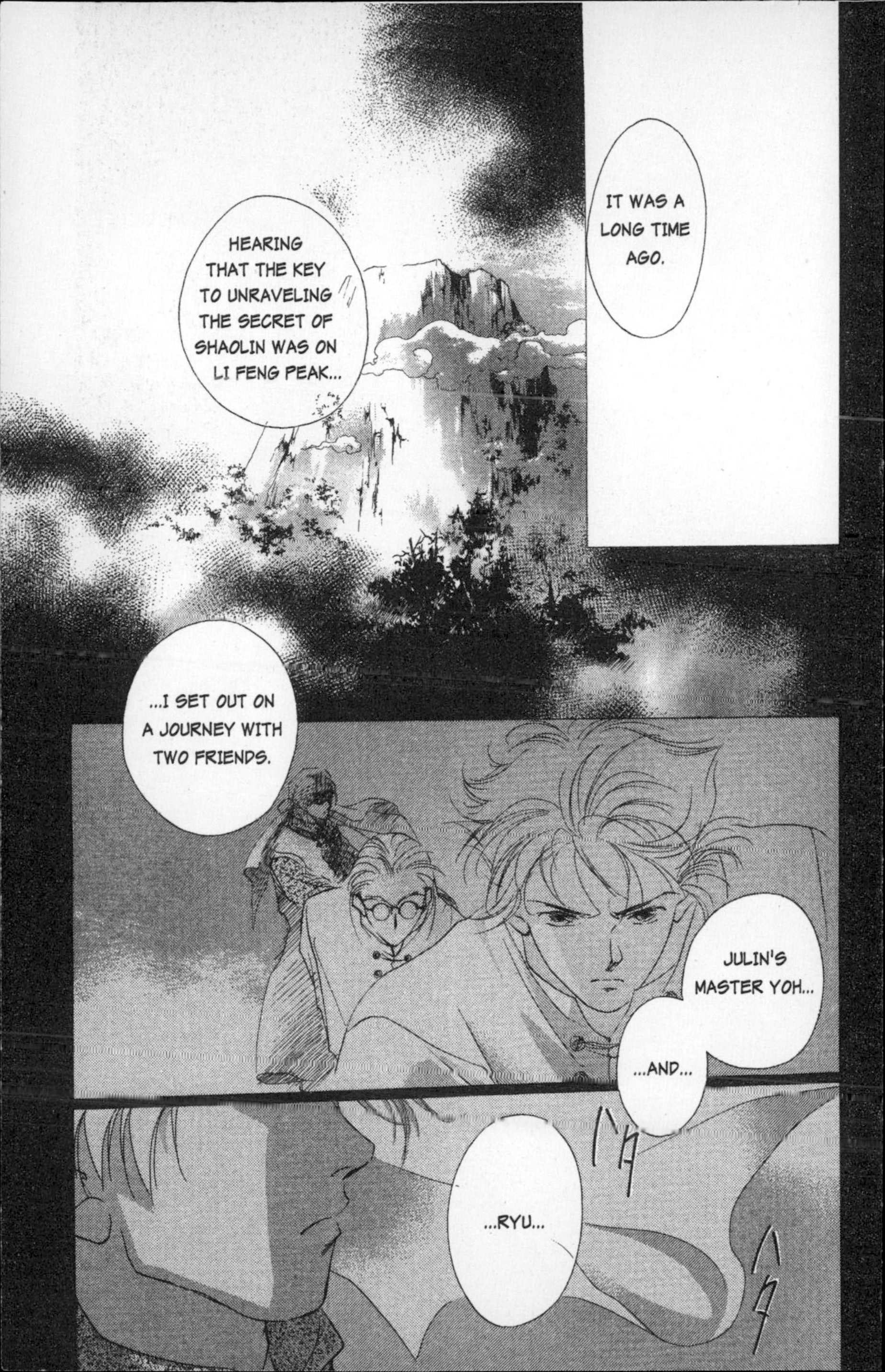
IT WAS A LONG TIME AGO.
HEARING THAT THE KEY TO UNRAVELING THE SECRET OF SHAOLIN WAS ON LI FENG PEAK...
...I SET OUT ON A JOURNEY WITH TWO FRIENDS.
JULIN'S MASTER YOH...
...AND...
...RYU...

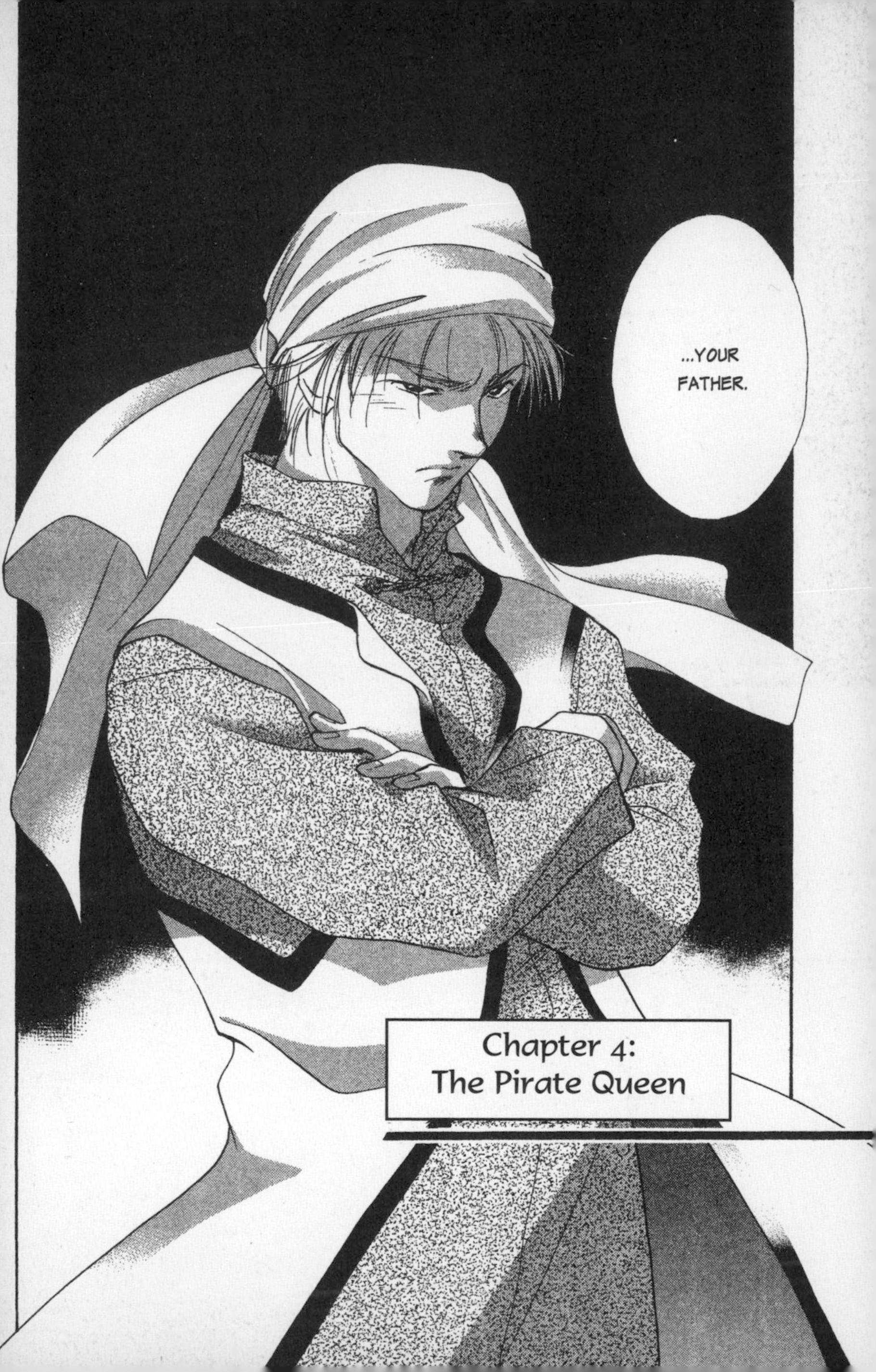
...YOUR FATHER.
Chapter 4: The Pirate Queen

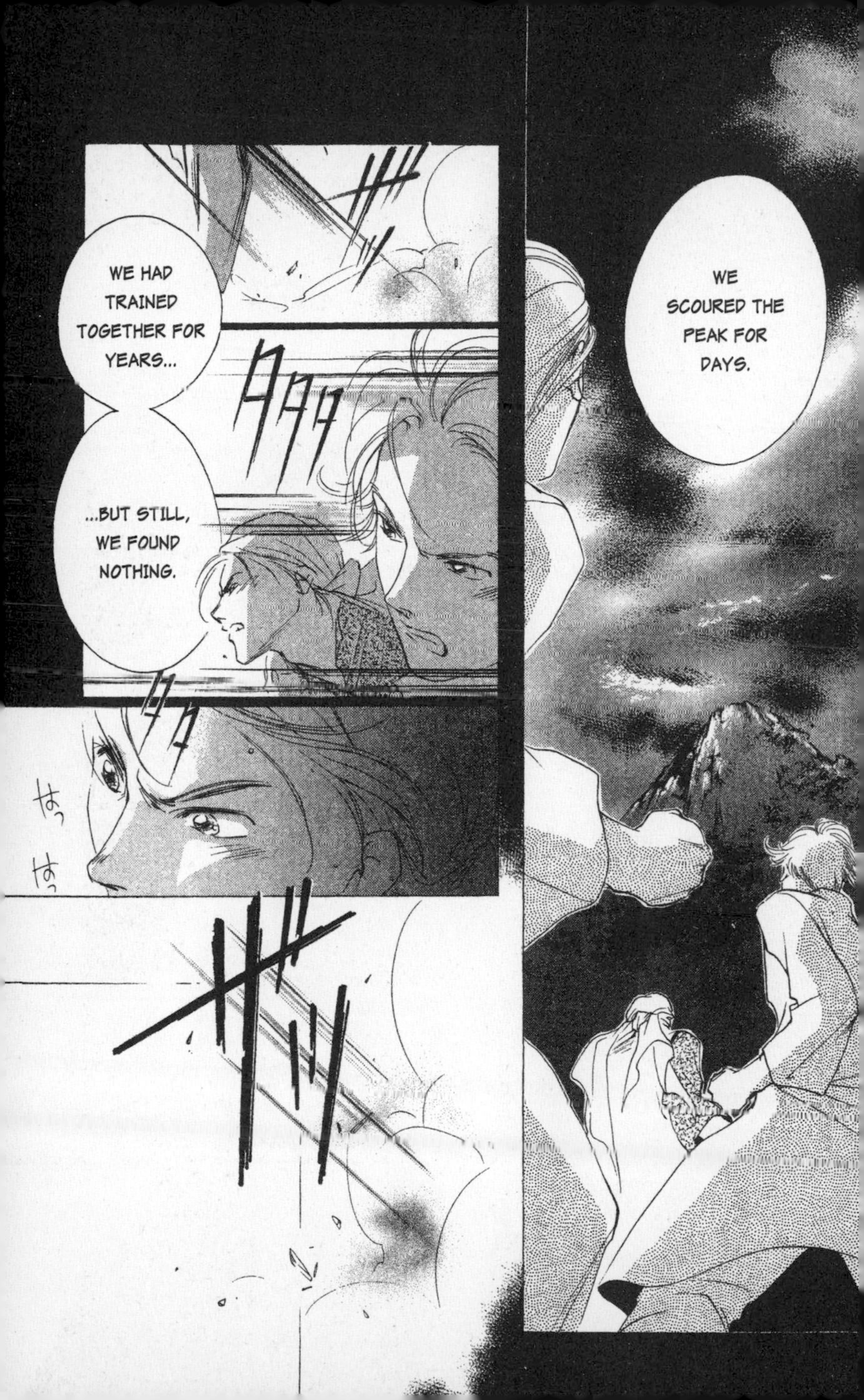
WE SCOURED THE PEAK FOR DAYS.
WE HAD TRAINED TOGETHER FOR YEARS...
...BUT STILL, WE FOUND NOTHING.
はっ
はっ

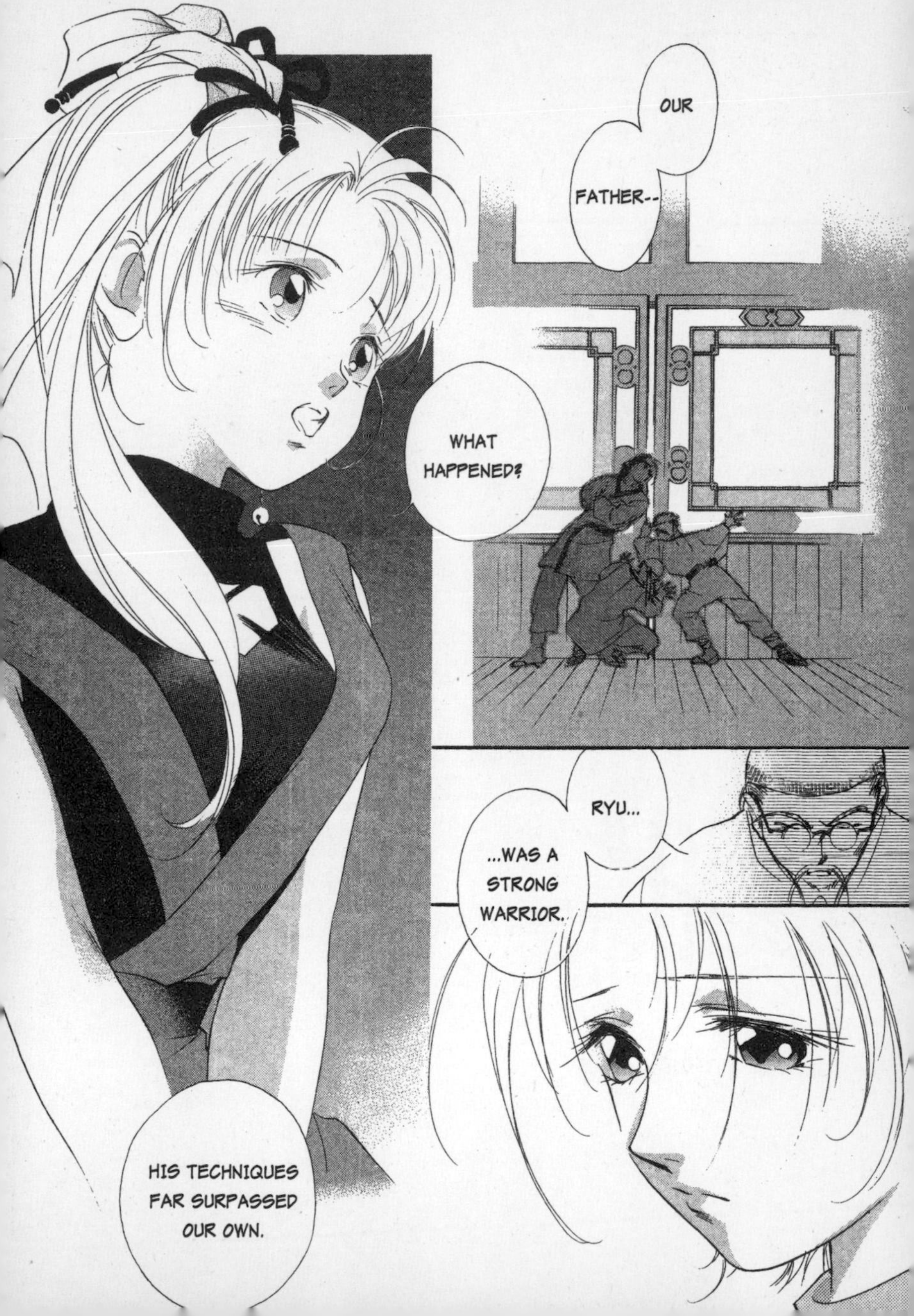
OUR
FATHER--
WHAT HAPPENED?
RYU...
...WAS A STRONG WARRIOR.
HIS TECHNIQUES FAR SURPASSED OUR OWN.

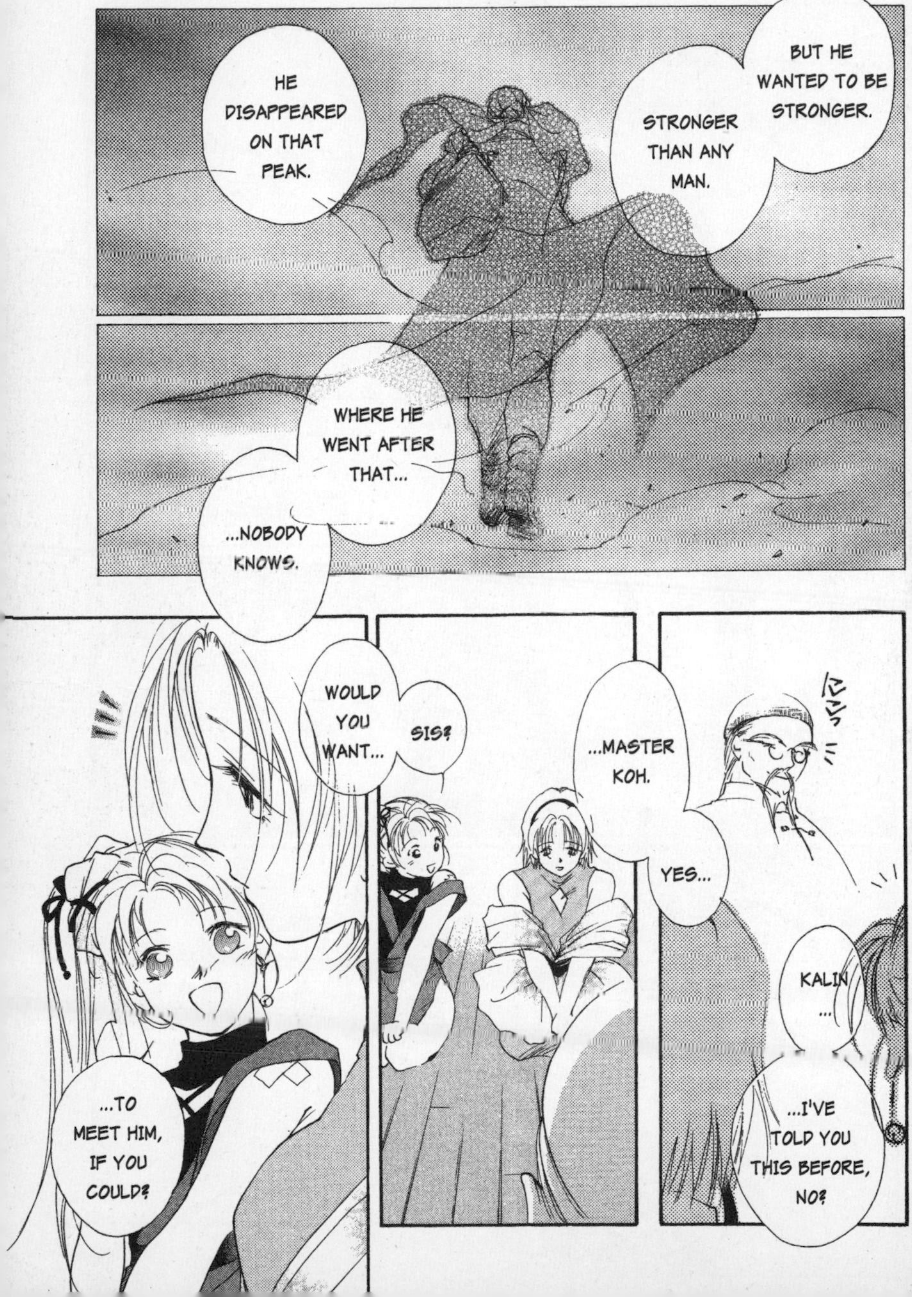
BUT HE WANTED TO BE STRONGER.
STRONGER THAN ANY MAN.
HE DISAPPEARED ON THAT PEAK.
WHERE HE WENT AFTER THAT...
...NOBODY KNOWS.
...MASTER KOH.
YES...
KALIN...
...I'VE TOLD YOU THIS BEFORE, NO?
WOULD YOU WANT...
SIS?
...TO MEET HIM, IF YOU COULD?

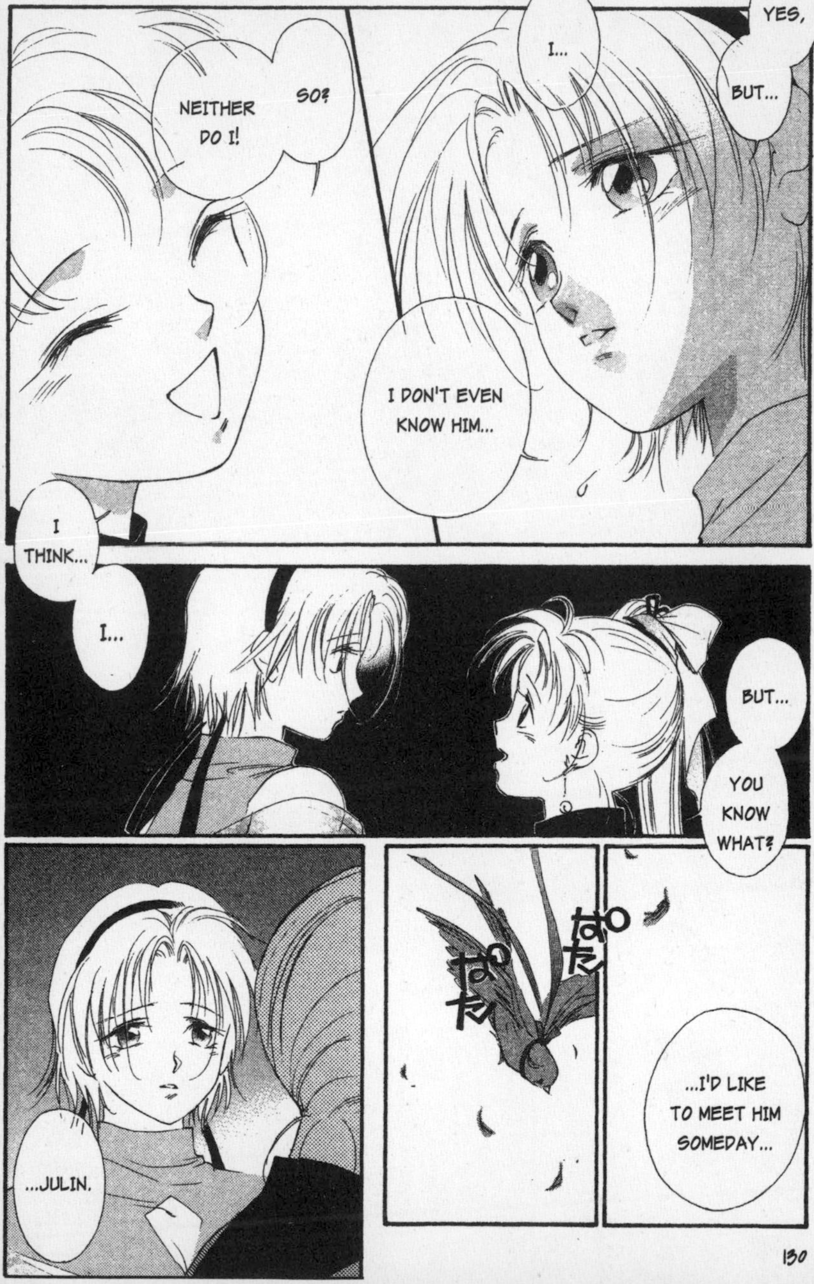
YES, BUT...
I...
I DON'T EVEN KNOW HIM...
SO? NEITHER DO I!
I THINK...
I...
BUT... YOU KNOW WHAT?
...I'D LIKE TO MEET HIM SOMEDAY...
ぱたぱた
...JULIN.

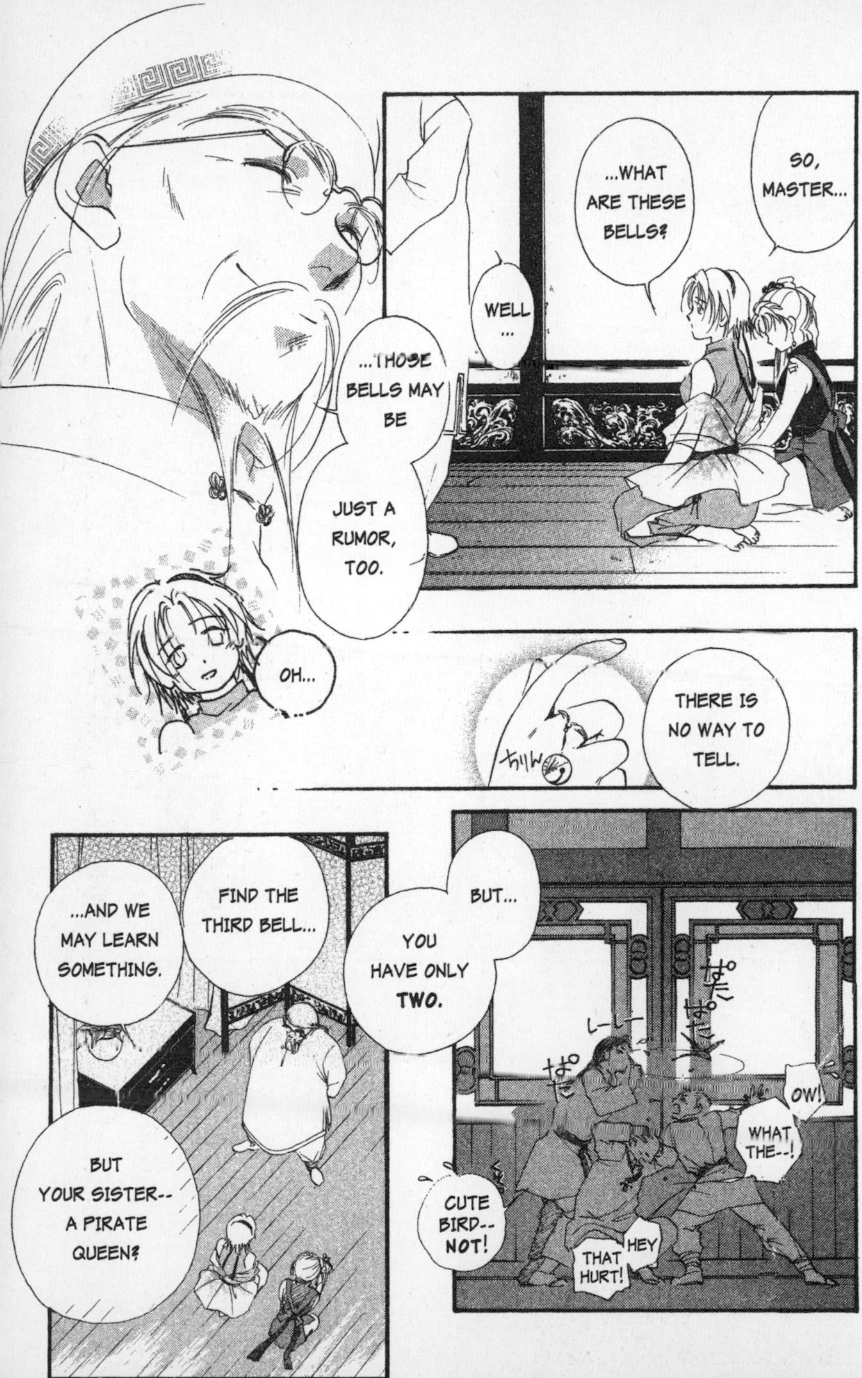
SO, MASTER...
...WHAT ARE THESE BELLS?
WELL...
...THOSE BELLS MAY BE
JUST A RUMOR, TOO.
OH...
THERE IS NO WAY TO TELL.
BUT...
YOU HAVE ONLY **TWO.**
OW!
WHAT THE--!
HEY
THAT HURT!
CUTE BIRD-- **NOT!**
FIND THE THIRD BELL...
...AND WE MAY LEARN SOMETHING.
BUT YOUR SISTER-- A PIRATE QUEEN?

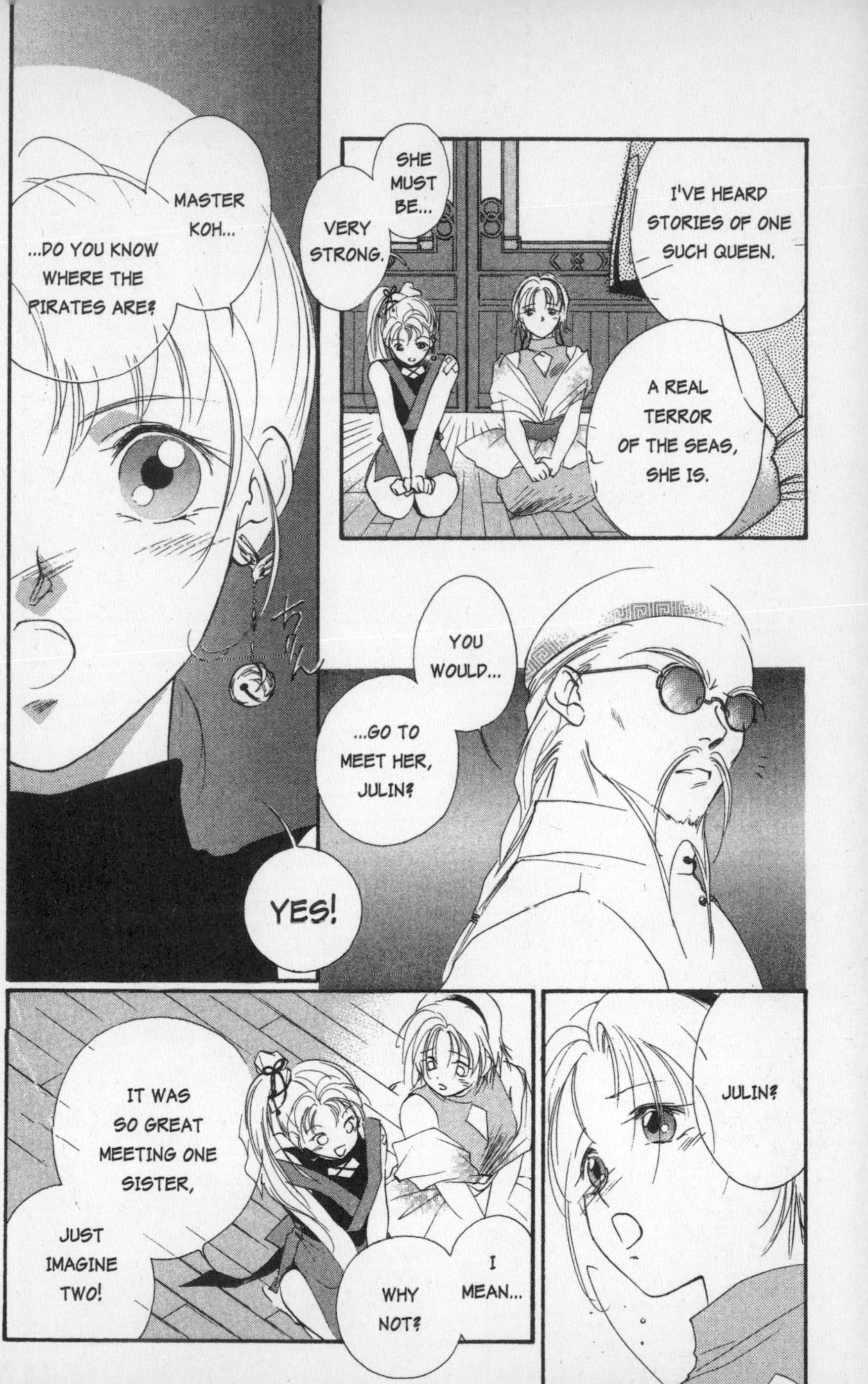
I'VE HEARD STORIES OF ONE SUCH QUEEN.
A REAL TERROR OF THE SEAS, SHE IS.
SHE MUST BE...
VERY STRONG.
YOU WOULD...
...GO TO MEET HER, JULIN?
MASTER KOH...
...DO YOU KNOW WHERE THE PIRATES ARE?
YES!
JULIN?
IT WAS SO GREAT MEETING ONE SISTER,
JUST IMAGINE TWO!
I MEAN...
WHY NOT?

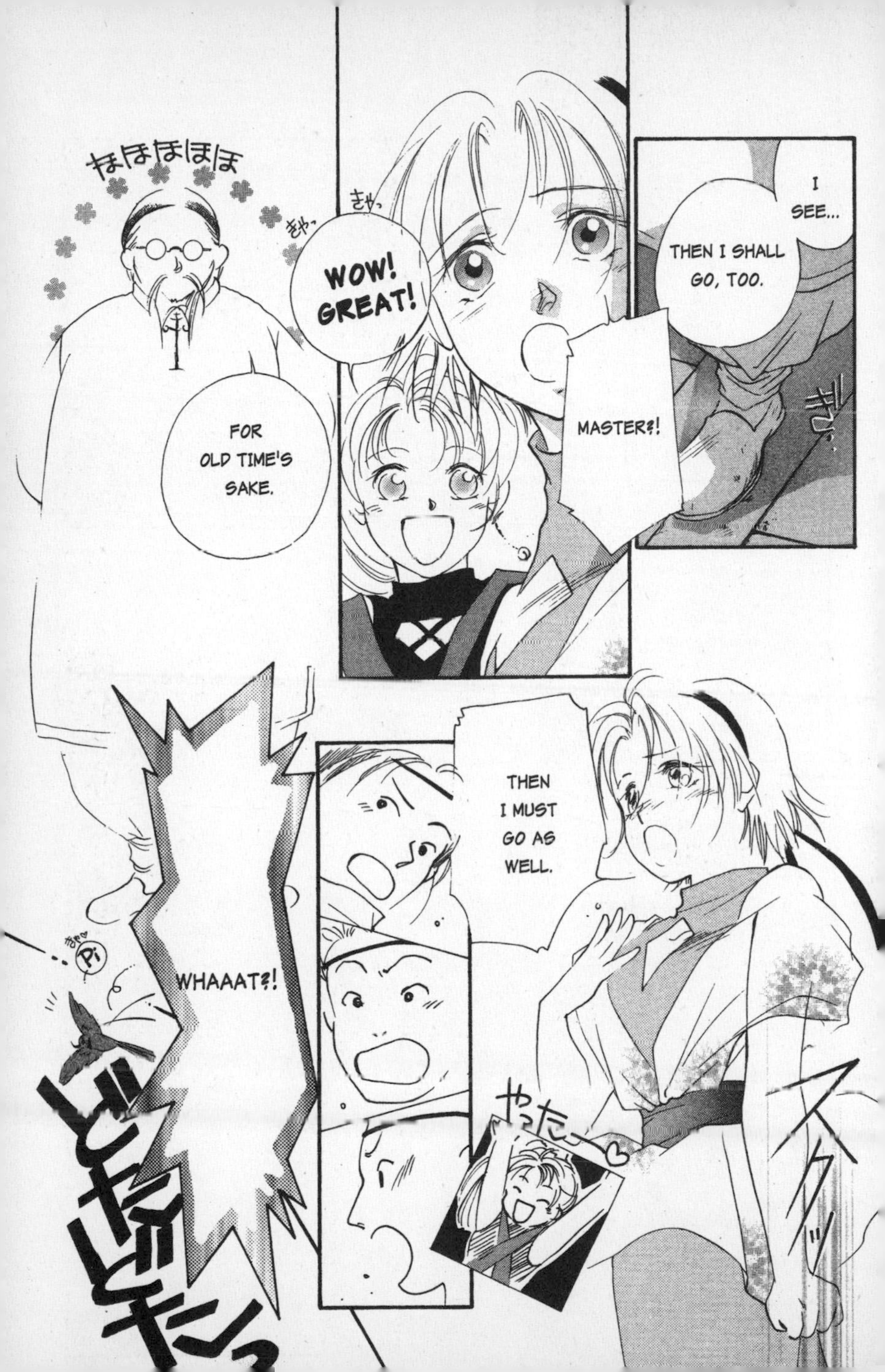
I SEE...
THEN I SHALL GO, TOO.
MASTER?!
きゃっ
きゃっ
WOW! GREAT!
ほほほほほ
FOR OLD TIME'S SAKE.
THEN I MUST GO AS WELL.
やったー
WHAAAT?!
Pi

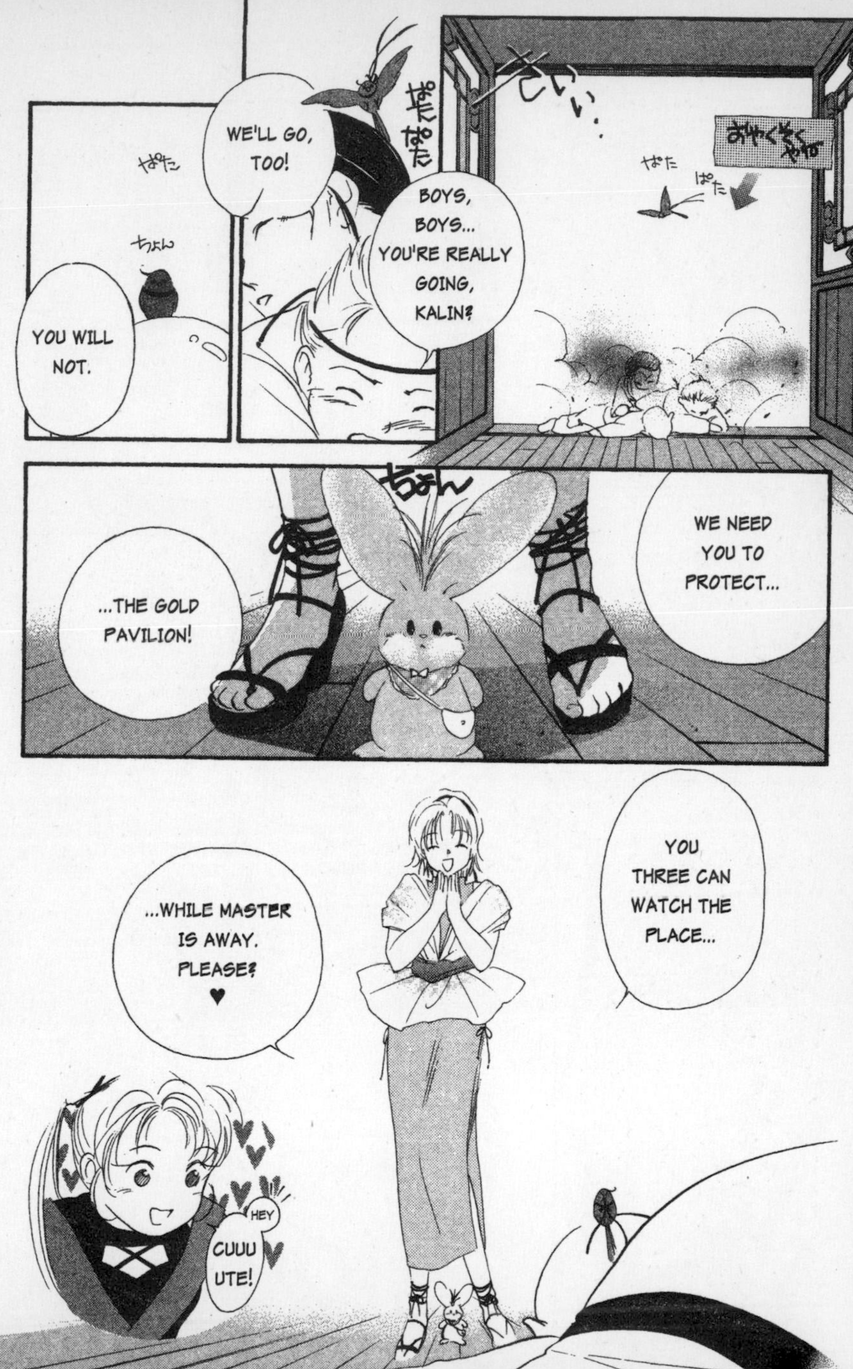
WE'LL GO, TOO!
BOYS, BOYS... YOU'RE REALLY GOING, KALIN?
YOU WILL NOT.
WE NEED YOU TO PROTECT...
...THE GOLD PAVILION!
YOU THREE CAN WATCH THE PLACE...
...WHILE MASTER IS AWAY. PLEASE? ♥
HEY
CUUU UTE!

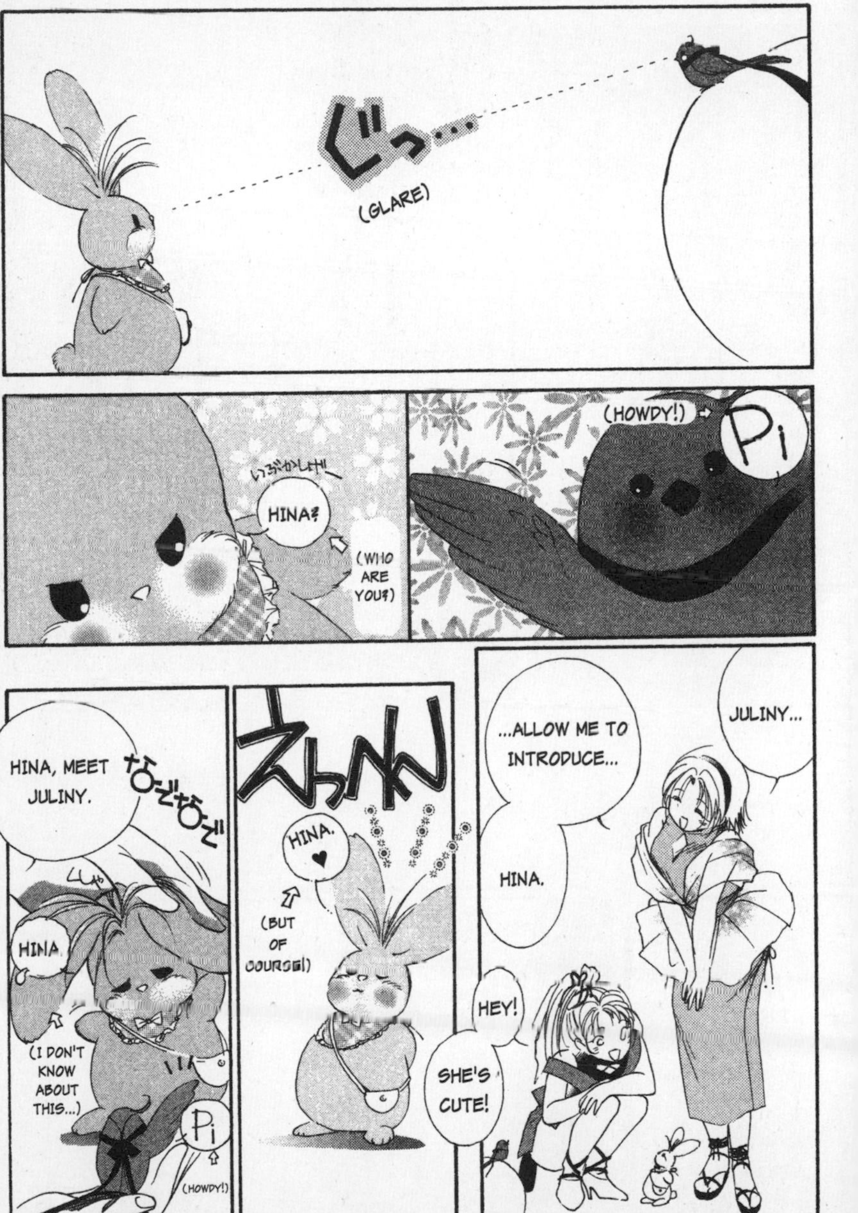
ぐっ...
(GLARE)
(HOWDY!)
Pi
いぶかしげ
HINA?
(WHO ARE YOU?)
JULINY...
...ALLOW ME TO INTRODUCE...
HINA.
HEY!
SHE'S CUTE!
えっへん
HINA. ♥
(BUT OF COURSE!)
HINA, MEET JULINY.
なでなで
HINA.
(I DON'T KNOW ABOUT THIS...)
Pi
(HOWDY!)

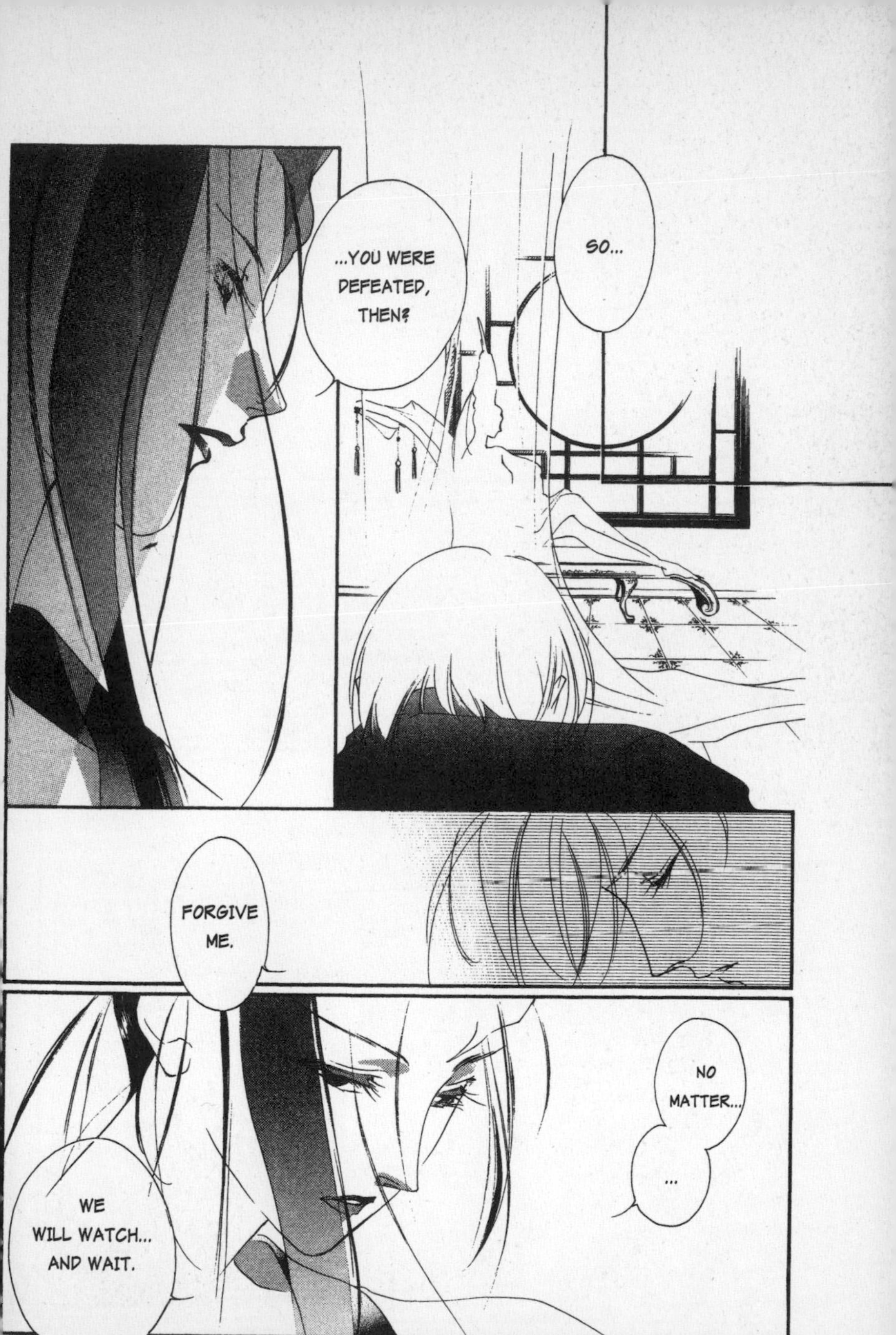
SO...
...YOU WERE DEFEATED, THEN?
FORGIVE ME.
NO MATTER...
...
WE WILL WATCH... AND WAIT.

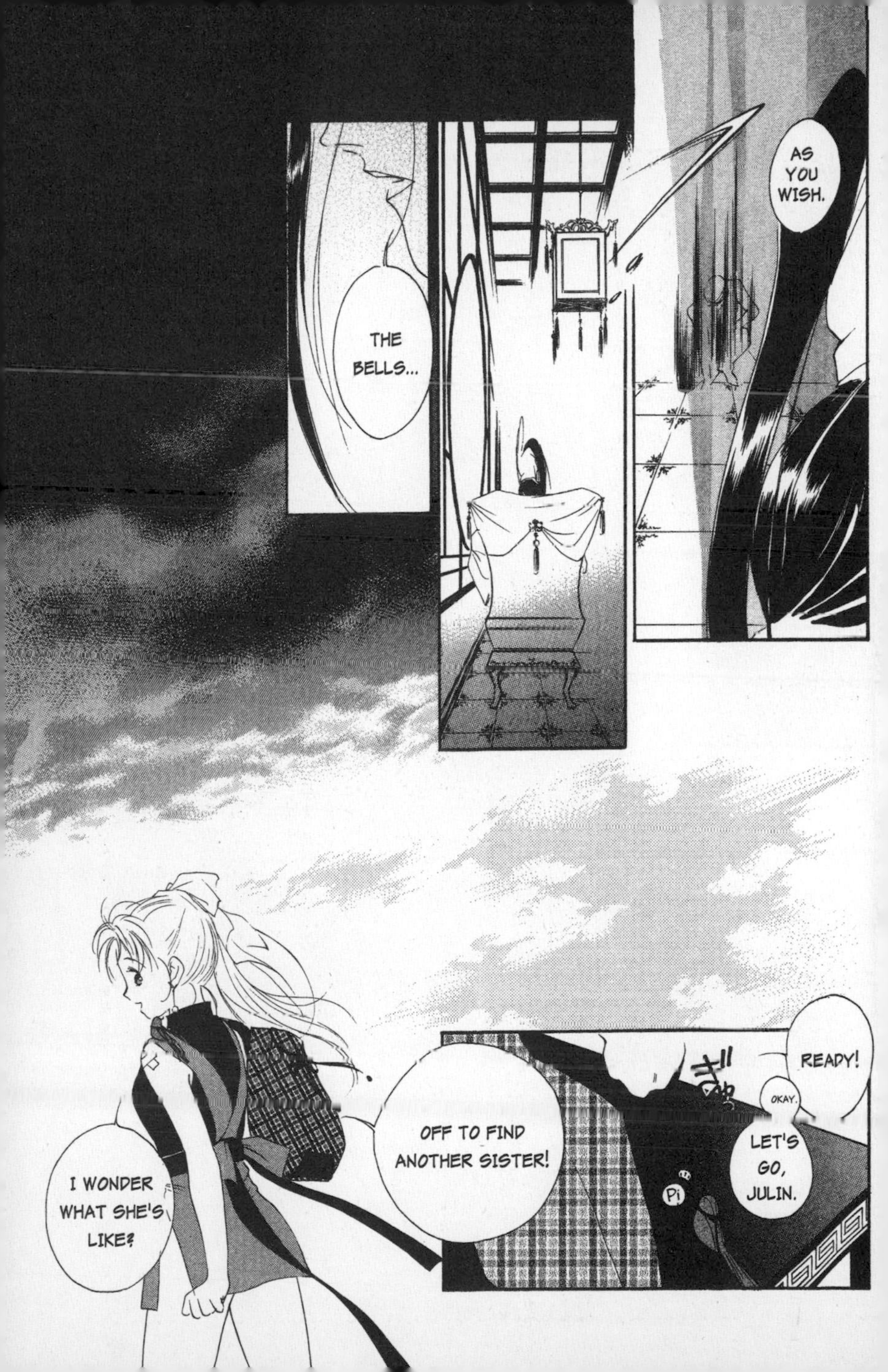
AS YOU WISH.
THE BELLS...
READY!
OKAY.
LET'S GO, JULIN.
Pi
OFF TO FIND ANOTHER SISTER!
I WONDER WHAT SHE'S LIKE?

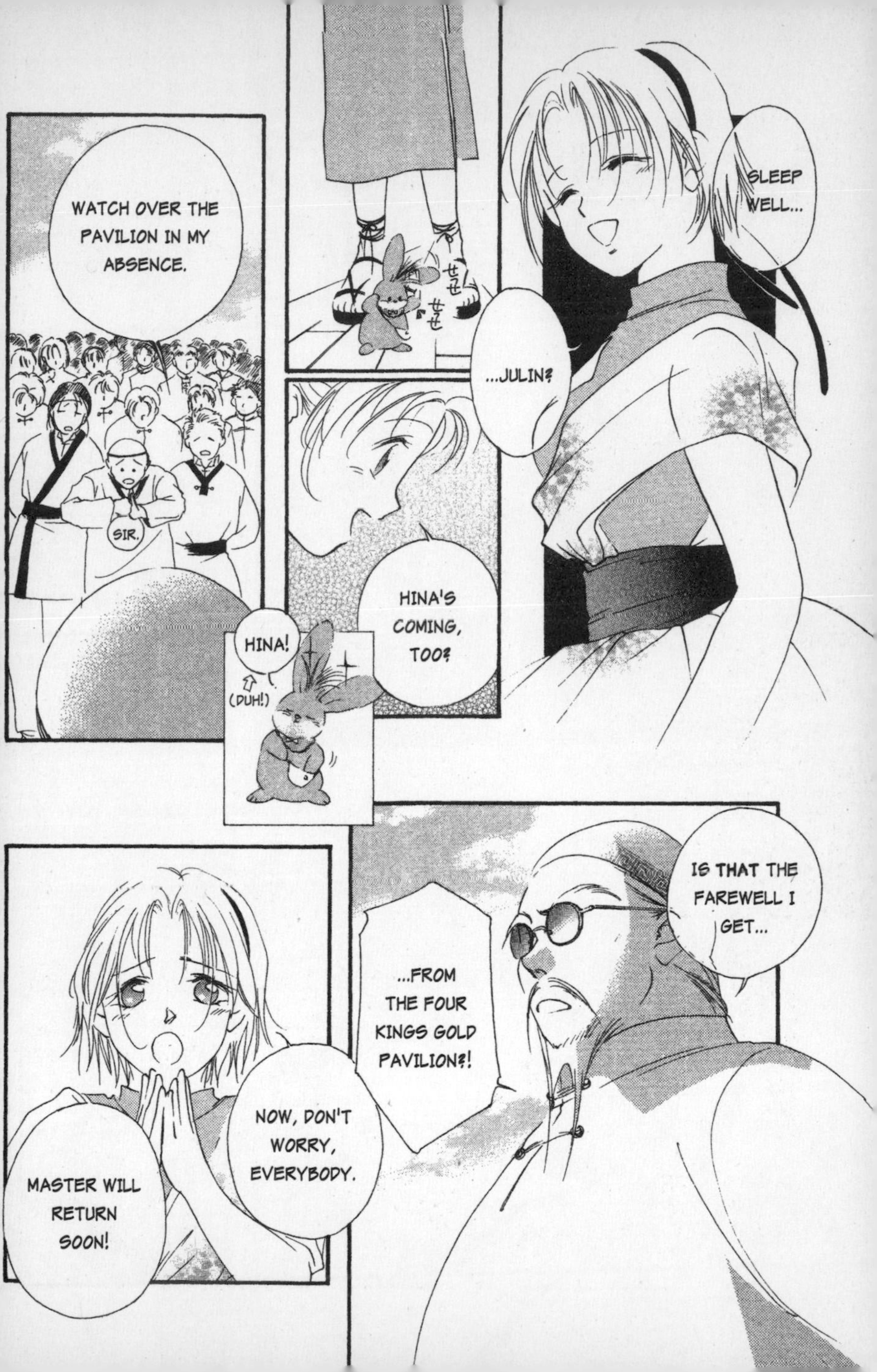
SLEEP WELL...
...JULIN?
HINA'S COMING, TOO?
HINA!
(DUH!)
WATCH OVER THE PAVILION IN MY ABSENCE.
SIR.
IS THAT THE FAREWELL I GET...
...FROM THE FOUR KINGS GOLD PAVILION?!
NOW, DON'T WORRY, EVERYBODY.
MASTER WILL RETURN SOON!

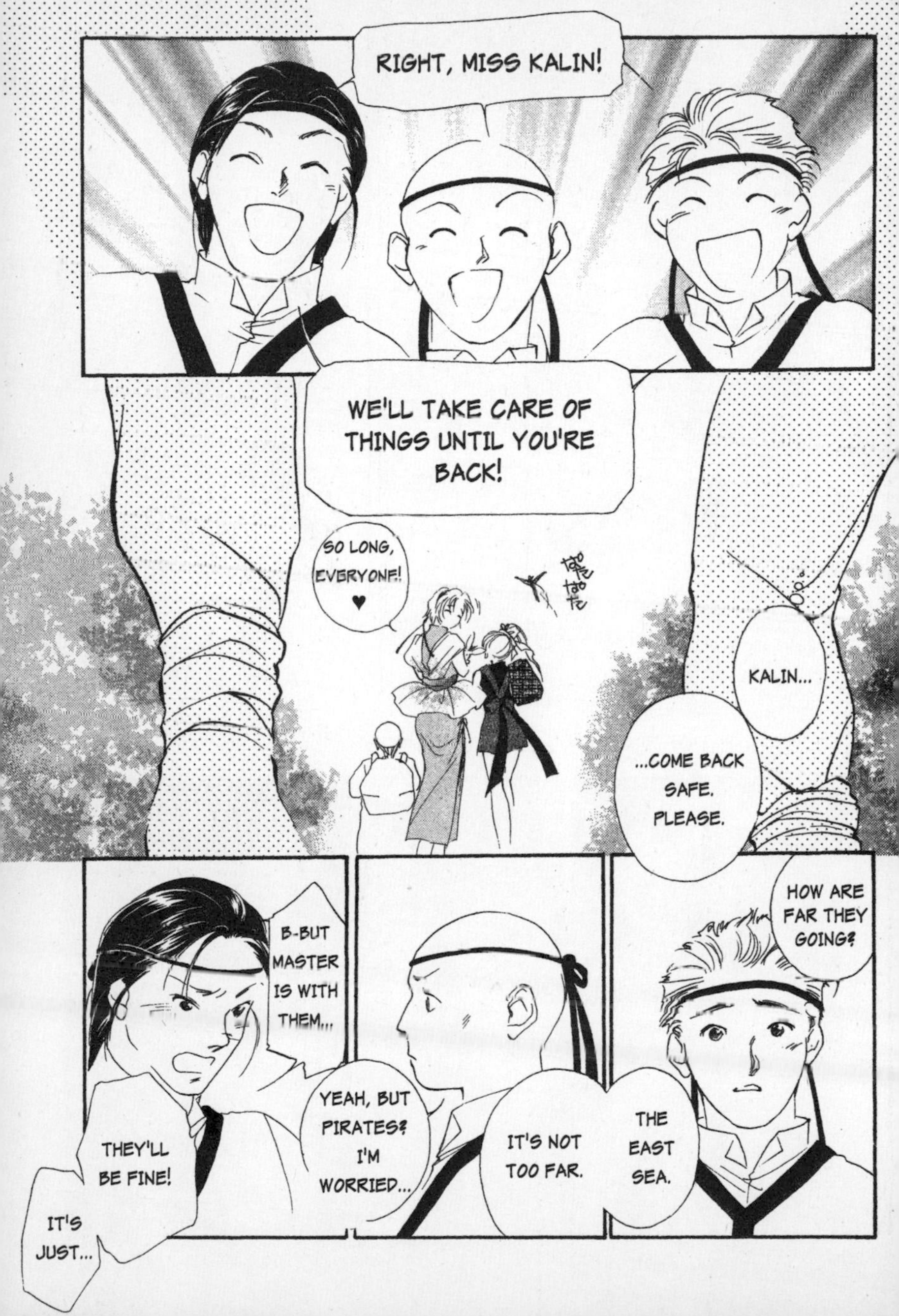
RIGHT, MISS KALIN!
WE'LL TAKE CARE OF THINGS UNTIL YOU'RE BACK!
KALIN...
...COME BACK SAFE. PLEASE.
ぱた ぱた
SO LONG, EVERYONE! ♥
HOW ARE FAR THEY GOING?
THE EAST SEA.
IT'S NOT TOO FAR.
YEAH, BUT PIRATES? I'M WORRIED...
B-BUT MASTER IS WITH THEM...
THEY'LL BE FINE!
IT'S JUST...

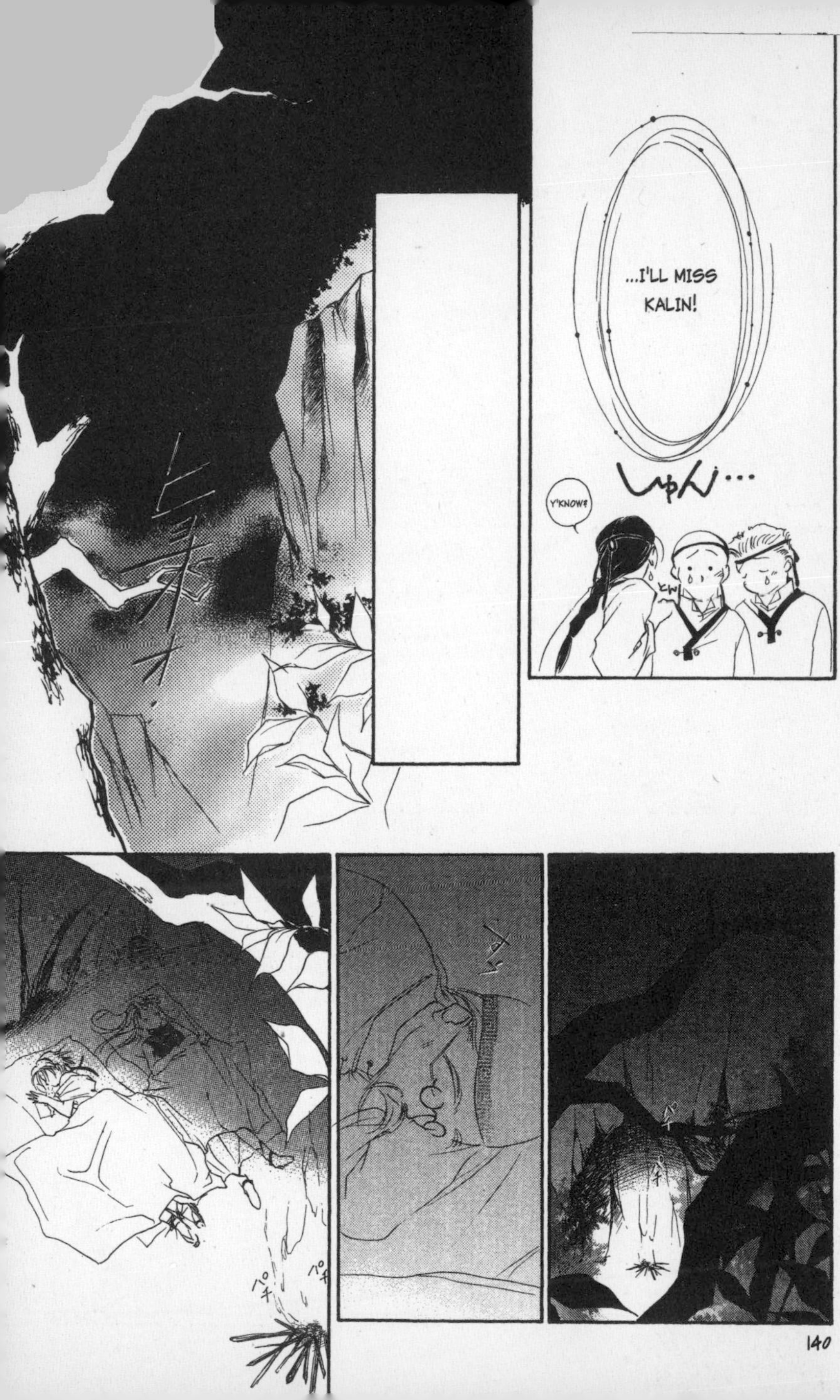
...I'LL MISS KALIN!
しゅん…
Y'KNOW?

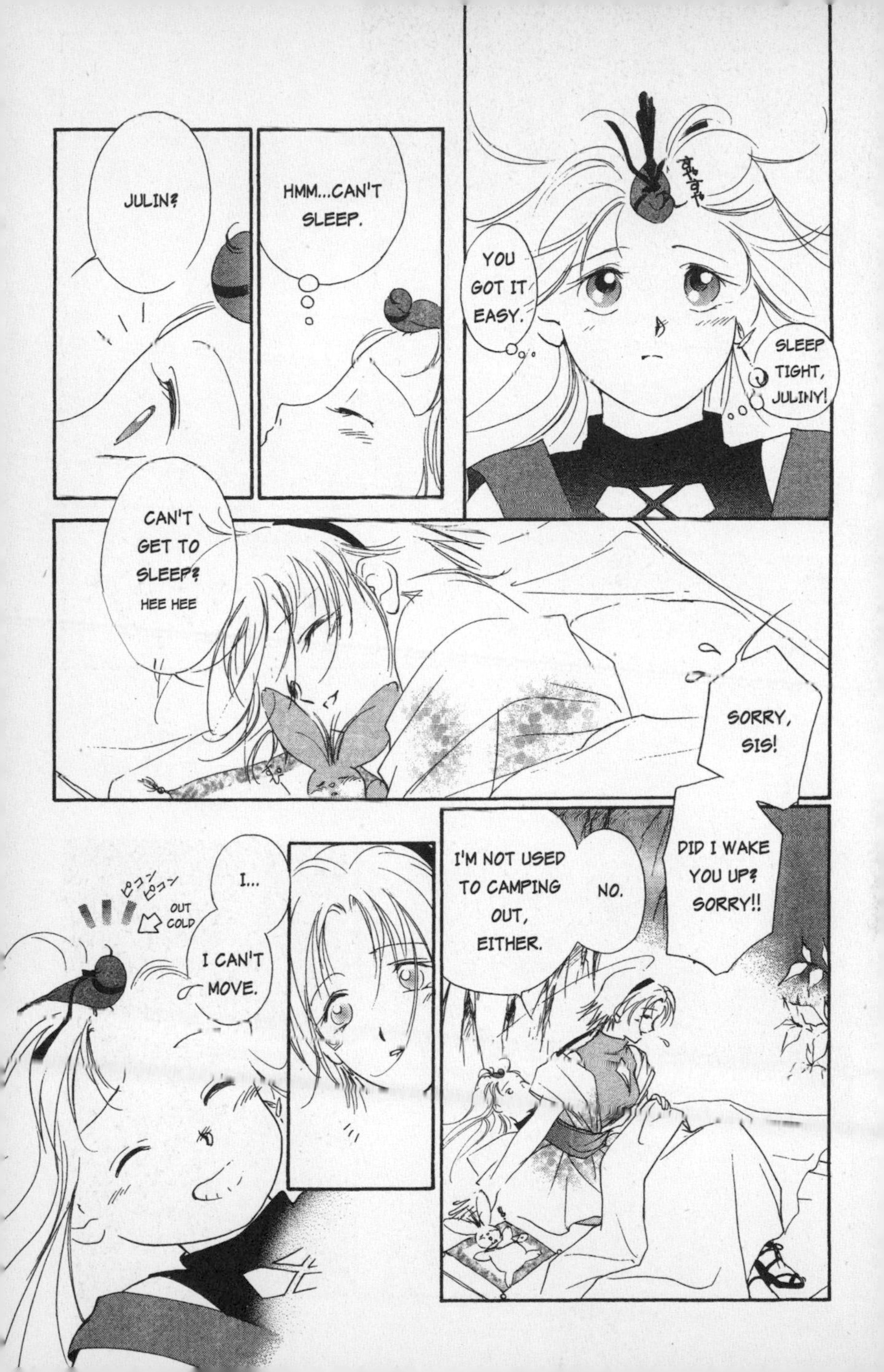
すやすや
SLEEP TIGHT, JULINY!
YOU GOT IT EASY.
HMM...CAN'T SLEEP.
JULIN?
SORRY, SIS!
CAN'T GET TO SLEEP? HEE HEE
DID I WAKE YOU UP? SORRY!!
NO.
I'M NOT USED TO CAMPING OUT, EITHER.
I...
I CAN'T MOVE.
ピコン ピコン
OUT COLD

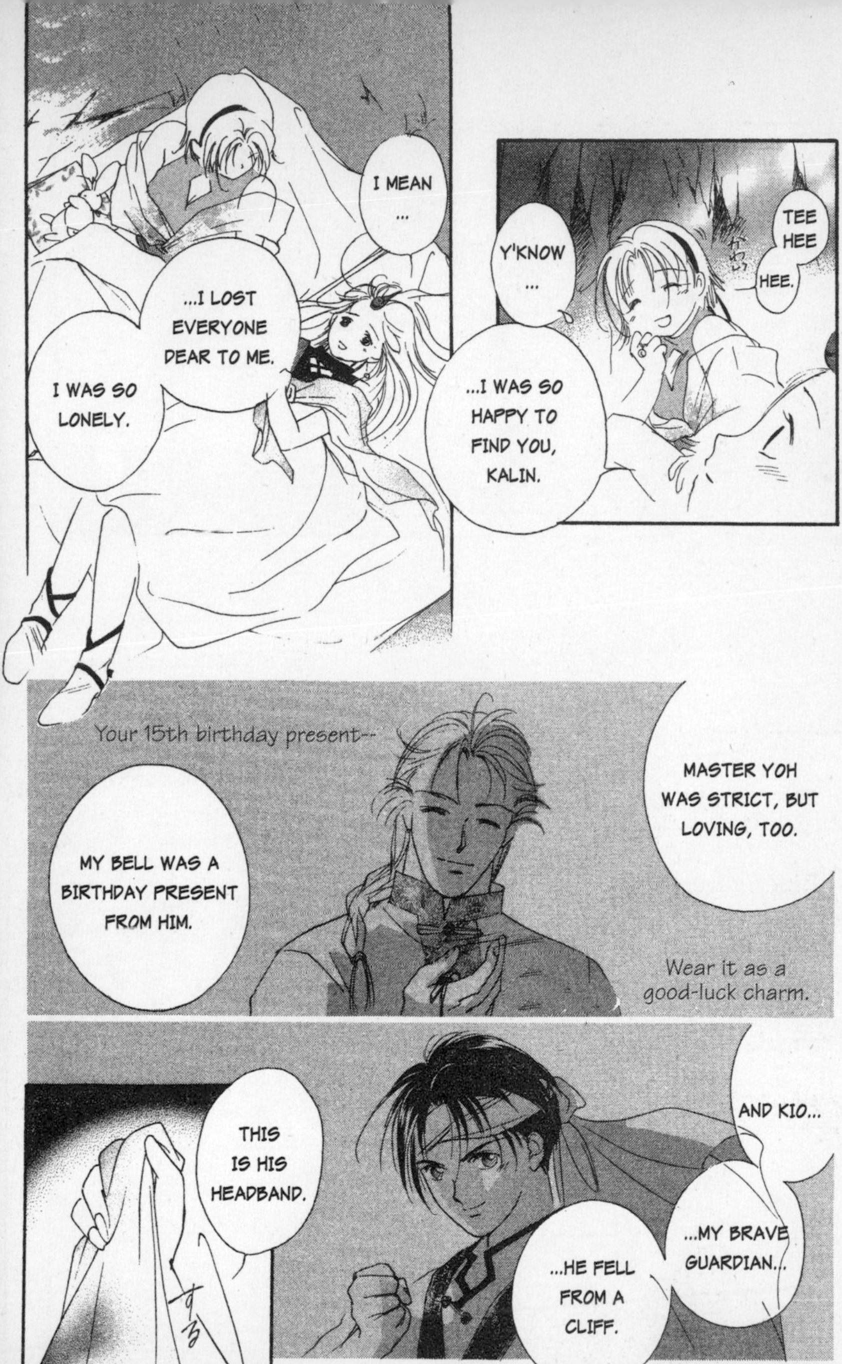
TEE HEE HEE.
Y'KNOW ...
...I WAS SO HAPPY TO FIND YOU, KALIN.
I MEAN ...
...I LOST EVERYONE DEAR TO ME.
I WAS SO LONELY.
MASTER YOH WAS STRICT, BUT LOVING, TOO.
Your 15th birthday present--
MY BELL WAS A BIRTHDAY PRESENT FROM HIM.
Wear it as a good-luck charm.
AND KIO...
...MY BRAVE GUARDIAN...
...HE FELL FROM A CLIFF.
THIS IS HIS HEADBAND.
する

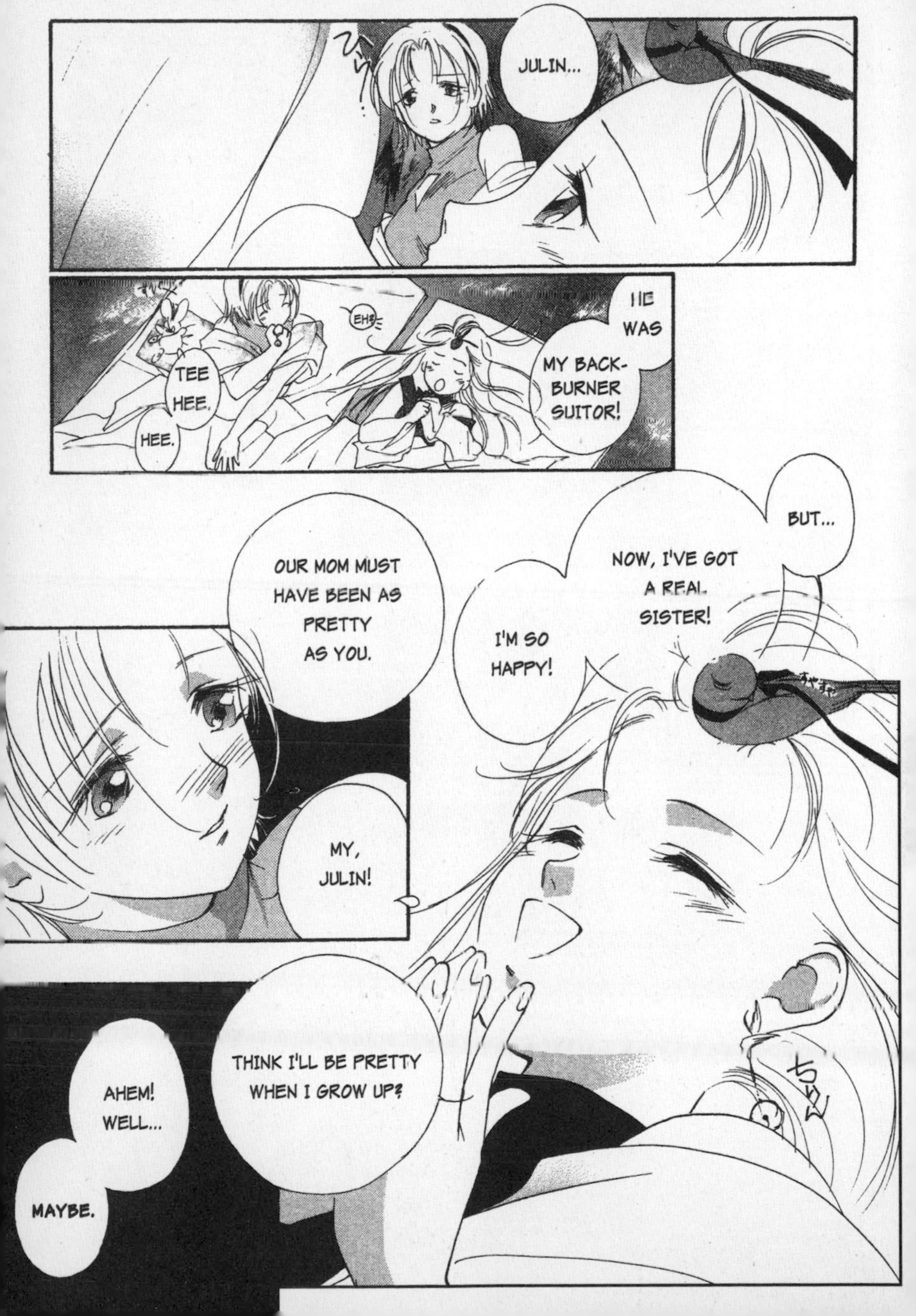
JULIN...
HE WAS MY BACK-BURNER SUITOR!
TEE HEE.
HEE.
BUT...
NOW, I'VE GOT A REAL SISTER!
I'M SO HAPPY!
OUR MOM MUST HAVE BEEN AS PRETTY AS YOU.
MY, JULIN!
THINK I'LL BE PRETTY WHEN I GROW UP?
AHEM! WELL...
MAYBE.

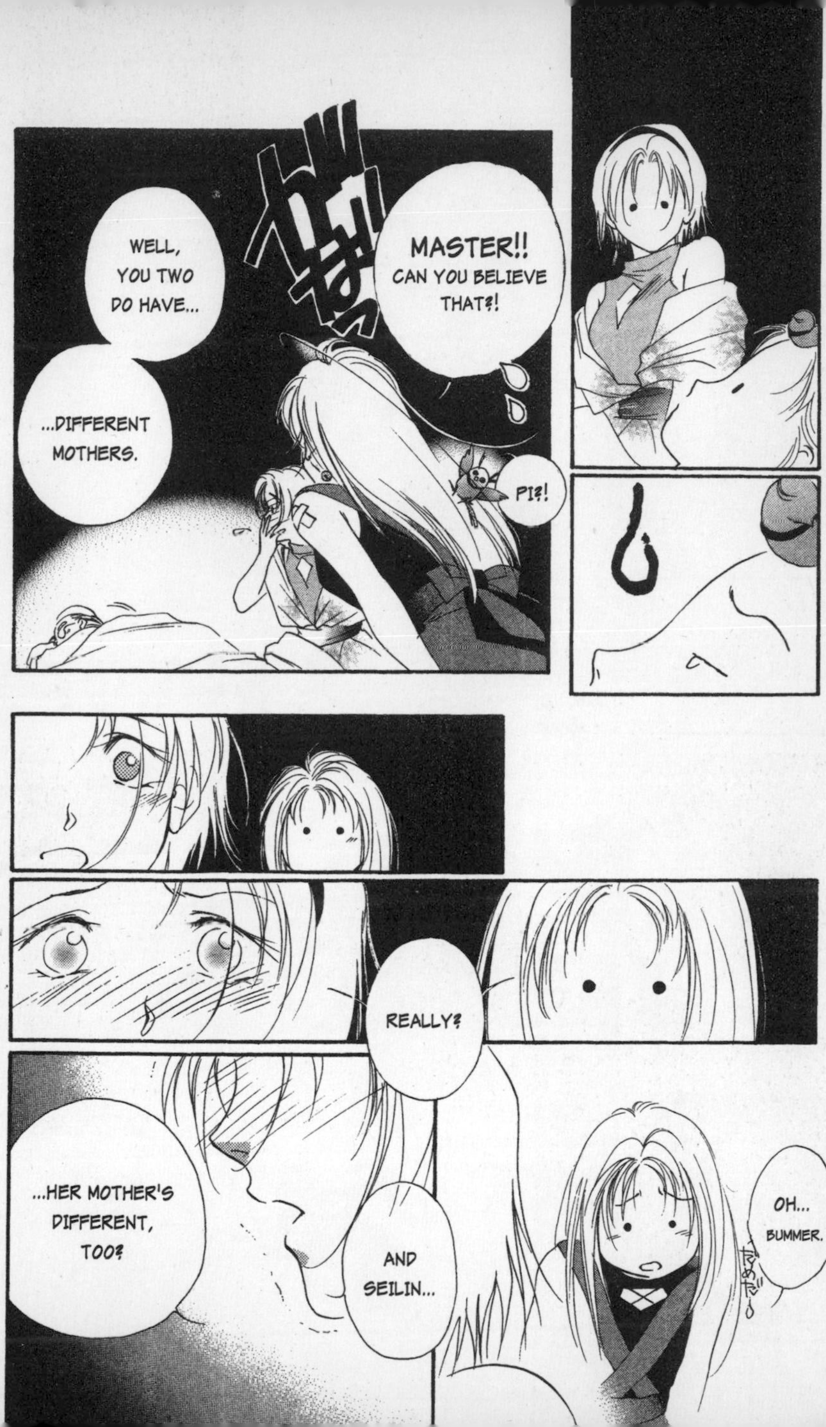
MASTER!! CAN YOU BELIEVE THAT?!
WELL, YOU TWO DO HAVE...
...DIFFERENT MOTHERS.
PI?!
REALLY?
OH... BUMMER.
AND SEILIN...
...HER MOTHER'S DIFFERENT, TOO?

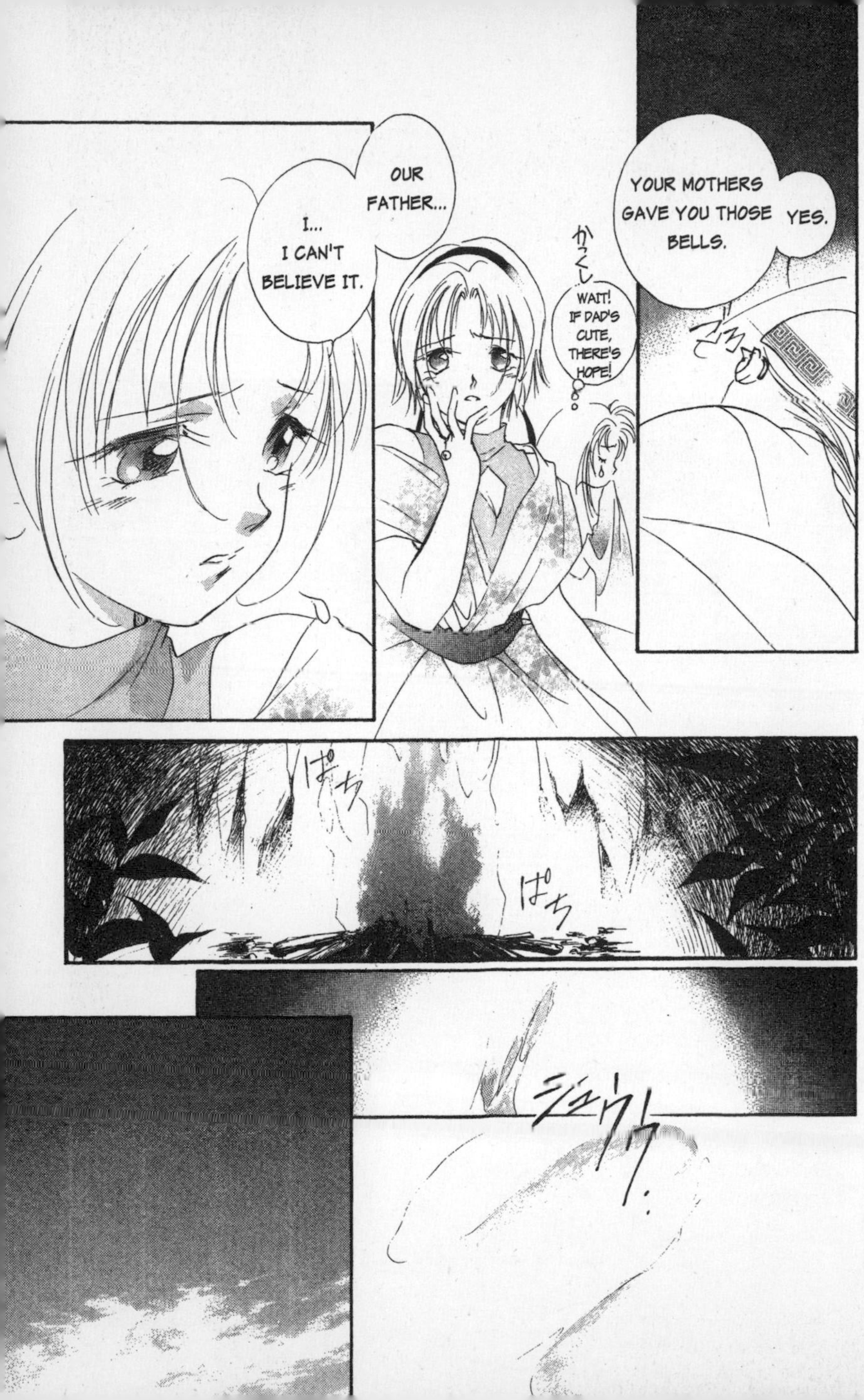
YES.
YOUR MOTHERS GAVE YOU THOSE BELLS.
OUR FATHER...
I... I CAN'T BELIEVE IT.
かっくし
WAIT! IF DAD'S CUTE, THERE'S HOPE!
ぱち
ぱち
ジュウ

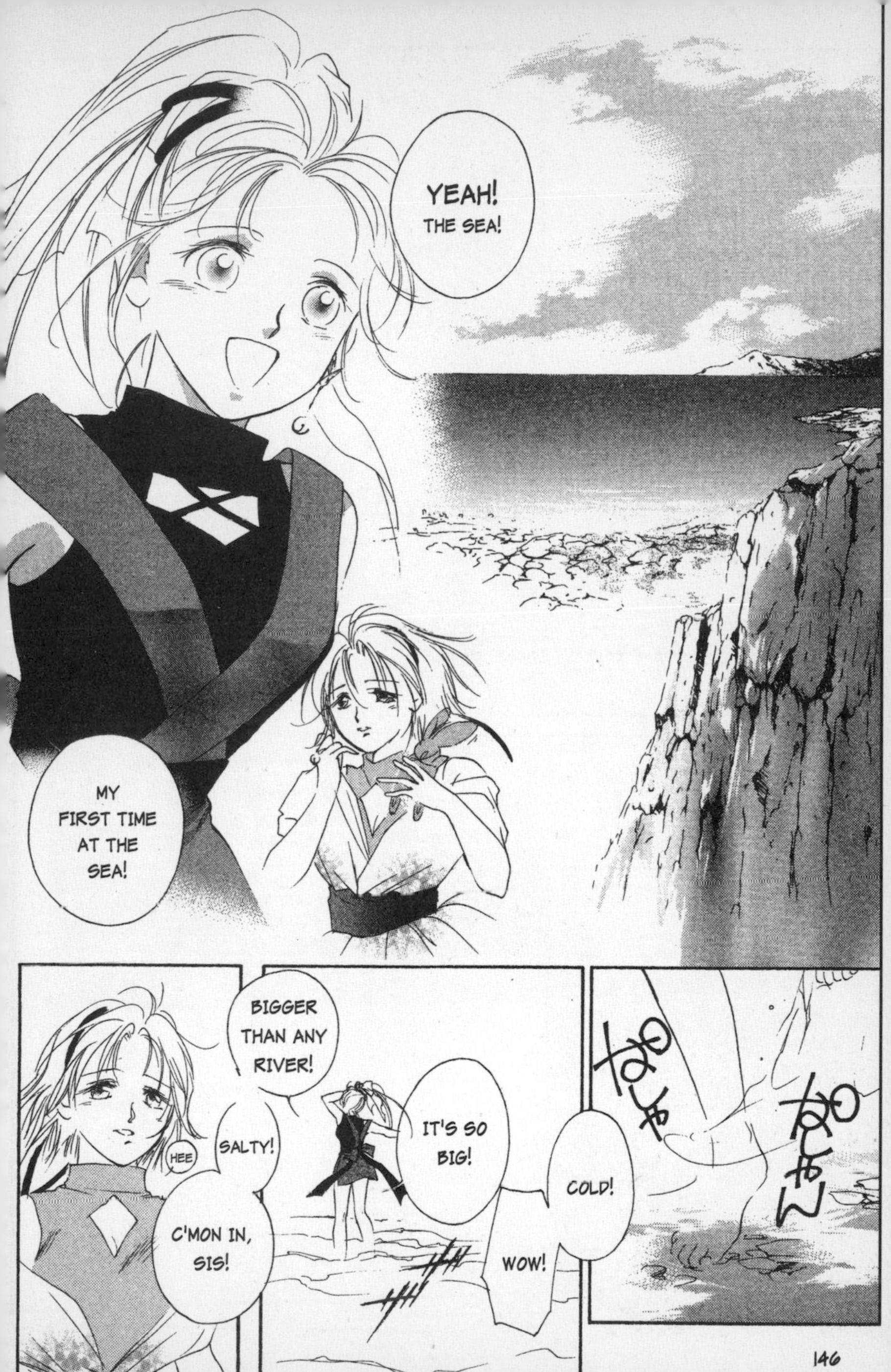
YEAH! THE SEA!
MY FIRST TIME AT THE SEA!
COLD!
IT'S SO BIG!
BIGGER THAN ANY RIVER!
SALTY!
WOW!
HEE
C'MON IN, SIS!

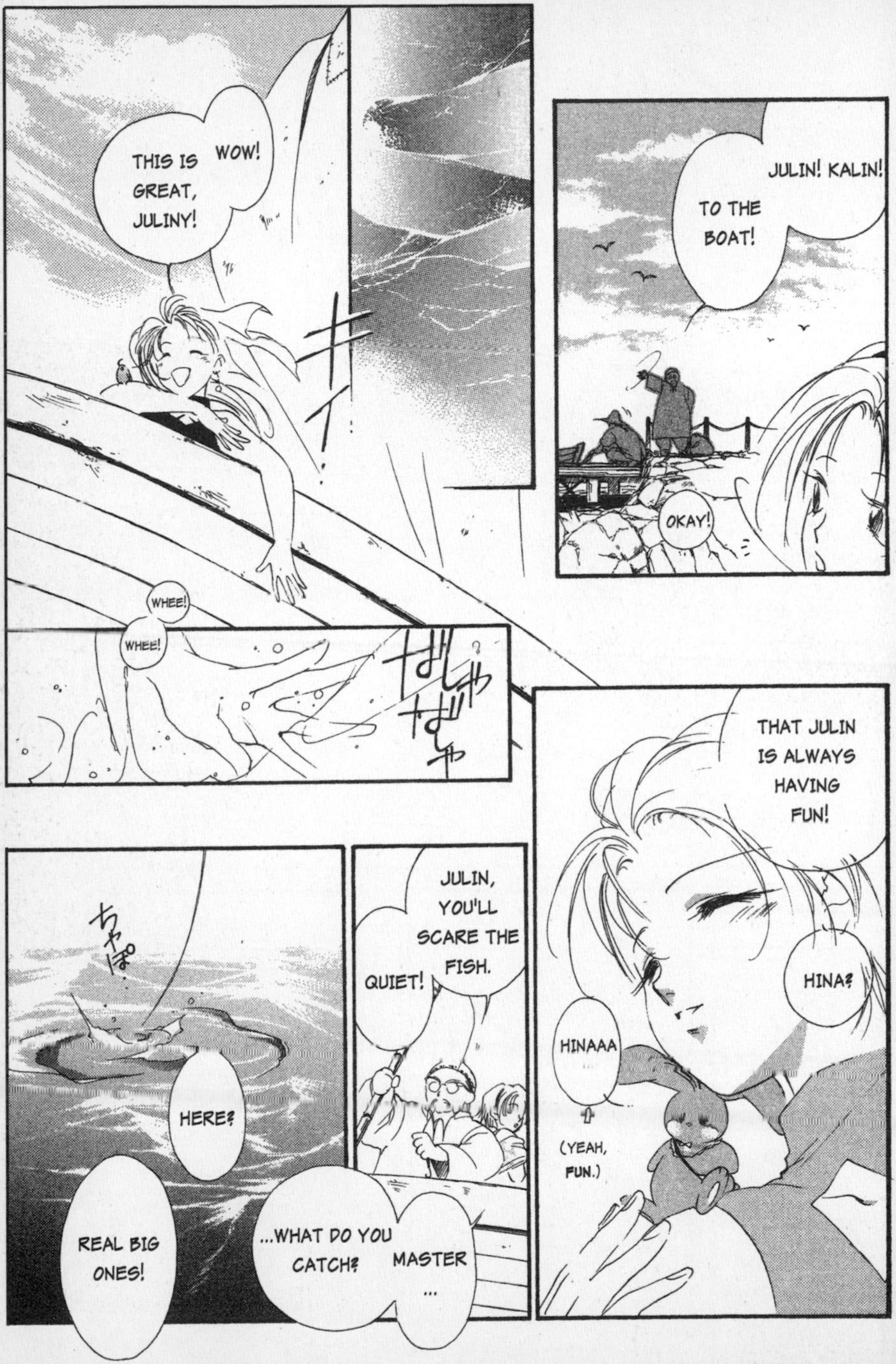

JULIN! KALIN! TO THE BOAT!
OKAY!
WOW! THIS IS GREAT, JULINY!
THAT JULIN IS ALWAYS HAVING FUN!
HINA?
HINAAA ...
(YEAH, FUN.)
WHEE!
WHEE!
ばしゃ ばしゃ
QUIET!
JULIN, YOU'LL SCARE THE FISH.
MASTER ...
...WHAT DO YOU CATCH?
ちゃぽ
HERE?
REAL BIG ONES!

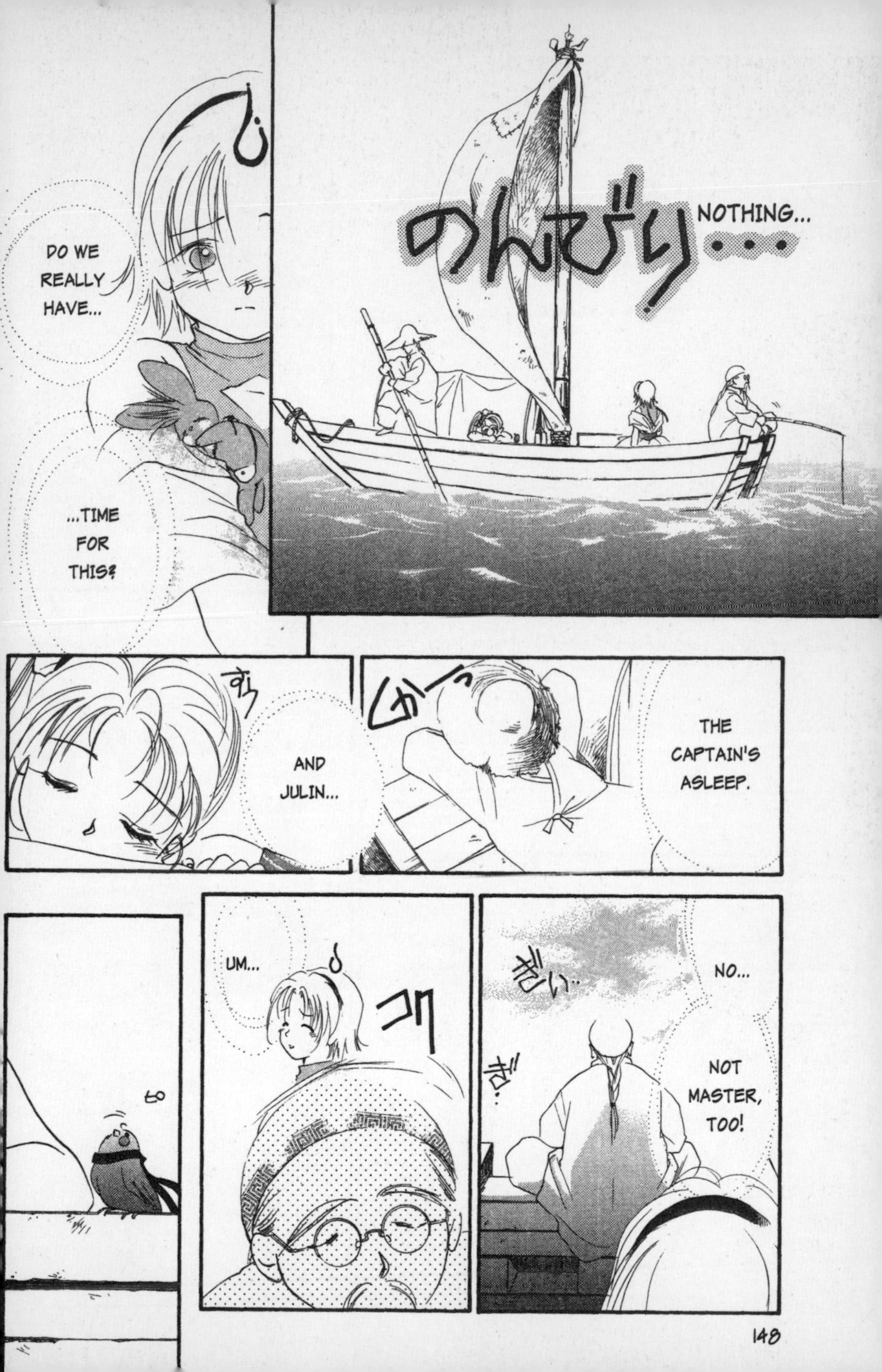
のんびり…
NOTHING...
DO WE REALLY HAVE...
...TIME FOR THIS?
THE CAPTAIN'S ASLEEP.
AND JULIN...
NO...
NOT MASTER, TOO!
UM...

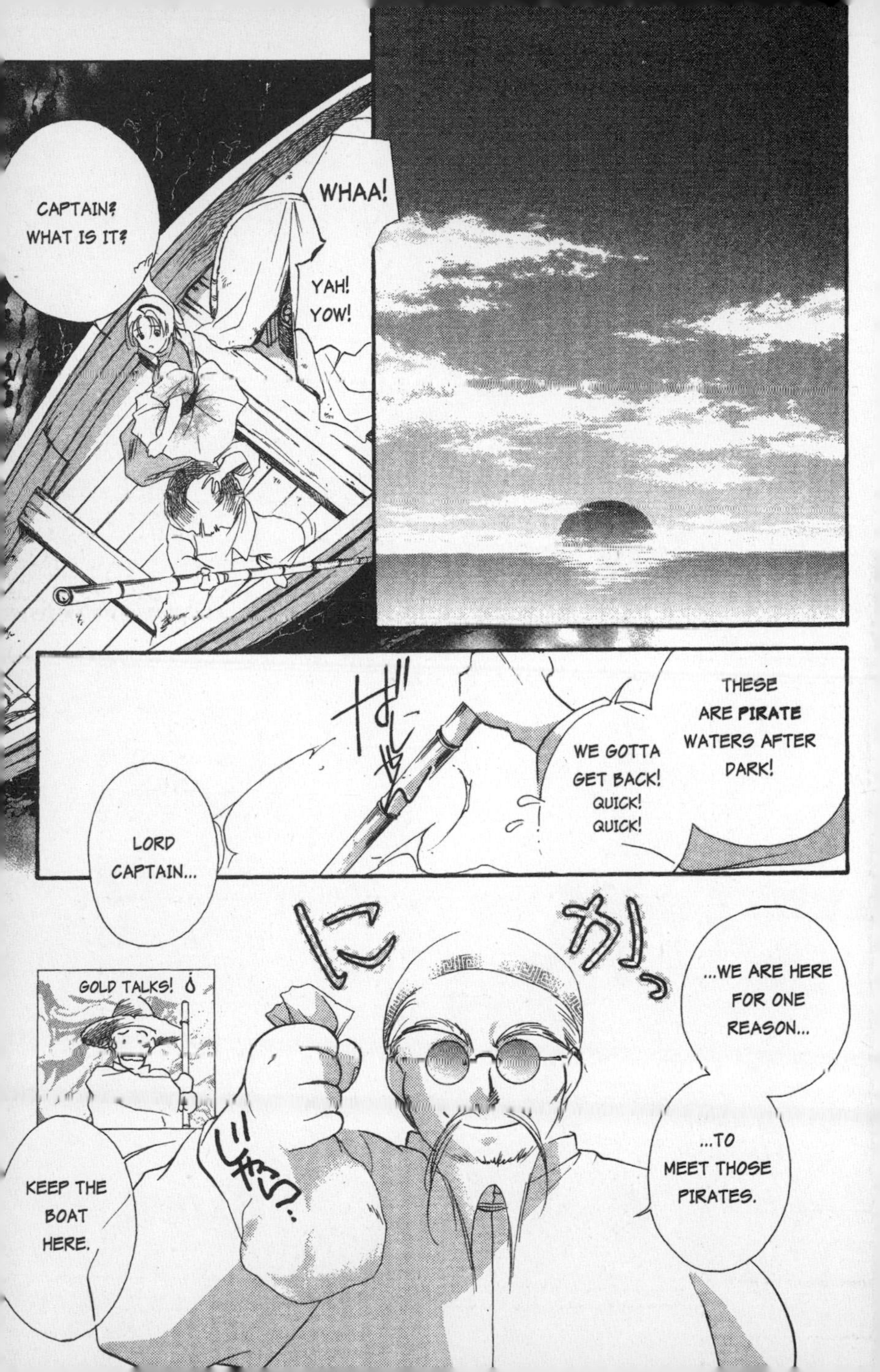
WHAA!
YAH! YOW!
CAPTAIN? WHAT IS IT?
THESE ARE PIRATE WATERS AFTER DARK!
WE GOTTA GET BACK! QUICK! QUICK!
LORD CAPTAIN...
にかっ
...WE ARE HERE FOR ONE REASON...
...TO MEET THOSE PIRATES.
GOLD TALKS!
KEEP THE BOAT HERE.

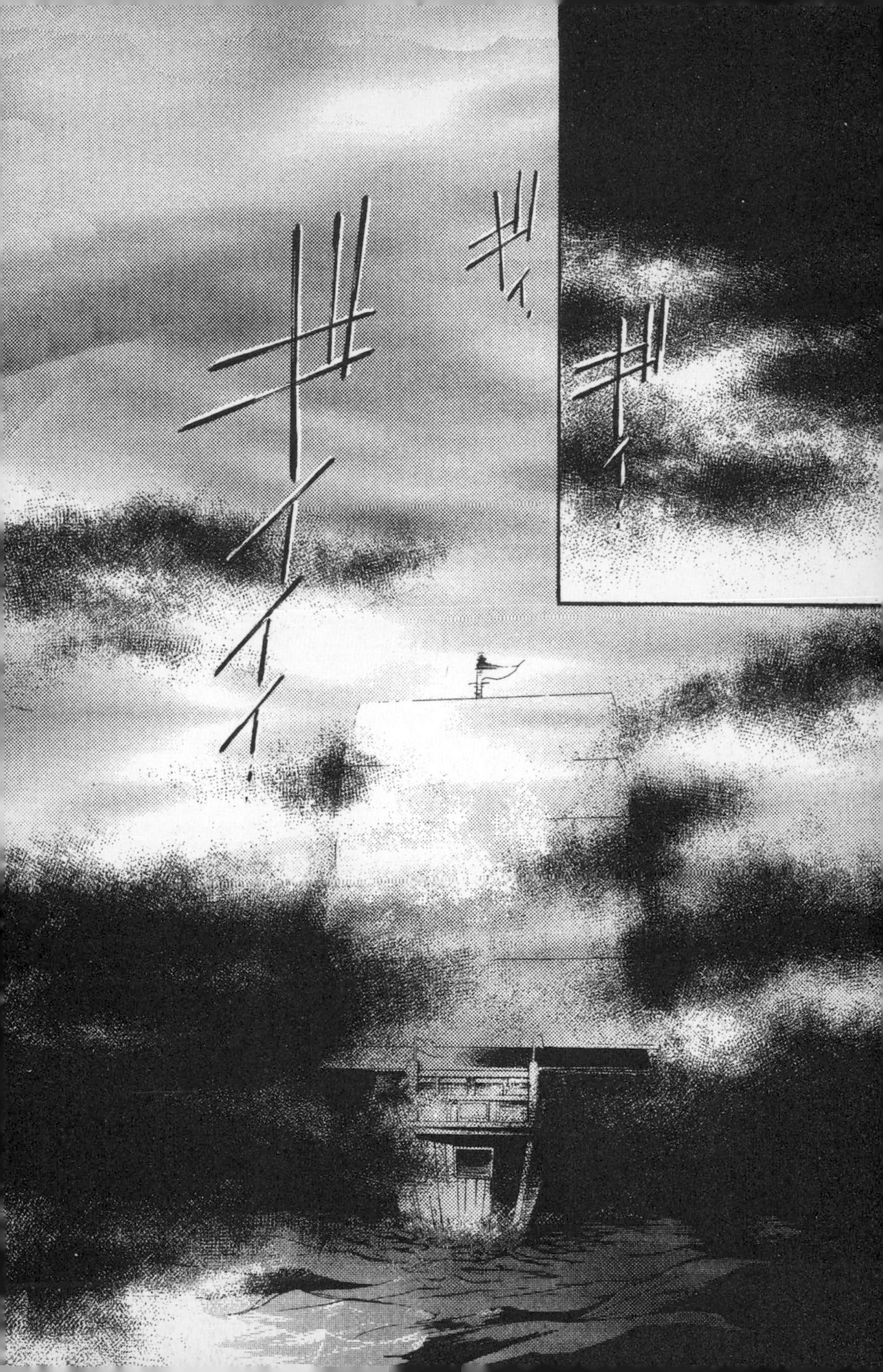
ギィ…
ギィ、
ギイイイイ…!

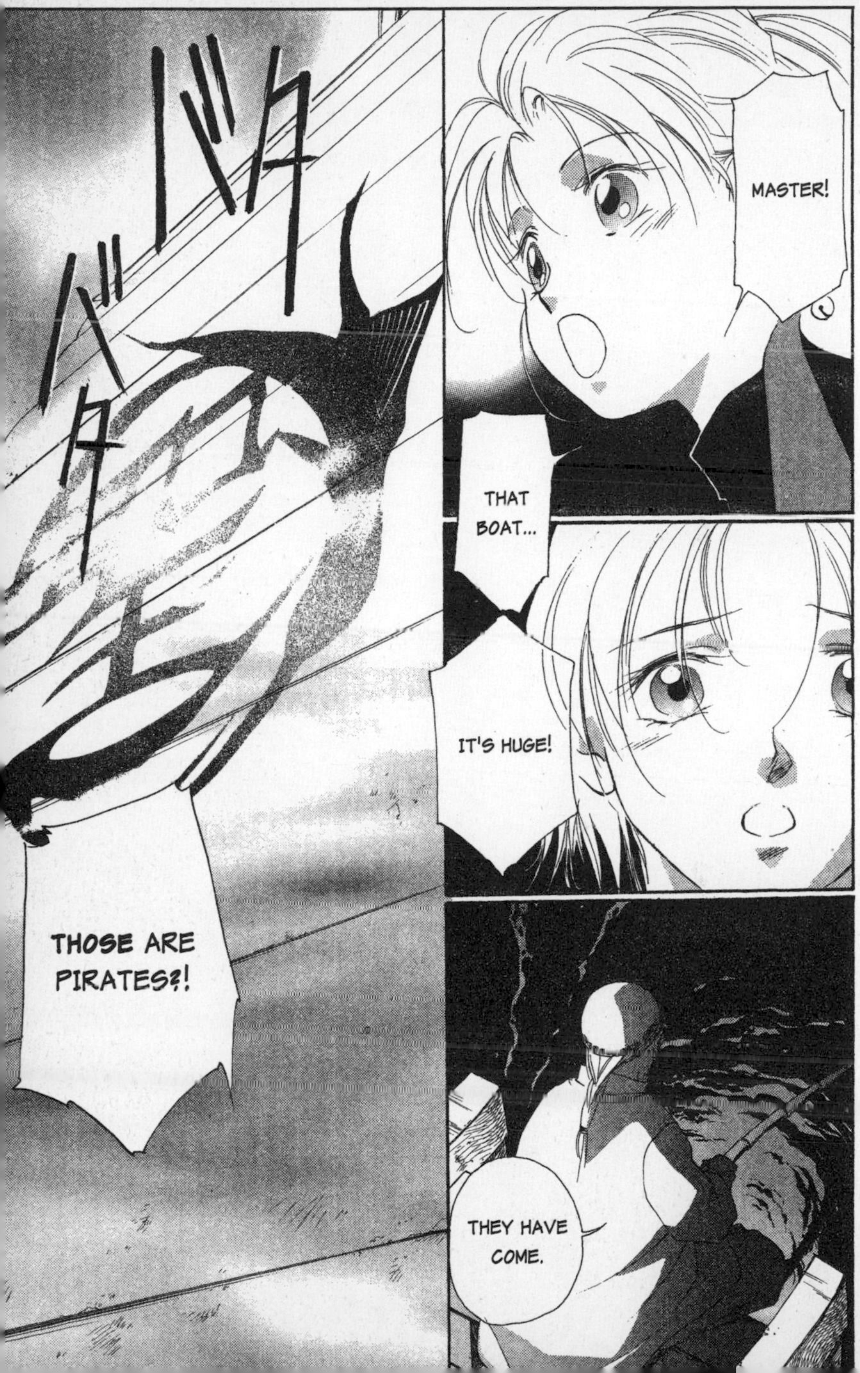
MASTER!
THAT BOAT...
IT'S HUGE!
THEY HAVE COME.
バタバタ
THOSE ARE PIRATES?!

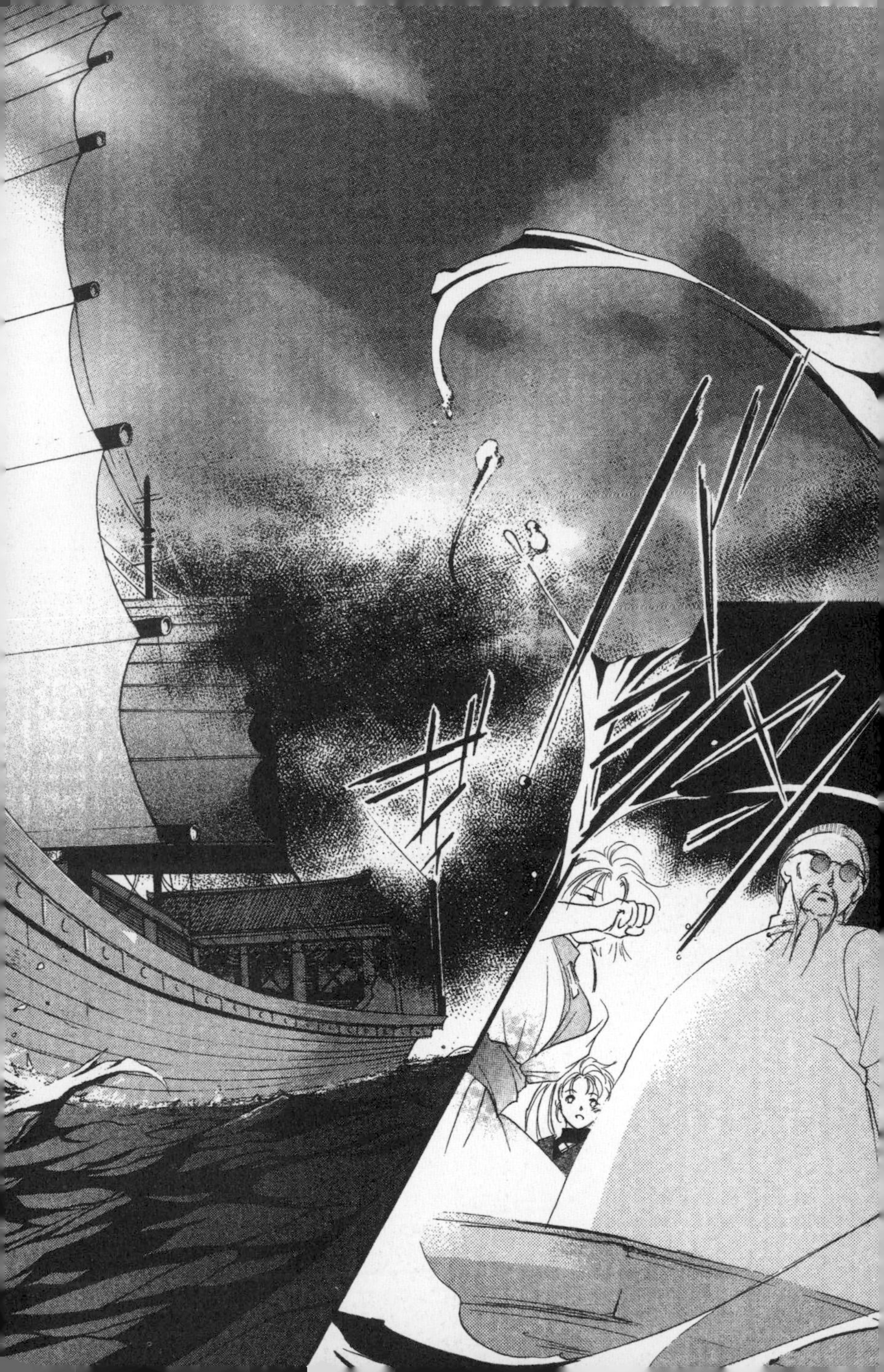

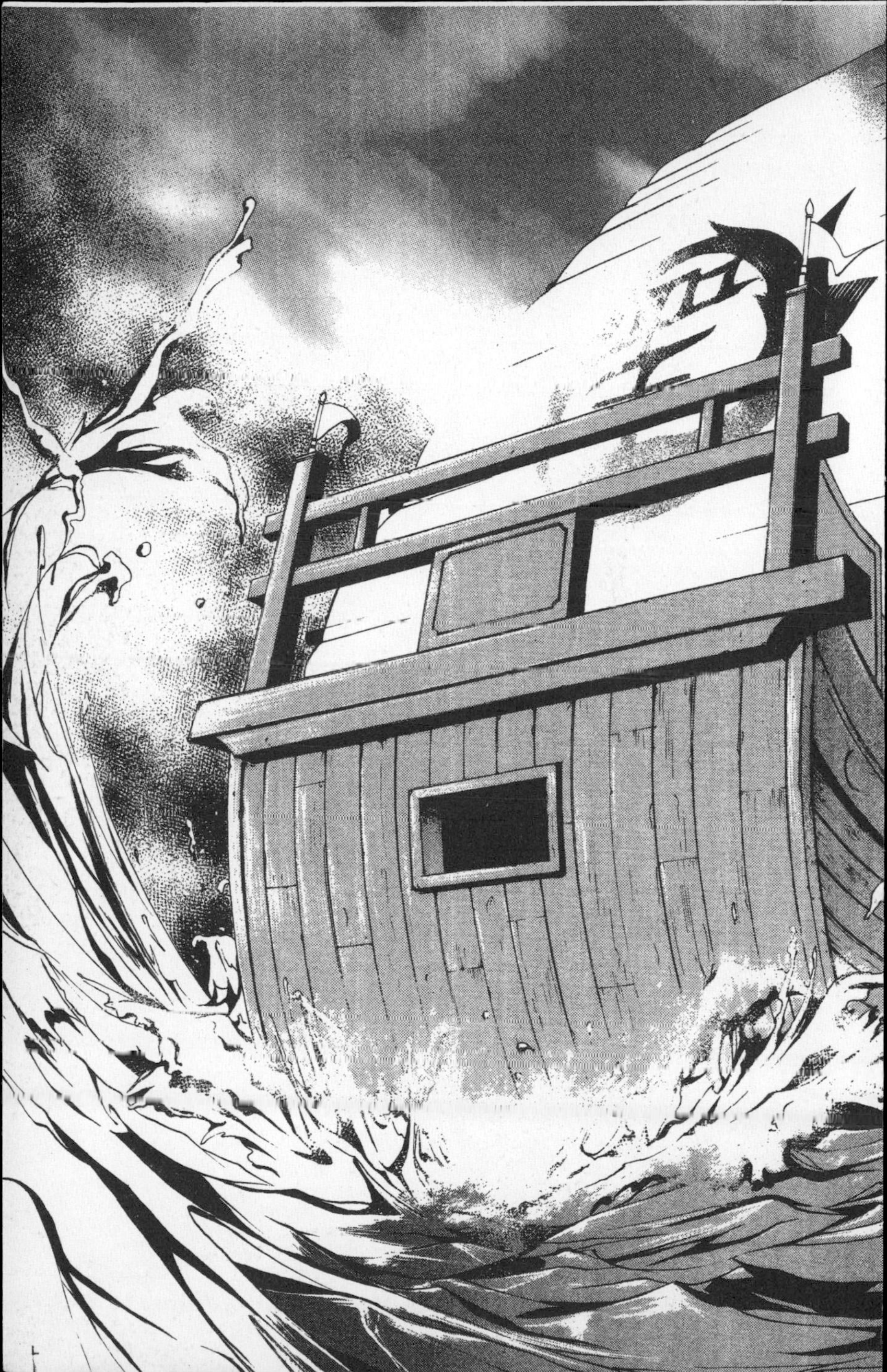

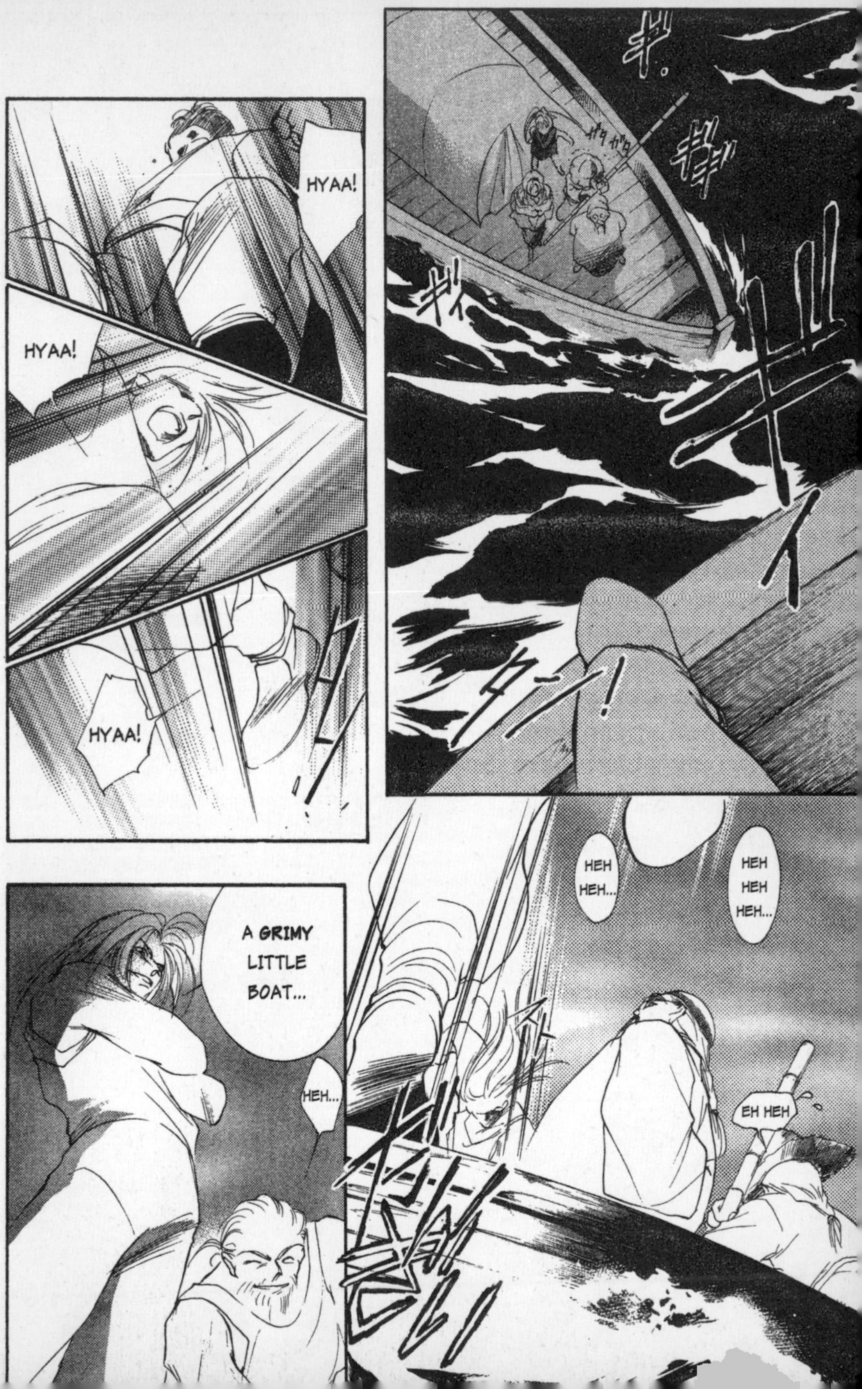
HYAA!
HYAA!
HYAA!
HEH HEH HEH...
HEH HEH...
EH HEH
A GRIMY LITTLE BOAT...
HEH...

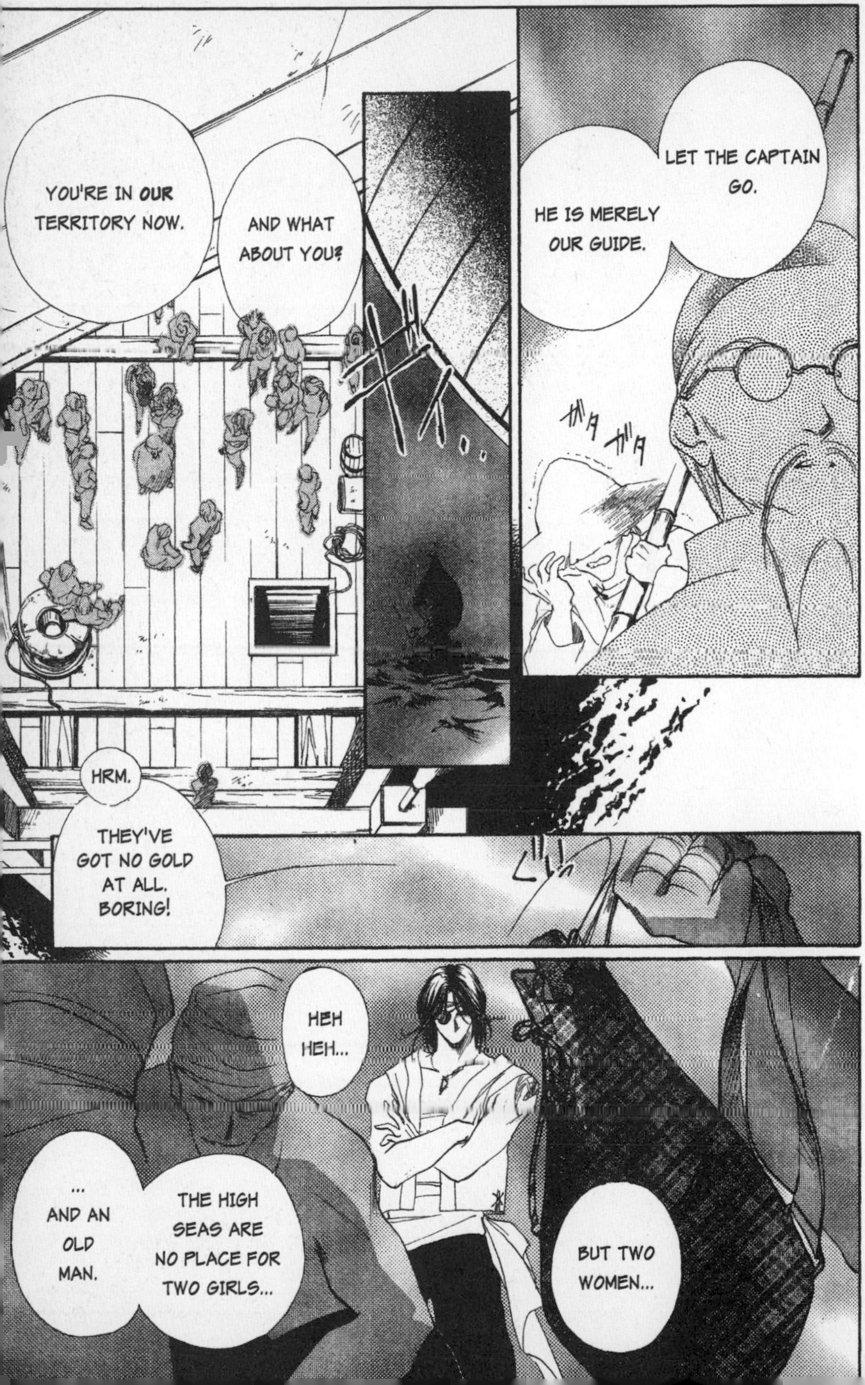
LET THE CAPTAIN GO.
HE IS MERELY OUR GUIDE.
ガタ ガタ
AND WHAT ABOUT YOU?
YOU'RE IN OUR TERRITORY NOW.
HRM.
THEY'VE GOT NO GOLD AT ALL. BORING!
HEH HEH...
BUT TWO WOMEN...
THE HIGH SEAS ARE NO PLACE FOR TWO GIRLS...
... AND AN OLD MAN.

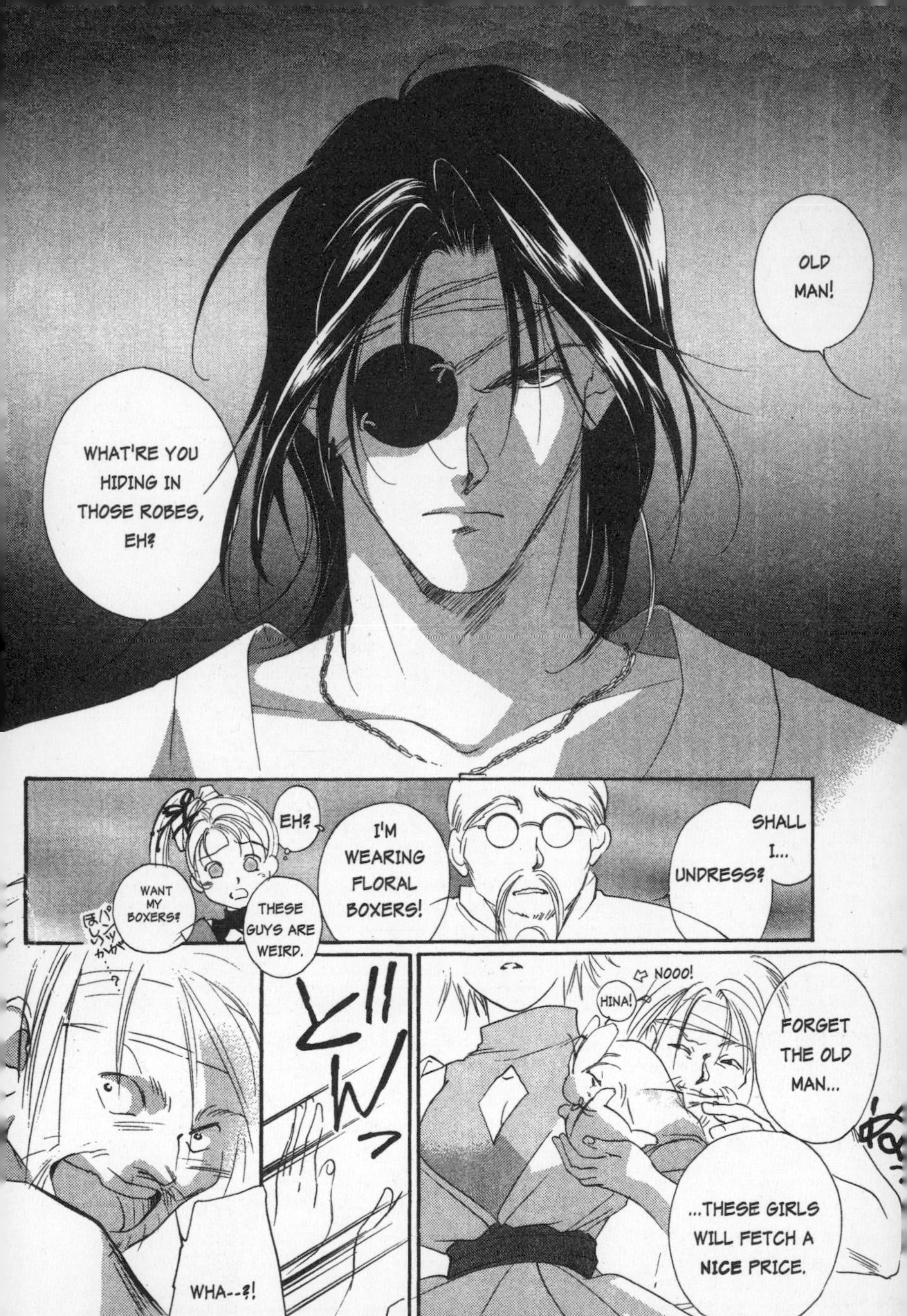
OLD MAN!
WHAT'RE YOU HIDING IN THOSE ROBES, EH?
SHALL I... UNDRESS?
I'M WEARING FLORAL BOXERS!
EH?
THESE GUYS ARE WEIRD.
WANT MY BOXERS?
FORGET THE OLD MAN...
NOOO!
HINA!
...THESE GIRLS WILL FETCH A NICE PRICE.
WHA--?!

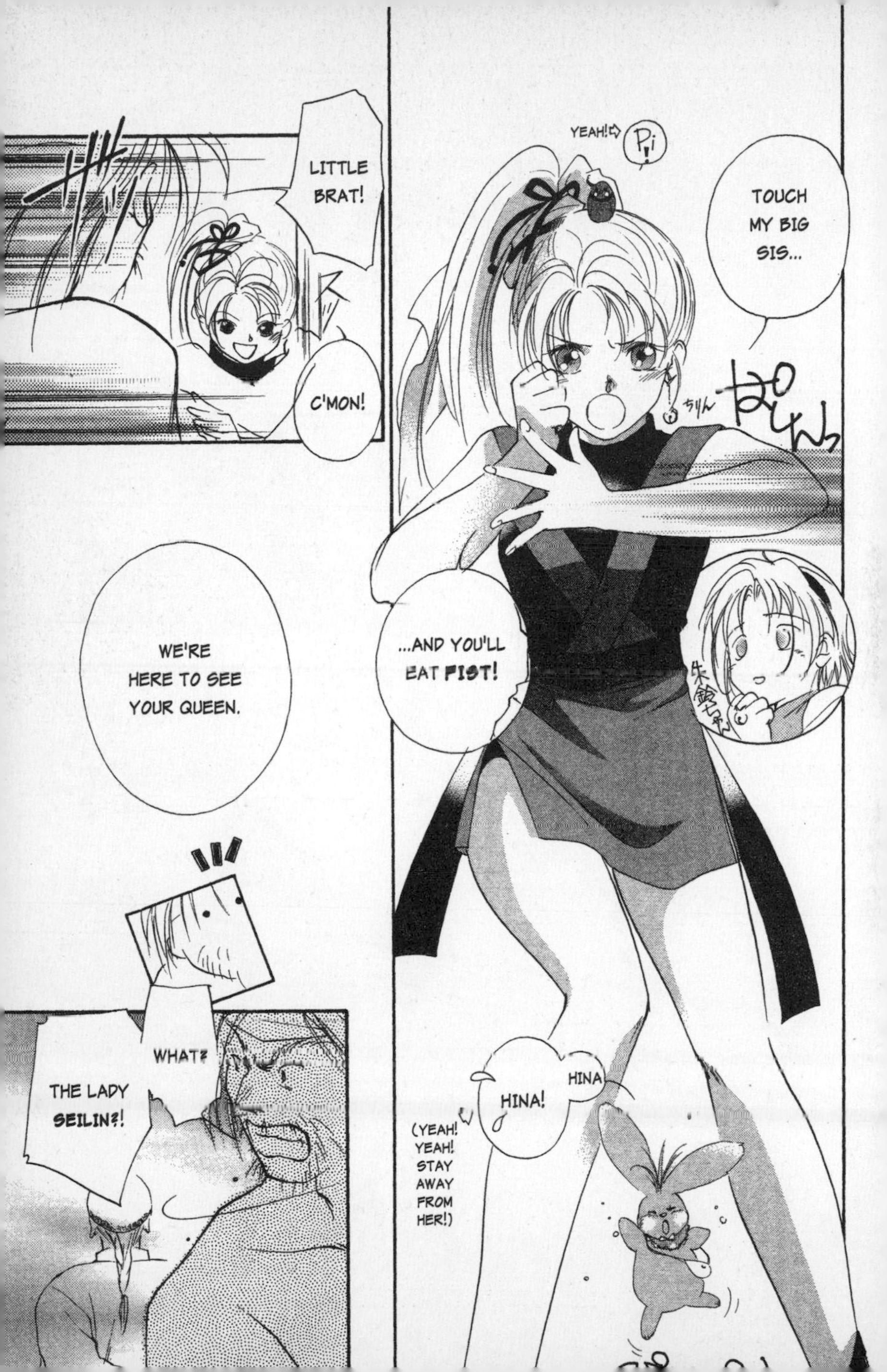
YEAH!⇨ Pi
TOUCH MY BIG SIS...
ちりん
...AND YOU'LL EAT FIST!
HINA
HINA!
(YEAH! YEAH! STAY AWAY FROM HER!)
LITTLE BRAT!
C'MON!
WE'RE HERE TO SEE YOUR QUEEN.
WHAT?
THE LADY SEILIN?!

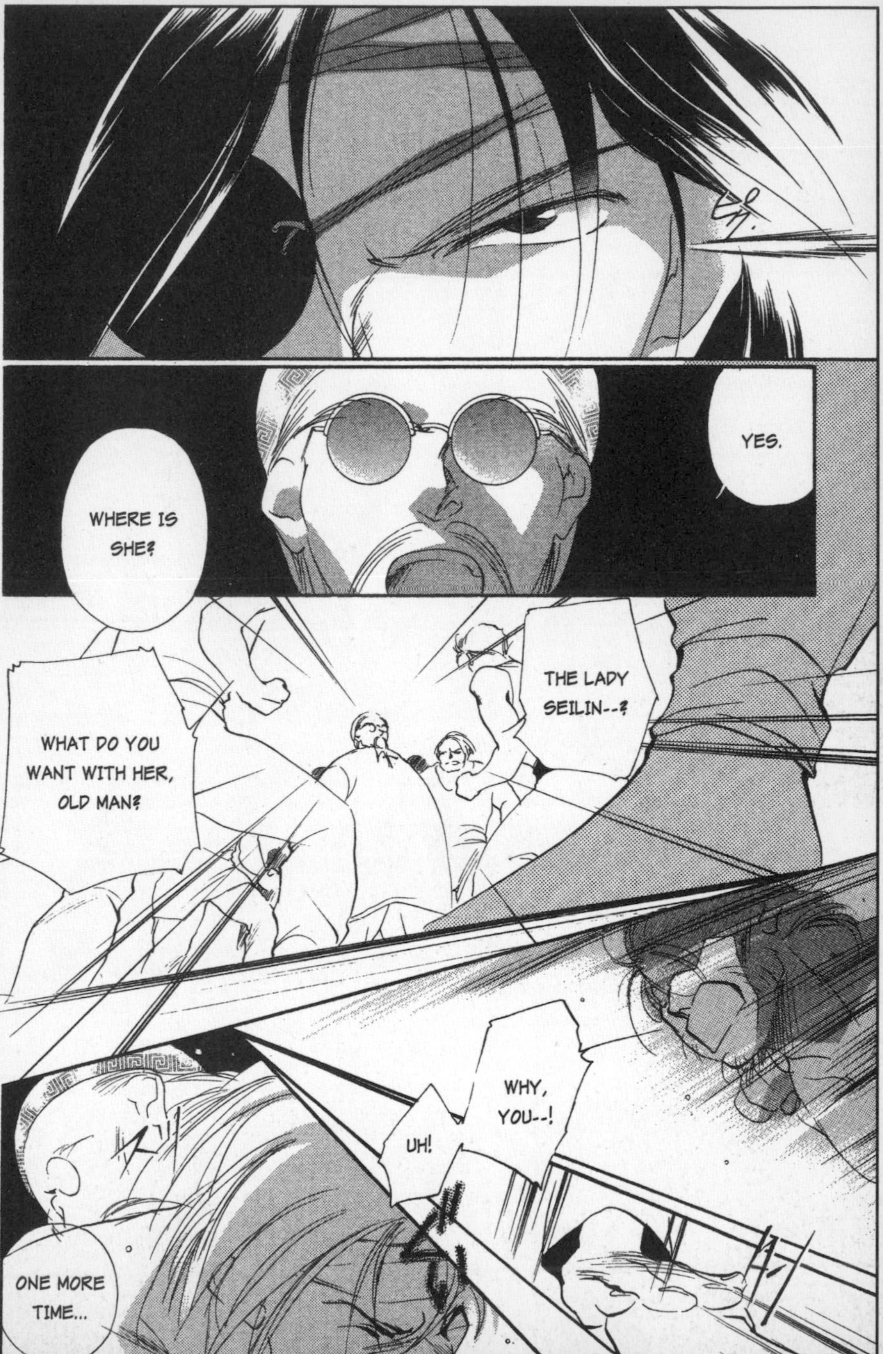
YES.
WHERE IS SHE?
THE LADY SEILIN--?
WHAT DO YOU WANT WITH HER, OLD MAN?
WHY, YOU--!
UH!
ONE MORE TIME...

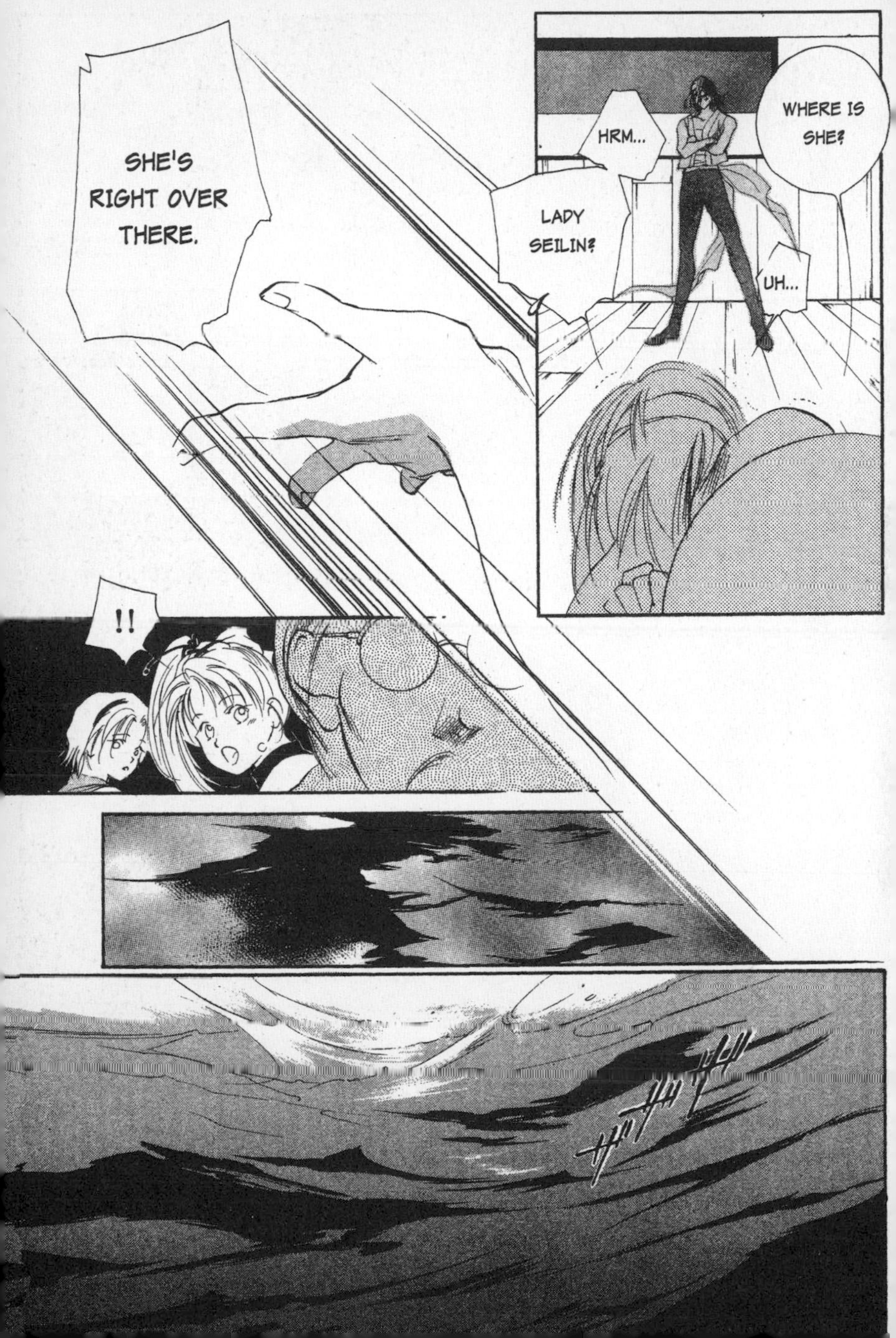
WHERE IS SHE?
HRM...
LADY SEILIN?
UH...
SHE'S RIGHT OVER THERE.
!!

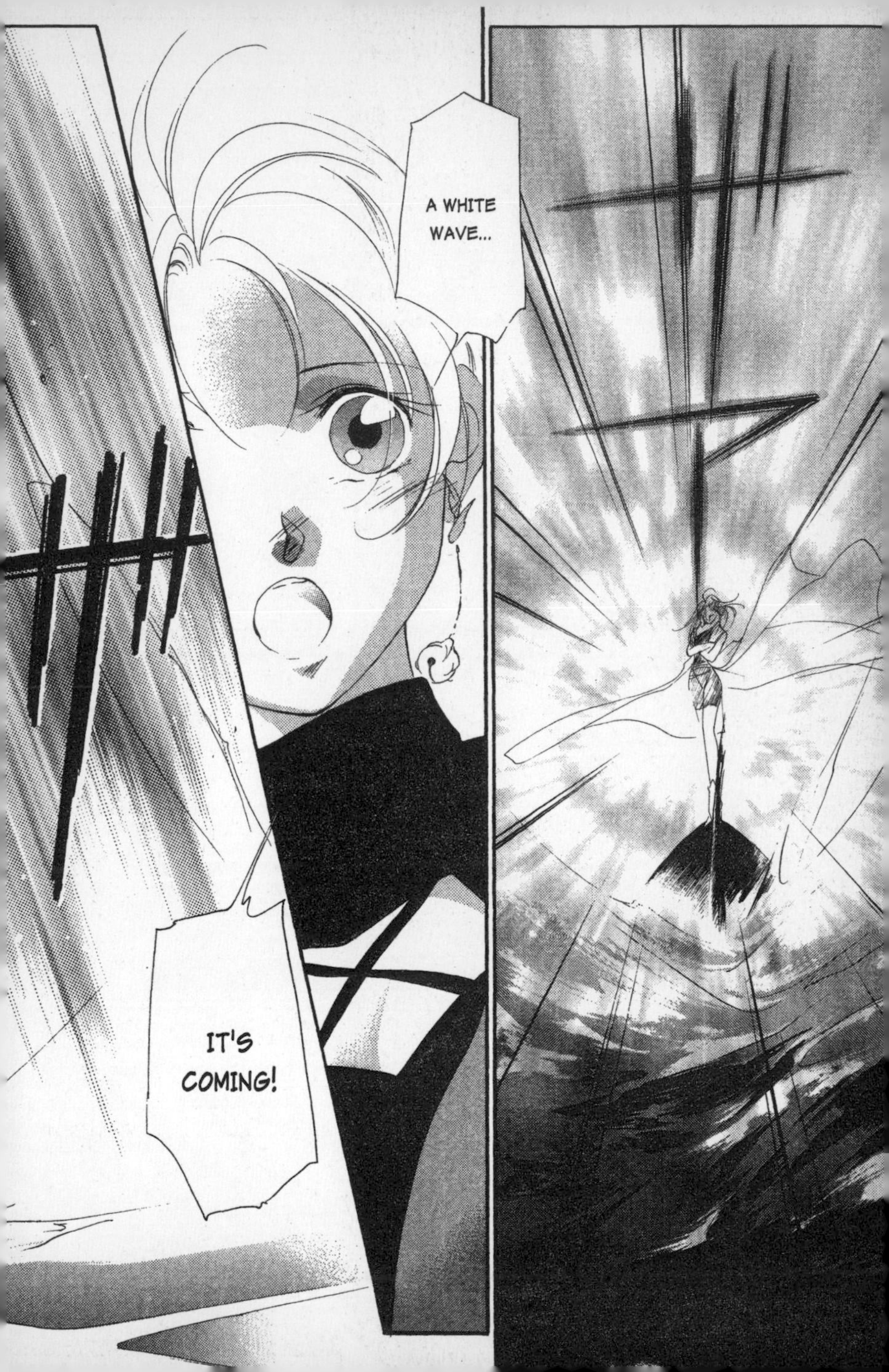
A WHITE WAVE...
IT'S COMING!

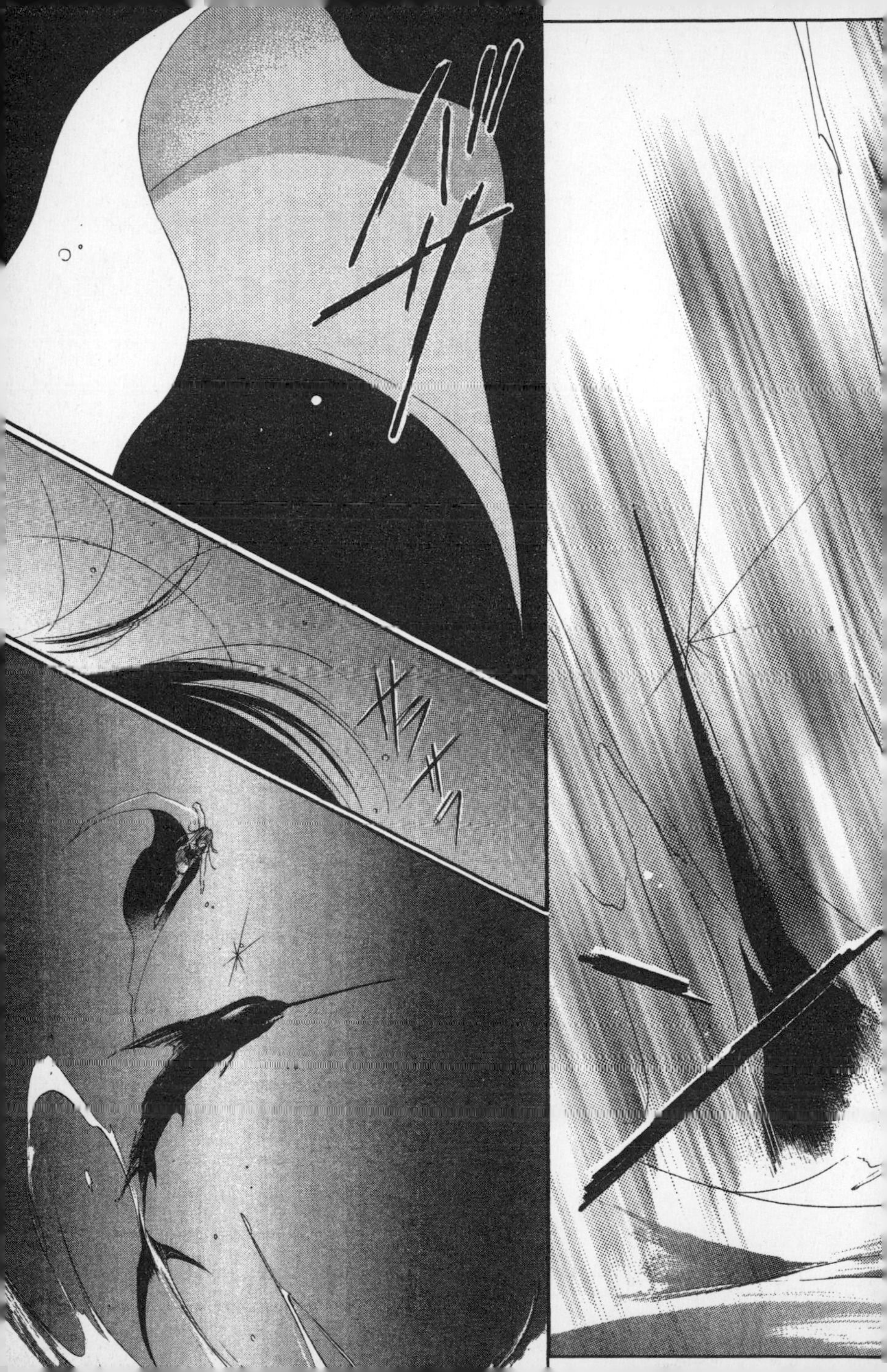
バサ

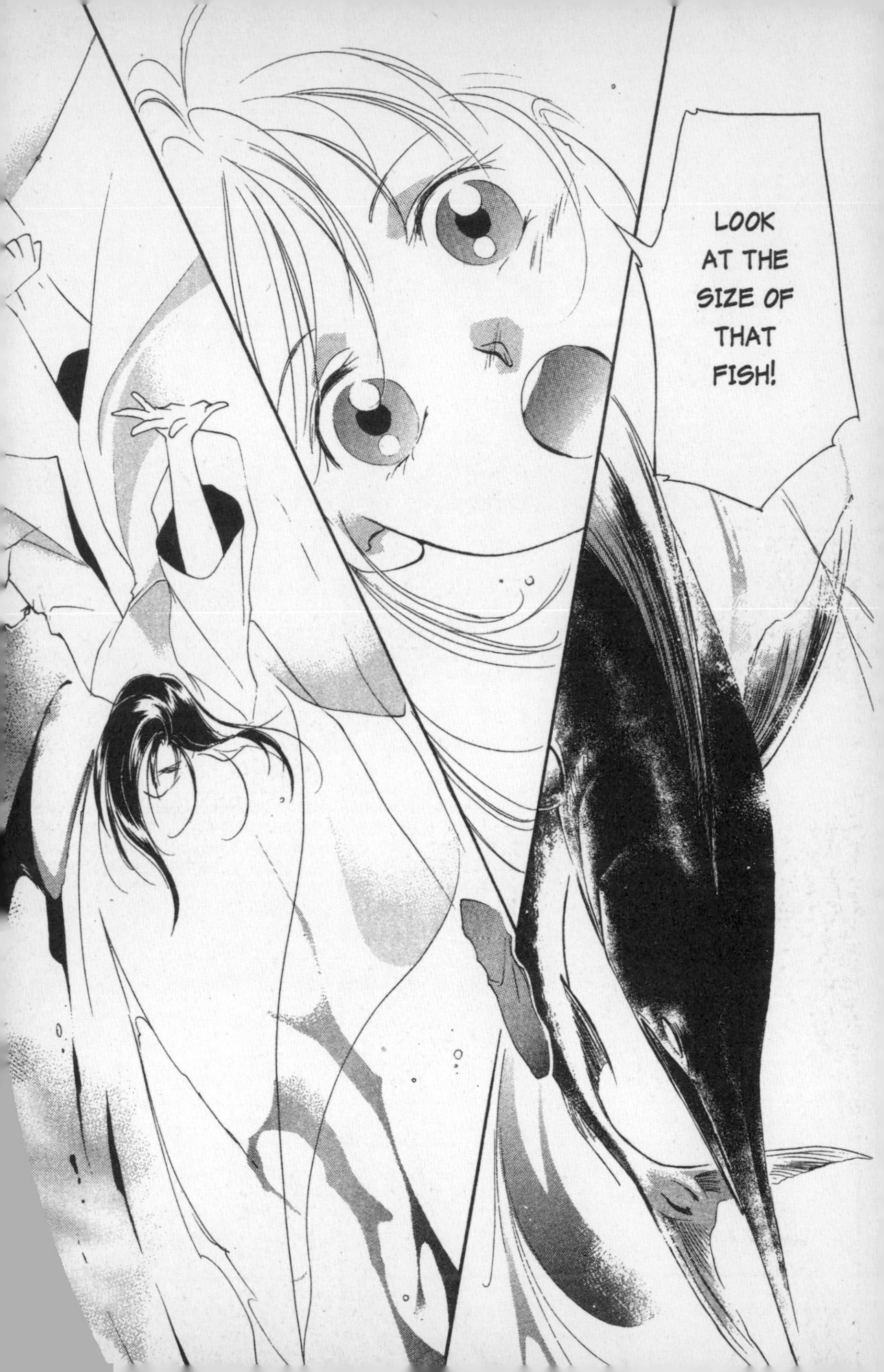
LOOK AT THE SIZE OF THAT FISH!

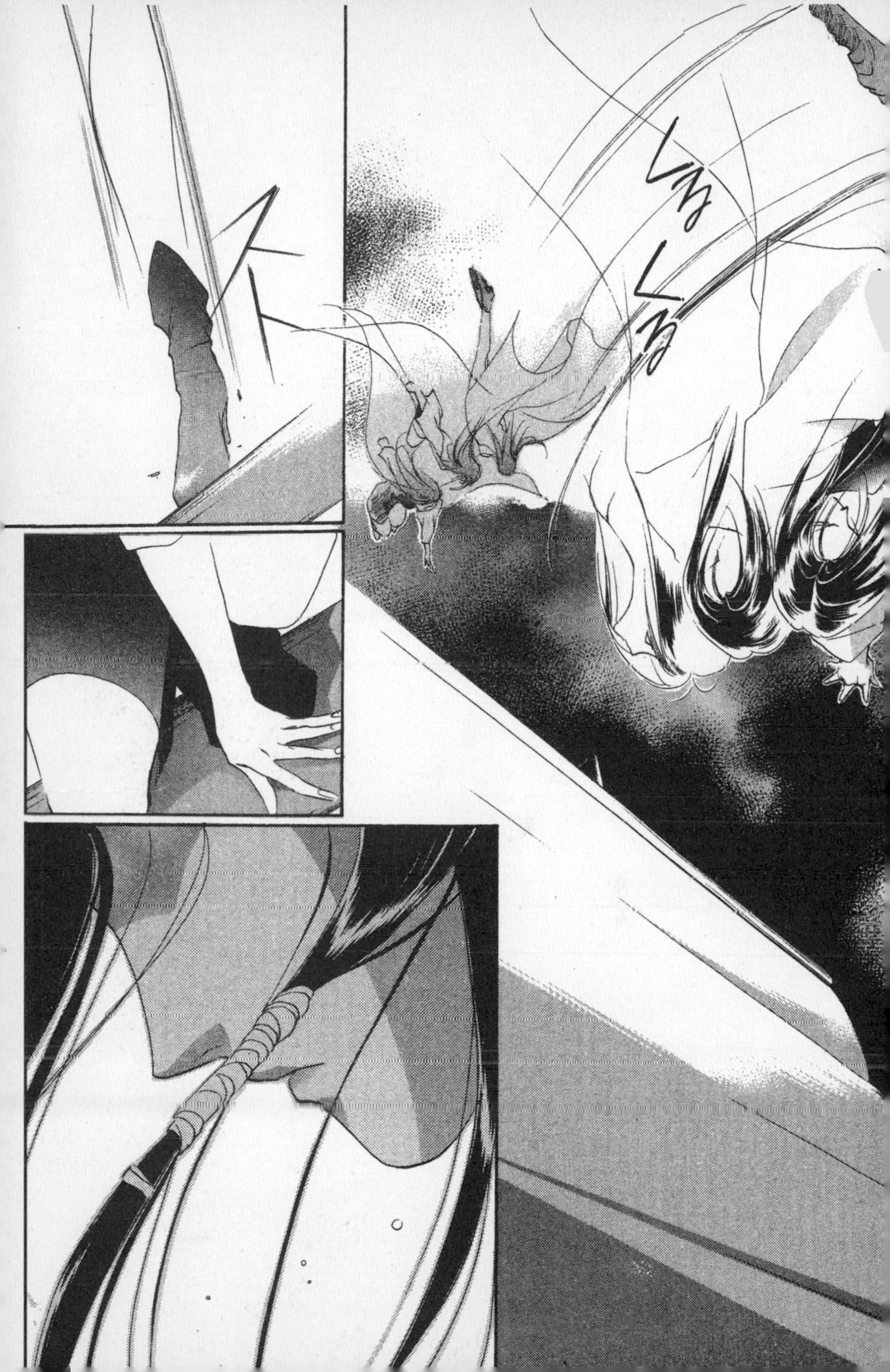
くるくる

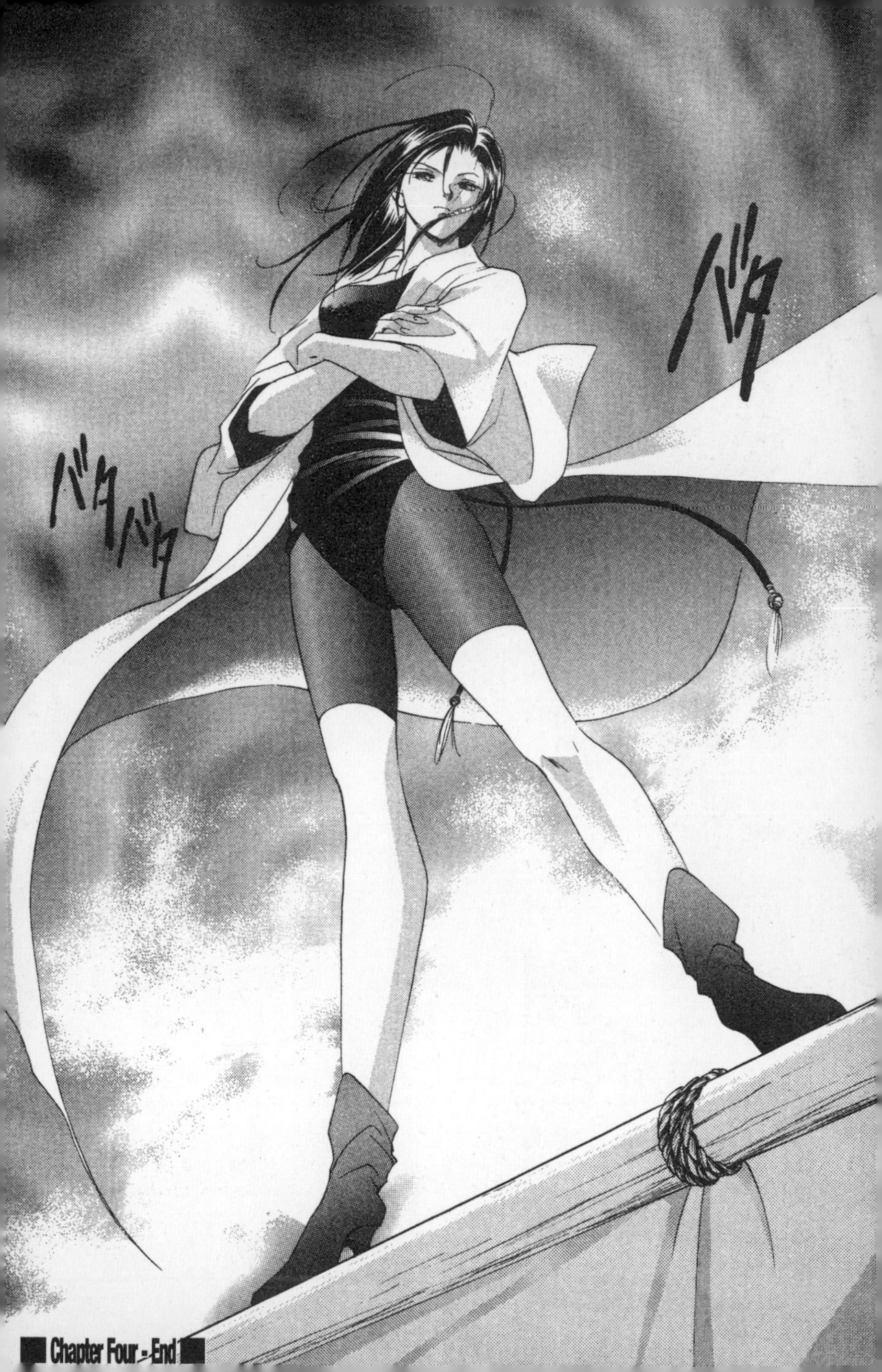
バタ
バタバタ

Chapter Four - End

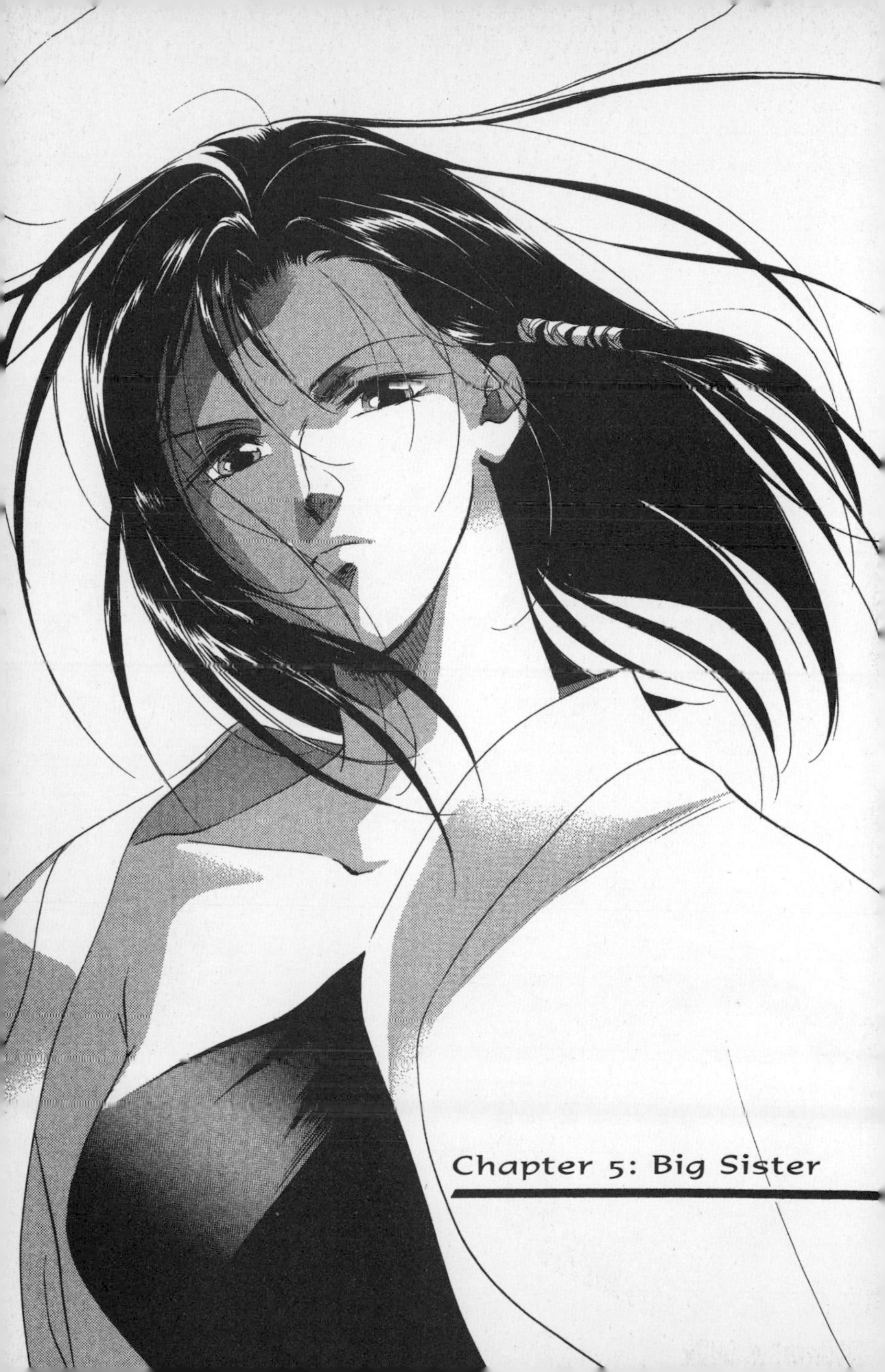

Chapter 5: Big Sister

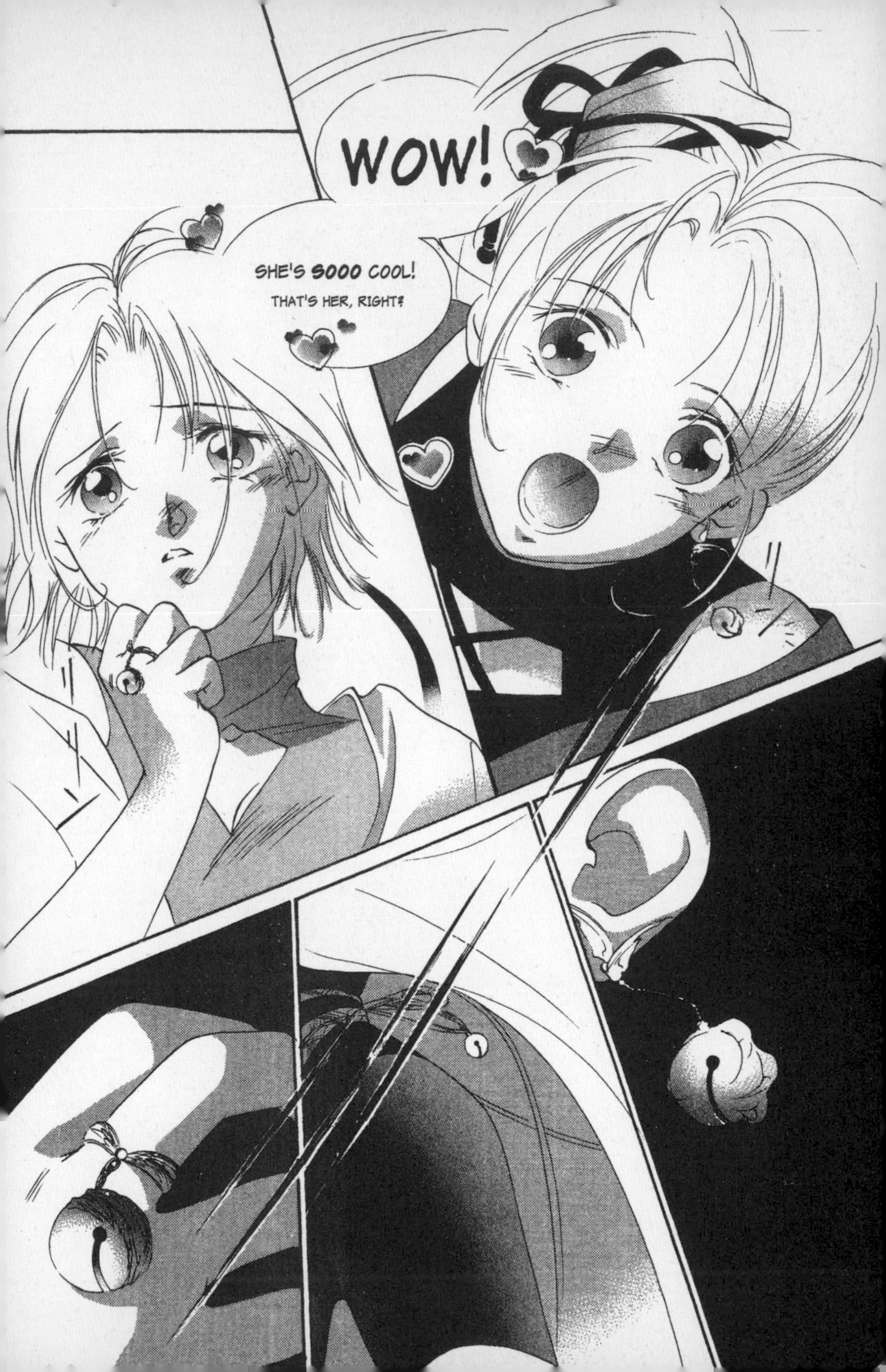
WOW!
SHE'S SOOO COOL!
THAT'S HER, RIGHT?

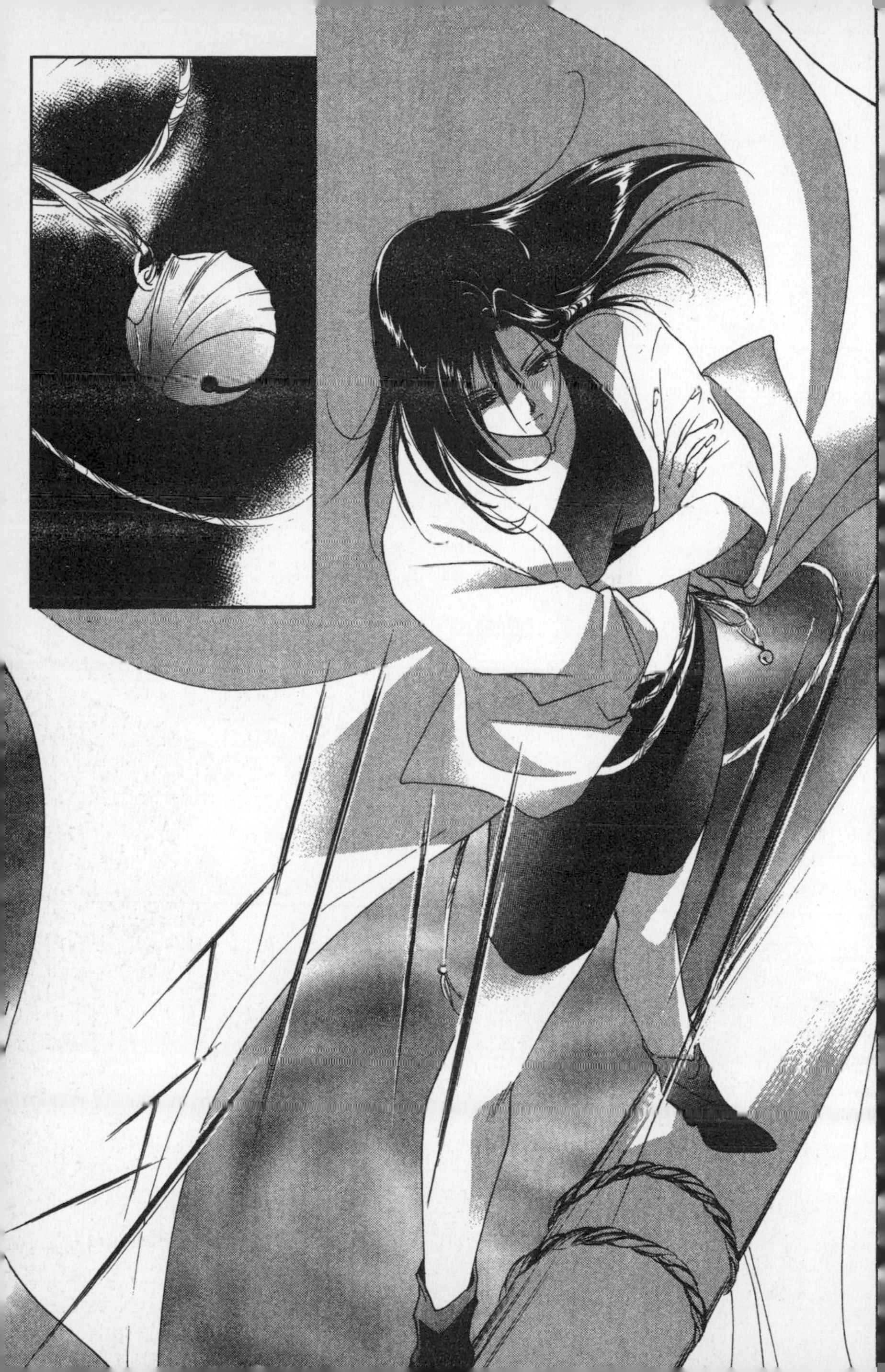

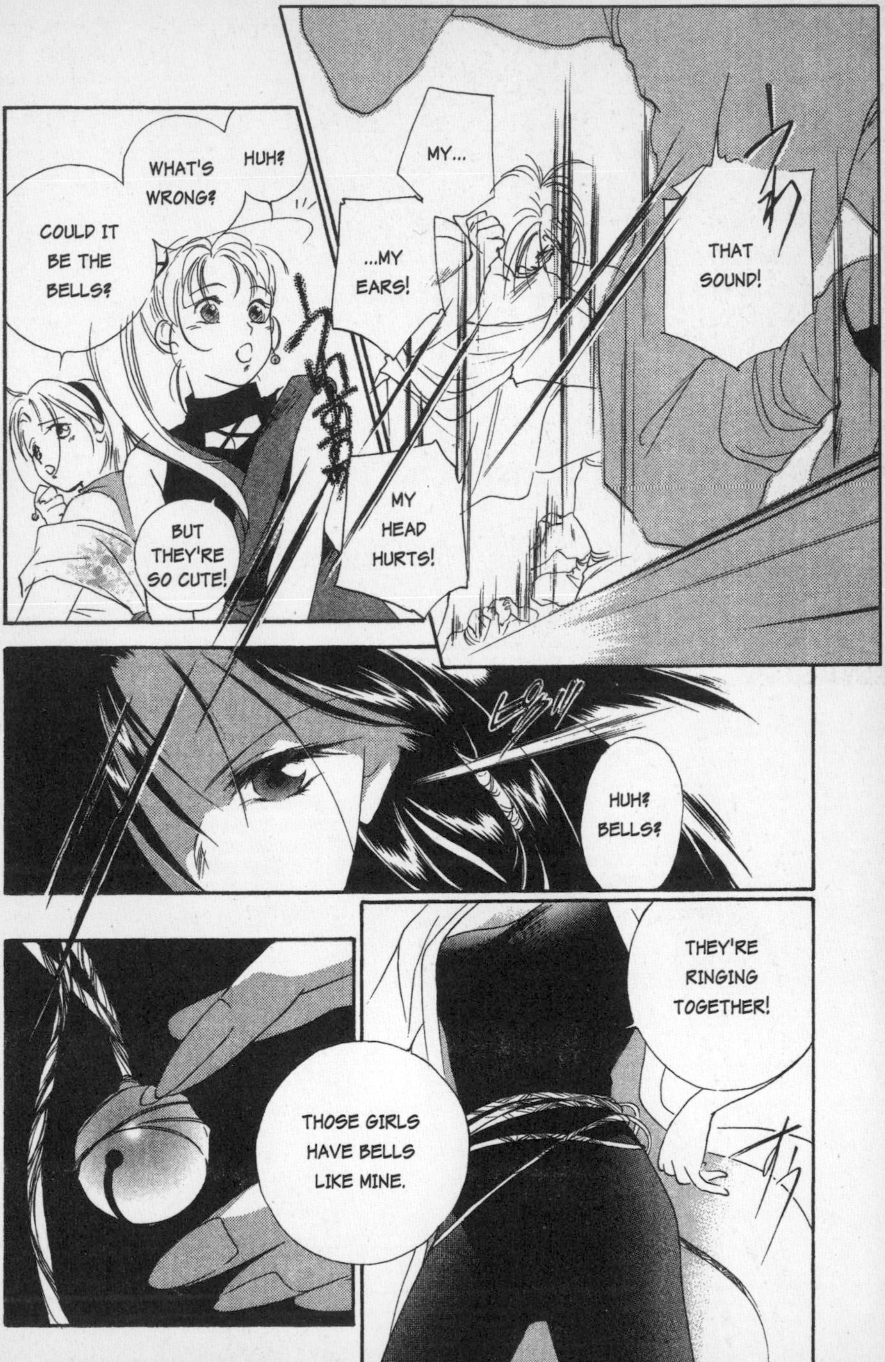
THAT SOUND!
MY...
...MY EARS!
MY HEAD HURTS!
HUH?
WHAT'S WRONG?
COULD IT BE THE BELLS?
BUT THEY'RE SO CUTE!
HUH? BELLS?
THEY'RE RINGING TOGETHER!
THOSE GIRLS HAVE BELLS LIKE MINE.

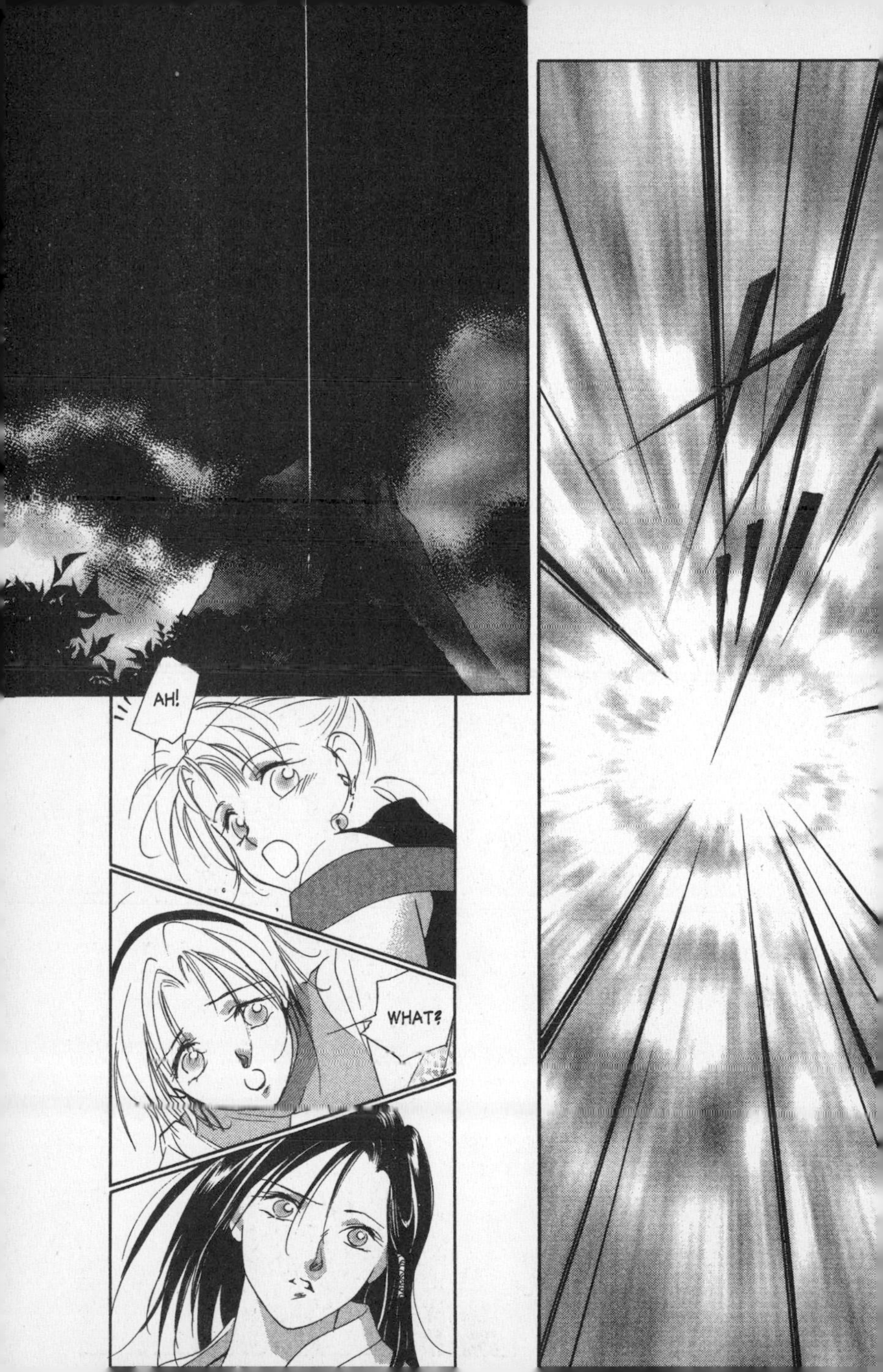
AH!
WHAT?

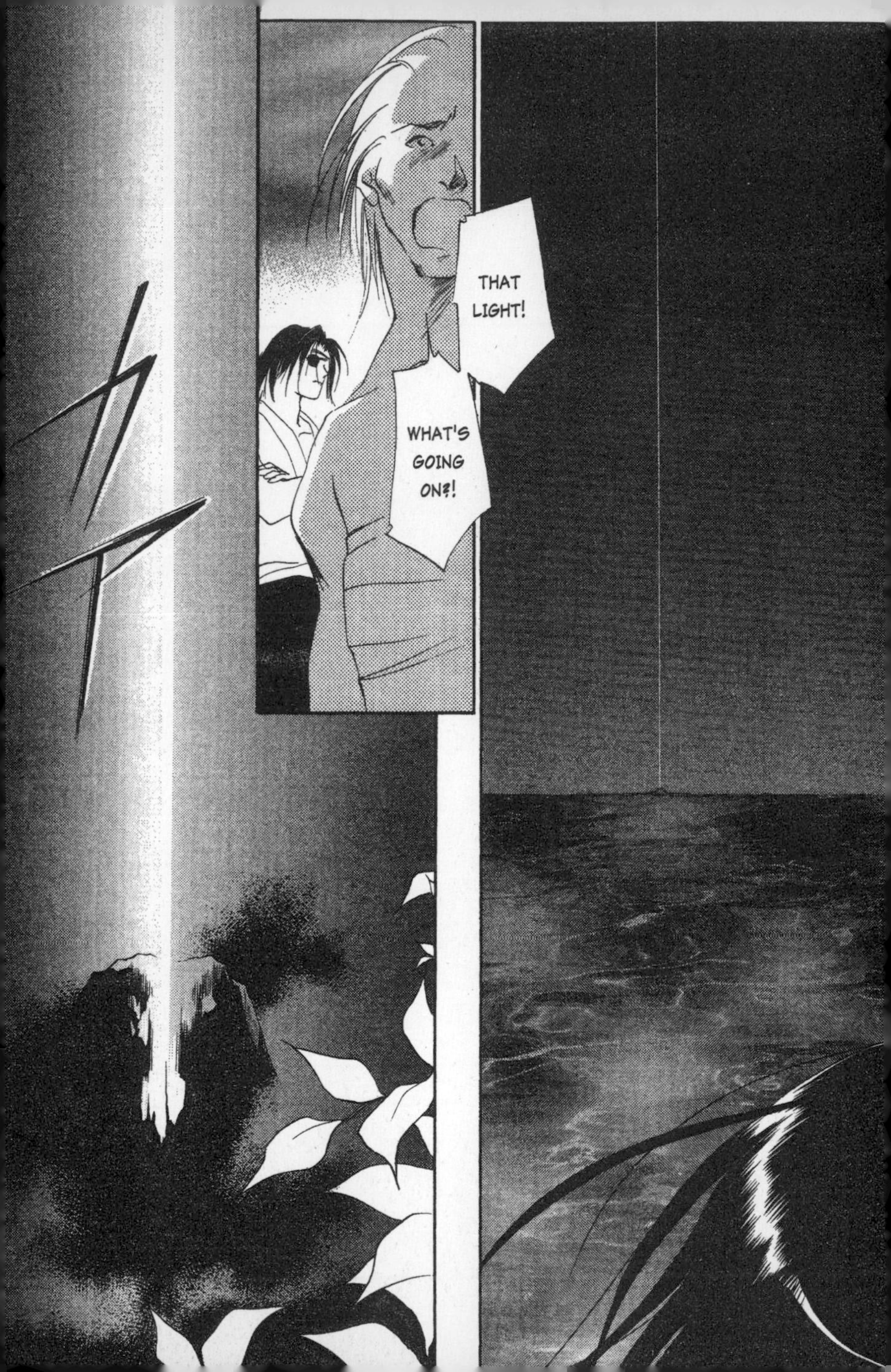
THAT LIGHT!
WHAT'S GOING ON?!

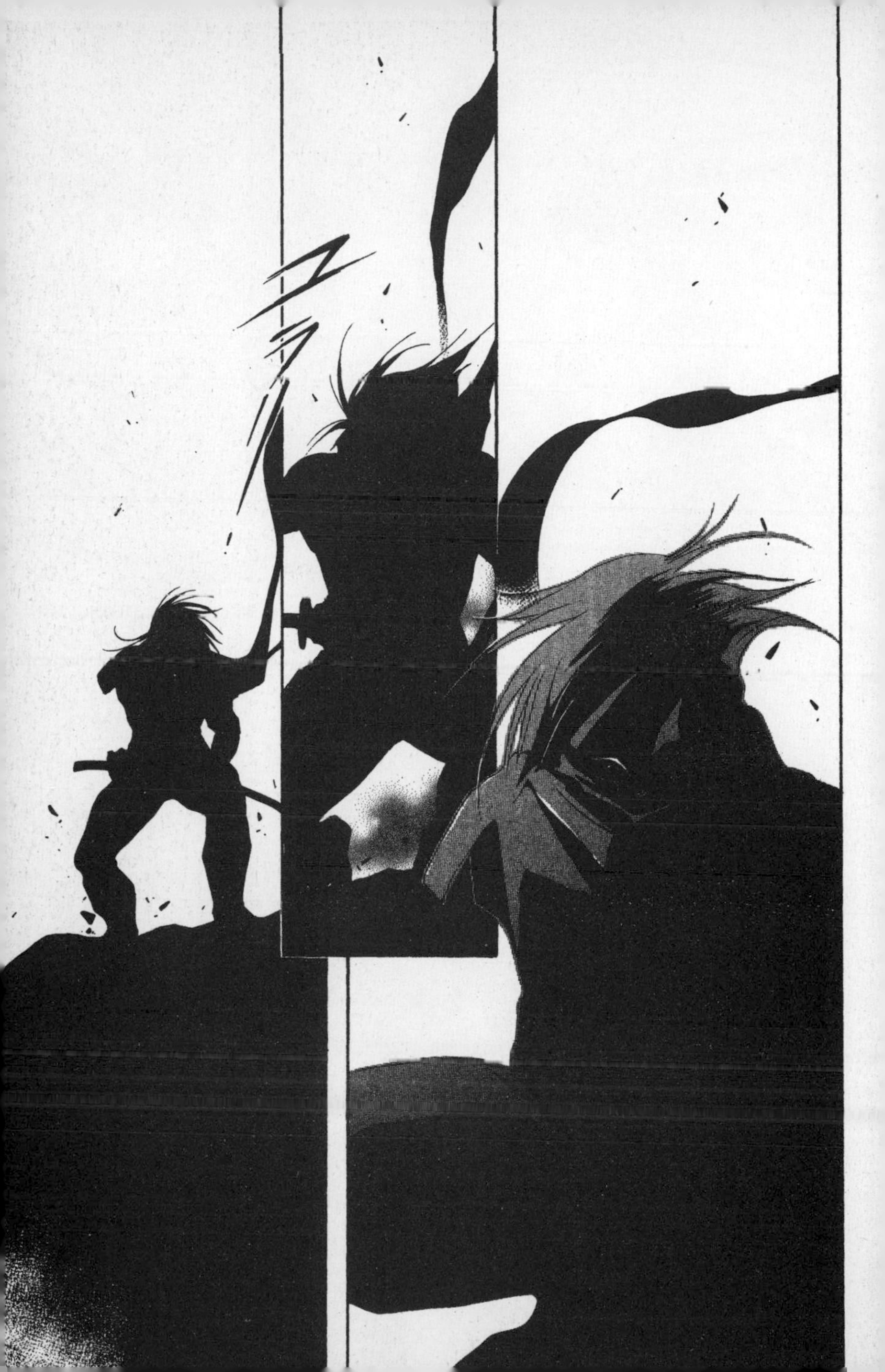

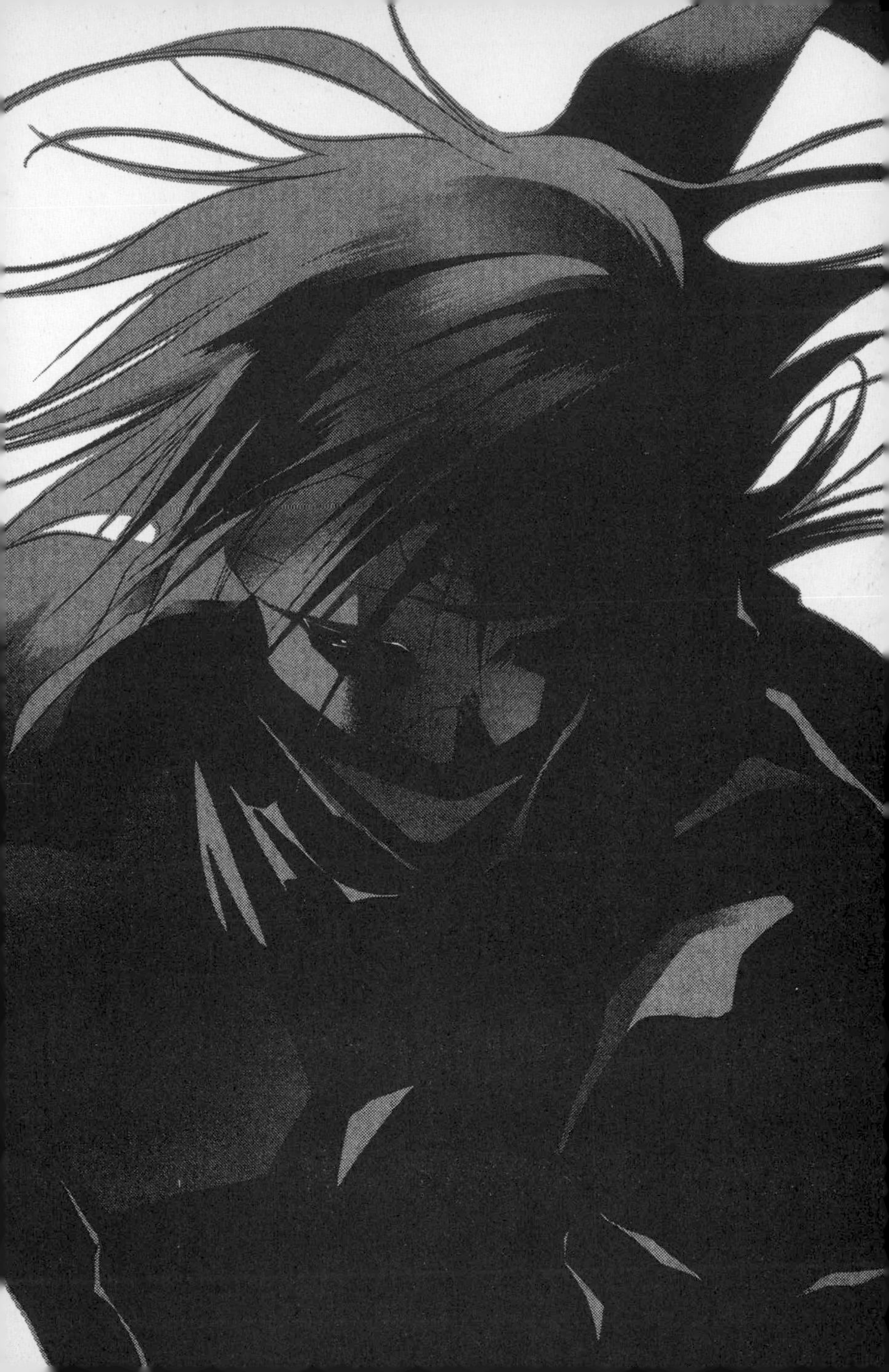

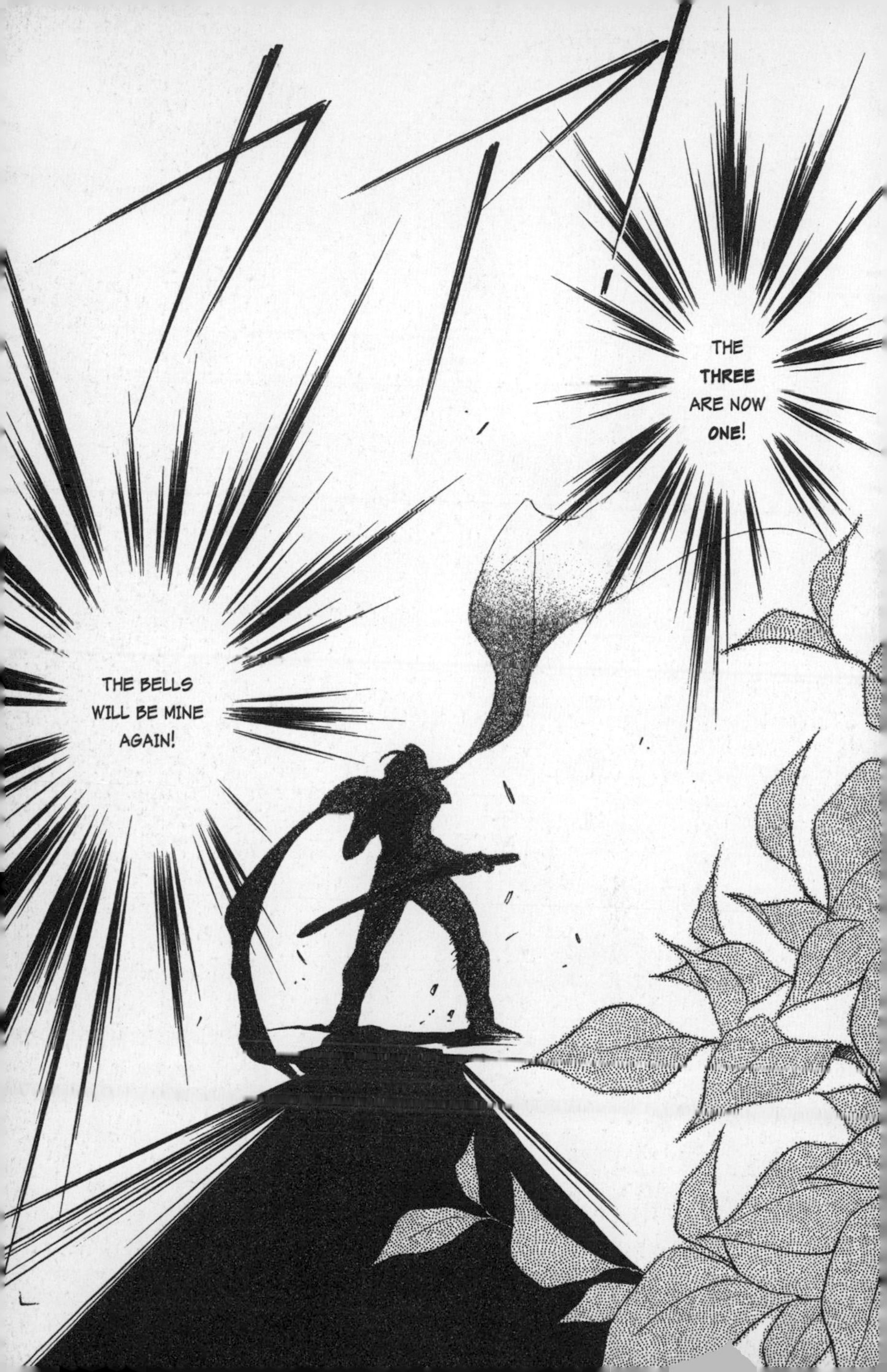
THE THREE ARE NOW ONE!
THE BELLS WILL BE MINE AGAIN!

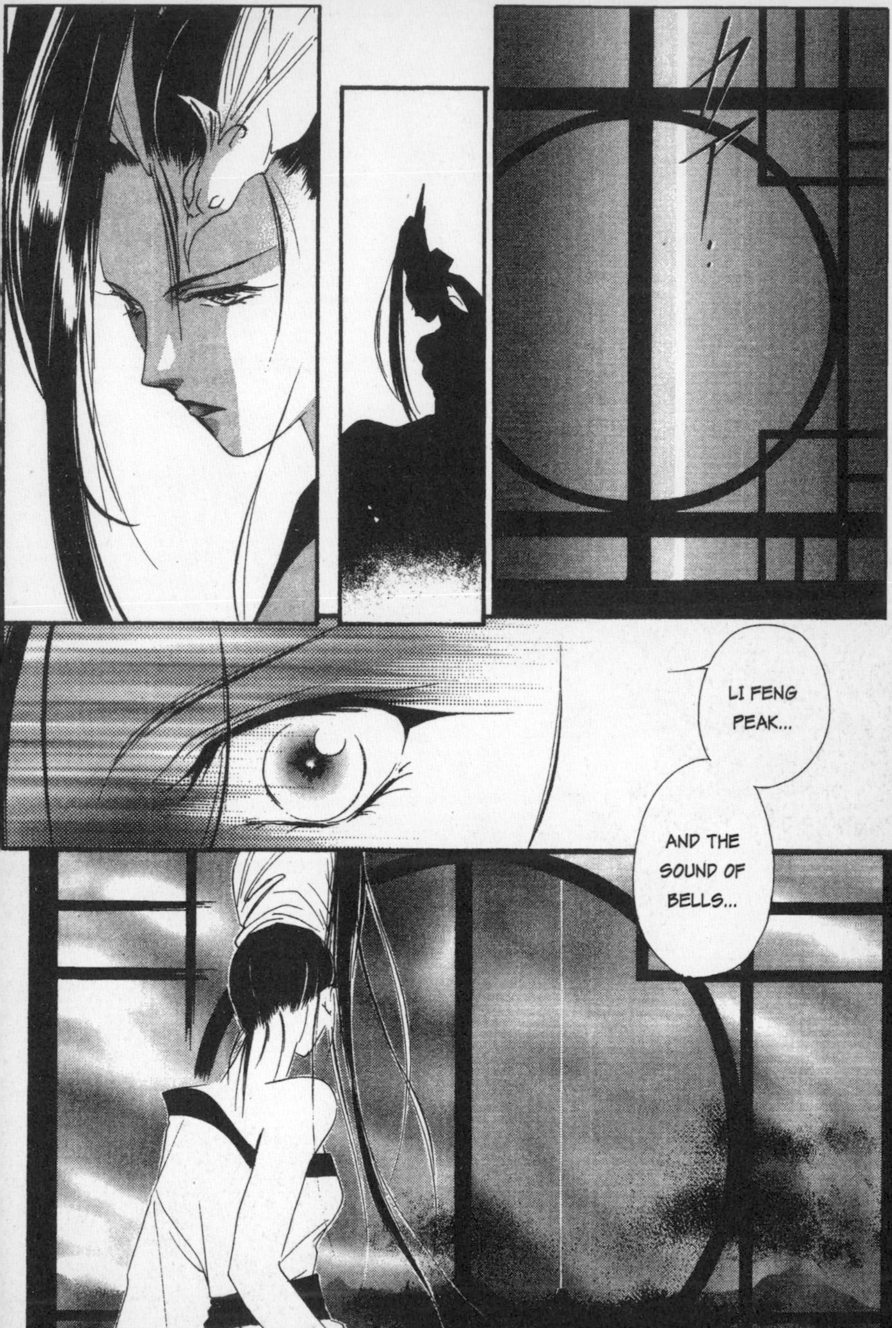
LI FENG PEAK...
AND THE SOUND OF BELLS...

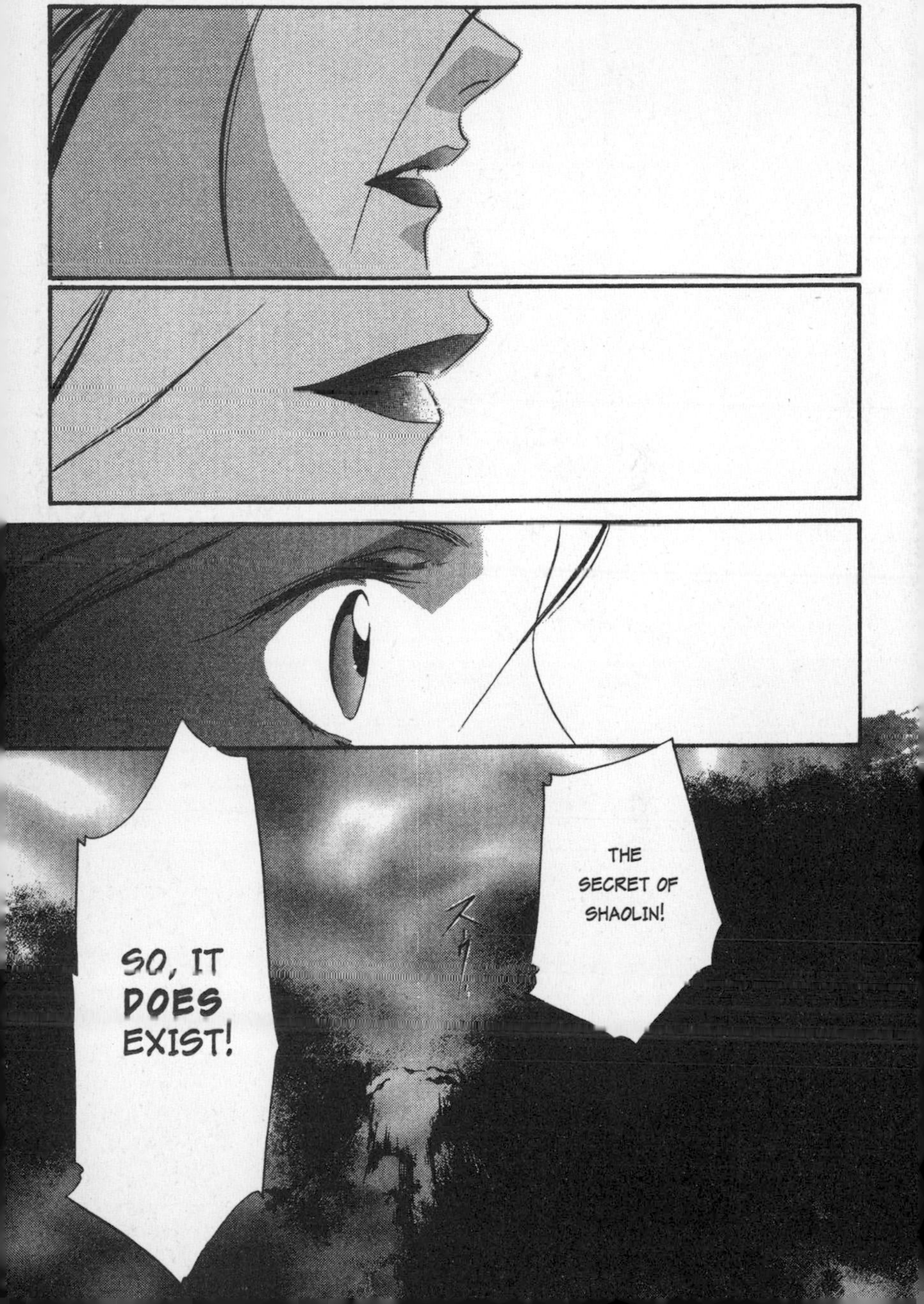
THE SECRET OF SHAOLIN!
SO, IT DOES EXIST!

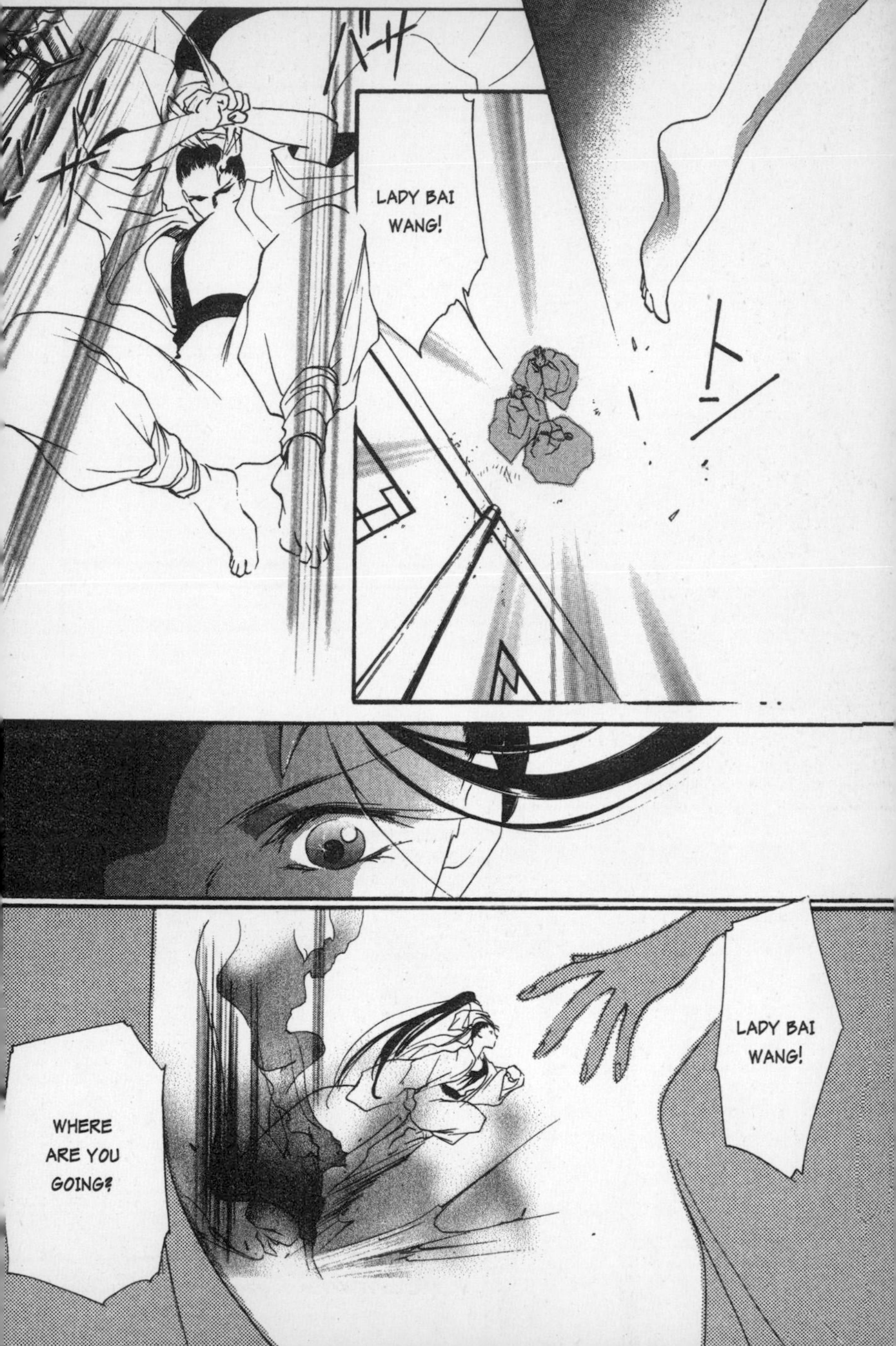
LADY BAI WANG!
LADY BAI WANG!
WHERE ARE YOU GOING?

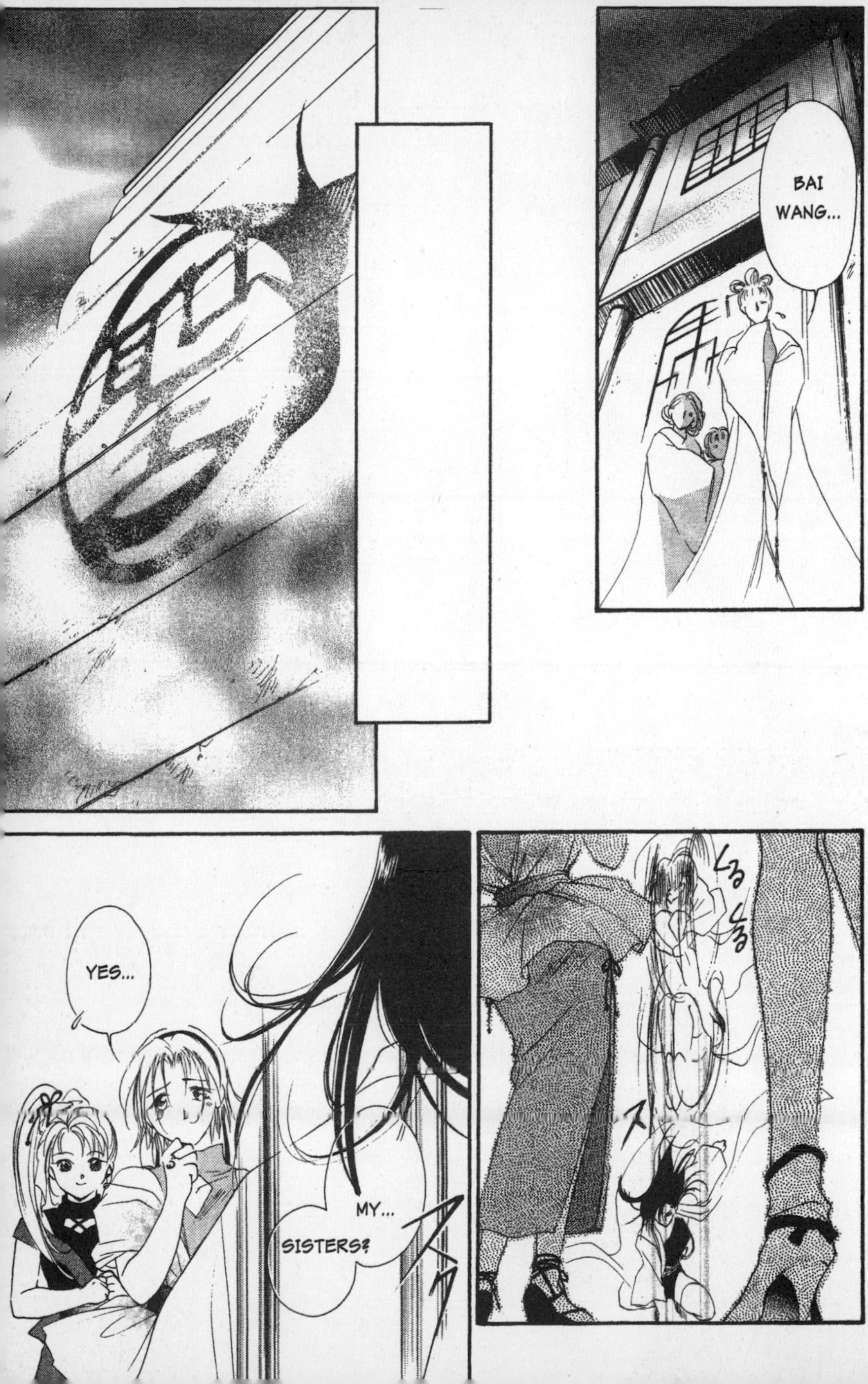
BAI WANG...
くる くる
ス
MY... SISTERS?
YES...

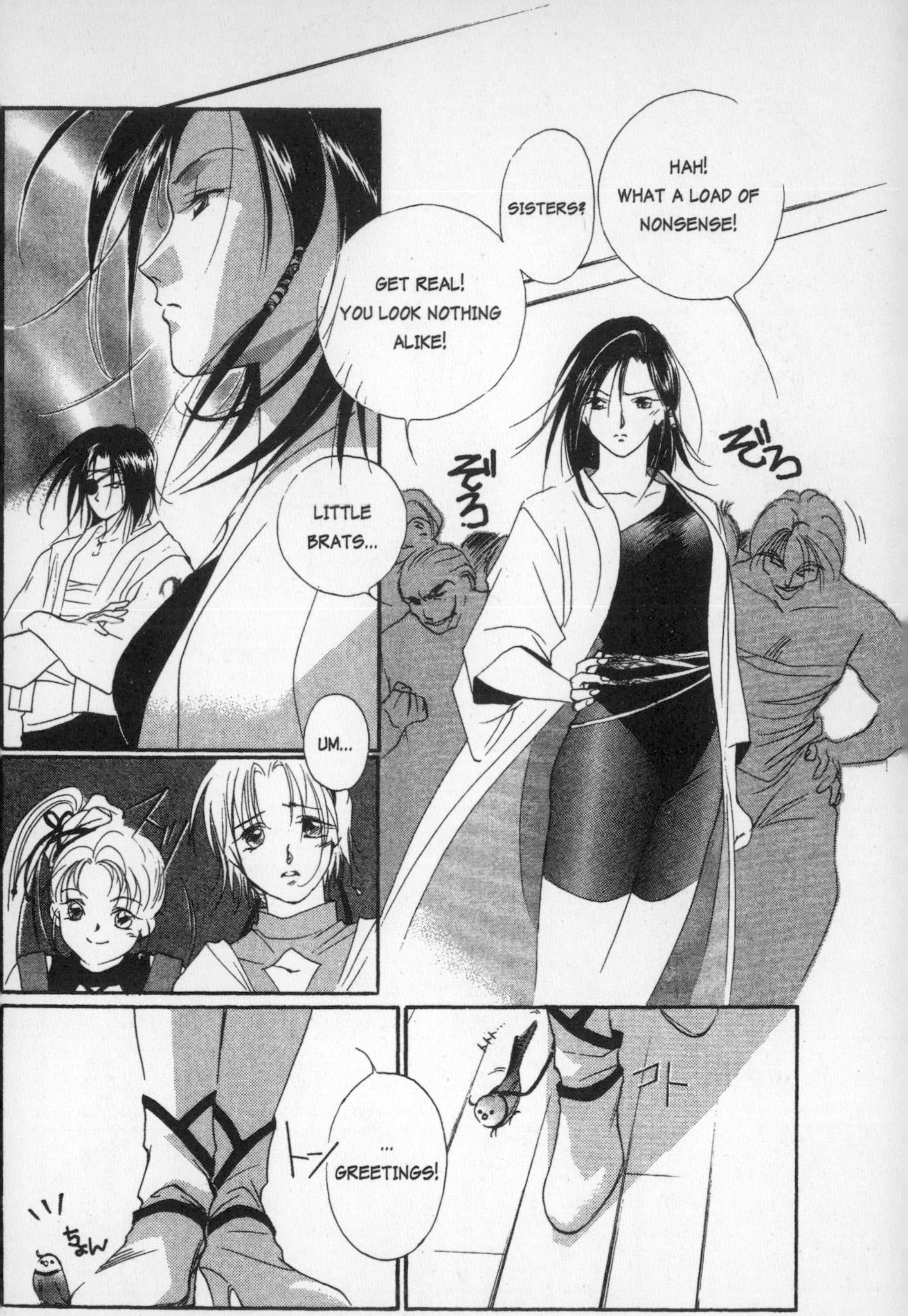
HAH! WHAT A LOAD OF NONSENSE!
SISTERS?
GET REAL! YOU LOOK NOTHING ALIKE!
ぞろ
ぞろ
LITTLE BRATS...
UM...
... GREETINGS!
ちょん

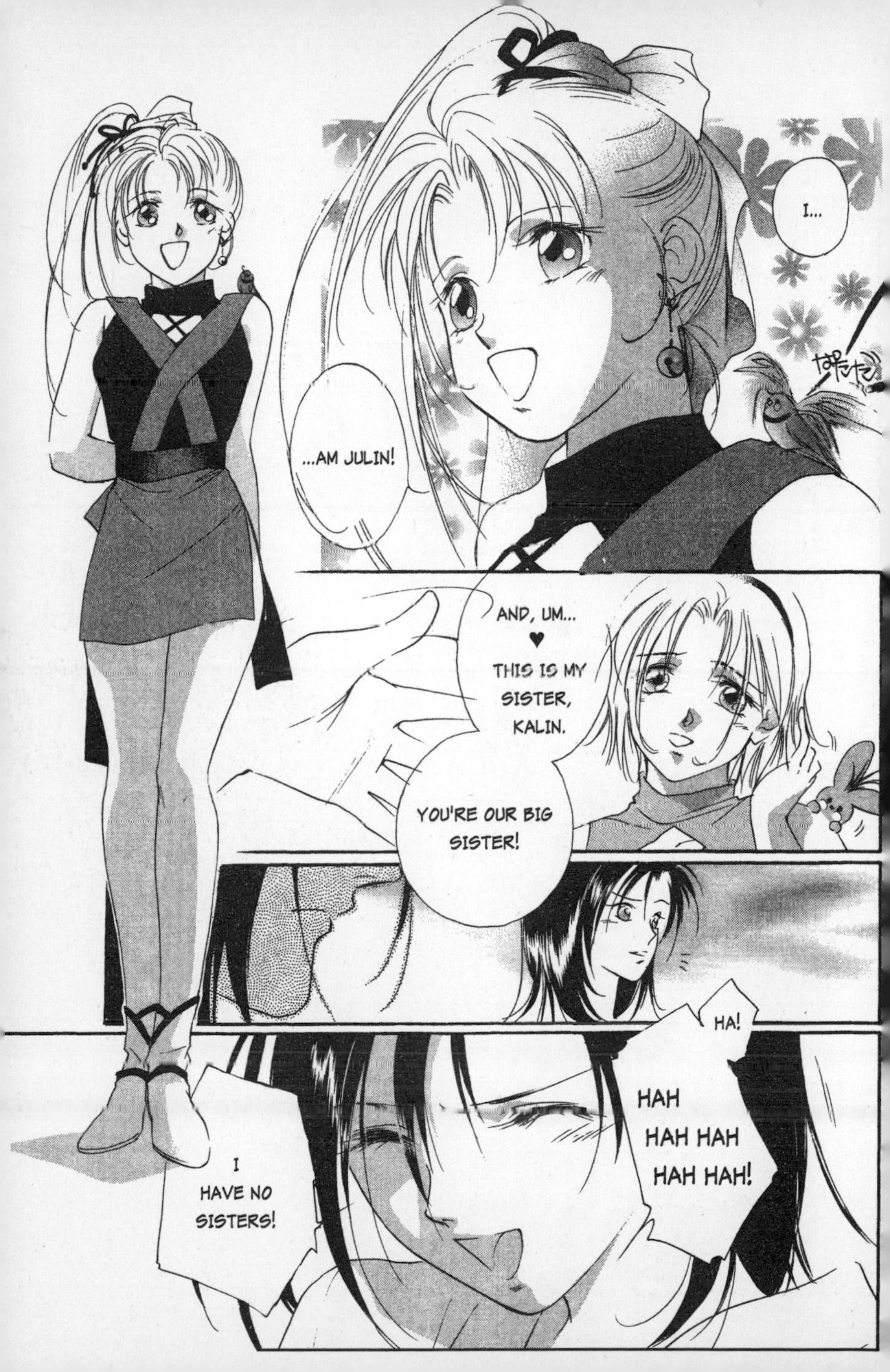
I...
...AM JULIN!
AND, UM... ♥ THIS IS MY SISTER, KALIN.
YOU'RE OUR BIG SISTER!
HA!
HAH HAH HAH HAH HAH!
I HAVE NO SISTERS!

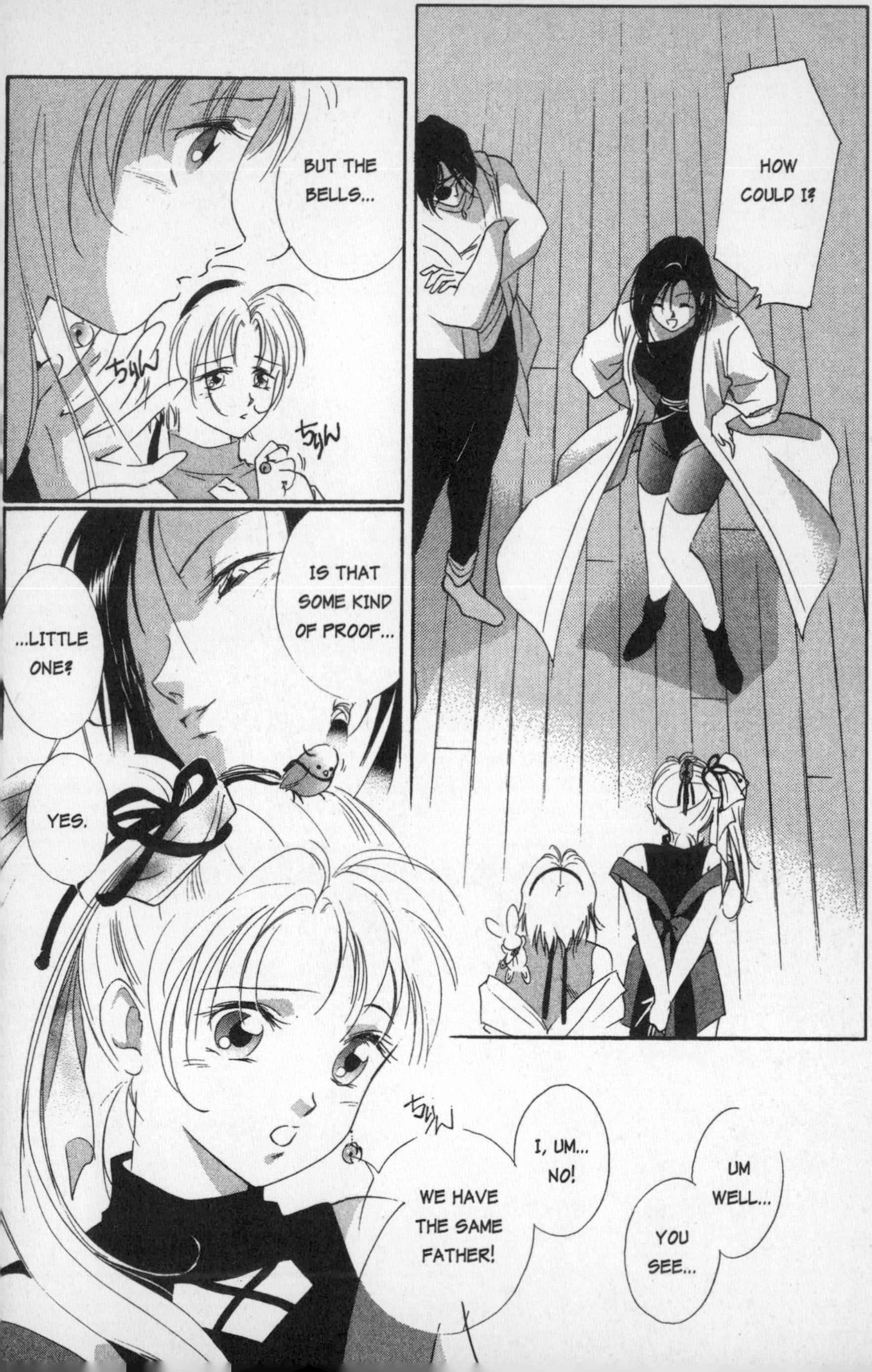
HOW COULD I?
BUT THE BELLS...
ちりん
ちりん
IS THAT SOME KIND OF PROOF...
...LITTLE ONE?
YES.
UM WELL...
YOU SEE...
I, UM... NO!
WE HAVE THE SAME FATHER!
ちりん

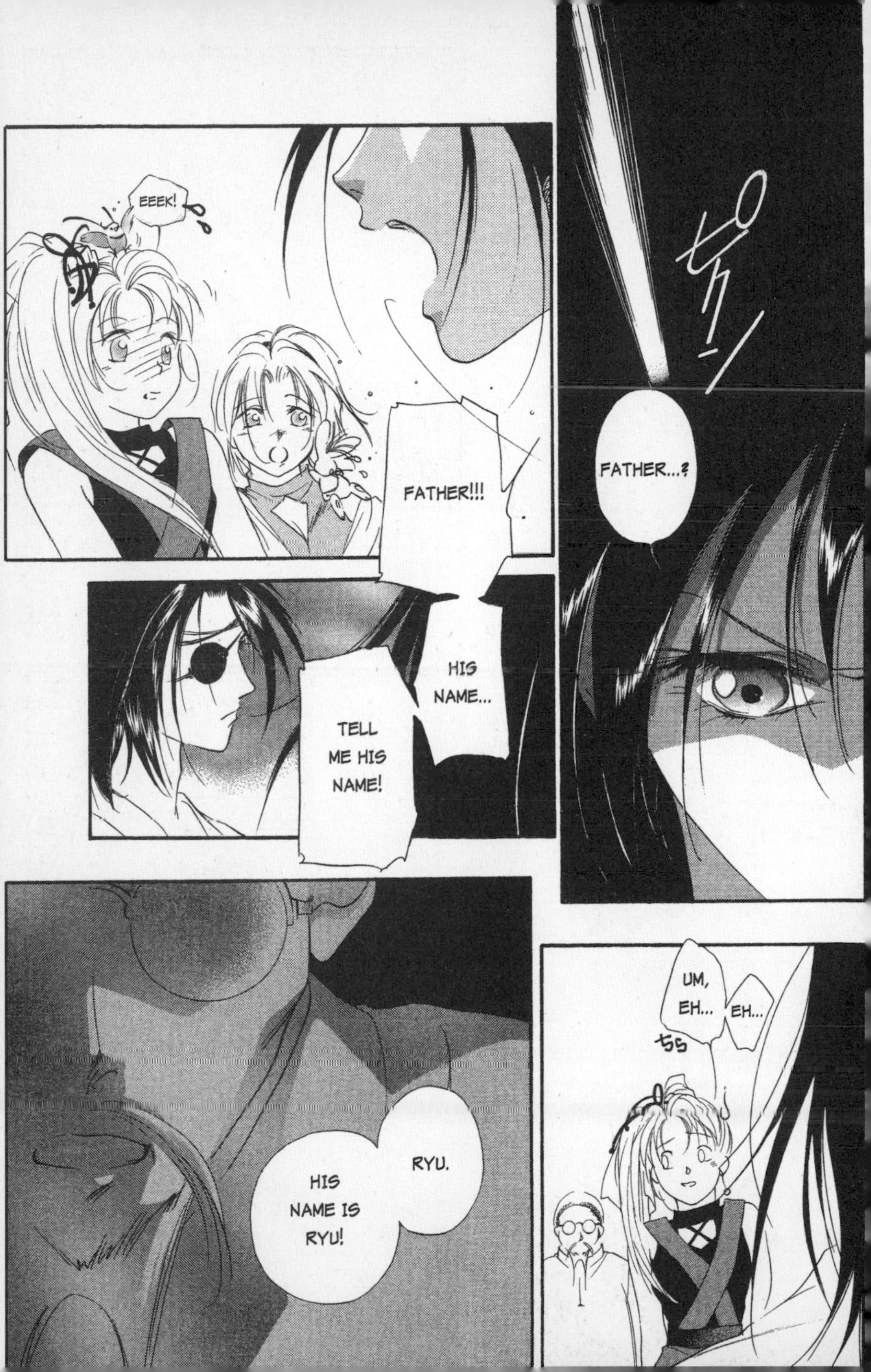
FATHER...?
EEEK!
FATHER!!!
HIS NAME...
TELL ME HIS NAME!
UM, EH...
EH...
ちら
RYU.
HIS NAME IS RYU!

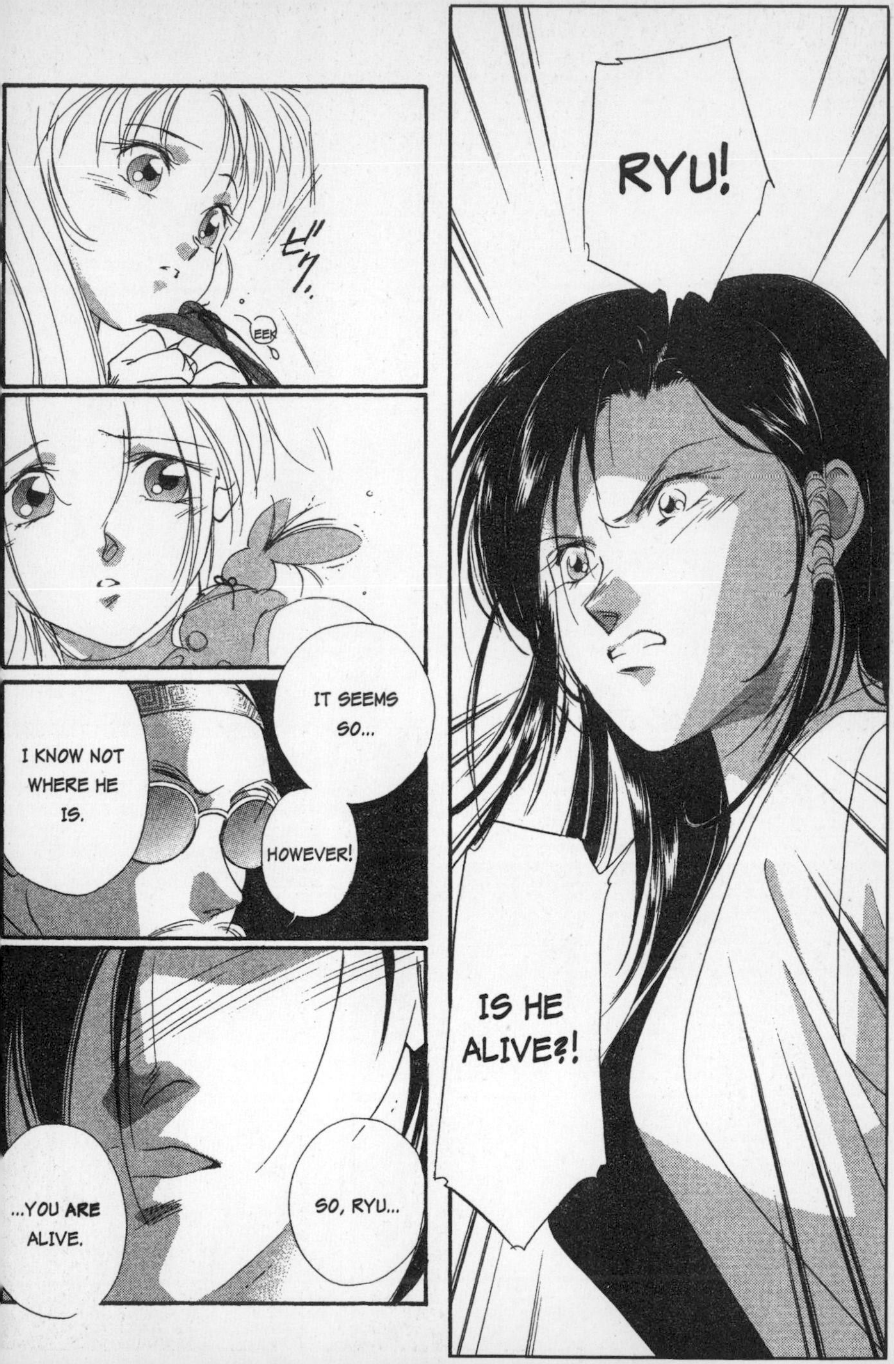
RYU!
IS HE ALIVE?!
EEK
IT SEEMS SO...
I KNOW NOT WHERE HE IS.
HOWEVER!
SO, RYU...
...YOU ARE ALIVE.

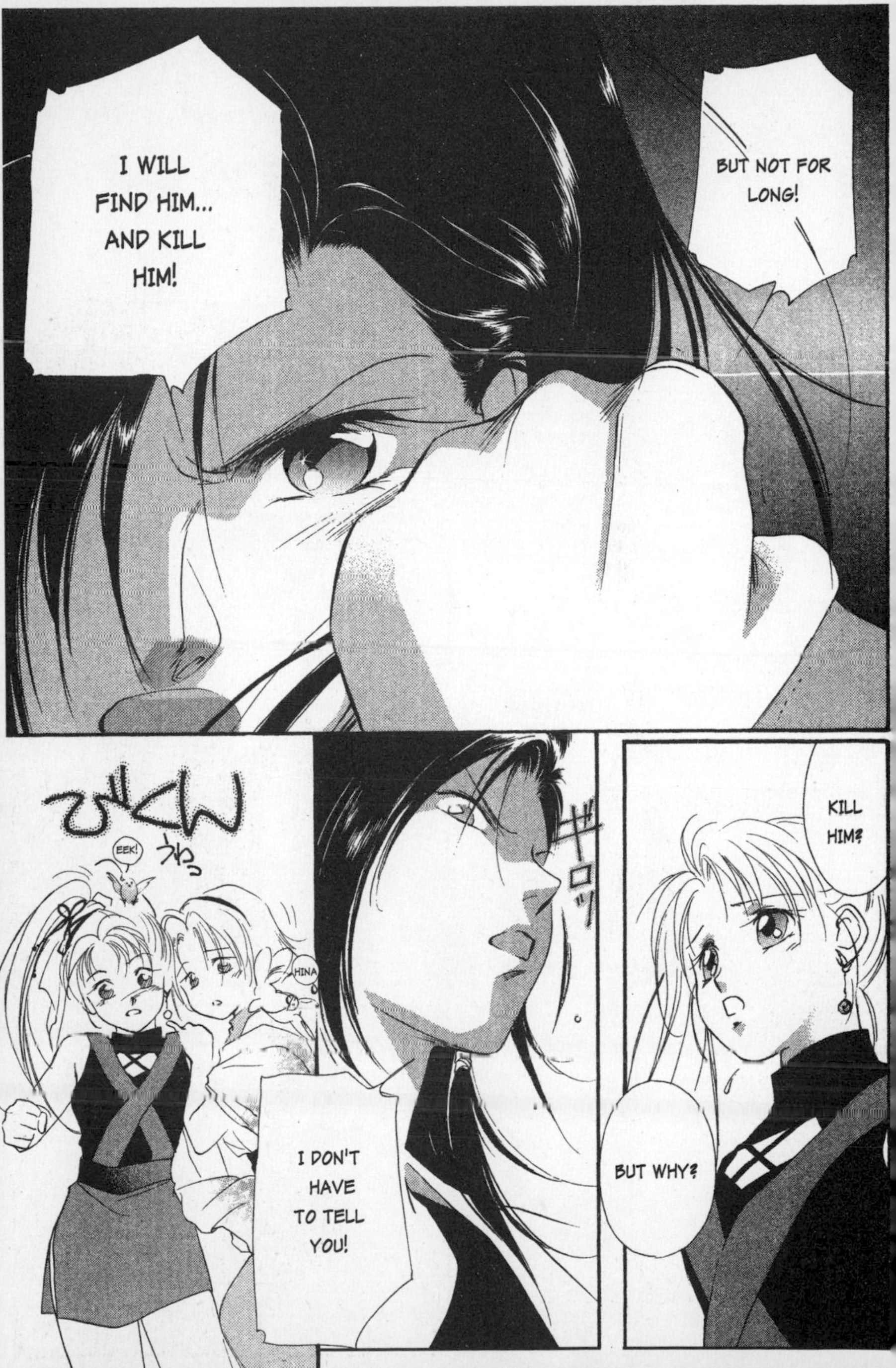
BUT NOT FOR LONG!
I WILL FIND HIM... AND KILL HIM!
KILL HIM?
BUT WHY?
ギロッ
I DON'T HAVE TO TELL YOU!
びくん
うわっ
EEK!
HINA

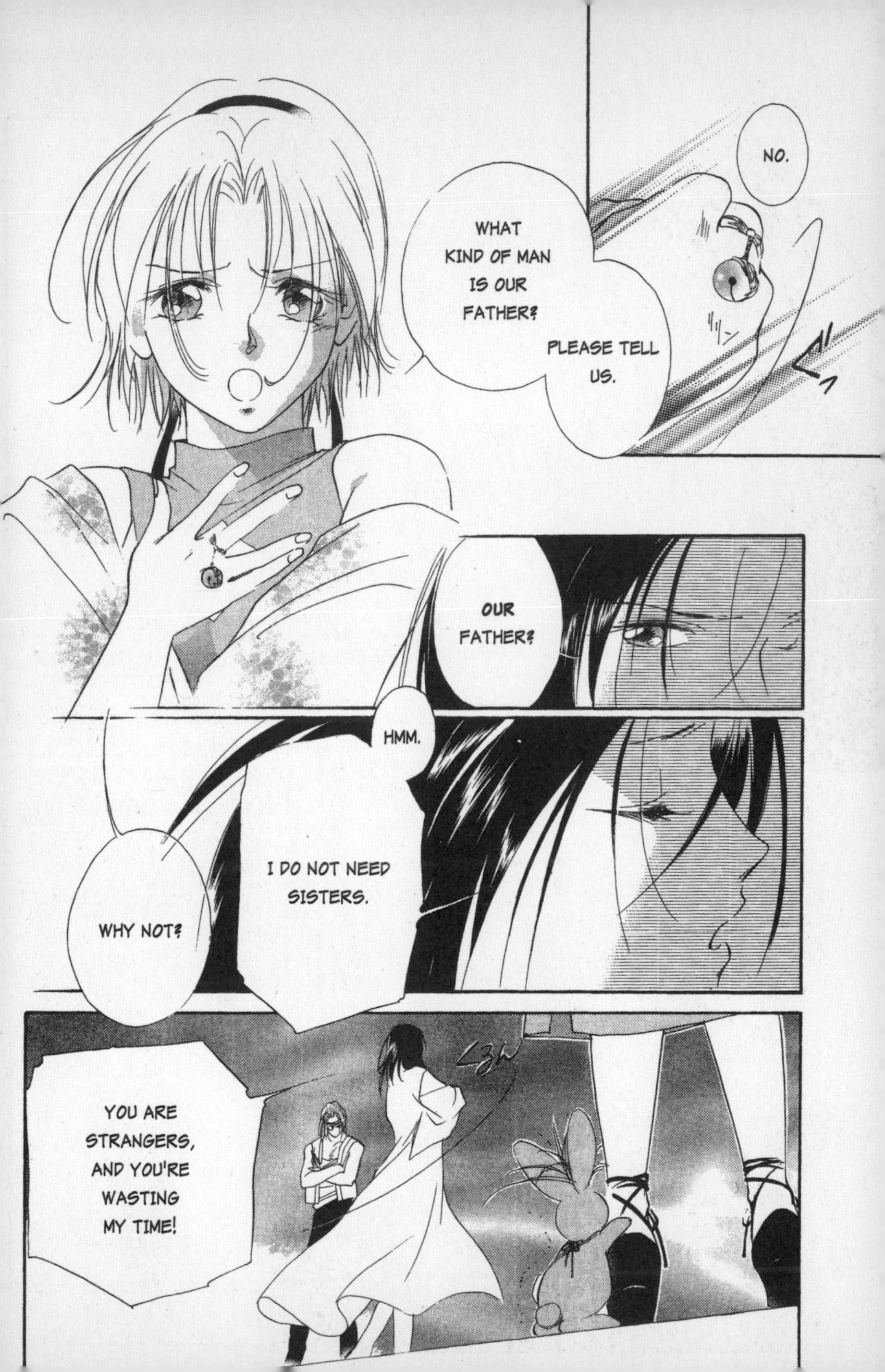
WHAT KIND OF MAN IS OUR FATHER?
PLEASE TELL US.
NO.
OUR FATHER?
HMM.
I DO NOT NEED SISTERS.
WHY NOT?
YOU ARE STRANGERS, AND YOU'RE WASTING MY TIME!

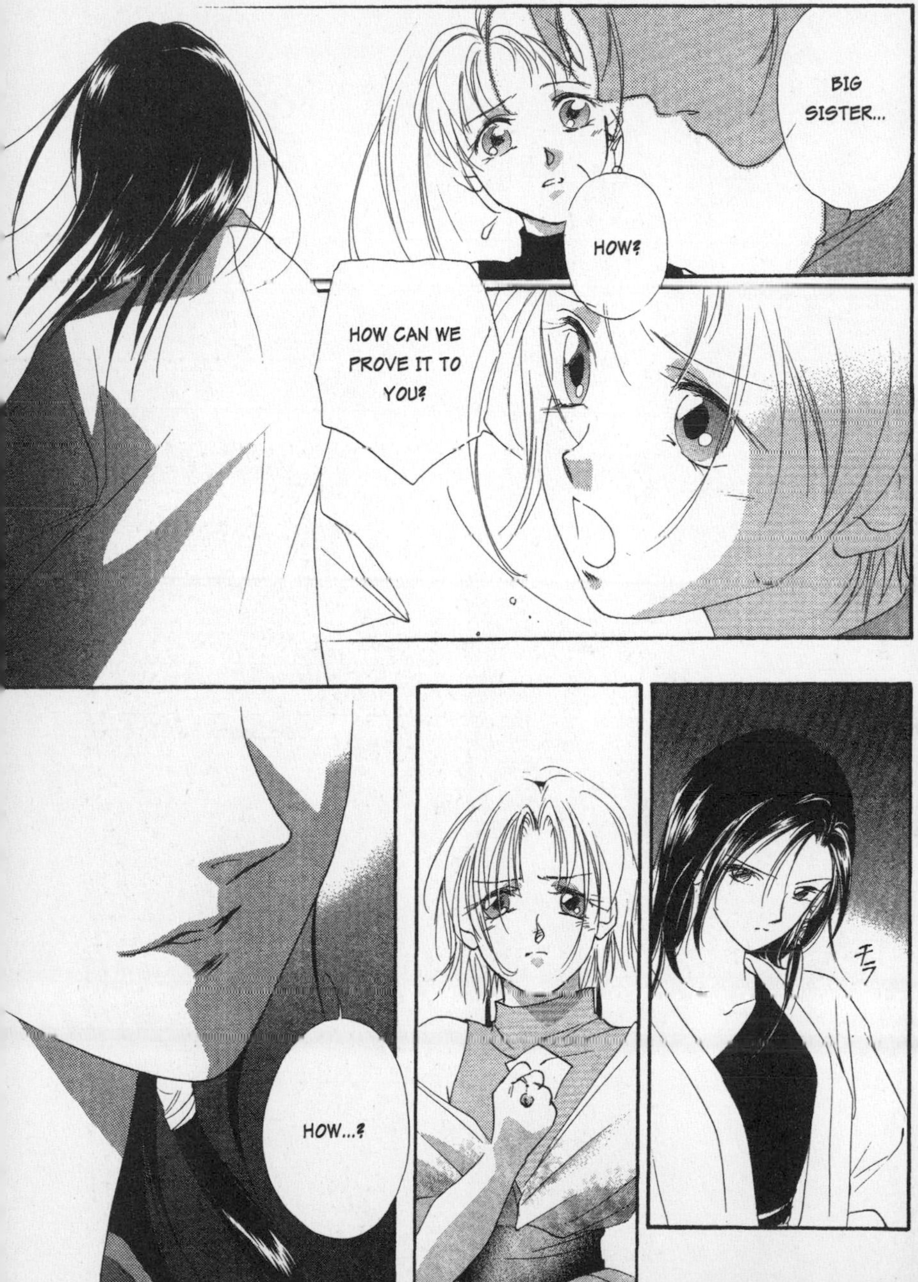
BIG SISTER...
HOW?
HOW CAN WE PROVE IT TO YOU?
チラ
HOW...?

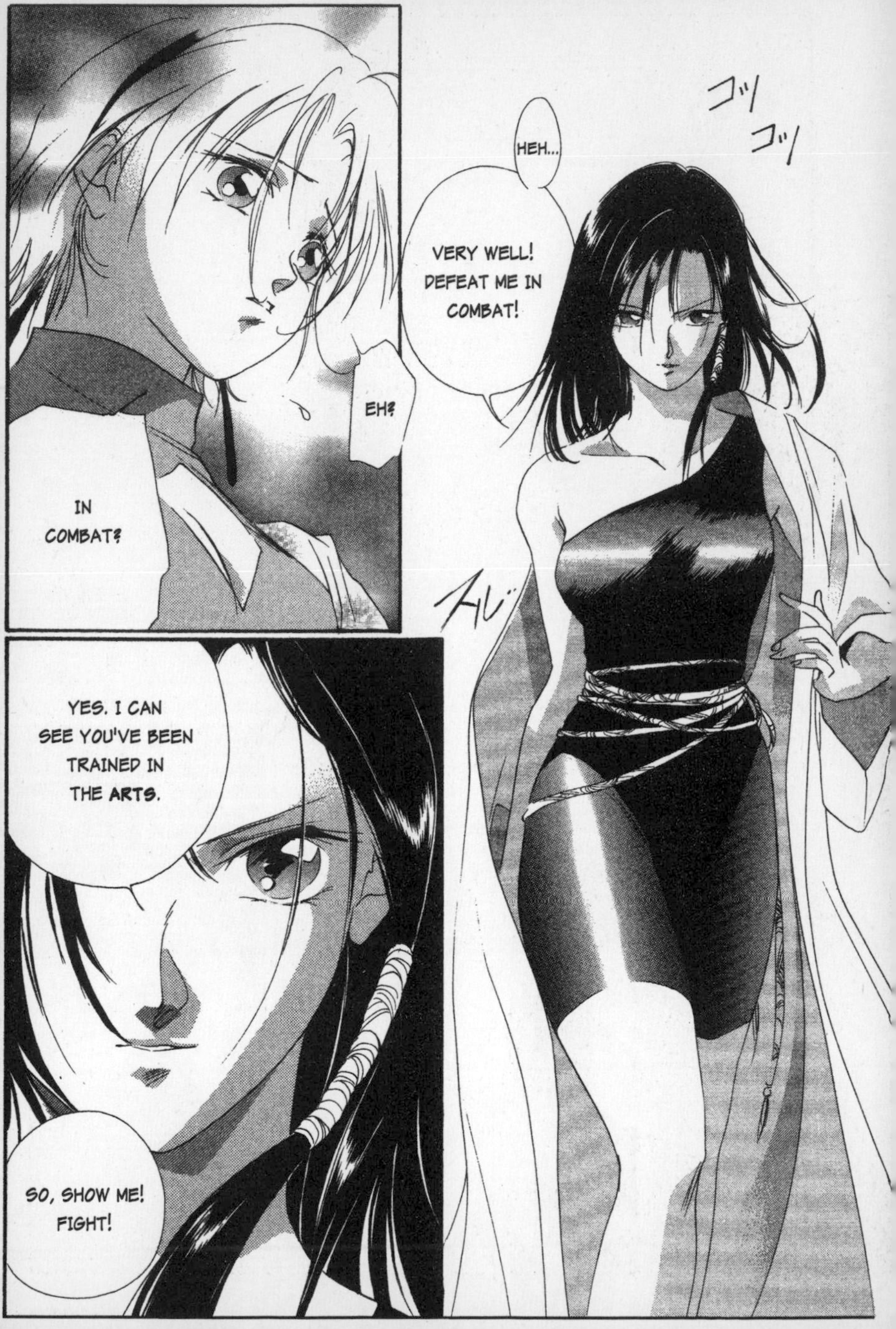
ゴッ
ゴッ
HEH...
VERY WELL! DEFEAT ME IN COMBAT!
EH?
IN COMBAT?
YES. I CAN SEE YOU'VE BEEN TRAINED IN THE ARTS.
SO, SHOW ME! FIGHT!

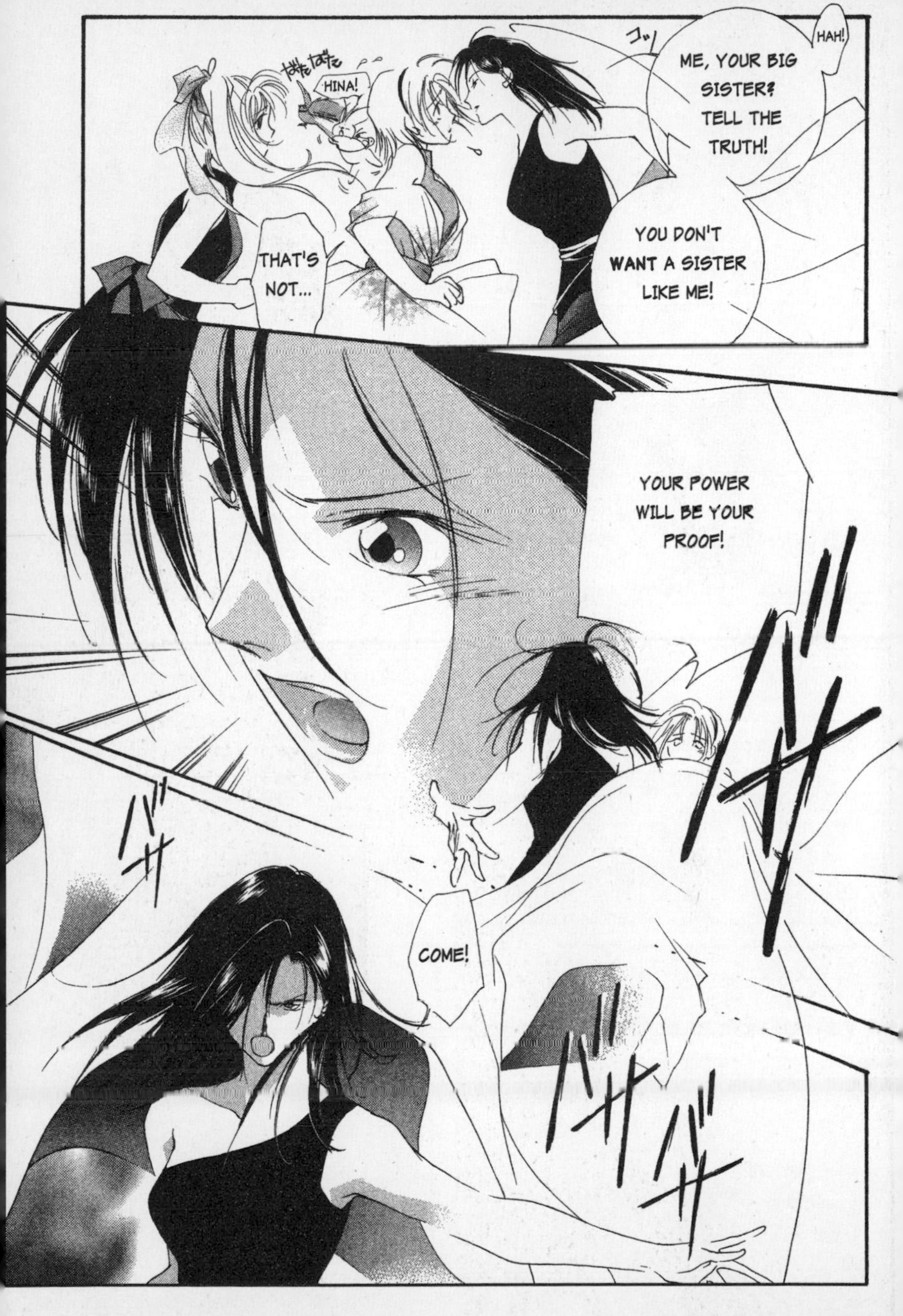
HAH!
ME, YOUR BIG SISTER? TELL THE TRUTH!
HINA!
YOU DON'T WANT A SISTER LIKE ME!
THAT'S NOT...
YOUR POWER WILL BE YOUR PROOF!
COME!

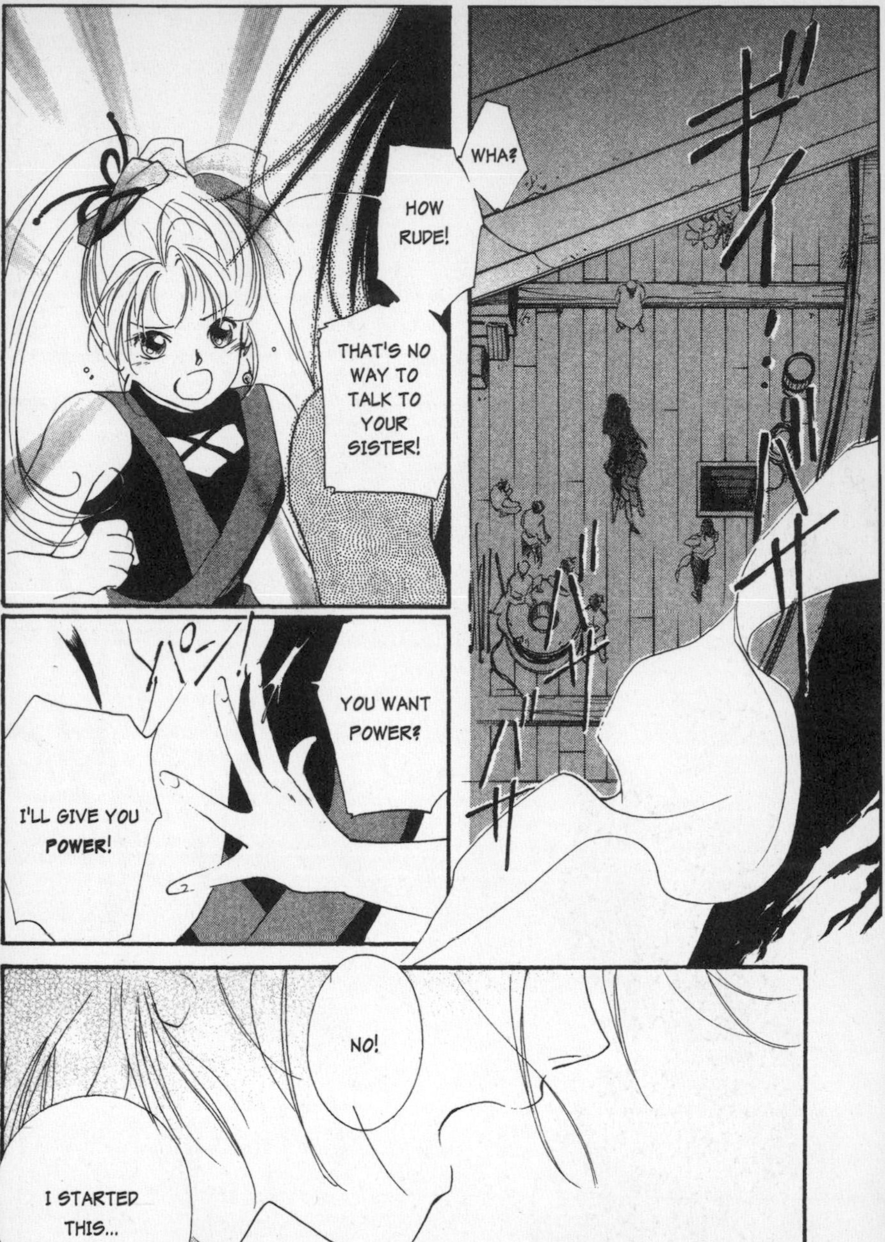
WHA?
HOW RUDE!
THAT'S NO WAY TO TALK TO YOUR SISTER!
YOU WANT POWER?
I'LL GIVE YOU POWER!
NO!
I STARTED THIS...

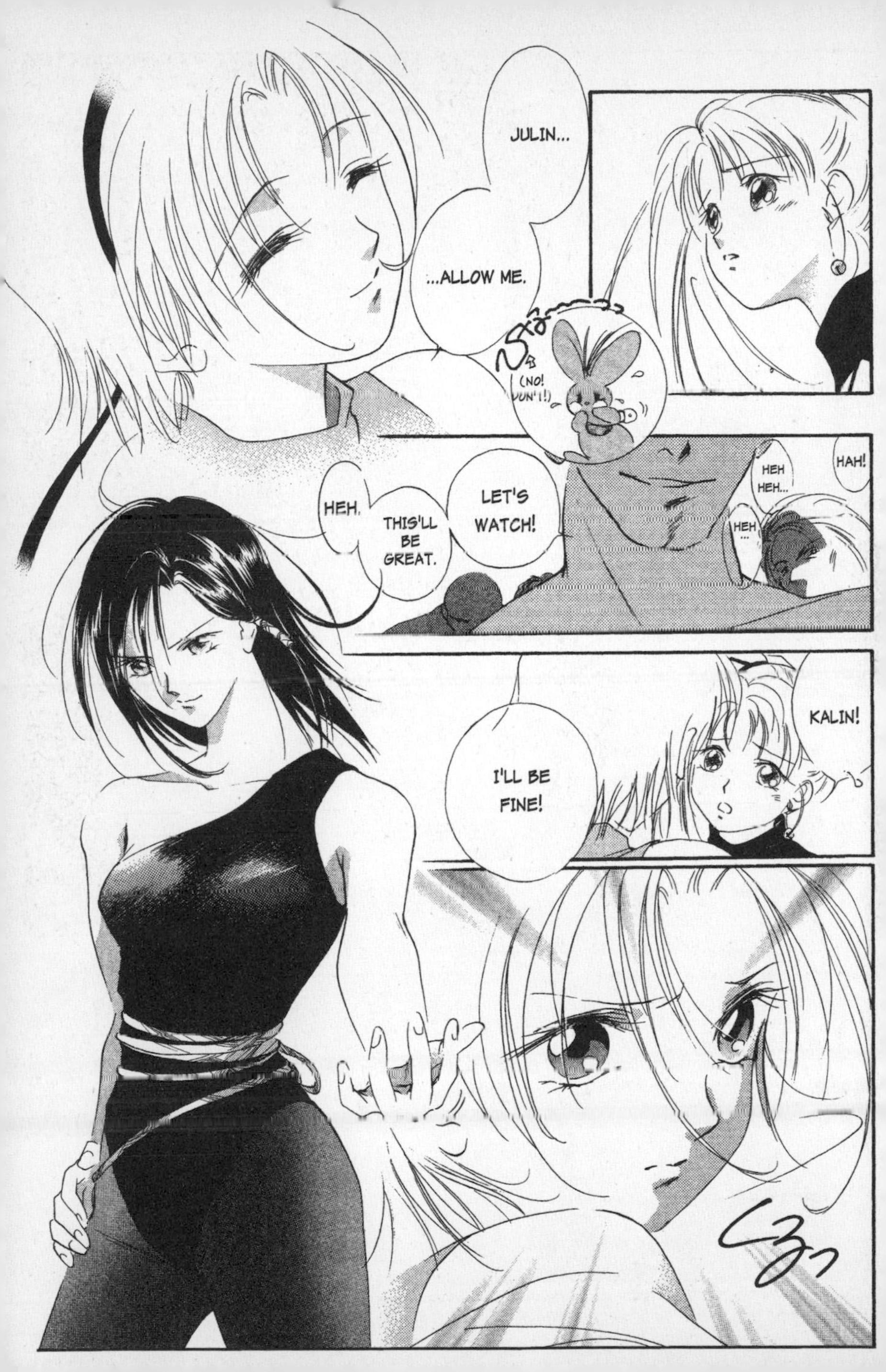
JULIN...
...ALLOW ME.
(NO! DON'T!)
HAH!
HEH HEH...
HEH...
LET'S WATCH!
THIS'LL BE GREAT.
HEH.
KALIN!
I'LL BE FINE!

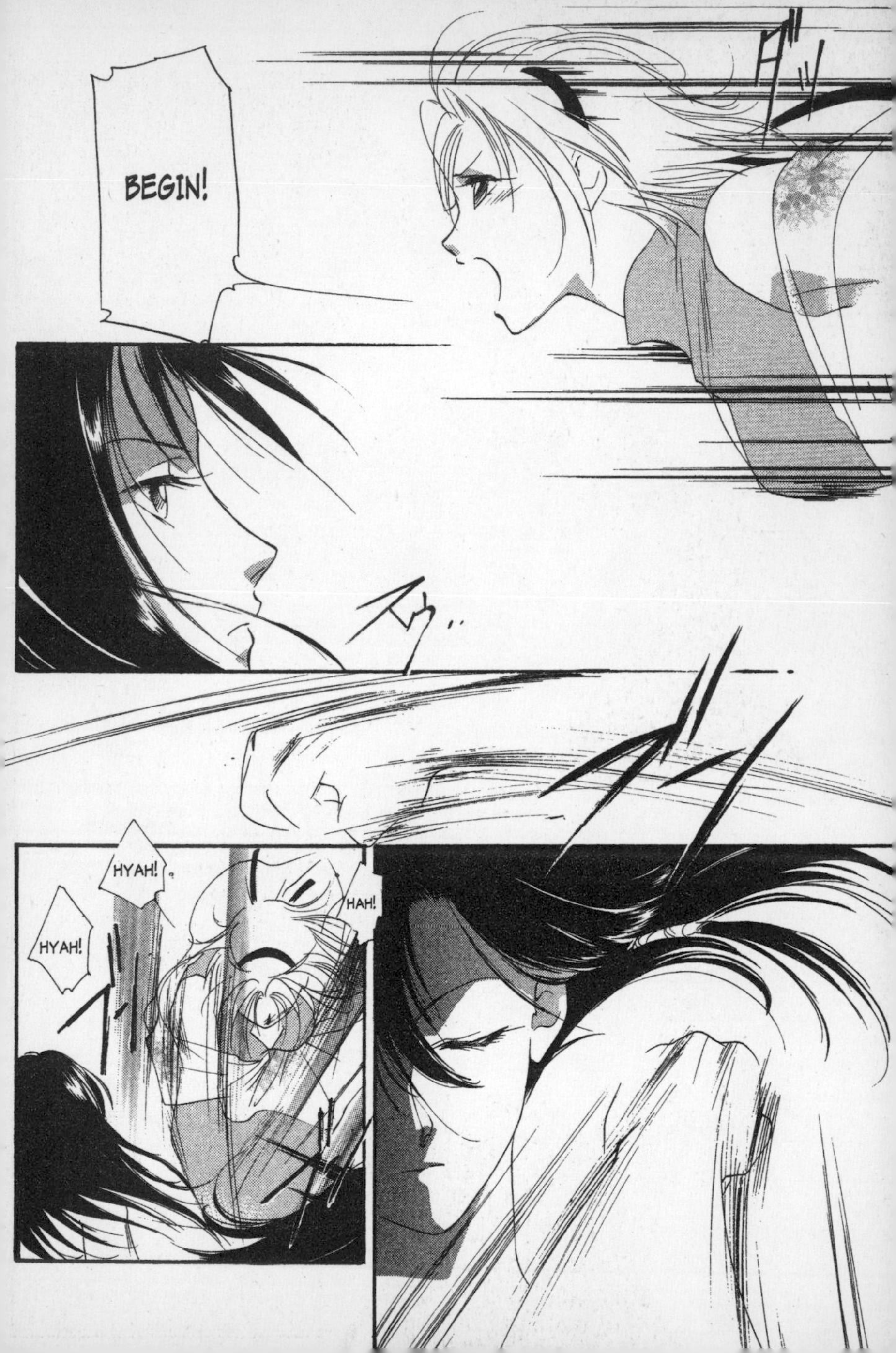
BEGIN!
HAH!
HYAH!
HYAH!

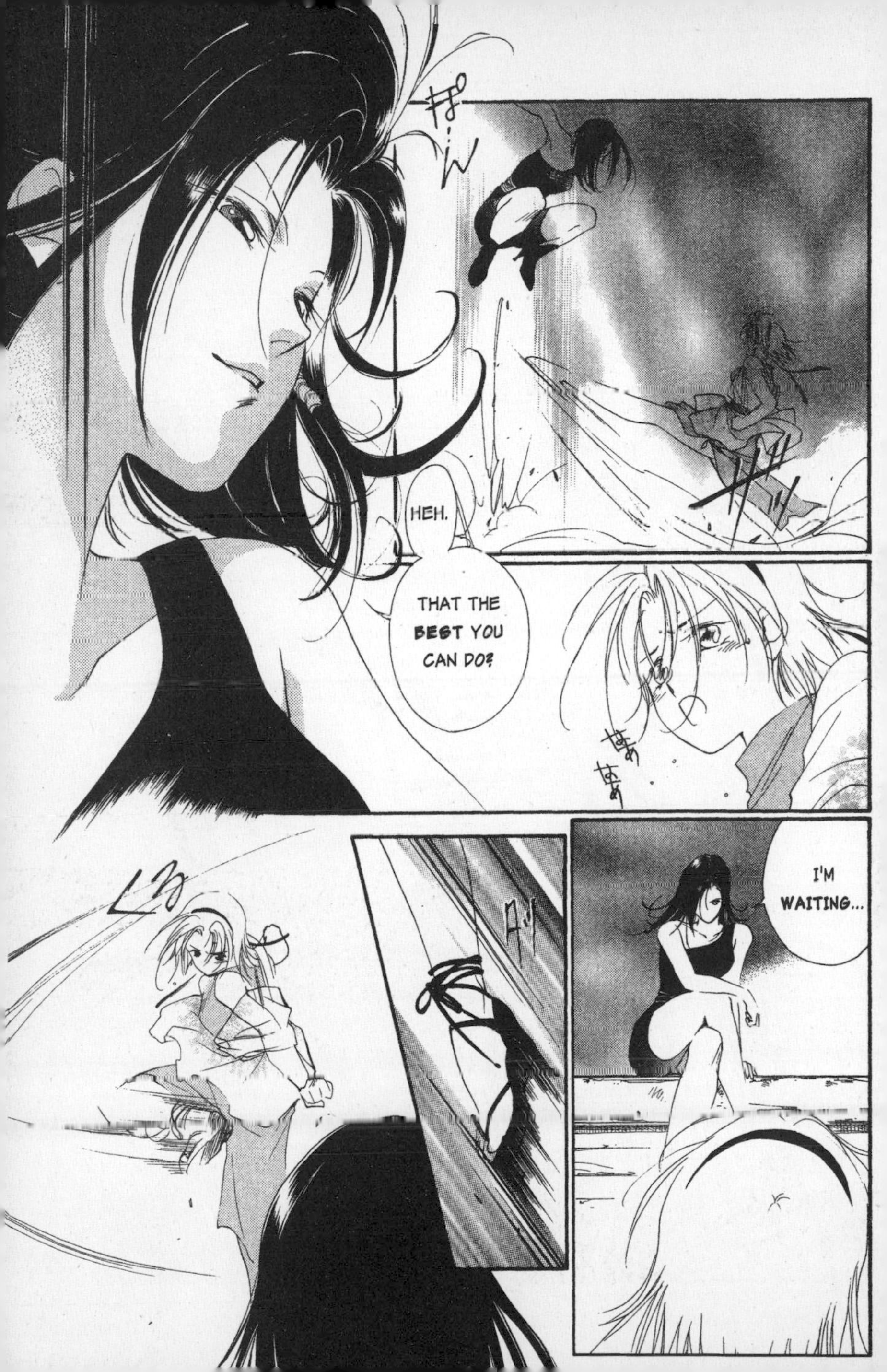
HEH.
THAT THE BEST YOU CAN DO?
I'M WAITING...

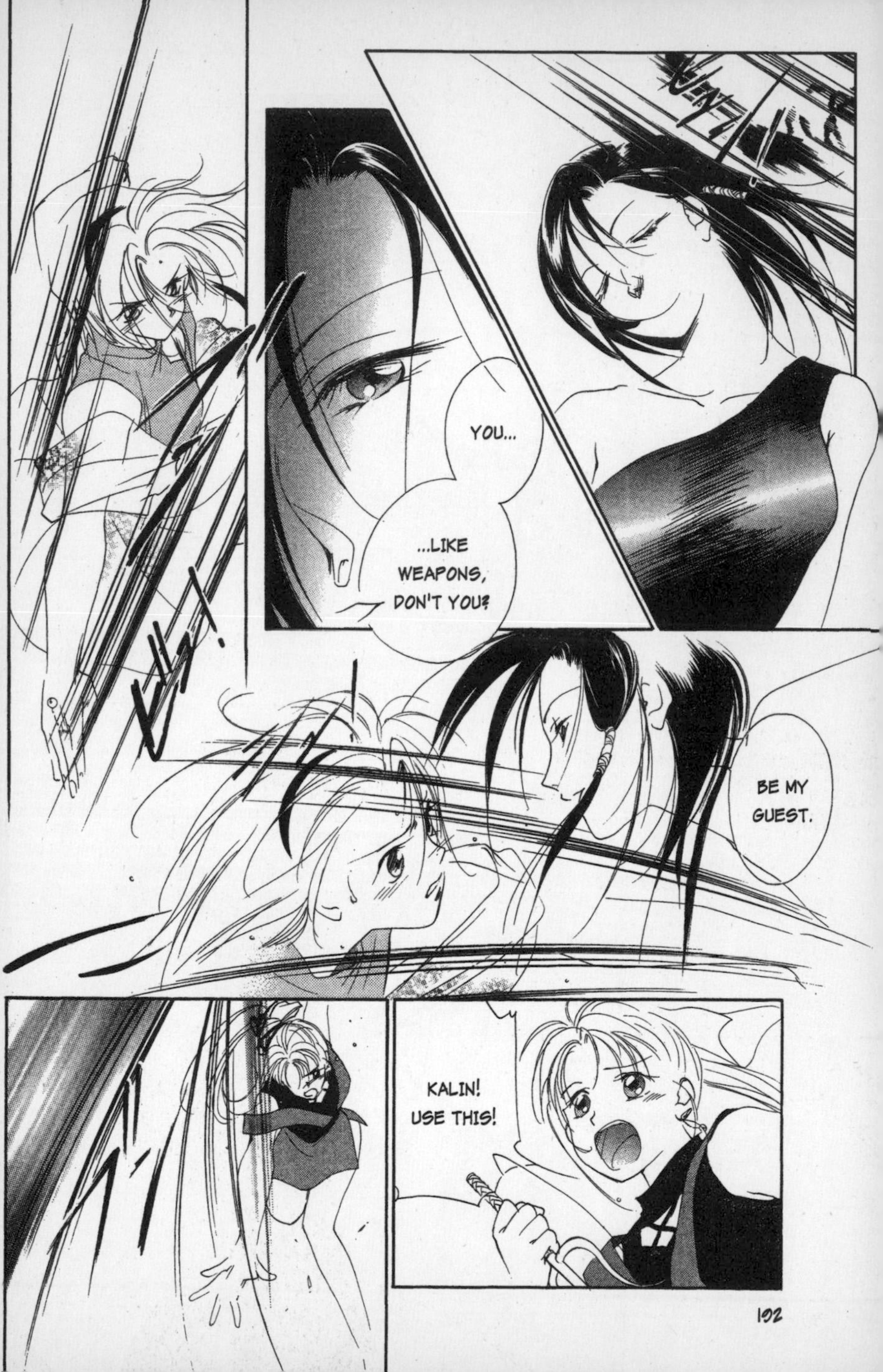
YOU...
...LIKE WEAPONS, DON'T YOU?
BE MY GUEST.
KALIN! USE THIS!

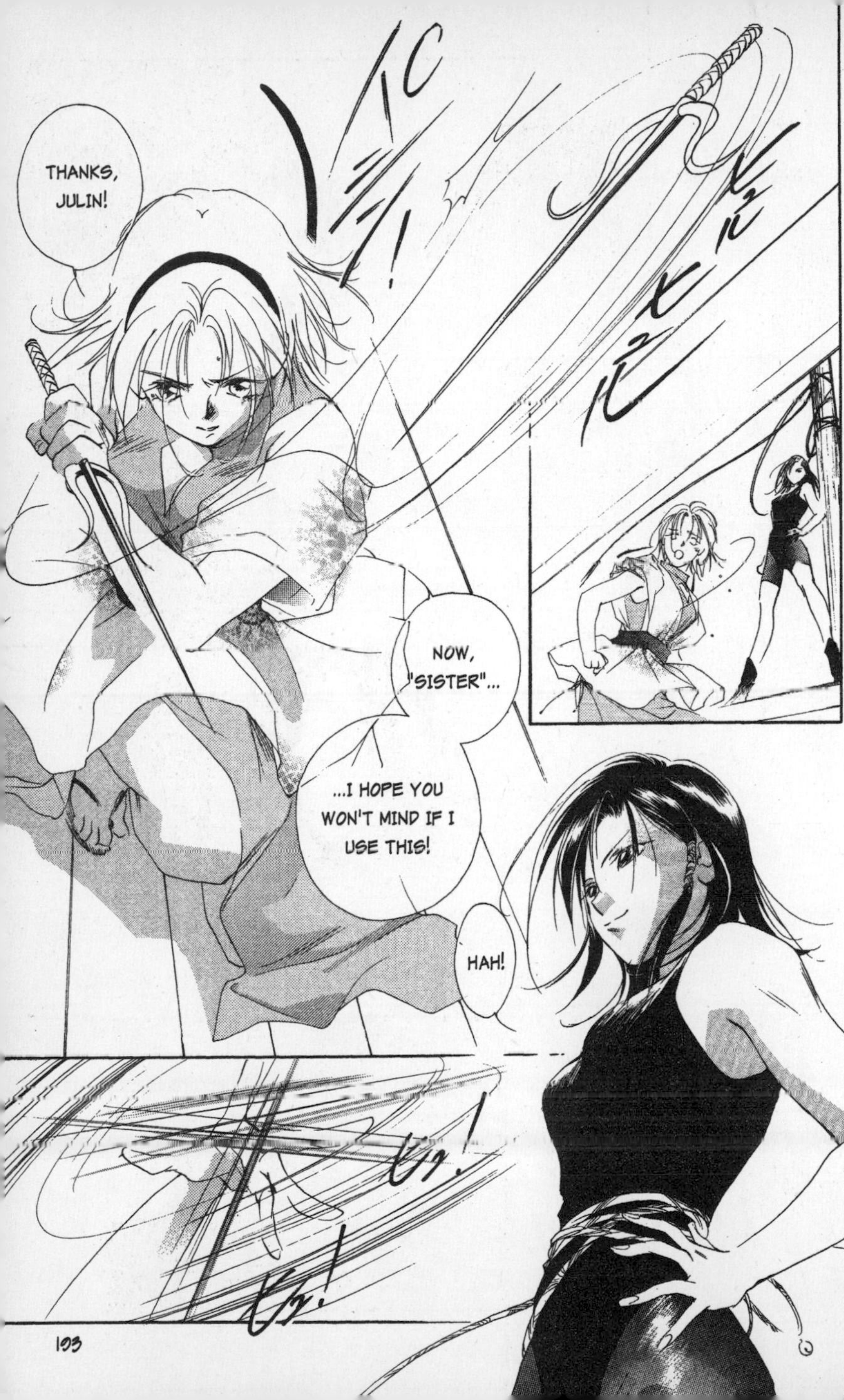
THANKS, JULIN!
NOW, "SISTER"...
...I HOPE YOU WON'T MIND IF I USE THIS!
HAH!

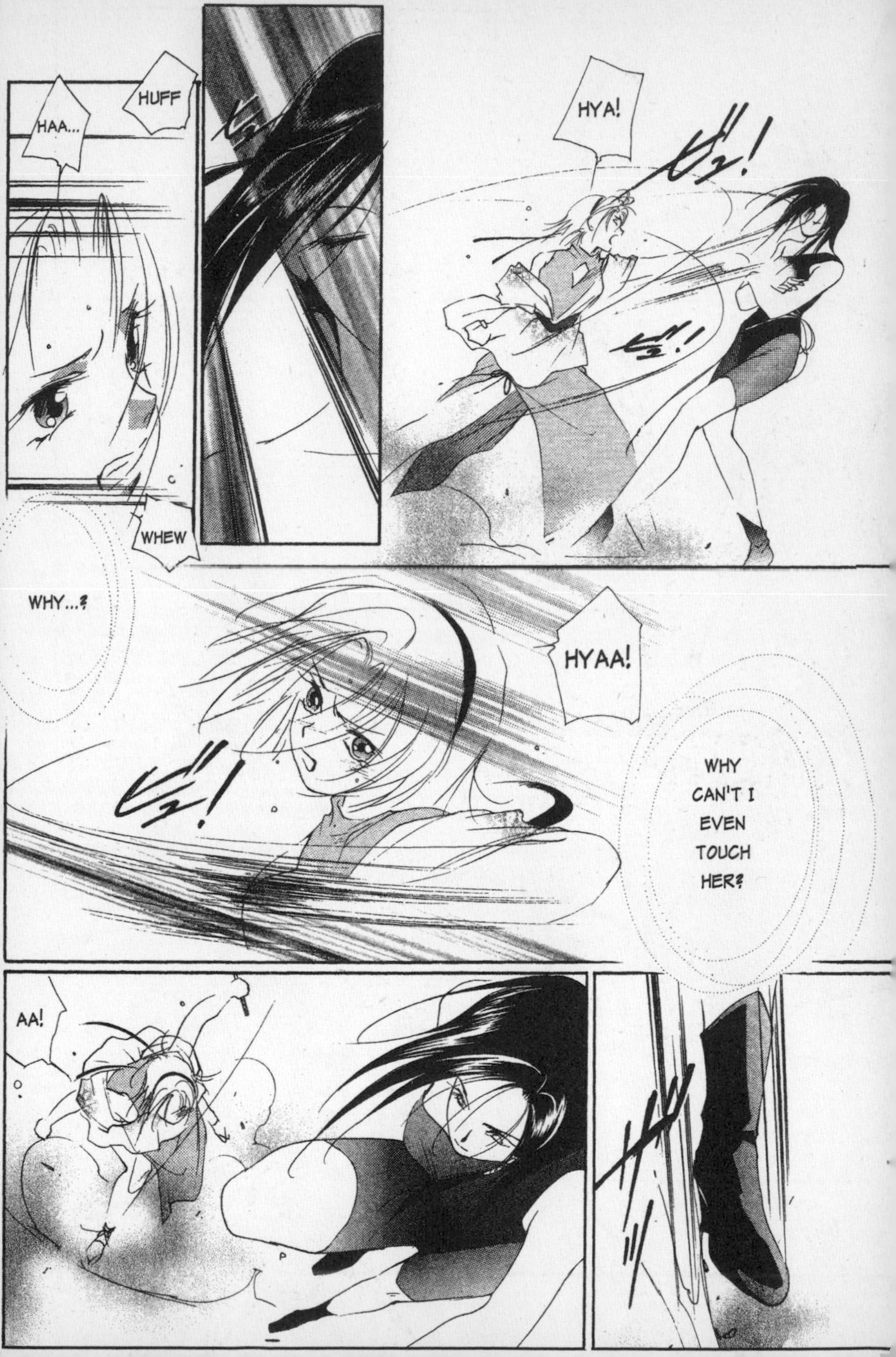
HYA!
HUFF
HAA...
WHEW
HYAA!
WHY...?
WHY CAN'T I EVEN TOUCH HER?
AA!

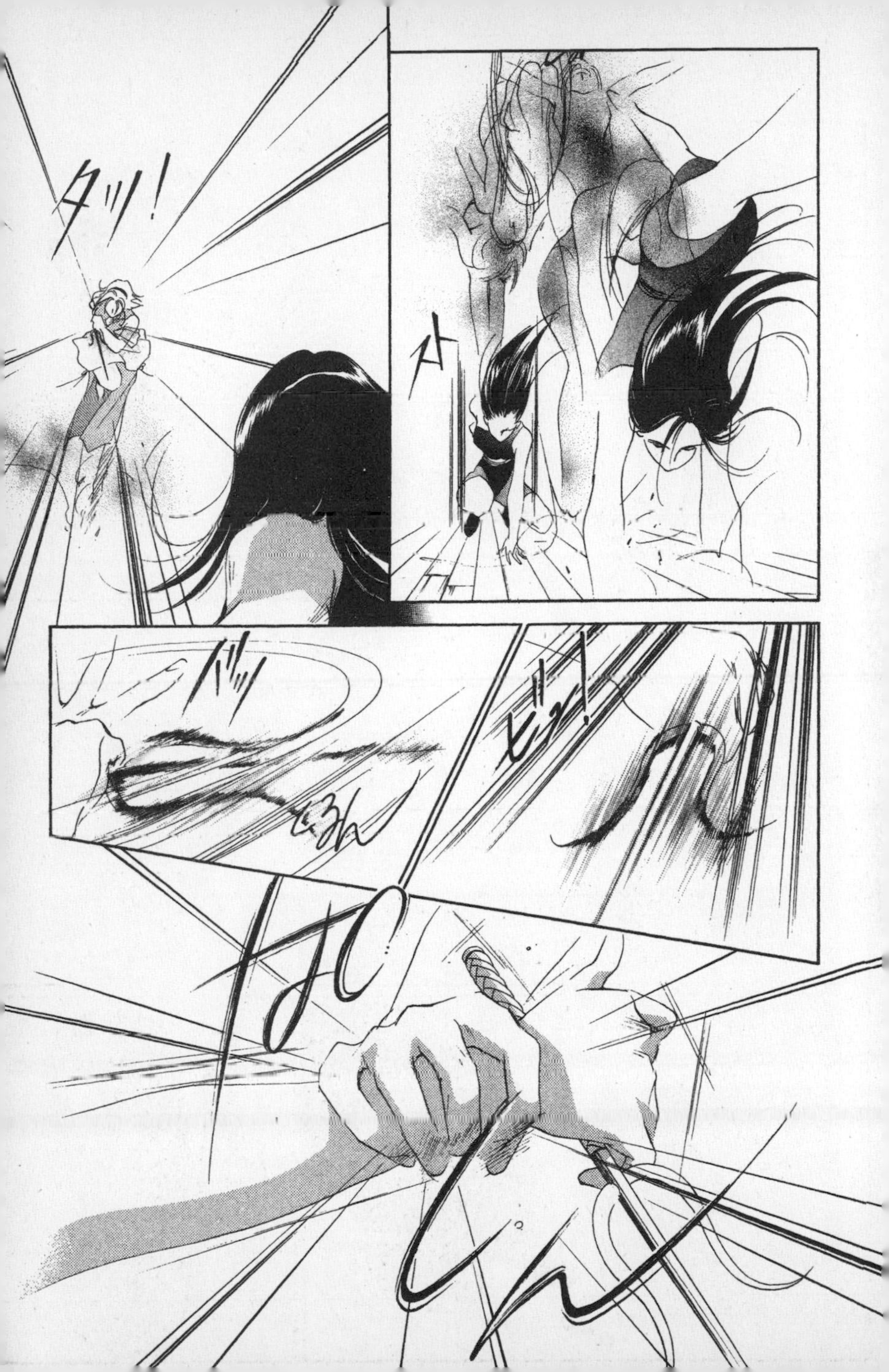
タッ！
ビュッ！
バッ

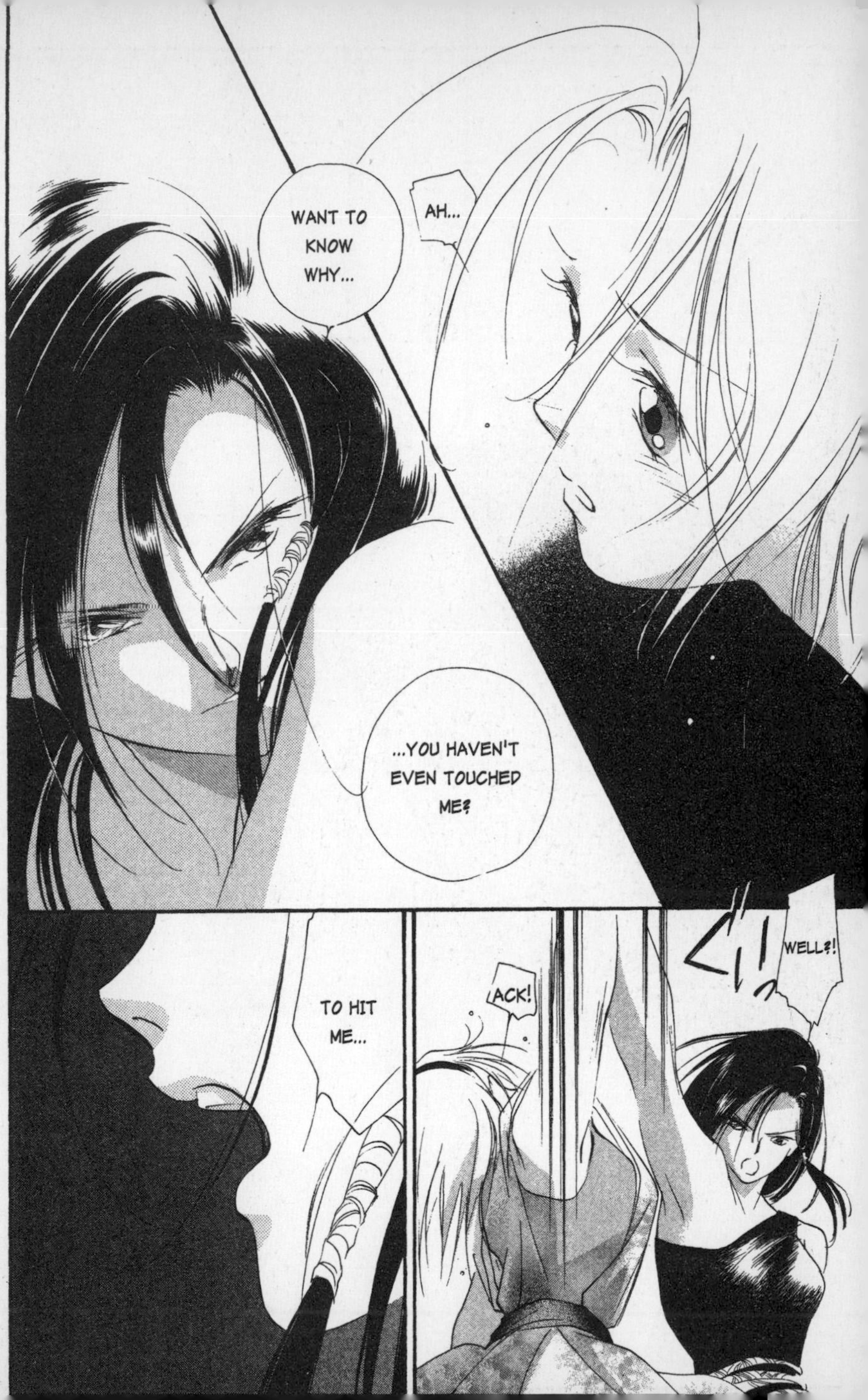
AH...
WANT TO KNOW WHY...
...YOU HAVEN'T EVEN TOUCHED ME?
ぐいっ
WELL?!
ACK!
TO HIT ME...

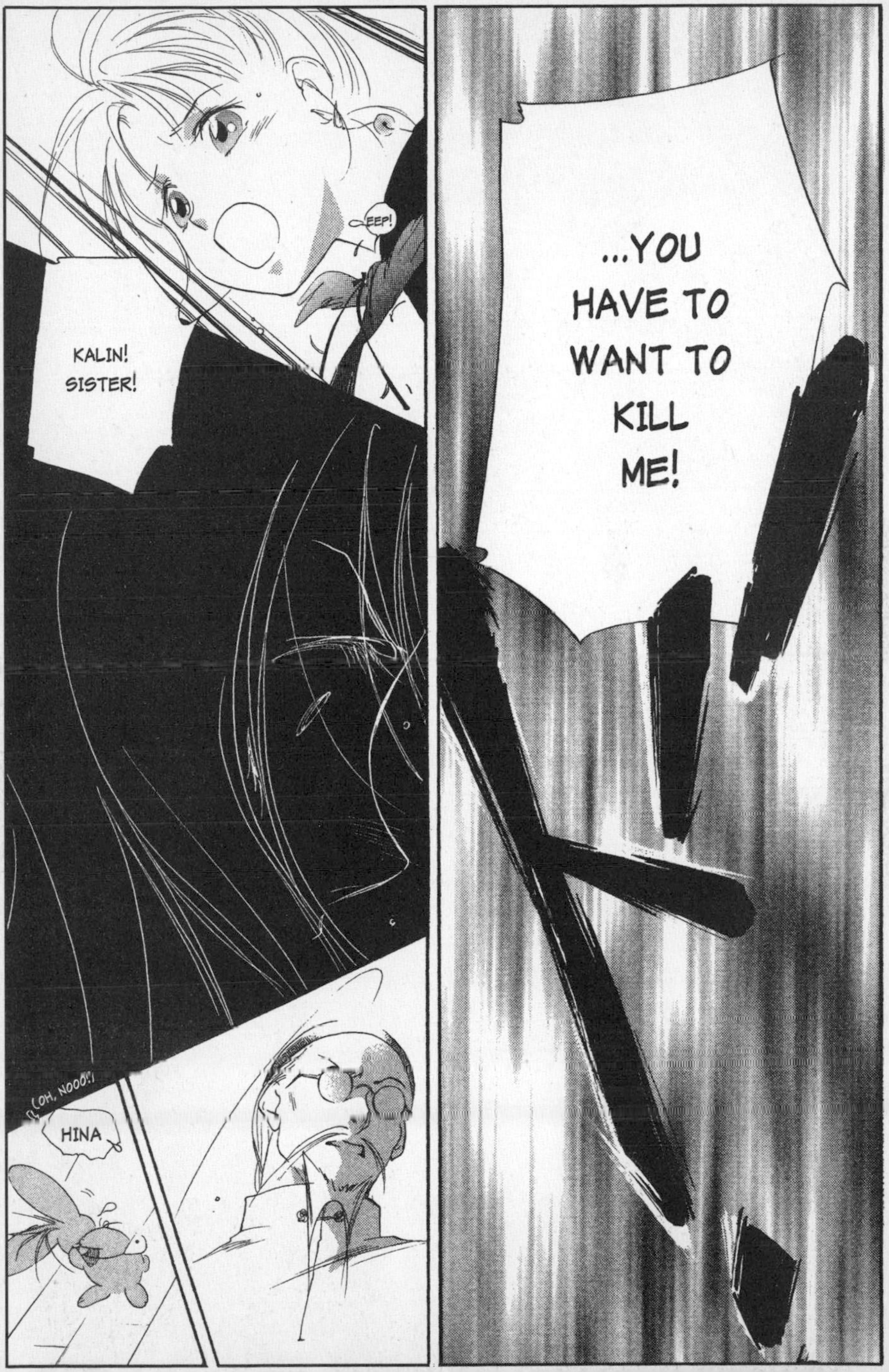
...YOU HAVE TO WANT TO KILL ME!
EEP!
KALIN! SISTER!
(OH, NOOO!)
HINA

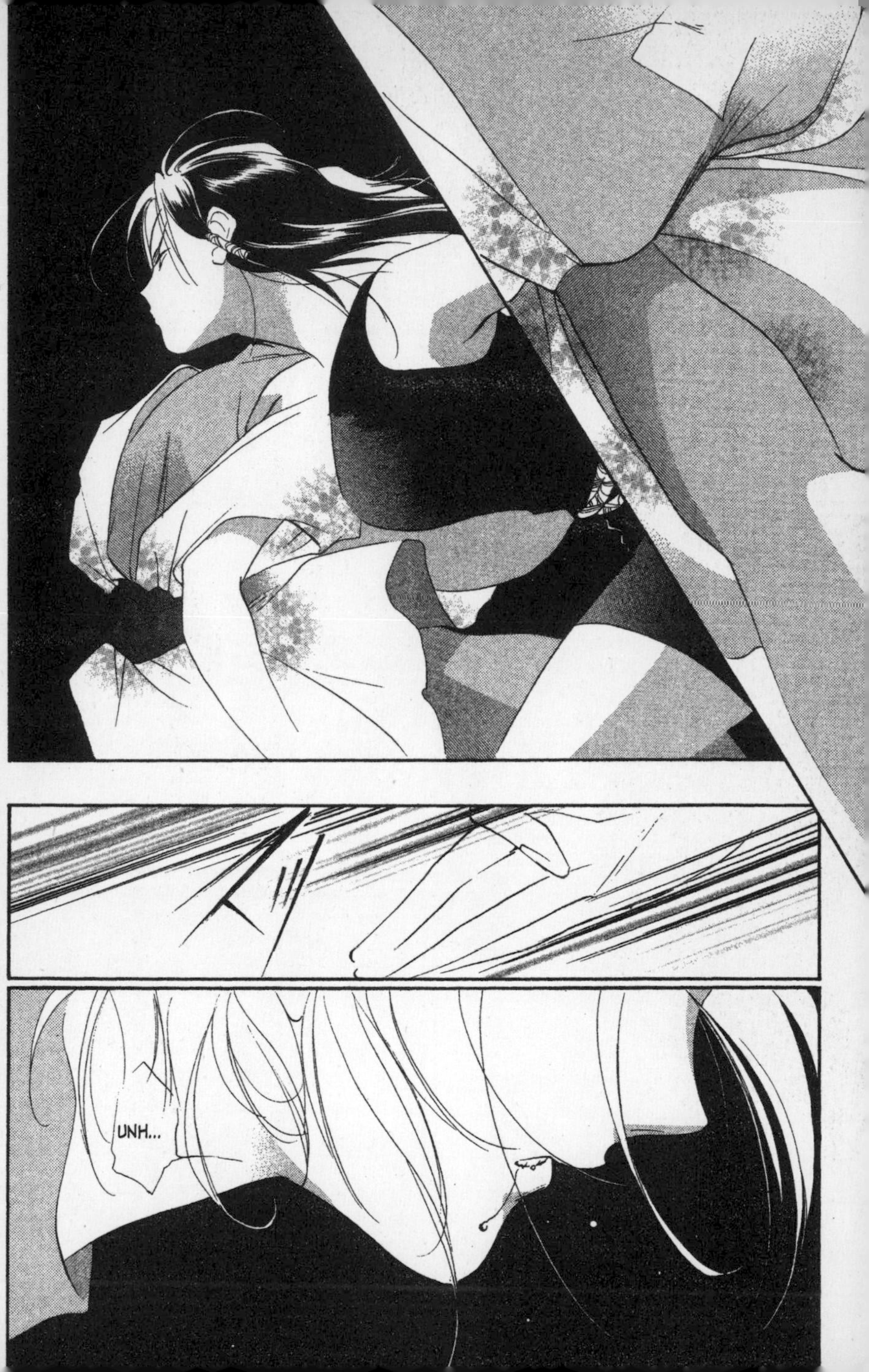
UNH...

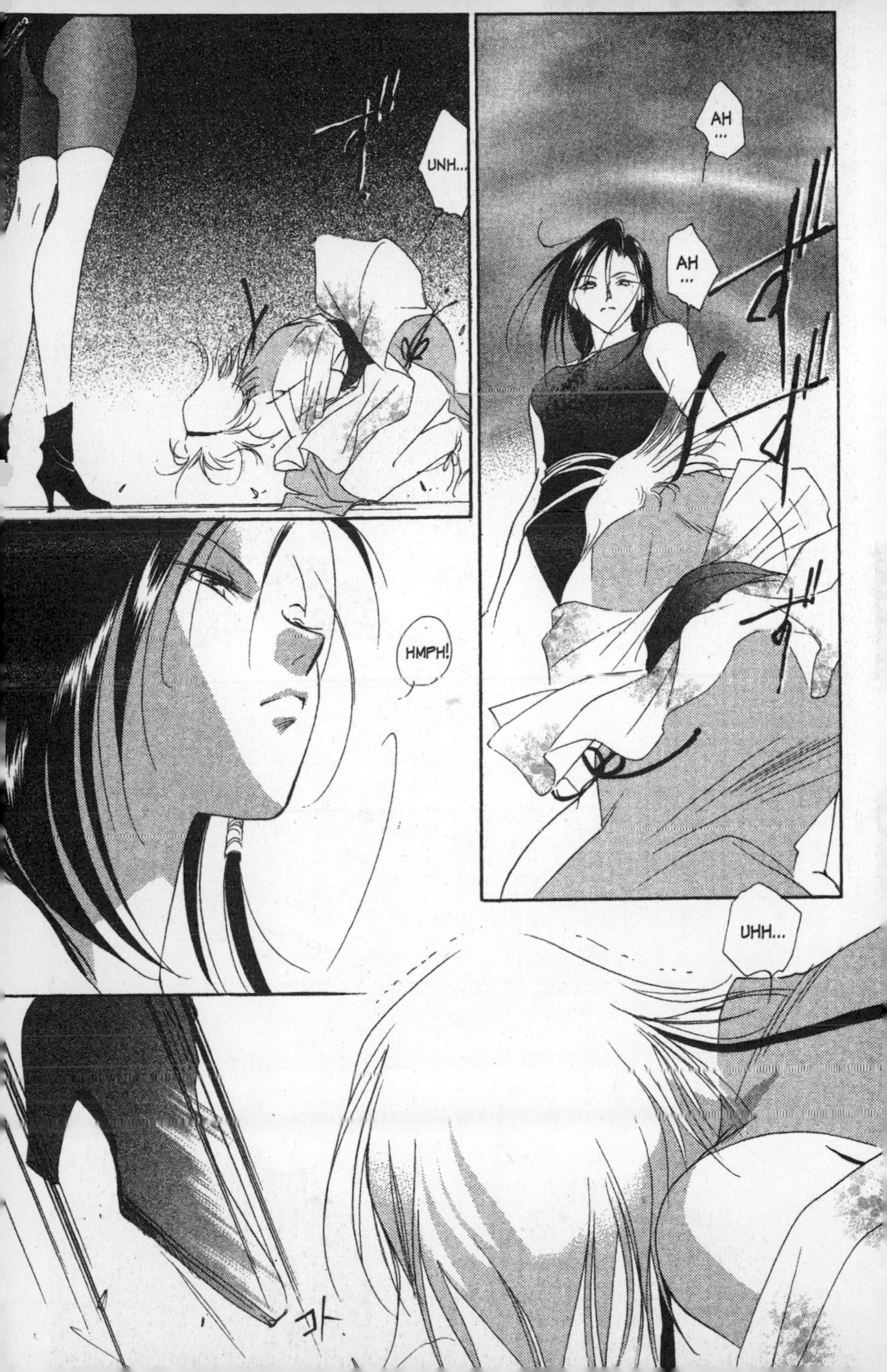
AH...
AH...
UNH...
HMPH!
UHH...
コト

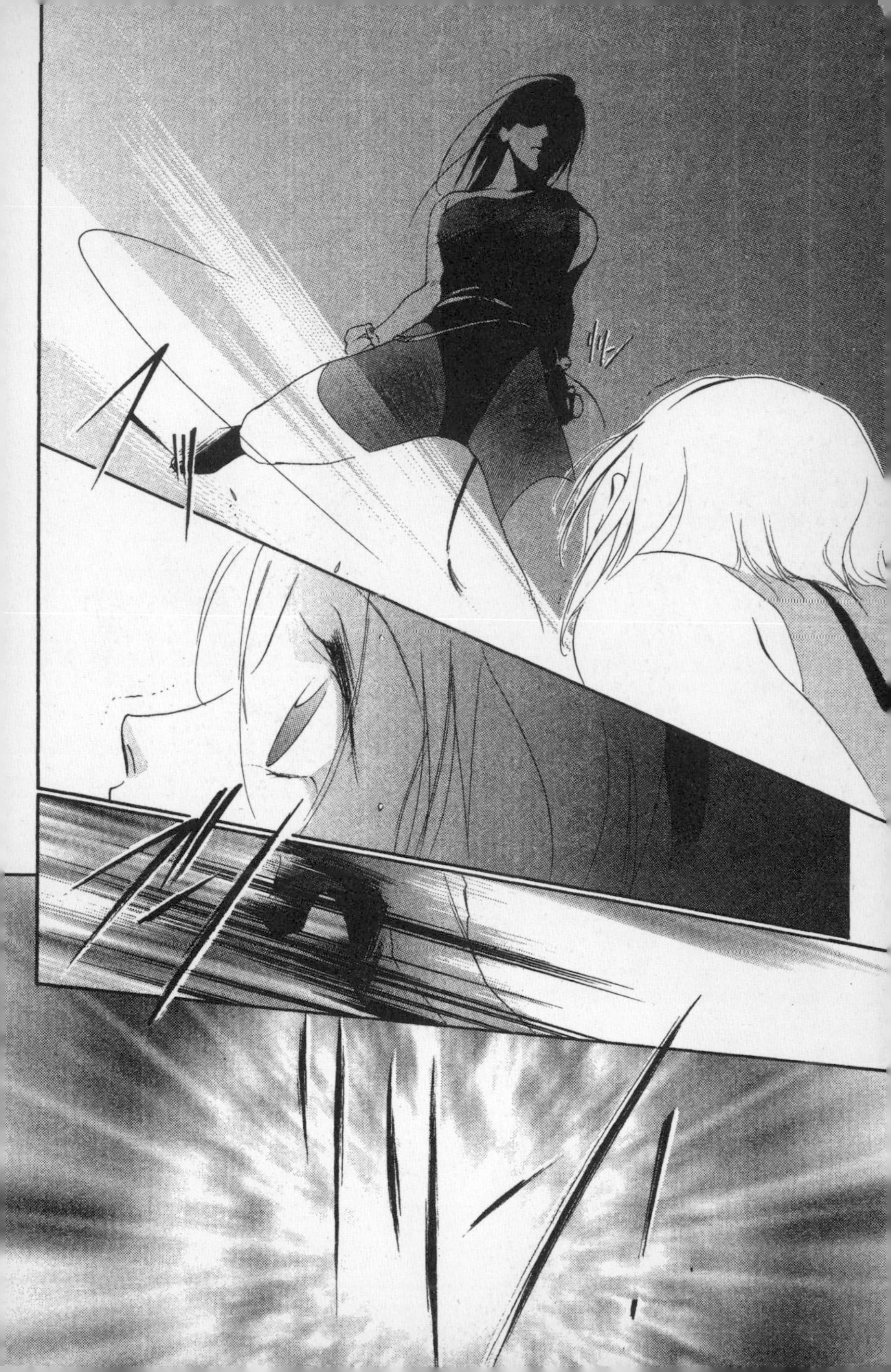
スッ

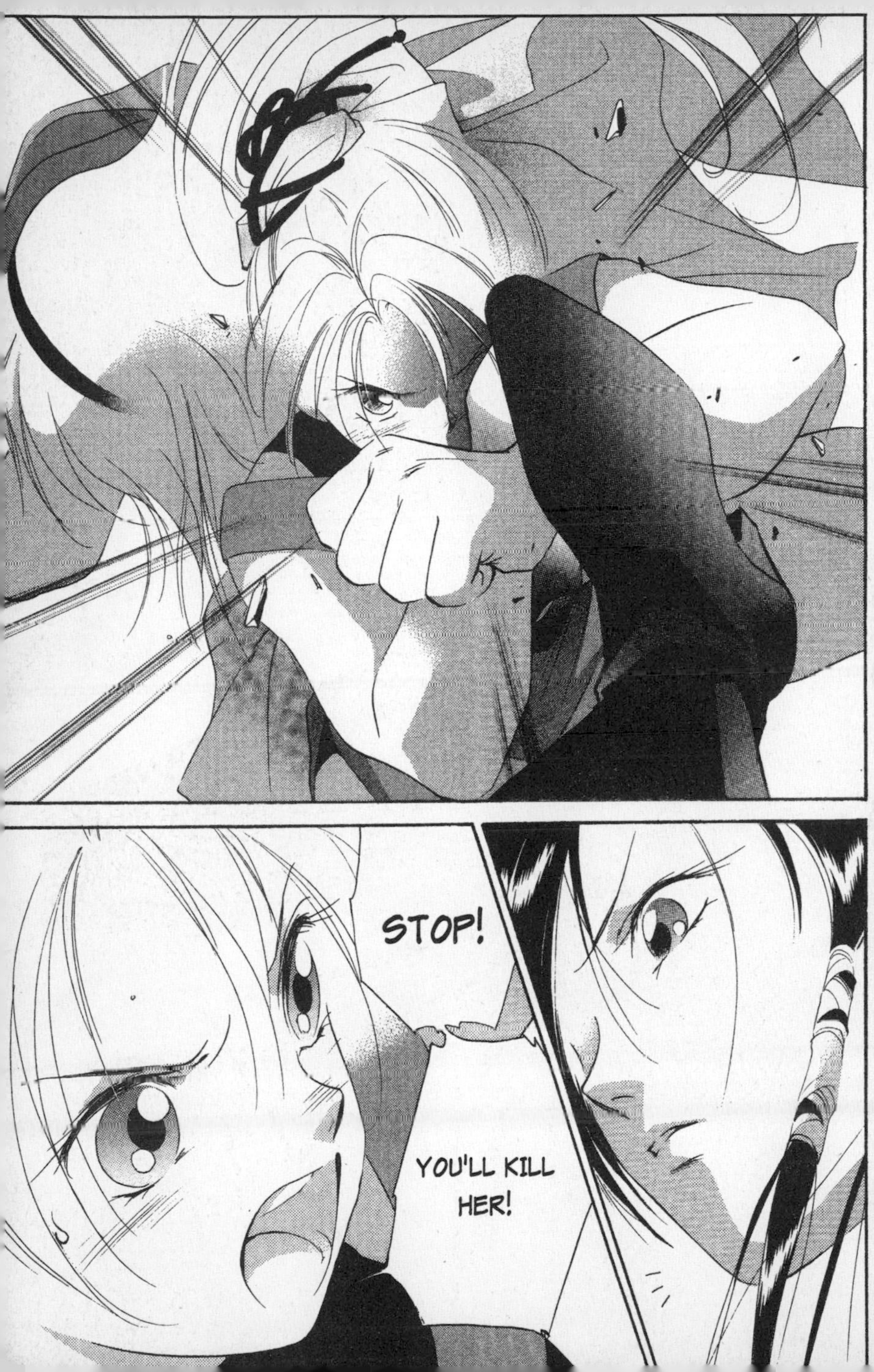
STOP!
YOU'LL KILL HER!

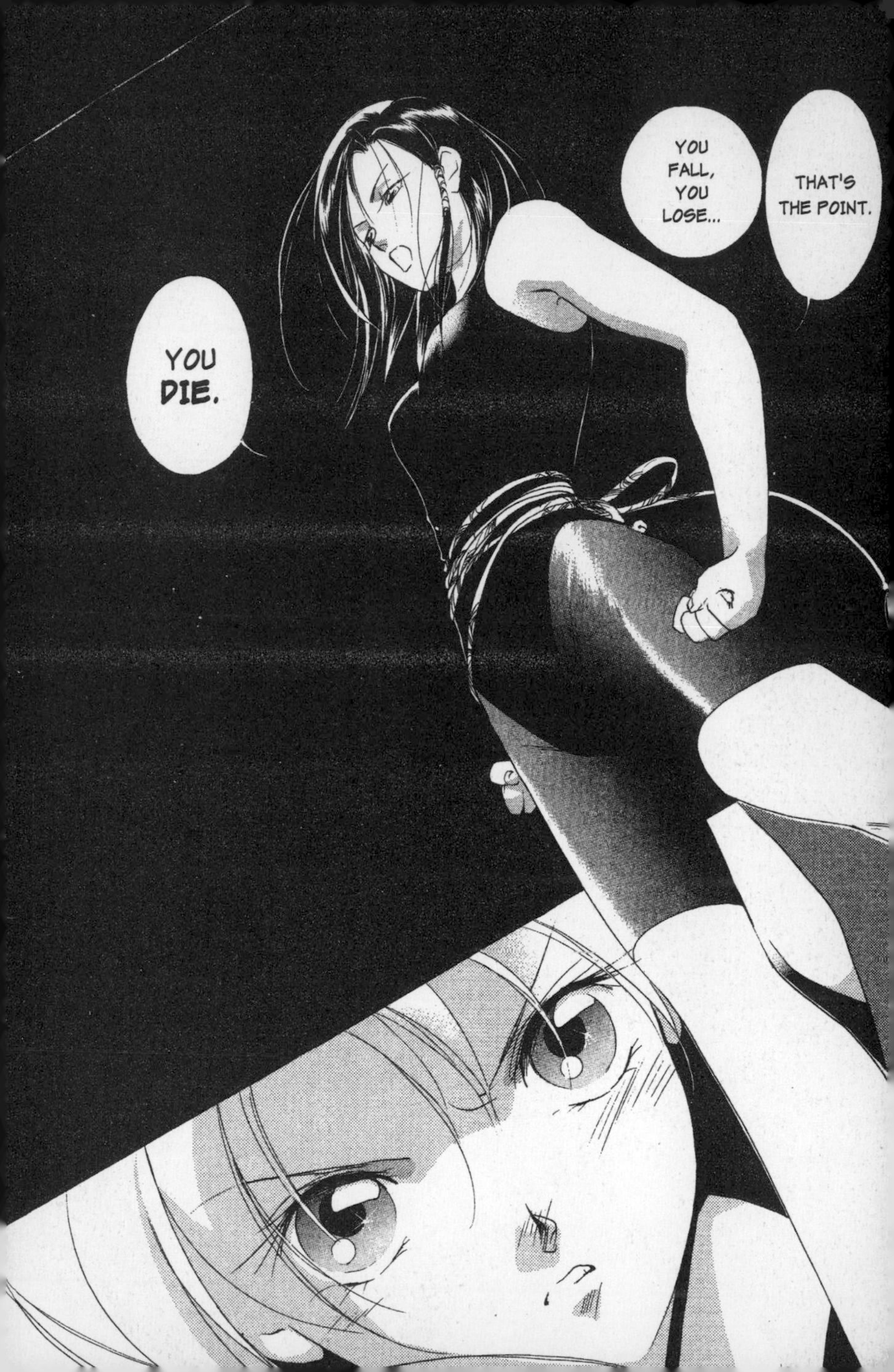
THAT'S THE POINT.
YOU FALL, YOU LOSE...
YOU DIE.

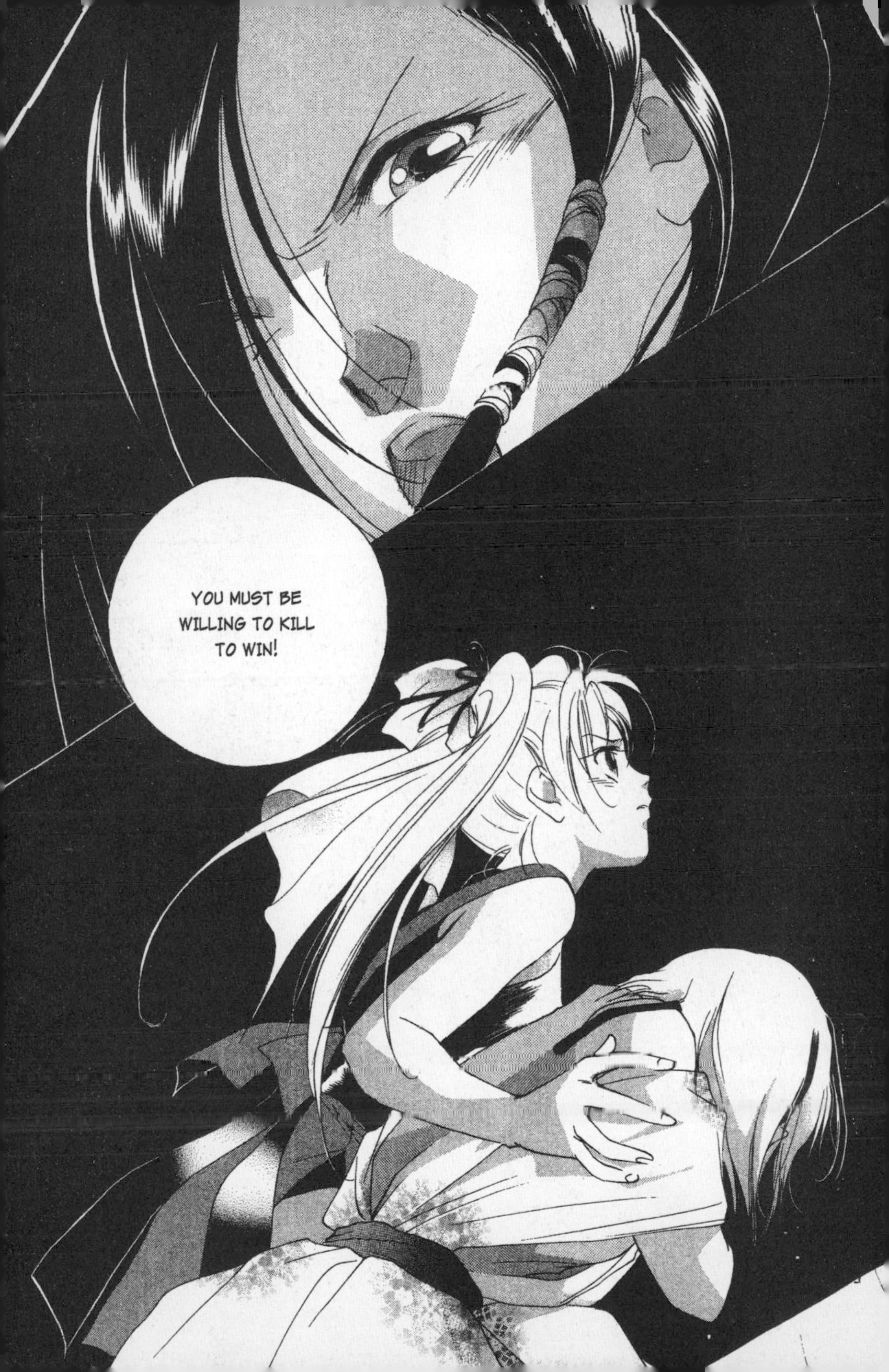
YOU MUST BE WILLING TO KILL TO WIN!

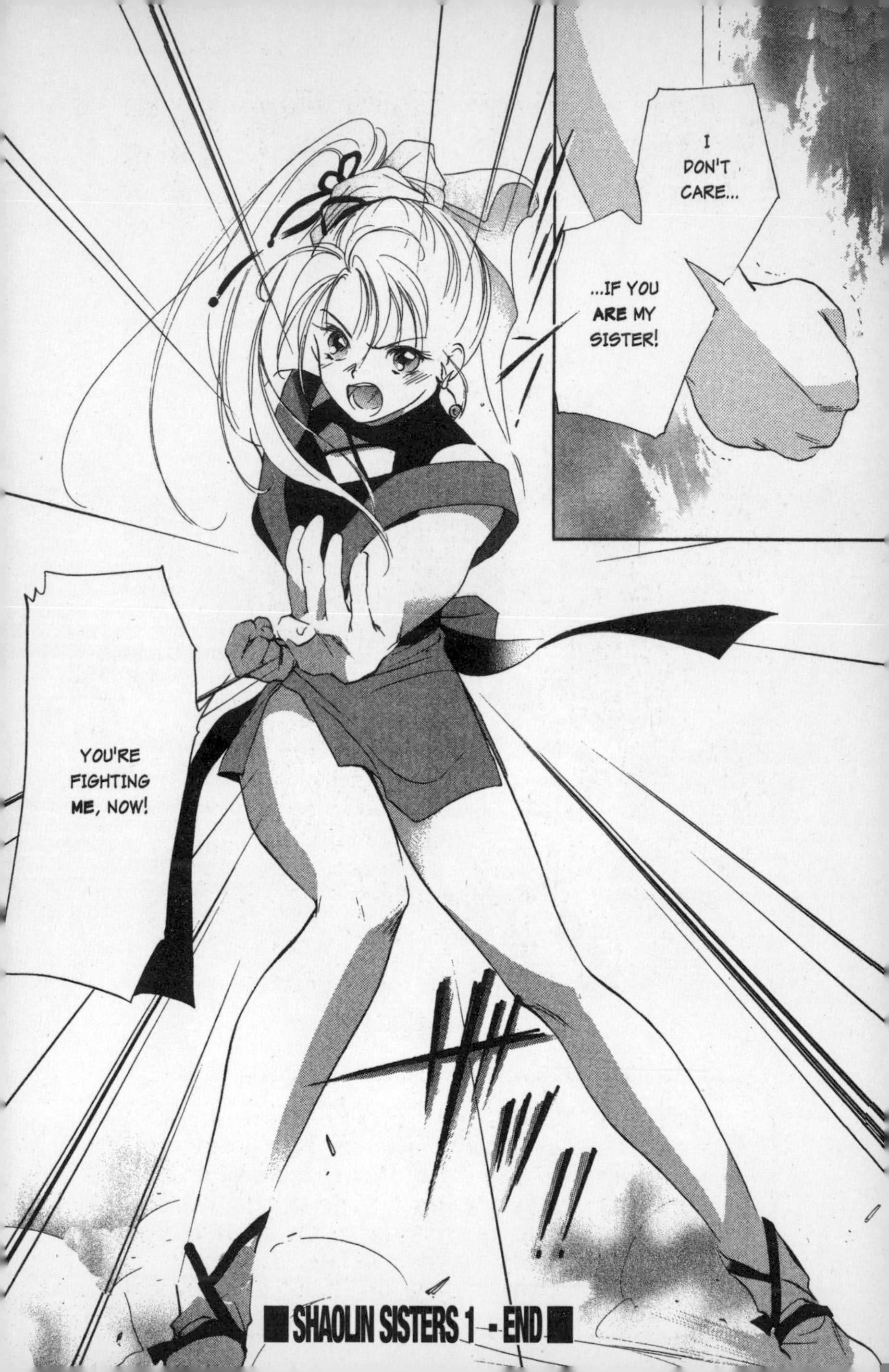
I DON'T CARE...
...IF YOU ARE MY SISTER!
YOU'RE FIGHTING ME, NOW!
!!
■SHAOLIN SISTERS 1 - END■

NEXT ISSUE

IN

SHAOLIN SISTERS

Julin and Kalin have found their long lost older sister, Seilin, but will Julin survive the family reunion? Bai Wang, the White Queen, has got her eyes on the magic bells, but a mysterious masked man named Drake claims they're his! All this and more in the next exciting issue of Shaolin Sisters!

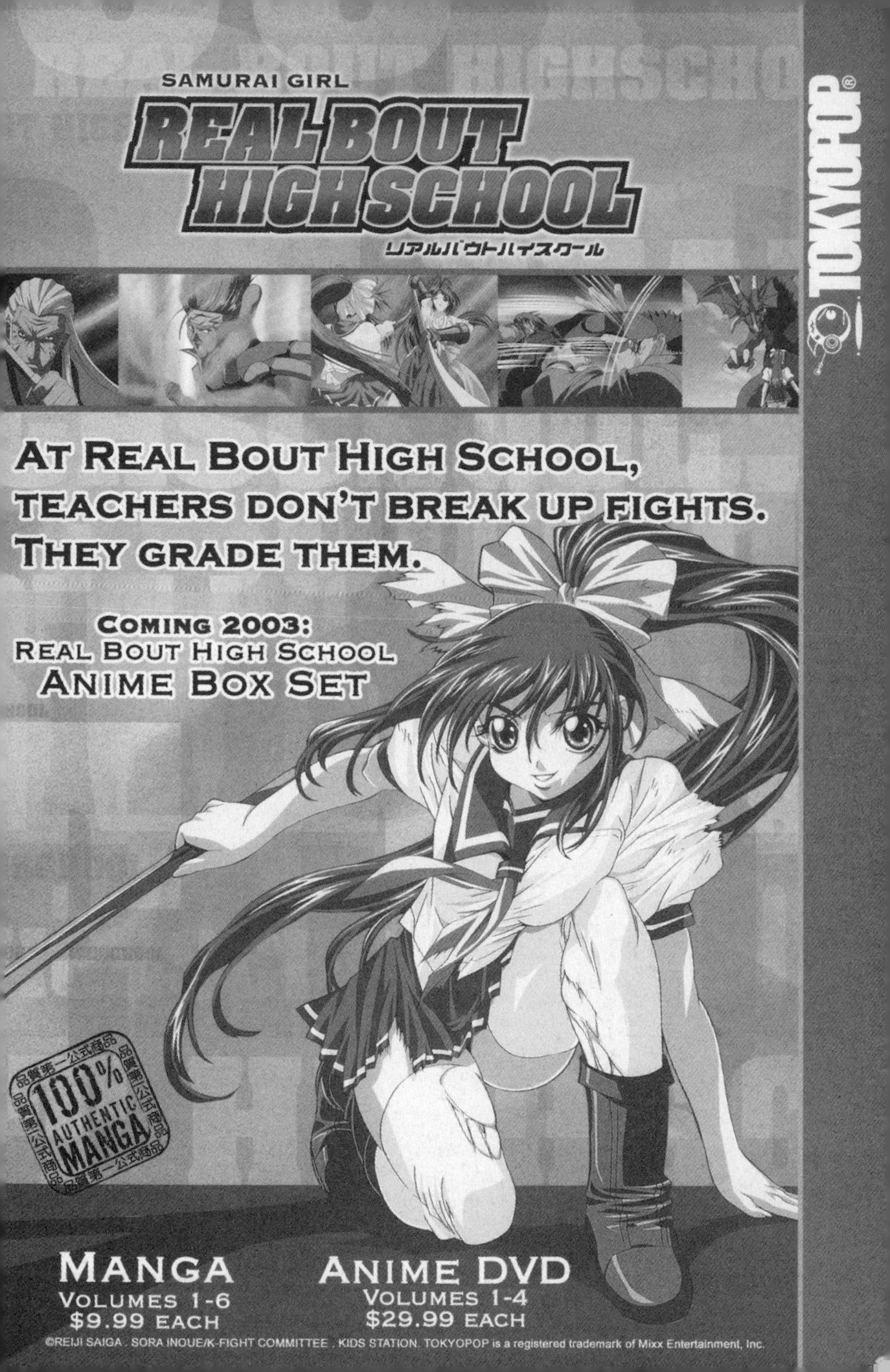
TOKYOPOP®
SAMURAI GIRL
REAL BOUT HIGH SCHOOL
リアルバウトハイスクール
AT REAL BOUT HIGH SCHOOL, TEACHERS DON'T BREAK UP FIGHTS. THEY GRADE THEM.
COMING 2003:
REAL BOUT HIGH SCHOOL
ANIME BOX SET
品質第一公式商品
100% AUTHENTIC MANGA
MANGA
VOLUMES 1-6
$9.99 EACH
ANIME DVD
VOLUMES 1-4
$29.99 EACH
©REIJI SAIGA . SORA INOUE/K-FIGHT COMMITTEE . KIDS STATION. TOKYOPOP is a registered trademark of Mixx Entertainment, Inc.

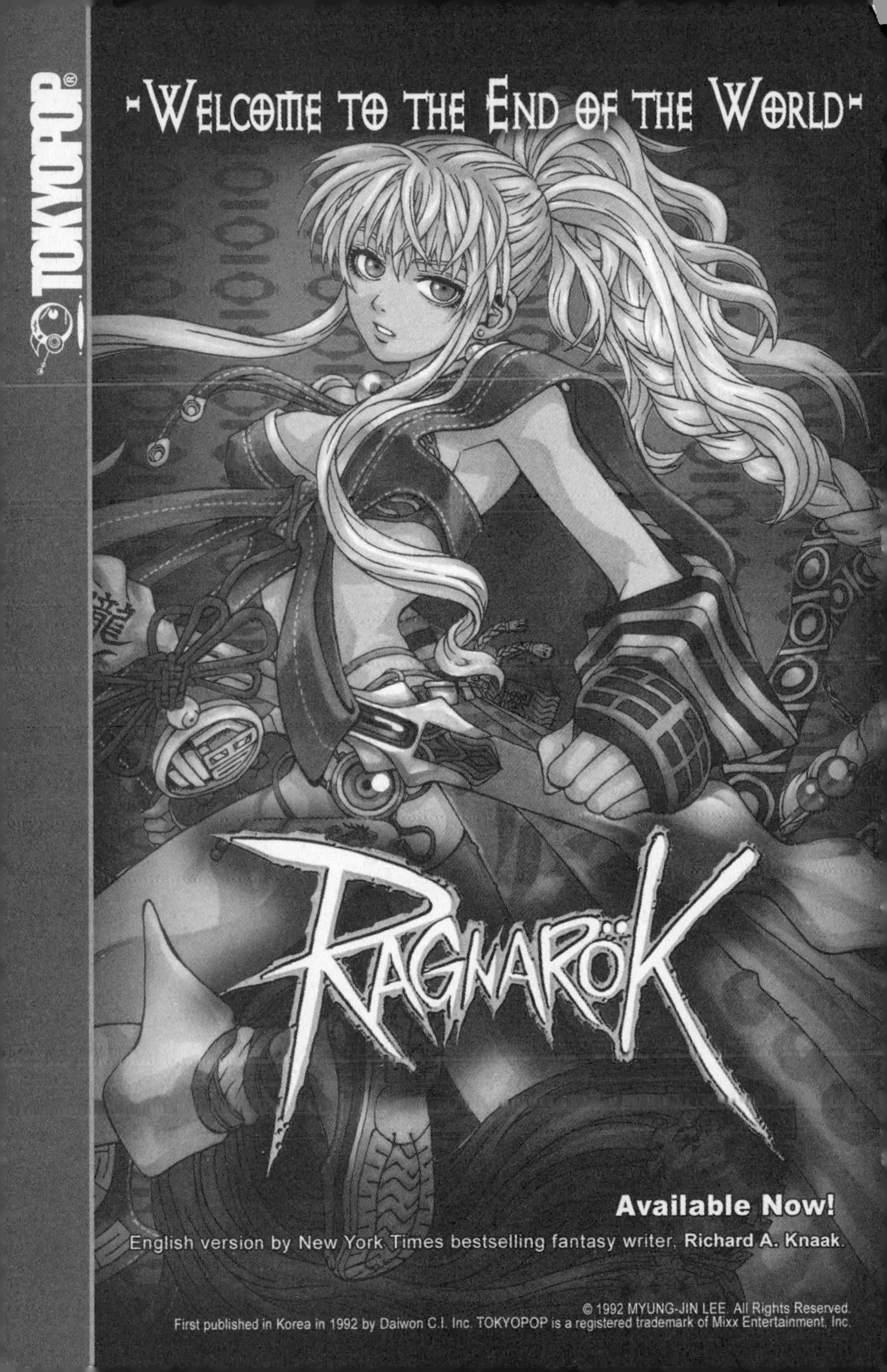
TOKYOPOP
-Welcome to the End of the World-
Ragnarök
Available Now!
English version by New York Times bestselling fantasy writer, Richard A. Knaak.
© 1992 MYUNG-JIN LEE. All Rights Reserved.
First published in Korea in 1992 by Daiwon C.I. Inc. TOKYOPOP is a registered trademark of Mixx Entertainment, Inc.

PCYAG

STOP!

This is the back of the book.
You wouldn't want to spoil a great ending!

This book is printed "manga-style," in the authentic Japanese right-to-left format. Since none of the artwork has been flipped or altered, readers get to experience the story just as the creator intended. You've been asking for it, so TOKYOPOP® delivered: authentic, hot-off-the-press, and far more fun!

DIRECTIONS

If this is your first time reading manga-style, here's a quick guide to help you understand how it works.

It's easy... just start in the top right panel and follow the numbers. Have fun, and look for more 100% authentic manga from TOKYOPOP®!

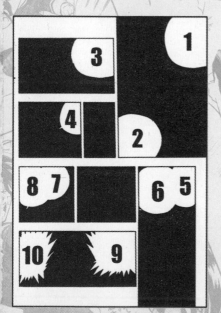